LAY MY BURDEN DOWN
A Folk History of Slavery

"SPLENDID."—*Commonweal*

"THE DEFINITIVE COLLECTION OF AMERICAN SLAVE NARRATIVES."—*Social Forces*

"No series of atrocities and certainly no idyll . . . the workaday world comes clear; the tanning, knitting, carding, spinning, cloth-dyeing, shoemaking, blacksmithing, plowing, hoeing, clearing of new land, the cultivating of tobacco, cotton, rice, and indigo, and the cooking of the famed diet of Dixie. . . . And suddenly across this world will flash the bright colors of melodrama—quarrels, fights, and murders."—*The Nation*

"The stories, often witty, often tall, and always flavorsome, make a sort of recital, in chorus, of what seems to have been a dreadful and brutalizing way of life."—*The New Yorker*

"Here are people—old and wise—talking over their lives, the little incidents—sights and sounds, tastes and smells—and the larger recollections of the feeling of living in slavery, being sold at public auction, being selected to breed more slaves, of working from can to can't ['They worked . . . from the time they could see until the time they couldn't']."—*Saturday Review*

"A record of permanent value. It takes the reader behind the scenes of the feudal economy of the plantation . . . good narrative and good material for the study of American culture."—*Yale Review*

Slave cabin, near Eufaula, Barbour County, Alabama

LAY MY BURDEN DOWN

A Folk History of Slavery

Edited by B. A. Botkin

Foreword by Jerrold Hirsch

Delta
Trade Paperbacks

A Delta Book
Published by
Dell Publishing
a division of
Bantam Doubleday Dell Publishing Group, Inc.
1540 Broadway
New York, New York 10036

Lay My Burden Down was first published in 1945 by the University of Chicago
Press.

Copyright © 1945, 1973 by B. A. Botkin
Foreword to the Brown Thrasher Edition © 1989
by the University of Georgia Press
Athens, Georgia 30602

Designed by GDS/Jeffrey L. Ward

The trademark Delta® is registered in the U.S. Patent and Trademark Office.

ISBN: 0-385-31115-X

Reprinted by arrangement with the University of Georgia Press

Manufactured in the United States of America
Published simultaneously in Canada

To the Narrators

No more sickness,
No more sorrow,
When I lay my burden down.

Contents

Foreword by Jerrold Hirsch   ix

Preface   xxxiii

Introduction   1

PART ONE: MOTHER WIT   7

Fooling Master and Catching John   9

Tall Tales and Tall Talk   17

How Come   20

Lincoln and Others   23

Birds and Beasts   29

Pastor and Flock   33

The Power   38

Hants   48

Anecdotes   59

PART TWO: LONG REMEMBRANCE   71

PART THREE: FROM CAN TO CAN'T   143

Count the Stars through the Cracks   145

Going High, Going Slow   159

Praying to the Right Man   170

The Slave's Chance   182

PART FOUR: A WAR AMONG THE WHITE FOLKS   199

They Made Us Sing "Dixie"   201

We've Come to Set You Free   212

PART FIVE: ALL I KNOW ABOUT FREEDOM   229

How Freedom Came   231

The Breaking-Up and After   238

The Equalization War   265

I Take Freedom   279

List of Informants and Interviewers   283

Index   307

Foreword

Listen to the voices of former slaves who speak in *Lay My Burden Down: A Folk History of Slavery*. They talk about the power of memory: "Does I 'member much about slavery times? Well, there is no way for me to disremember unless I die" (p. 71). They introduce us to the workaday world of slavery: "When the day begin to crack, the whole plantation break out with all kinds of noises, and you could tell what going on by the kind of noise you hear" (p. 121). They often define freedom and slavery in terms of the power whites had over the most meaningful relationships in their lives: "I never will forgive that white man for not telling me [after the Civil War that] I was free, and not helping me to git back to my mammy and pappy! Lots of white people done that" (p. 112). The personal and communal functions of memory, ways of living and ways of wresting a living from the land, the meaning of slavery and freedom, the struggle to create a family and community life in a world of slavery and racial conflict—these are some of the great themes of this folk history.

The voices of former slaves written down by members of the New Deal's Federal Writers' Project (FWP), a WPA relief program, can forever speak to readers who care to listen. They tell the story of the generation of Afro-Americans who were born under slavery, who lived to see the institution's demise, and who struggled to obtain the promise of freedom. It is their story to tell, for as B. A. Botkin, the editor of *Lay My Burden Down,* pointed out: "From the memories and the lips of former slaves have come the answers which only they can give to questions which Americans still ask: What does it mean to be a slave? What does it mean to be free? And, even more, how does it *feel?*" (p. 1). They speak to us not only about a specific time and place, but also about the ability of people to create for themselves a culture that even in the face of oppression allows them to build a sense of community and to assert their dignity. They remind us of the burdens and the promise of the American experience: "The first war [the Civil War] was 'bout freedom and the war right after it [Reconstruction] was equalization" (p. 265).

When *Lay My Burden Down* was published, the FWP interviews with former slaves from which Botkin shaped his book were virtually unknown. "The book is a new thing," declared black poet and former national FWP Negro affairs editor, Sterling Brown, in his review of *Lay My Burden Down* in the *Nation*.[1] Brown saw the book as a departure from the way previous popular and scholarly writings on slavery had ignored black sources. In poetry and fiction created by white southern authors, the words put into the mouths of Afro-American characters became the voices that reached the public forum: Comic darkies. Contented darkies. Devoted darkies. Childlike darkies. Ridiculously superstitious darkies. These white authors created black voices that shaped the dominant understanding of slavery. Virginia author Thomas Nelson Page created characters such as Sam, a former slave, who in "Marse Chan" (1887) testifies: "Dem wuz good ole times, marster—de bes' Sam ever see! Niggers didn' hed nothin' 't all to do—jes hed to 'ten' to de feedin' an' cleanin' de hawses an' doin' what de marster tell 'em to do . . . Dyar warn' no trouble nor nothin'." Page's darkies were the models for countless other literary, popular, and folk creations.[2] In *Lay My Burden Down* Botkin intended to bring into the public discussion of slavery a black oral tradition that countered the romanticized plantation tradition created by white southerners.

With the publication of the multivolume series *The American Slave: A Composite Autobiography* in 1972 (nineteen volumes in the first series and subsequent supplemental volumes) under the editorship of George Rawick, the entire FWP collection, which had previously only been available either in manuscript form at the Library of Congress or on microfilm, became more accessible to scholars.[3] The publication of these materials has helped change forever the study of American slavery.[4] Recent historians of American slavery have drawn heavily on the FWP interviews with former slaves in describing the development of a rich and distinctive Afro-American culture that gave slaves a way of resisting the dehumanizing forces of slavery, a sense of community, and a world view. Today it would be impossible to write a history of American slavery without using the narratives of former slaves. The multivolume set of FWP slave narratives is an important research tool, but it does not meet the need of nonscholars for a selection from this material that can help them understand the experience of slavery as seen from the perspective of the former slaves themselves.

National FWP officials intended for the interviews conducted with former slaves to reach a general audience. When Henry Alsberg, national FWP director, hired B. A. Botkin as national folklore editor in the summer of 1938, one of his goals was to have Botkin edit a volume of stories by former slaves that could reach a wide variety of readers. The FWP was not able to fulfill that goal largely because the conservative reaction to the New Deal in the late thirties and the coming of World War II curtailed FWP activities. In editing *Lay My Burden Down* Botkin was fulfilling one of the great visions of national FWP officials. He tried to orchestrate a careful selection of black voices from the FWP former slave narrative collection to tell the story of slavery, the Civil War, and Reconstruction entirely in the words of former slaves. Every time the book is read it becomes again "a new thing," as voices recorded over half a century ago come alive for receptive readers.

More than a sample of the evidence about slavery collected by the FWP, *Lay My Burden Down* provides a way of entering the slave's world, a way of understanding slavery and the opportunities, struggles, and disappointments that the Civil War and Reconstruction offered Afro-Americans. The book, as Botkin argued, is both history and literature. The authors are former slaves, "the narrators" to whom the book is dedicated. Botkin thought it was a new kind of history—a "history from the bottom up, in which the people become their own historians" (p. 5). An active reader can be vicariously present at a turning point not only in Afro-American history but also in American history—present at events whose full meaning we continue to debate, for part of the answer to their meaning lies in the society we want to try to achieve.

Botkin, in his title, introduction, and arrangement of the selections in *Lay My Burden Down: A Folk History,* raised enduring questions about both a past way of life and the way we go about trying to understand and interpret our history. What kind of history is a folk history? What does folklore have to do with history? The directors of the FWP had seen the stories of the former slaves as part of a great American epic. In his introduction to *Lay My Burden Down* Botkin used the term *saga.* He also subtitled the book *A Folk History.* These weighty terms reflect Botkin's effort to find an appropriate label for a book that in many ways remains a new kind of history. What are we to make of a history based on oral tradition—folk literature, folk reminiscence, and folk knowledge? Are the former slaves who speak in this volume reliable witnesses? Are the Federal Writers who interviewed the former slaves trustworthy interviewers? Trying to understand how and why the Federal Writers' Project set out to capture the voices of former slaves on paper can not only answer the questions about the origins of these documents, which we ask regarding any historical source, but can also help us consider the ways in which *Lay My Burden Down* continues to address in a fresh way seemingly permanent questions surrounding American life and history.

Lay My Burden Down is divided into five sections: "Mother Wit" (folk literature); "Long Remembrance" (life histories of former slaves); "From Can to Can't" (daily life, social structure, and social conflict in the slave's world); "A War Among the White Folks" (the Civil War experience); and "All I Know About Freedom" (the struggles of the Reconstruction period). The stories the former slaves tell take the reader from the world of antebellum slavery through the struggles of Civil War and Reconstruction, and occasionally into the segregated and impoverished world of the American South in the 1930s. Arranging the selections from the FWP interviews to narrate a story that begins in slavery and ends in Reconstruction was only one of Botkin's goals. An equally important goal was to convey a sense of the pattern of slave society, of the development of an Afro-American culture. Botkin wanted to give the narrators the opportunity to share their experience of the changes they had witnessed, what might be visualized as the horizontal unfolding of events over time. At the same time he aimed to arrange the former slaves' stories so that together the narrators could describe in depth aspects of the slave's world, what might be visualized as a vertical analysis of a past time.

In *Lay My Burden Down* the dynamics of cultural and social history, the relationship between the individual and the community, tradition and change, social structure and social conflict are captured in the relationship between the horizontal and vertical dimensions of the stories the slaves tell, the way the chapters are organized, and the way selections from the interviews are organized within chapters. It is a complex form, developing what Botkin saw as the possibilities for folk history—"history produced by the collaboration of the folklorist and the historian with each other and with the folk." A history in which "the people are the historians as well as the history, telling their own story in their own words." He saw the form as relevant to all types of social history: "If we admitted no impediments to the marriage of true minds between folklore and history, the product of their union would be folk history," he declared before a 1939 meeting of the American Historical Association. In each section of *Lay My Burden Down,* folklore and oral history are the basis of this folk history.[5]

One of the difficulties many readers have faced in *Lay My Burden Down* is overcoming their preconceptions about what the terms folk and folklore mean and the relationship this material has to history. Members of literate societies tend to give written documents primary status as the authoritative source of their history and the guarantee that their history will be transmitted to future generations (Afro-American slaves could make none of these assumptions). In literate societies oral traditions come to be viewed as unreliable sources of information about public events or sources largely about allegedly trivial private matters. In this way a public record is created that obscures the historical relationship between individual lives and public events, that writes whole groups and classes out of the historical record, and that treats only the prominent as historical actors who make choices and help shape their world. This reliance on the written public record results in a history that ignores the ways the same events were experienced by different groups and individuals and that largely treats only events and not ways of life as part of the historical record. Trying to convince both scholars and general readers that folklore was a neglected source of social history, Botkin faced an uphill struggle.

Botkin's view that a group's folklore was an important historical source flew in the face of conventional wisdom. One reviewer who praised *Lay My Burden Down* for giving the slave's perspective on slavery also wondered why Botkin found it necessary to include so much folklore and superstition, the products, in his view, only of ignorance. He feared that such material would only reinforce racist stereotypes.[6] As late as 1974, historian C. Vann Woodward could write that "B. A. Botkin published a small book of excerpts from the FWP interviews consisting mainly of anecdotes and folklore, but containing quite enough material of historical value."[7] Among historians that view of folklore has changed somewhat, and among students of American slavery the battle has been won. Although Botkin was aware that many historians and most readers thought of folklore as false, dead, phony stuff—a totally unreliable account—that was vanishing with progress, he proceeded on the assumption that folklore was an essential part of the cultural and social history of a people.

Unlike many historians, Botkin did not dichotomize folklore and history, nor did he privilege written sources over oral ones, because he knew that the voices that could be recovered from written sources did not represent the variety of people who had helped create the world we have inherited. By the term *folk* Botkin did not mean only the rural and the isolated, the marginalized groups that urbanites commonly referred to as folk—people they saw as keeping alive yesterday's traditions. In the folklore manual he had written for Federal Writers, Botkin explained that, in his view, "every group bound together by common interests and purposes, whether educated or uneducated, rural or urban, possesses a body of traditions which may be called its folklore."[8] Folklore was an important source for the writing of the history of every group, but even more so for those like the former slaves who had left few written records.

Lay My Burden Down begins with what is still probably the most difficult material for many readers to see as a historical source, a section on "Mother Wit" —stories about slaves tricking masters, material about conjure, stories about hants (ghosts), birds and beasts, etc. And yet it is the slaves' stories about these matters that provide a basis for understanding the accounts, in later chapters, of the lives of individual slaves, the cooperation and conflict that took place within the daily round and seasonal rhythms of plantation life, and the way Afro-Americans responded to the Civil War and Reconstruction. These topics can only be understood in relationship to the emergence of a distinctive Afro-American cultural identity and world view that developed in slavery and that is embodied in the folk literature, knowledge, and testimony of the former slaves.

Botkin sought to move beyond those students of Afro-American life who were preoccupied with the origins of cultural traits. He wanted to convey an understanding of the process by which Afro-American slaves created their own distinctive culture, rather than debate the origins of discrete items in that culture. In seeking to move the debate away from origins, he was trying to shift attention to cultural dynamics, to the interaction between past and present, tradition and experience, in shaping consciousness, cultural identity, and world view. Only in recent years has this shift in focus become characteristic of studies of slave life and culture. Nevertheless, there has also been a renewed attention to the African heritage of the slaves, not as a static survival, but as one of the significant and dynamic strands out of which slaves created their culture. Although Botkin did not stress the importance of the African heritage, his interest in cultural processes led him to concentrate on many of the questions about the Afro-American experience that remain central to the effort to understand emergence of an Afro-American culture. It was one of the reasons he wanted to let the slaves describe what they meant by "mother wit" and the role it played in their individual lives and the cultural community in which they lived.[9]

By mother wit, Botkin explained, slaves meant the folk wisdom and knowledge accumulated over generations, the product of both tradition and improvisation. The individual both draws on and contributes to a living tradition of "mother wit," the "other things [that] got to build you up 'sides learning" (p. 7). The proverbs, beliefs, and stories that gave a slave "mother wit" embodied an inherited wisdom that, through the interaction between the individual and the group, grew and changed in response to new situations. Actual incidents, through repetition and variation, become stories that project the views of the slave community. Stories like those about fooling Master and the power of conjure demonstrate the existence of a cultural pattern that integrated blacks into a slave community with its own perspective on slave life and that saw itself both tied to and in conflict with the white world. Although Botkin organized the material in the "Mother Wit" chapter by genre, he also arranged the material to give a sense of cultural change over time. Many of these selections organized by genre conclude with stories about the Civil War and Reconstruction. Such stories, as Botkin observed, reflected the way "oppression has taught the art of evasion and irony as a compromise between submission and revolt." To understand the stories "of those whom cruelty has made wary" (p. 7) requires a suspension of preconceptions, an openness to irony. It served the slaves' interests that the whites they lived with ignored or missed the irony in much of black folklore. That fact helped them create a cultural space in which they could have a degree of autonomy and could forge a communal and family life. It would now serve our interests, and theirs, to understand their need to be wary, evasive, and ironic.

The life histories in the "Long Remembrance" section of *Lay My Burden Down* create a sense of how individual lives developed in dynamic relationship to a cultural pattern that bound together an Afro-American community. They also testify to the variations on a pattern, to a complexity in the social structure of antebellum slavery that readers living in a postindustrial society might tend to underestimate. The narrators describe the different experiences of house servants, drivers, artisans, and field hands, of slaves on small farms and large plantations, and of slaves who lived on the frontier (including slaves owned by Indians) and those in the older plantation areas. Accounts also vary in significant ways because of the complex interaction of personality and culture. They provide a window on the slave experience from the perspective of the individual.

Through these life histories we learn how individual slaves used folk knowledge in coping with their world. In the course of the daily and seasonal rhythms of work and holidays they drew on a rich store of folk knowledge. Individual slaves knew how to card, spin, weave, and dye. They could plant and harvest crops such as cotton, corn, indigo, and tobacco. Slave artisans "hauled up the cypress logs and sawed them and frowed out the clapboards by hand" (p. 120). There were fiddlers who knew how to play so the "fiddle could almost talk" (p.

74). Slaves possessed knowledge that was essential to the world in which they lived: knowledge that made the farms on which they lived more productive, thus improving their lives as well as that of their owners, and knowledge that served only themselves and their community. As individuals they contributed from their experience to the folk literature and knowledge that allowed the group to express, in stories, prayer, and music, the fears, hopes, and ties that bound them together.

For these former slaves the line between private life and public events was not as sharply drawn as late twentieth-century Americans often imagine it to be for themselves. The individual's experience of family relationships, of place and community, the stages of his or her life—childhood, marriage, the birth of children—were inextricably tied to slavery, war, and emancipation. These accounts illustrate the way individual slaves responded to private and public events that both shaped and disrupted the patterns of their lives. Memories of events, as well as the events themselves, shape lives, and the memories of one generation help shape relationships with the next. A former slave tells an FWP interviewer that she is busy sewing dresses for her grandchildren and then the memories come: "I can see lots of little children just like my grandchildren, toting hoes bigger than they is, and they poor little black hands and legs bleeding where they scratched by the brambledy weeds, and where they got whippings 'cause they didn't git out all the work the overseer set out for 'em. I was one of them little slave gals my own self, and I never seen nothing but work and tribulations till I was a grownup woman, just about" (p. 112).

In testifying and bearing witness—"I saw slaves sold. I can see that old block now" (p. 162)—the former slaves inevitably told stories. These stories, as the last three sections of *Lay My Burden Down* demonstrate, are both part of an oral history of slavery and "on their way to becoming folklore—the folklore of ex-slaves" as they are told again and again (p. 5). When Federal Writers wrote down the answers to the questions they asked they were often recording stories that had been shared many times before, memories that had been and were being passed on.

The former slaves told stories of the contest for control in both the pre-Civil War world and the postemancipation world: "If they hollered, 'Lord, have mercy!' Marse Jim didn't hear 'em, but if they cried, 'Marse Jim, have mercy!' then he made 'em stop the beating. He say, 'The Lord rule Heaven, but Jim Smith rule the earth'" (p. 170). But they also had memories of laughing at Master's funeral, of both men and women who couldn't be whipped, of slaves who committed suicide rather than be whipped—"They say Negroes won't commit suicide, but Isom told us of a girl that committed suicide. . . . They intended to make her an example to the rest of the slaves. But they didn't get Lucy" (p. 192)—of a runaway slave who hid in a cave for seven years, of slaves who worked to buy their freedom, and of those who helped their fellow slaves escape.

When historians first began using the FWP slave narratives, they tended to focus exclusively on their relevance to writing the history of slavery. National FWP officials had had a broader vision. FWP director, Henry Alsberg, thought that part of the appeal of the stories told by the former slaves and a book based on these stories would be that they were a source of information about both the Old and the New South: "In many instances we have been able in these stories to carry the picture of slavery in the United States back to the beginning of the nineteenth century and on the other side through the Reconstruction era and later period in the South."[10]

Listen carefully to the former slaves and it is clear that the coming of freedom was a watershed for both the individual and the group: "Everybody went wild. We all felt like heroes, and nobody had made us that way but ourselves" (p. 231). It was a moment none forgot. "How Freedom Came" (pp. 231–37) was, as *Lay My Burden Down* illustrates, not only a moment in the lives of individual slaves, but also a group of stories about an experience that became part of Afro-American folk literature and history. The stories of war and emancipation embodied not only joy but also disappointment and tragedy. Stories told about the coming of freedom passed on lessons learned, as had the slaves' animal stories.

Within the limits of slave society and the restricted opportunities freedom created, Afro-Americans made choices and those choices became part of their folk history. In *Lay My Burden Down* the emergence of a new postwar agricultural system is depicted not in abstract legal and economic terms but as a social structure partly created by the choices former slaves made in their struggle with white landowners. In addition to describing a past social structure, historians need to provide an understanding of the options available to individuals in the society they are studying. As their own historians, the former slaves undertook both tasks.

Postwar freedom was not the realization of an ideal abstraction. During Reconstruction former slaves struggled with white southerners to fulfill the promise of freedom. The fourteenth and fifteenth amendments to the United States Constitution that the defeated southern states had to ratify provided for equal treatment under the law regardless of race and for universal male suffrage. Nevertheless, southern whites found ways to deny these constitutional rights to southern blacks. The federal Freedmen's Bureau created to assist the freed slaves proved a weak and temporary agency. White southerners struggled to recreate in new circumstances the racial and economic hierarchy they had fought to protect. Blacks struggled with an active Ku Klux Klan that "would watch you just like a chicken rooster watching for a worm" (p. 270), that used its knowledge of white and black folk beliefs to psychologically intimidate, and that shot and lynched former slaves in a successful effort to reestablish white supremacy. The contradictions between words and deeds and between abstract freedom and political and economic realities helped shape the life histories of the former slaves and the folk history that they kept alive, a history that countered the official white version. No former slave thought of the overthrow of Reconstruction governments, through the use of intimidation, voting fraud, and violence, as "Redemption," although the overwhelming majority of southern whites did.

Former slaves interviewed by the FWP in the 1930s were often living in an abject poverty that in many areas of the South was demonstrably worse than what they had known in slavery. They nevertheless kept alive an oral tradition that both prized freedom and was realistic about economic realities: "There is something 'bout being free, and that makes up for all the hardships. I's been both slave and free and I knows" (p. 279). "If they would have freed the slaves and give them a piece of ground, I think that would have been a heap better than the way they did" (p. 280). In his introduction, written during World War II, Botkin maintained that the words of former slaves "take on new meaning and relevance in the light of the present, with its new freedoms and new forms of slavery" (p. 5). His assessment transcends the moment in which it was written, for *Lay My Burden Down* is a history both of Afro-Americans who experienced slavery and freedom and of the centrality to the American experience of the struggle to define freedom in a multiethnic society.

In *Lay My Burden Down* the former slaves are not all heroes, though there are heroes in this account, nor are they all helpless victims, though there are stories of victimization. The former slaves present themselves as a people who created a group identity and culture, kept alive a desire for freedom and justice, and preserved a record of their experience. This was their triumph. That triumph now belongs to those who choose to learn from it. To learn from it is to inherit an obligation. Together Botkin and the former slave he quoted said it best: "Neither Negroes nor whites could stop fighting for freedom until it could truly be said that 'this country is a free country; no slavery now' " (p. 230).

Paradoxically, the story of how these interviews came to be recorded can help illuminate the ways in which the significance of the stories told in *Lay My Burden Down* transcends the historical moment in which these stories were written down. National FWP officials were romantic nationalists who assumed that the experience of ordinary Americans would contribute to the creation of a revitalized culture and art. Unlike many romantic nationalists they rejected racist and reactionary approaches that stressed homogeneity and looked to a past golden age in trying to define a national tradition. Instead they argued that in America all groups should be taken into account in defining the national tradition and that the various groups that constituted America could benefit from learning about groups different from themselves. They looked at the American heritage, not simply as a received tradition, but as a tradition embodying values and hopes that had not yet fully been achieved. They sought to reconcile romantic nationalism and cultural pluralism.[11]

National FWP director Henry Alsberg regarded the collecting of former slave narratives as a key part of the work of the Writers' Project. In the spring of 1937, John Lomax, Botkin's predecessor as FWP folklore editor, issued instructions to southern and border state units on interviewing former slaves. Lomax's instructions emphasized how "to get the Negro talking about the days of slavery." A few months later, Alsberg sent state directors additional questions focusing on life since 1865, what the slaves had hoped freedom would mean and what they had actually experienced.[12]

Alsberg saw the FWP's first and major project, a series of encyclopedic guides to every state in the Union and to numerous cities, as only the initial phase in the Writers' Project's rediscovery of a diverse American culture. In the second phase that he initiated in 1938, Alsberg intended that the FWP would study American culture in greater depth. He thought studies of former slaves, urban workers, ethnic minorities, and southern tenant farmers and textile workers would contribute to a redefinition of American identity along more democratic pluralistic lines. To help pursue these studies he hired B. A. Botkin as FWP folklore editor, a position that Lomax's earlier resignation had left open. Alsberg planned for Botkin to work closely with Sterling Brown, FWP Negro affairs editor, and Morton Royse, FWP social-ethnic studies editor, on projects that would examine the participation of diverse groups in creating a pluralistic American culture. He envisioned books entitled *A Guide to Composite America* and *The Negro as American.* The personal interview, the individual life history, that would only much later be called oral history, emerged as a key element of these studies. The project ended before any of the studies could be completed.[13]

The contention of national FWP officials that black history was representative of important aspects of the American experience was a culturally radical assumption that held out the possibility of transforming the definition of American culture and identity. Botkin saw studies of Afro-American life and history, especially the transition from slavery to freedom, as essential to achieving this redefinition. Thus, studies of the Afro-American experience were regarded as a central part of the vision national FWP officials had of the contribution their agency could make to American culture. The desire of national FWP officials to reopen not only the subject of slavery but also the question of the Negro's place in American life led them to emphasize interviews that dealt with both slavery and freedom.

In the 1930s most folklorists still perceived the modern world as a mortal threat to folklore and regarded isolated and homogeneous communities as the places in which a pure and uncontaminated folklore survived. Botkin took a different approach. In his view folklore was not only survivals from the past that were fast disappearing, but also something that was still being created. Botkin regarded much of the study of folklore as a study in acculturation—the process by which the folk group adapts itself to its environment and to change, assimilating new experiences and generating new forms.[14] Thus, rather than searching for the allegedly pure and uncontaminated, Botkin wanted to use folklore as a source for studying the life and history of Americans living in a state of transition—one definition of the modern condition—such as recent immigrants and their children, urban workers, and former slaves. He was convinced that life histories and folklore materials obtained through interviews could give an artistic and historical account of the dynamics of cultures in a state of transition.[15] Botkin thought the FWP slave narratives would allow the former slaves to present an account of their experience that had value both as history and literature and that would contribute to a rewriting and revisioning of dominant literary and historical traditions.

National FWP officials thought that a rediscovery and reexamination of indigenous traditions could contribute to the creation of an American epic that could claim for Americans all the national significance and glory that had been attributed to Greek and Roman epics. Unlike conservative romantic nationalists, however, they did not have in mind an epic focusing on the heroic deeds of heroes with superhuman characteristics set in the tribe or nation's distant past— an epic that explained and justified present social and cultural arrangements. Like Emerson and Whitman, the Federal Writers found an American epic in the doings of ordinary as well as great men, and in the present as well as in the past. They saw the story of ordinary Americans such as former slaves, not the elite, as providing the basis for a new epic. It would be an epic centered on the group, but told through the accounts of ordinary individuals, not an epic centered on famous individuals with the masses as background.[16] In collecting former slave narratives Federal Writers were focusing on the institution and people whose social position constituted the greatest challenge to America's democratic claims. In envisioning such accounts as the basis of an American epic, Botkin affirmed a commitment to a definition of America as an inclusive, egalitarian, and democratic community.

The local Federal Writers who conducted the interviews with the former slaves were overwhelmingly white and southern. Their point of view differed greatly from that of national FWP officials. White southern Federal Writers, with few exceptions, were determined to make their interviews confirm the white South's traditional view of the Negro and slavery. The way the interviewers formulated their questions and the commentary they included in their interviews reveal that they worked within the conventions of the plantation tradition familiar to them through folklore, literature, and popular culture. In this tradition, inferior, dependent, and contented black slaves lived with gentlemen masters and crinolined belles in an idyllic world devoid of conflict. Since the Civil War many white southern writers had worked to convince the rest of the nation (and perhaps themselves) of the Arcadian nature of this lost plantation world and that race relations on antebellum plantations provided an ideal model for race relations in the New South.[17]

In the plantation tradition the folklore of the black community as interpreted by whites was used to justify the necessity of slavery in the past and rigid segregation in the present. This reflected the white southern view that paternalism and a caste system were a new way of continuing the allegedly benevolent race relations of the antebellum era in the New South. A similar outlook on the part of the interviewer is often evident in the unedited interviews white southern Federal Writers conducted with former slaves. The plantation tradition as a romantic national myth of a lost Camelot stood in sharp contrast to the pluralistic definition of America national FWP officials were trying to help create. The plantation myth celebrated inequality and posed no challenge to the status quo.[18]

Ignoring the commentary provided by the interviewers and focusing on the words of the former slaves, Botkin put together a volume that let the former slaves portray a much more complex world than that allowed by the plantation tradition from which many of the interviewers worked. *Lay My Burden Down* fulfilled the FWP goal of contributing to a romantic nationalism that looked forward, not backward, to a world better than the present. Botkin and the University of Chicago Press presented *Lay My Burden Down* to the American reading public as a work that spoke to inherited and unresolved questions about democracy and freedom. The shift in the discussion of slavery Botkin aimed for was reflected in the advertisement for the book the publisher ran in major newspapers: "This is no *Uncle Tom's Cabin.* It is closer to being the *Book of Exodus* of the American Negro. . . . From its rich kaleidoscope of themes, attitudes, tones, and styles, emerges the true character of the slave and his descendants as *human beings and partners in America*" (emphasis added).[19] Harriet Beecher Stowe's Uncle Tom transcended slavery through his Christian martyrdom. In *Exodus* slavery is transcended both spiritually and politically through movement into a new state of freedom. *Exodus,* but not Uncle Tom, was part of black oral tradition.

Botkin's metaphoric use of terms like epic and saga was more self-conscious than that of most other Federal Writers. He was well aware that in *Lay My Burden Down* he was putting between the covers of a book material that had been gathered from a living and changing black oral tradition. He wanted to put in print a living epic from the oral tradition and to close the gap between oral and written literature by turning to a living American oral tradition to give us a saga —in book form. The folk history of the former slaves, Botkin argued, was an American saga about the struggle for freedom, a saga that had to be understood if Americans were to understand their history, to understand the political and social order they had created, and to envision a freer and more democratic future.

For Botkin the stories of the former slaves composed a story of extraordinary adventure and heroic achievement. Like the Icelandic sagas, they were ultimately stories about family obligations and conflicts that resulted in changes in the nature of the state, for the families in the Icelandic sagas embodied the state as did the family relationships that constituted the South's peculiar institution. In both cases changes in family relationships meant changes in the state. In the saga told in *Lay My Burden Down* fratricidal war promised to recast political relationships between North and South, and between whites and blacks.

Botkin knew that *Lay My Burden Down* denied the basic assumptions of a tradition that had dominated public discourse: "there is no attempt here to gloss over the physical and mental effects of slavery, as in the sentimental distortions and cheap caricatures of fiction, the stage, and popular song. Instead, the slave emerges as an individual rather than a type, a person rather than a symbol, with normal sensibilities and intelligence, portrayed as only the Negro can portray his own kind" (p. 143). Contrary to the plantation tradition, former slaves expressed not only "humorous" philosophy but also a sense of life's tragic dimension that spoke for the common humanity they shared with white southerners and that white caricaturizations had denied them.

The tragedy at the heart of the white southern plantation tradition was the destruction of an allegedly grand way of life, an American Camelot. *Lay My Burden Down* puts a different tragedy at the heart of the story. The former slaves in *Lay My Burden Down* testify to the tragedy of a system that treated them and their families as things and a post-Civil War world in which fraud and violence were used to reestablish an oppressive racial order. If the sense of the tragedy that comes across in *Lay My Burden Down* contradicts the values of the plantation tradition, it is also broad enough to include both master and slave. As Botkin put it, "In a world torn by fear, passion, and violence, all classes were inevitably demoralized and brutalized." The tragedy was not the loss of a past world, but the continuing tragedy of the failure to create a new democratic and egalitarian society: "the tragic beginnings of what was most degrading of all— slavery's legacy of race prejudice and hatred, which has left its mark on the whole country" (p. 144). This sense of tragedy affirmed the human dignity of slaves and the primacy of democratic values. It envisioned a new social order.

Black Americans and their white allies worked during the New Deal to place the issue of civil rights on the national agenda for the first time since Reconstruction. They took advantage of the ideological aspect of World War II as a war for freedom and democracy against an abhorrent racist and totalitarian enemy to press their case for reform at home. There was a dynamic relationship between the effort to reopen discussion of slavery and Reconstruction and the effort to challenge the status quo of Jim Crow and segregation.

Assessing the usefulness of the FWP interviews with former slaves involves not only questions about the reliability and authenticity of the materials, but also questions about their relationship to Afro-American written and oral literature and history dealing with slavery. *Lay My Burden Down* is part of an Afro-American literary tradition that both protested the situation of blacks in America and offered a picture of black life to counter white racist portrayals. Deeply embedded in the slave narrative genre was a quest for freedom and a protest against slavery and racism. Botkin understood that slave narratives had always been a weapon against slavery and a defense of black culture. Slave narratives, he insisted, were the basic texts of Afro-American history and literature.

The Civil War closed the phase of the tradition in which fugitive slave narratives were a direct weapon against de jure slavery. The FWP interviews with the last of the former slaves closed a genre that had begun with the narratives of the fugitive slaves. As the Federal Writers knew well, the chance to interview former slaves was quickly passing. It was not the black oral tradition that was passing, but the opportunity to put into print the particular mix of black folklore and the individual oral history that only former slaves could provide.

But the destruction of slavery did not end the debate over slavery. After the Civil War that debate remained as much a fight over the place of Afro-Americans in American culture as it had been before the war. In each case, there was a dialectical relationship between texts created by blacks and their antislavery allies in protest and those created by whites who aimed to protect the status quo. The antebellum slave narrative helped shape its antithesis—the plantation novel defending slavery. The antithesis of prewar slavery for the vast majority of Afro-Americans was not postwar freedom, but new forms of subjugation embodied in the southern caste system. In history, literature, white folklore, and popular culture, the white southern plantation tradition justifying slavery triumphed. From roughly the end of Reconstruction until the Harlem Renaissance in the 1920s, writings by blacks could not gain the attention of a white audience unless they were written within the conventions of the plantation tradition. *Lay My Burden Down* was one of the first successful attempts since the pre-Civil War era to gain a white, as well as a black, audience for the slave's perspective.

The pre-Civil War slave narratives were written by fugitive slaves, sometimes with the assistance of a white editor, to challenge the existence of slavery. The FWP narratives are the products of the interviewers' request that the former slaves share their memories. The literacy of the fugitive slave was offered to antebellum white readers as evidence of the escaped slave's intelligence and of blacks' potential to acquire "civilization." These narratives were written more in relationship to other written texts than out of an oral tradition.[20] For the FWP interviewers and the former slaves they interviewed a different set of goals existed. The former slaves, who had not initiated these interviews, had only limited ways of influencing the interviewers' agenda. For the most part, white southern Federal Writers asked the questions. In theory, they were to do no more than faithfully transcribe oral interviews with former slaves, but it is clear that the structure of race relations in the thirties shaped the collaborative narrative form that emerged from the interviews. Nevertheless, the FWP interviews are closer to an oral tradition than the antebellum narratives, closer to the experience and the stories that created slave culture. As part of the slave's oral literature and history they reflect both tradition and change and place the reader in touch with a tradition much older than the narrators.

When Botkin edited the narratives for *Lay My Burden Down* he eliminated the presence of the interviewer from the main body of the book and confined information about individual interviewees and interviewers to an appendix. While this limits the readers' ability to analyze the interviewer/interviewee relationships, it also eliminates a barrier between the former slave and readers of *Lay My Burden Down*. Botkin focused on the self-contained story or anecdote, that part of the interview where the former slaves assumed control of the interview and told stories they had told many times before.[21] In this way, Botkin's editorial method makes for both a more powerful and more accurate story than a collection of unedited interviews would provide.

Unlike most of the authors and editors of the antebellum narratives, Botkin claims that the black oral tradition is already in itself a form of literature and history. While this history had to be printed to be shared with other Americans, it did not have to be transformed into an existing written genre to become a history. *Lay My Burden Down* works to overturn a cultural hierarchy that placed Africans and Afro-Americans at the bottom rung, that regarded blacks as inferior because they did not possess a written tradition. Rather, Americans were urged to regard black folk literature and oral history as part of "our national literature."[22]

Many readers will want to delve further into the FWP slave narrative collection after reading *Lay My Burden Down*. A critical literature dealing with the nature and scope of the former slave narrative collection and with the opportunities and problems these interviews present for researchers has developed in recent years along with studies of slavery using interviews with the former slaves. It is possible to make some generalizations about the FWP former slave narrative collection from which Botkin drew in editing *Lay My Burden Down*. While the collection represents all types of occupations and all sizes of plantations, the sample was not collected on a scientifically random basis. Interviewees were usually selected on the basis of previous contact or proximity. The slave experience in the upper South and border states is greatly underrepresented. A large majority of the interviewees were less than fifteen years old when the Civil War began. Thus the great majority had experienced the life of a slave as children. Approximately two-thirds of the slaves who were interviewed were over eighty, and, since such a long life span was unusual for a former slave, it is possible that these interviewees had been better fed and treated than most slaves. Many of the former slaves resided in the same areas as their master's descendants and were economically dependent on whites. Interviewers were often members of the local white community and sometimes descendants of the former owners of the individuals they were interviewing.[23]

Understandably, the former slaves often tried not to violate the etiquette of race relations that governed their interactions with whites. As one interviewee explained it: "Lots of old slaves closes the door before they tell the truth about their days of slavery. . . . You can't blame them for this, because they had plenty of early discipline making them cautious about saying anything uncomplimentary about their masters" (p. 280). Or, "Everything I tells you am the truth, but they's plenty I can't tell you" (p. 95). Outside of Virginia, Louisiana, and Florida, which had special black writers' units, few blacks were employed on the state Writers' Projects in the South. The efforts of national FWP officials to change this mostly failed. And that failure limited their ability to reopen the discussion about Afro-American history. In general, former slaves talked more openly with black interviewers than they did with whites.[24]

Drawn from the relief rolls, few Federal Writers had any previous experience relevant to interviewing. They often failed to pursue important topics and asked leading questions. Far too often they were totally unreflective regarding their assumptions about slavery and blacks, and they sought, perhaps unconsciously, to have the interviewees confirm their preconceptions. Federal Writers did not use tape recorders. That fact alone raises questions about whether the interviews are verbatim accounts. Furthermore, it is almost impossible for untrained outsiders to write down oral communication of another group without making it conform to some extent to rules governing oral and written communication in their own culture. Many Federal Writers were willing to edit interviews in ways that would be unacceptable to historians and folklorists today. In some cases the goal seems to have been to make the interview conform to the notions of Federal Writers about what constituted an orderly and coherent presentation. Sometimes the changes reflect the biases of the Federal Writers involved.[25]

The study of American slavery has been one of the most exciting and dynamic fields in American historical writing in the last quarter century—and the FWP interviews with former slaves have been a central part of this work. While questions about how to read and interpret the FWP interviews have engendered a lively dialogue, scholars no longer simply dismiss these sources because they contain folklore and are based on memory and oral tradition. Rather they argue that all historical documents have strengths and limitations.

Lay My Burden Down and more recent studies of slavery should be viewed as complementary works that need to be read together in the effort to understand American slavery. A major strength of *Lay My Burden Down* is the evocative way it uses stories to create a narrative history out of the folk literature, knowledge, and experience of former slaves. Ironically, in drawing on oral tradition *Lay My Burden Down* can remind readers that written history, along with several other nonfiction genres, was once widely regarded as an important part of literature.

Readers of *Lay My Burden Down* will find that this book can keep the discussion of slavery from becoming an abstraction and can give them a sensitivity to the human dynamics of slavery. No single work, however, can exhaust the complex history of so rich a topic. Historians relying on a wide variety of sources can treat economic, political, and demographic matters hardly mentioned in *Lay My Burden Down*. The work of recent scholars can send us back to these texts with new sensitivity to what the former slaves experienced and what they have to tell us. And reading *Lay My Burden Down* can provide readers with their own sense of the slave experience to match against the debates among historians about slave culture, religion, personality, family life, and relationships between masters and slaves.

There is no direct continuity between the views of FWP national officials and recent historians of slavery, and yet the underlying themes of these recent works echo the goals of Henry Alsberg and B. A. Botkin. The echoes are evidence of persistent issues in American life and cultural studies. FWP officials asked questions about black history and culture that would not again become central issues until the 1960s and 1970s. They advocated going directly to the former slaves to obtain a black perspective on slavery. Like the new social historians who came to dominate their profession in the 1970s, national FWP officials wished to create a history of America that paid attention to the great majority of people, particularly those on the lowest social rungs—the workers, the poor, the ethnic and racial minorities. And they sought alternatives to traditional literary sources that primarily reflected the viewpoint of small elites. The end they envisioned, however, was not simply a greater understanding of social change, processes, and structures, but also a flowering of American culture growing out of a more democratic community in which all citizens participated equally. They thought that the voices of people such as former slaves could not only change the way Americans understood the past, but also in doing that help create the future.

The story the former slaves told remains forever unfinished, for through the ongoing act of retelling and rereading, in oral tradition and in print, it contributes to continuing efforts to create and maintain a freer and more democratic and egalitarian society. The effort to define and achieve a democratic society is still, and will forever, remain a challenge. Listening to the voices in *Lay My Burden Down* can aid us in understanding the American experience and in meeting that challenge. We owe it to the former slaves and to ourselves to listen to these voices that, through the work of B. A. Botkin and the Federal Writers' Project, found a permanent way to reach across time and speak to later generations of Americans.

JERROLD HIRSCH

Notes

1. Sterling Brown, "By the Rivers of Babylon," review of *Lay My Burden Down, Nation* 146(May 11, 1946):534–35.

2. Thomas Nelson Page, *In Ole Virginia; or, Marse Chan and Other Stories* (New York, 1887), p. 10. For an overview of the pervasive popularity of the plantation tradition see Francis Pendelton Gaines, *The Southern Plantation: A Study in the Development of the Accuracy of a Tradition* (New York, 1924).

3. George Rawick, ed., *The American Slave: A Composite Autobiography,* 19 vols.; Supplemental Series no. 1, 12 vols.; Supplemental Series no. 2, 10 vols. (Westport, Conn., 1972, 1977, 1979).

4. David Brion Davis, "Slavery and the Post World War II Historians," *Daedalus* 103(1974):1–16.

5. B. A. Botkin, "Folklore as a Neglected Source of Social History," in *The Cultural Approach to History,* ed. Caroline Ware (New York, 1940), p. 308.

6. Ben Burns, review of *Lay My Burden Down, Chicago Defender,* December 1, 1945. Melville J. Herskovits, an anthropologist who stressed the importance of the African strand in Afro-American culture, wrote Botkin: "The ambivalence of the reviewer [in the Chicago *Defender,* a black newspaper] toward it [*Lay My Burden Down*] is, of course, the perfect documentation of what seems to me to be the real inner tragedy of the Negro in this country." Herskovits to Botkin, November 28, 1945, B. A. Botkin Papers, University of Nebraska Archives, Lincoln, Nebraska.

7. C. Vann Woodward, "History from Slave Sources," *American Historical Review* 79(1974):470.

8. B. A. Botkin, "Manual for Folklore Studies," August 15, 1938, Federal Writers' Project files, Works Progress Administration, Records Group 69, National Archives, Washington, D.C. (hereinafter FWPNA).

9. Botkin's views need to be placed in a historical context. Many involved in the debate over origins assumed whites were racially superior. Some scholars emphasized aspects of black culture that they saw as inferior imitations of white culture, while others called attention to what they saw as survivals from an inferior African culture. Among scholars, white and black, who did not make racist assumptions, anthropologist Melville Herskovits was virtually alone in emphasizing the importance of the African strand in Afro-American culture. His conclusions were widely dismissed as a strained and exaggerated interpretation of the evidence. See his now classic *The Myth of the Negro Past* (New York, 1941). For a discussion of the historical development of this issue and the theoretical issues involved see Charles Joyner, "Introduction to the Brown Thrasher Edition," in *Drums and Shadows: Survival Studies Among the Georgia*

Coastal Negroes (Athens, Ga., 1946, 1984), pp. ix–xxiv; Charles Joyner, *Down by the Riverside: A South Carolina Slave Community* (Urbana, Ill., 1984), pp. xix–xxii; and Lawrence Levine, *Black Culture and Black Consciousness* (New York, 1977), pp. 5, 19–30, 154–55.

10. Alsberg to Ellen Woodward, assistant WPA director, July 22, 1938, FWPNA.

11. These are key themes in Jerrold Hirsch, "Portrait of America: The Federal Writers' Project in an Intellectual and Cultural Context" (Ph.D. diss., University of North Carolina at Chapel Hill, 1984), especially pp. 30–67, where Hirsch examines the outlook of key national FWP officials.

12. Lomax's questionnaire and Alsberg's letter to State Directors of the Federal Writers' Project, July 30, 1937, are reprinted in Rawick, *From Sunup to Sundown: The Making of the Slave Community,* vol. 1 of *The American Slave: A Composite Autobiography,* pp. 173–76.

13. Alsberg to Lewis Mumford, October 4, 1938; Alsberg to Ellen Woodward, July 22, 1938, Box 195, FWPNA.

14. For an overview of Botkin's career and ideas see Jerrold Hirsch, "Folklore in the Making: B. A. Botkin," *Journal of American Folklore* 100(1986):3–38.

15. B. A. Botkin, "We Called it 'Living Lore,'" *New York Folklore Quarterly* 14(1958):189–98.

16. Jerrold Hirsch, "Portrait of America," pp. 192–213, 641–53; Henry Bennett to Mrs. Wharton, February 21, 1941, Box 192, FWPNA.

17. Gaines, *The Southern Plantation,* pp. 1–17, 95–142, supports my analysis. Gaines is sympathetic to the tradition he purports to be probing for its accuracy, and thus his work is valuable as both a primary and a secondary source. Paul H. Buck, *The Road to Reunion: 1865–1900* (Boston, 1937), pp. 196–235, 282–97, provides an analysis similar to mine. Buck, however, views the fruits of the plantation tradition positively. For a critical view see Paul Gaston, *The New South Creed: A Study in Southern Mythmaking* (New York, 1970), pp. 167–186.

18. Gaines, *The Southern Plantation,* pp. 1–5.

19. From the full page advertisement run in the Chicago *Sun* Book Week, November 25, 1945. The advertisement was also run in other major metropolitan newspapers. University of Chicago Press Records, Box 64, University of Chicago Archives.

20. Henry Louis Gates, Jr., "The Language of Slavery," in *The Slave Narrative,* ed. Charles T. Davis and Henry Louis Gates, Jr. (New York, 1985), pp. xxiii–xxix.

21. For an insightful analysis that supports this point see John Edgar Wideman, "Charles Chestnutt and the WPA Narratives: The Oral and Literate Roots of Afro-American Literature," in *The Slave Narrative,* pp. 69–78.

22. From the full page advertisement run in the Chicago *Sun* Book Week, November 25, 1945.

23. For a discussion of these issues see David T. Bailey, "A Divided Prism: Two Sources of Black Testimony on Slavery," *Journal of Southern History* 46(1980):381–404; "Using the Testimony of Ex-Slaves: Approaches and Problems," *Journal of*

Southern History 41(1975):473–92; Paul D. Escott, *Slavery Remembered: A Record of Twentieth-Century Slave Narratives* (Chapel Hill, 1979); Jerrold Hirsch, "Reading and Counting," *Reviews in American History* 8(1980):312–17; C. Vann Woodward, "History from Slave Sources"; and Norman R. Yetman, "The Background of the Slave Narrative Collection," *American Quarterly* 19(1967):533–53, and "Ex-Slave Interviews and the Historiography of Slavery," *American Quarterly* 36(1984):181–210.

24. Monty Penkower, *The Federal Writers' Project: A Study in Government Patronage of the Arts* (Urbana, Ill., 1988), pp. 66–67. The FWP's Negro Studies File contains Sterling Brown's repeated and mostly futile effort to encourage black employment on the southern state FWP projects, Boxes 201 and 202, FWPNA.

25. Blassingame, "Using the Testimony of Ex-Slaves," p. 487; Rawick, "General Introduction," in *The American Slave* Supplemental Series no. 1, vol. 1, pp. xvi–xxvi; Hirsch, "Reading and Counting," pp. 314–16. Fortunately, it is possible in Rawick's collection of the slave narratives to see examples of editorial procedures, since he reproduces more than one version of an interview and leaves intact all of the editorial comments, deletions, and additions. The correspondence of Chalmers Murray to Mabel Montgomery, South Carolina State FWP director, July 1 and July 8, 1937, FWPNA, provides insight into the outlook that guided many white southern field workers interviewing ex-slaves.

LAY MY
BURDEN DOWN

Preface

This book is a selection and integration of excerpts and complete narratives from the Slave Narrative Collection of the Federal Writers' Project, whose history and method are discussed below. The present note concerns my own part in a work which has passed through many hands and minds, as well as several stages of completion.

Since the work of collection had been nearly completed when I became folklore editor of the Federal Writers' Project in 1938, my efforts have been devoted chiefly to utilization. From 1939 to 1941, as chief editor of the Writers' Unit of the Library of Congress Project, I planned and supervised the work of organizing and preparing the collection for deposit in the Library of Congress.

In February, 1944, I was asked to prepare for publication a selection of the narratives "which would give at once the flavor of the entire collection and the social patterns revealed in the series, while keeping literary excellence to the forefront." This meant not only a reduction in scope and scale but also a revision of my thinking about the narratives to the point where I could see them not as a collection of source material for the scholar but as a finished product for the general reader. Specifically, it meant (1) reducing the bulk of the collection from over ten thousand to five or six hundred manuscript pages; (2) concentrating on its broadly human and imaginative aspects and on those oral, literary, and narrative folk values for which in 1928 I coined the word "folk-say"; and (3) fitting the selections into some sort of sequence that would give pattern to the book and to slavery.

To do all this in the narrow compass of some three hundred pages required the use of excerpts in preference to complete narratives, except where the latter constituted an irreducible minimum, as in the autobiographical section, "Long Remembrance," which balances the picture of slavery with the picture of the individual life. At the same time, the excerpts required considerable pointing up, by careful cutting, arranging, and titling, to give proper emphasis where there was none or where, out of context, there might be a wrong emphasis.

In accordance with the same criteria of truth and readability, the original attempts at dialect-writing, successful and unsuccessful, were abandoned, except for a few characteristic and expressive variations. Although they had been instructed to put truth to idiom first, many interviewers were betrayed by their zeal for accurate recording into stressing truth to pronunciation, which led them into new and worse inaccuracies. It is true that a word like "master" may have a half-dozen variants—"marster," "moster," "mastuh," "maussa," "marsa," and "massa"—but the fine distinctions of phonetic spelling (due to differences as much in the way a sound is heard or represented as in the sound itself) are for the specialist and get in the way of the essential qualities of spoken language, which are qualities of style, of word choice and word order.

To preserve the narrative flow and the collective tone of many voices speaking as one, the source of each selection is given in the appended "List of Informants and Interviewers." For the rest, except for an occasional omission or emendation to clarify meaning or the change of a name here and there, my job has been that of the original interviewers, namely, to let the ex-slaves, and through them slavery and freedom, speak for themselves.

The photograph on the cover was made in Greene County, Georgia, in 1941, by Jack Delano for the Farm Security Administration. For valuable aid or encouragement, of one kind or another, I am indebted to the Librarian of Congress, Dr. Luther H. Evans, and the staff of the Rare Books Division of the Library of Congress; to Joseph A. Brandt and the editors and production department of the University of Chicago Press; and to Sterling Brown, Joseph L. Leach, and Gertrude F. Botkin.

B. A. BOTKIN
Washington, D.C.
September 1945

Introduction

Everything I tells you am the truth, but they's plenty I can't tell you.

From the memories and the lips of former slaves have come the answers which only they can give to questions which Americans still ask: What does it mean to be a slave? What does it mean to be free? And, even more, how does it *feel?* The writing and recording of slave autobiographies goes back to the latter part of the eighteenth century, which produced the narratives of Briton Hammon, John Marrant, and Gustavus Vassa. During the antislavery movement, fugitive slaves not only joined in the struggle for freedom but also supplied it with an effective weapon in the form of narratives of their "Uncommon Sufferings and Surprising Deliverance." Slavery itself, as experienced and reported by the slave, was the best argument against slavery. This autobiographical propaganda, a kind of nonviolent slave revolt, represents the first attempts of Negroes to write their own history and their earliest literature of self-portraiture and social protest. As contemporary social history, from the bottom up, it completes the picture of slavery which we get, on the one hand, from planters' and overseers' records, diaries, and letters and, on the other hand, from the journals of travelers like Harriet Martineau, Fanny Kemble, and Frederick Law Olmsted.

Both during and since slavery times the experiences of ex-slaves have been recorded and used in several different ways. First and perhaps best of all is the method of taking down the informant's own words as he speaks or as soon after as convenient. This method was employed by Benjamin Drew, of Boston, in *The Refugee: or The Narratives of Fugitive Slaves in Canada, Related by Themselves* (1856), a collection of over a hundred graphic sketches in the first person. Another method is that of the editorialized interview, used by James Redpath in *The Roving Editor: or, Talks with Slaves in the Southern States* (1859), which weaves conversations into a narrative and descriptive commentary, sprinkled with dialect and exhortation. A variation of the moralizing approach is seen in Octavia V. Rogers Albert's *The House of Bondage, or Charlotte Brooks and Other Slaves* (1890), with its sentimental and retrospective pen pictures and narratives of old slaves. Finally, there are collections of biographical sketches and anecdotes in the third person, from Isaac T. Hopper's "Tales of Oppression" (originally published in Northern newspapers and revised and reprinted in Lydia Maria Child's life of the Quaker abolitionist in 1853) to William Still, the Negro antislavery agent's *The Underground Rail Road: A Record of Facts, Authentic Narratives, Letters, &c., Narrating the Hardships Hair-breadth Escapes and Death Struggles of the Slaves in Their Efforts for Freedom, as Related by Themselves and Others, or Witnessed by the Author.* . . . (1872).

In our own day, slave narratives and interviews have continued to be used in one or another of these two main fashions: for serious historical and sociological documentation, as in Frederic Bancroft's *Slave-trading in the Old South* (1931), Charles S. Johnson's *Shadow of the Plantation* (1934), and John B. Cade's "Out of the Mouths of Ex-Slaves" (*Journal of Negro History,* July, 1935); or for nostalgic character and local-color sketches of old times, as in Orland Kay Armstrong's *Old Massa's People: The Old Slaves Tell Their Story* (1931) and Bernard Robb's *Welcum Hinges* (1942).

In 1934 Lawrence D. Reddick proposed to Harry L. Hopkins, director of the Federal Emergency Relief Administration, a Negro project "to study the needs and collect the testimony of ex-slaves" in the Ohio River Valley and the lower South. In 1936 the work thus begun was continued and extended under the Works Progress Administration by white and Negro workers of the Federal Writers' Project in the states of Alabama, Arkansas, Florida, Georgia, Indiana, Kansas, Kentucky, Louisiana, Maryland, Mississippi, Missouri, North Carolina, Ohio, Oklahoma, South Carolina, Tennessee, Texas, and Virginia. To this type of large-scale collection of life-history and interview material the program and personnel of the Federal Writers' Project were well adapted. Established primarily to give employment to unemployed writers, newspaper men, research workers, and other qualified persons in the preparation of a series of state and local guides, the Project also made collections of folklore and life-histories, representing, in addition to former slaves, people of various occupations, nationalities, and regions, as in *These Are Our Lives* (1939).

Beginning in 1939, when the Work Projects Administration passed from federal to state control, the Library of Congress Project prepared for deposit in the Library, along with other surplus products of the Writers' Program, the bulk of the slave-narrative collection, including photographs of former slaves, interviews with descendants of slaves and white informants concerning slavery, transcripts of laws, and notices and records of sale, transfer, and manumission of slaves. Collated and arranged in seventeen volumes in thirty-three parts (now available in microfilm copy), the original typescripts of over two thousand narratives, with several hundred photographs, were bound and deposited in the Rare Books Division. Other narratives (notably those gathered by the Virginia and Louisiana projects) are still in the states, in specially designated depositories for unpublished materials of the Federal Writers' Project. A number of narratives have been published in two Writers' Project publications, *The Negro in Virginia* (1939) and *Drums and Shadows: Survival Studies among the Georgia Coastal Negroes* (1940).

The workers of the Federal Writers' Project approached their task of interviewing ex-slaves frankly as amateurs. Those associated with the direction and criticism of the work in the national office[1] had a variety of special interests, from folklore to race relations; but they all had in common a preoccupation with the materials of American culture and a desire to give the Negro fair representation in both the program and the personnel of the Project.

In 1937 a set of simple and "homely" instructions and questions was issued with a view to getting the ex-slave to thinking and talking freely about the days of slavery. The questions covered the following subjects: Place and date of birth; parents' names and origin; brothers' and sisters' names; recollections or stories of grandparents; life in the quarters; kind of work; money earned, if any, and how, and what was purchased with it; food and cooking; clothing; owner and his family; the big house; overseer or driver and poor-white neighbors; size of plantation and number of slaves; daily schedule; punishments; slave sales and auctions; education; religion; runaway slaves; trouble between blacks and whites; patrollers; leisure-time activities; holidays, weddings, funerals, etc.; games, songs, stories, superstitions, etc.; health, medicine, and folk cures; the Civil War; the Yankees; the news of freedom; the first year of freedom; the Ku Klux Klan and night riders; marriage and children; opinions concerning Negro and white leaders; attitude toward slavery and the church. As the need of more information on life after freedom was felt, the following subjects were subsequently added: What the slaves expected of freedom and what they got; attitude toward Reconstruction; the influence of secret organizations; experience in voting and holding office; life since 1864; attitude toward the younger generation and the present; slave uprisings; stories of the Nat Turner Rebellion; songs of the period.

In reading the narratives one is impressed first by their very bulk, whose variety and repetition provide a broad basis for interpretation. They are, at the same time, uneven. Many are damaged or weakened by internal contradictions and inconsistencies; obvious errors of historical fact; vague, confused, or ambiguous statements; lapses of memory; and reliance on hearsay rather than firsthand experience. By comparison with the first-person accounts, the few written in the third person seem completely lacking not only in flavor but also in reliability. In the absence of accompanying information on the interviewer, however, all judgments of reliability must be based on purely internal evidence. Here the form, as well as the content, of the narrative may inspire confidence or arouse distrust. Still, one can often be fooled, since even the most tortuous and painfully misspelled narrative may conceal excellent passages. In spite of instructions against editing or censorship, some narratives show signs of having been retouched. And, in spite of instructions against taking sides, the interviewer, in his edito-

---

[1] Directly involved were Henry G. Alsberg, director of the Federal Writers' Project; George Cronyn, associate director; John A. Lomax, national advisor on folklore and folkways (1936–37); Sterling A. Brown, editor on Negro affairs; Mary Lloyd, editor in the Essay Department; and B. A. Botkin, folklore editor (1938–39).

rial introductions and asides, his notes and leading questions, often betrays his personal prejudices and sympathies.

The informant himself is often guilty of flattery and exaggeration, of telling only what he wants to tell or what he thinks the interviewer wants to hear. No less interesting than what he says is how he says it, on account of the many subtly implied acceptances and resistances which one interviewer describes as the "quick, smooth cover-up when something is to be withheld," the "unexpected vigor of the mind when the bait is attractive enough to draw it out," the "reserve in her manner which makes questioning beyond a certain point impertinent," the apparent "lack of resentment that lies behind the words that sound vehement when read." The whole complex of Negro adjustment, including personal loyalties and white controls, past and present, and the ex-slave's status in his community, affect his attitude and expression, particularly on the questions of slavery and freedom. Thus the ex-slave on relief is likely to be more bitter about the present than about the past. In other cases, as when the narrator may belong to an ex-slave association or may even have found it profitable to be an object of curiosity or awe, he obviously enjoys the role he is playing.

> The former slaves have not only retained memories of their earlier status, but have maintained a certain dignity and prestige for themselves by contrasting these memories with the pretensions to freedom of the younger generation. For these older ones it has become a part of the technique of survival to rationalize the social adjustments made. There are, at the same time, former slaves who, with a certain defiance, refer to slavery as an ill which they were fortunate and grateful to escape. This they do with vigor and eloquence, but also with a becoming caution. There is enough spirit in their recital of slave conditions, however, to set them apart from some of their brethren, who, like many of their masters, find these memories glowing with increasing charm and romance as time separates them from the period [Charles S. Johnson, in *Shadow of the Plantation,* pp. 18–19].

Finally, the narratives display considerable variation in style and treatment, ranging from fragmentary and scrappy accounts to full, well-rounded recitals, from correct to colloquial English, from modified to extreme dialect, from rambling and at times senile garrulousness to clear-cut reconstruction of the past, from mere generalization to rich circumstantial detail, from stilted self-consciousness to complete naturalness and spontaneity, from sheer triteness to highly imaginative and dramatic realism. The best results are obtained when a good informant and a good interviewer get together and the narrative is the product of the conscious or unconscious collaboration of the two, or when the interviewer succeeds in eliminating himself entirely and the reader is brought face to face with an informant who has a rewarding experience to share or a good story to tell.

As the last of the ex-slaves speak, with the urgency of the "historic few," their words take on new meaning and relevance in the light of the present, with its new freedoms and new forms of slavery. For what they have to say of race, caste, and class, of cultural conflict and change, as well as slavery, the narratives have prime importance for the sociologist and the social anthropologist. As folk history—history from the bottom up, in which the people become their own historians, they directly concern the cultural historian, fully aware that history must study the inarticulate many as well as the articulate few.

The best of the slave narratives also belong to literature. "With the exception of his folk songs," writes Vernon Loggins, in *The Negro Author,* "the Negro's most valuable contributions to American literature have been in the form of personal memoirs." In contrast to the more consciously produced narratives of racial leaders, many of which, like those of Josiah Henson (the original Uncle Tom) and Frederick Douglass, have become classics, the oral statements of ex-slaves may seem crude and casual. But as folk-say—what the people have to say about themselves—and oral literature on an illiterate or a semiliterate level, they will be found to possess literary qualities of their own, close to folk literature. They have the forthrightness, tang, and tone of people talking, the immediacy and concreteness of the participant and the eyewitness, and the salty irony and mother wit which, like the gift of memory, are kept alive by the bookless world.

But it is not only as folk history and folk literature that the narratives interest the folklorist. In its static structure, "extra-organizational" and "extra-techno-logical," slave society was a folk society, here revealed in all its multiplicity of folkways and folk notions, differentiated by occupation, region, and economy—field hand, house servant, and artisan; Sea Islands, Tidewater, and Deep South; cotton, tobacco, and sugar plantations. As a self-taught, self-contained group, moreover, on the make-it-yourself-or-do-without level of culture, slaves had their folk handskills and mindskills, their play of popular fantasy in both the real and the unreal world, their songs (omitted here), stories, sayings, games, pastimes, and superstitious beliefs and practices. Finally, slaves had their own code of behavior with respect to the whites, to complement the latter's slave code; and ex-slaves have kept alive their own tradition of slavery to match the white plantation tradition. As a mixture of fact and fiction, then, colored by the fantasy and idealization of old people recalling the past, the narratives constitute a kind of collective saga of slavery. In it the characters themselves are the narrators, revealing themselves as natural storytellers, who draw, for both their material and their expression, upon group experience and traditional symbols, upon the folklore of slavery which outlives slavery. Thus the narratives, as they develop certain common and traditional patterns of their own, may be said to be on their way to becoming folklore—the folklore of ex-slaves.

Since any written record of an interview is necessarily a visual arrangement, the reader should bear in mind that he "can't get the whole story by reading the words" but has to "hear the tones and the accents, and see the facial expressions and bodily movements, and sense the sometimes almost occult influence," as one interviewer puts it. Yet in spite of the difficulty of making the "pen become a

tongue for the dumb," in these pages the dumb speak; and history and humanity cannot fail to listen and heed. Now, even as Benjamin Drew announced in
1856:

> While his informants talked, the author wrote: nor are there in the whole
> volume a dozen verbal alterations which were not made at the moment of
> writing, while in haste to make the pen become a tongue for the
> dumb. . . .
>
> He will endeavor to collect, with a view to placing their testimony on
> record, their experience of the actual workings of slavery—what experience
> they have had of the condition of liberty—and such statements generally as
> they may be inclined to make, bearing upon the weighty subjects of op-
> pression and freedom.

PART ONE

Mother Wit

Course, the people be more intelligent in learning these days, but I'm telling you there a lot of other things got to build you up 'sides learning. There one can get up to make a speech what ain't got no learning, and they can just preach the finest kind of speech. Say they ain't know one thing they gwine say 'fore they get up there. Folks claim them kind of people been bless with plenty good mother wit.

We begin with people talking and swapping stories—the way all literature and history began in the days before writing. The talk is canny talk, full of shrewd meaning and sly humor. The stories have the unaffected sincerity of honest folk plus the reticence of those whom cruelty has made wary and whom oppression has taught the art of evasion and irony as a compromise between submission and revolt.

Where there is no tradition of learning or any tradition, for that matter, save an oral one, the folk fall back on mother wit, a kind of inspired wisdom and eloquence, based on intuition and experience. "How I larnt such?. . . . It come to me." "I ain't talking 'bout what I heard; I'm talking 'bout what I done seed." "This is a fact; 'taint no lie. It's what I done." ". . . Most of them things works iffen you tries them." Mother wit tells you what to say and do and think, on the spur of the moment; and yet its promptings come from away back; for there is a kind of accumulated mother wit of generations, which has the weight of tradition behind it and which gives the quality of proverb and ritual to improvisation. How else can one explain the rich allusiveness of language which is both plastic and patterned?

"Mean a man as God ever wattled a gut in." "He done ever'thing he could 'cept eat us." "I nussed babies till I got against nussing babies." "Right smart spends it foolish." "They [the snakes] commenced to rattle like dry butterbeans." And the power of aphorism: "White folks do as they pleases, and the darkies do as they can." "The laws of the country were made for the white man. The laws of the North were made for man." "You take a one-armed man, and he can't do what a two-armed man can. The colored man in the South is a one-armed man. . . ." "I didn't quite make slavery. Me and freedom come here together." "She said they didn't know what to do with freedom. She said it was like weaning a child what never learned to eat yet." "People *raised* children in them days. Folks just feeds 'em now and lets 'em grow up." And the power of fancy, poetic or humorous: "When you is gwine along the road and feel some warm air, then that is where the spirits has just been. The wings of the dead has done fanned that air till it's hot. . . ." "You says why did I run? These feets was made to take care of this body, and I used 'em is all."

But bright sayings and funny stories were part of a cultural pattern as well as of mother wit. In slavery's "state of perpetual war" (in Redpath's phrase), folklore was a weapon of both master and slave. Through the whole code of luck signs, of omens, charms, and taboos, as well as through "fireside training" in "mannerableness" and the good-timing of folk gatherings, the master kept a fearful and a restless people in hand. "Old training is best, and I cannot forget my manners." "Old Master was good to us. He said he wanted us singing and shouting and working in the field from morning to night." At the same time, the slave used the power of luck for his own protection, as in conjuring the hounds or carrying a rabbit's foot in his pocket to keep from getting whipped. And in his folk stories and anecdotes he took a subtle revenge on his master by turning the tables on him. Just as Br'er Rabbit, in a politer form, for the entertainment of the whites, symbolizes the triumph of cunning over superior force, so among themselves the Negroes told more realistic and more caustic tales of Old John, the slave who outwits his master, even though he sometimes gets caught. Take the sardonic jest, "Old Massa's Gone to Philameyork": While the slaves were feasting, the master returned from a pretended trip ("He just wanted to see what they would do if they thought he was away"), "disguised as a tramp—face smutty and clothes all dirty and raggedy. They couldn't tell who he was. He walked up just as though he wanted to eat and begged the boys for something to eat. The boys said to him: 'Stand back, you shabby rascal, you. Iffen they's anything left, you get some; iffen they ain't none left, you get none. This is our time. Old Massa done gone to Philameyork, and we're having a big time.' "

Although themes and motifs may be traced to Old World sources, the slave made them distinctly his own, so that much that is characteristic in Negro folklore may be traced to slavery. His hard-hitting lore reflects the way in which the Negro has adapted himself to a white man's world by "hitting a straight lick with a crooked stick."

Fooling Master
and Catching John

I fooled Old Master seven years,
Fooled the overseer three.
Hand me down my banjo,
And I'll tickle your bel-lee.

FOOLING MASTER

Mr. Whitehead owned Dirtin Ferry down to Belmont, and they had a darky there named Dick what claim sick all the time. So the master man said, "Dick, damn it, go to the house. I can't get no work outen you." So Dick went on. He was a fiddler, so they just took his victuals to him for seven years. Then one day, Old Master say to the overseer man, "Let's slip up there and see what Dick doing." So they did, and there sot Dick, fat as he could be, a-playing the fiddle and a-singing,

> Fool my master seven years.
> Going to fool him seven more.
> Hey diddle, de diddle, de diddle, de do.

About that time Old Master poked his head in the door, said, "Damn if you will. Come on outen there, you black rascal, and go to work." And I ain't never heard of Dick complaining no more.

CATCHING JOHN

He had one, do call him John, and it come a traveler and stayed all night. Old Master pointed out John and said, "He ain't never told me a lie in his life." The traveler bet Master a hundred dollars 'gainst four bits he'd catch John in a lie 'fore he left. Next morning at the table the mice was pretty bad, so the traveler caught one by the tail and put him inside a coverlid dish what was setting there on the table, and he told Old Master tell John he could eat something out of every dish after they got through but that coverlid one, and not to take the cover offen it. And John said, "No, sir, I won't." But John just naturally had to see what was in that dish, so he raise the lid and out hopped the mouse. Then here come Old Master and asked John iffen he done what he told him not to do, and John 'nied it. Then the traveler look in the dish and the mouse wa'n't there, and he said, "See there, John been lying to you all the time, you just ain't knowed it." And I reckon he right, 'cause us had to lie.

IT WAS A POSSUM A WHILE AGO

One day a nigger killed one of his master's shoats, and he catch him and when he ask him, "What's that you got there?" the nigger said, "A possum." The master said, "Let me see." He looked and seen it was a shoat. The nigger said, "Master, it may be a shoat now, but it sure was a possum while ago when I put 'im in this sack."

PIG-OOIE, PIG

Master John Booker had two niggers what had a habit of slipping across the river and killing Old Master's hogs and hiding the meat in the loft of the house. Master had a big blue hog, and one day he missed him and he sent Ned to look for him. Ned knowed all the time that he had killed it and had it hid in his loft. He hunted and called, "Pig-ooie, pig. Somebody done stole Old Master's big blue hog." They couldn't find it, but Old Master thought Ned knowed something 'bout it. One night he found out Ned was gonna kill another hog and had asked John to go with him. He borrowed John's clothes and blacked his face and met Ned at the river. Soon they find a nice big one, and Ned say, "John, I'll drive him round and you kill him." So he drove him past Old Master, but he didn't want to kill his own hog, so he made like he'd like to kill him but he missed him. Finally Ned got tired and said, "I'll kill him, you drive him by me." So Master John drove him by him, and Ned knock the hog on the head and cut his throat and they load him on the canoe. When they was nearly 'cross the river, Old Master dip up some water and wash his face a little, then he look at Ned and he say, "Ned, you look sick. I believe you've got leprosy." Ned row on little more and he jump in the river, and Master had a hard time finding him again. He had the overseer whip Ned for that.

MALITIS

. . . I remember Mammy told me about one master who almost starved his slaves. Mighty stingy, I reckon he was.

Some of them slaves was so poorly thin they ribs would kinda rustle against each other like corn stalks a-drying in the hot winds. But they gets even one hog-killing time, and it was funny, too, Mammy said.

They was seven hogs, fat and ready for fall hog-killing time. Just the day before Old Master told off they was to be killed, something happened to all them porkers. One of the field boys found them and come a-telling the master: "The hogs is all died, now they won't be any meats for the winter."

When the master gets to where at the hogs is laying, they's a lot of Negroes standing round looking sorrow-eyed at the wasted meat. The master asks: "What's the illness with 'em?"

"Malitis," they tells him, and they acts like they don't want to touch the hogs. Master says to dress them anyway for they ain't no more meat on the place.

He says to keep all the meat for the slave families, but that's because he's afraid to eat it hisself account of the hogs' got malitis.

"Don't you all know what is malitis?" Mammy would ask the children when she was telling of the seven fat hogs and seventy lean slaves. And she would laugh, remembering how they fooled Old Master so's to get all them good meats.

"One of the strongest Negroes got up early in the morning," Mammy would explain, "long 'fore the rising horn called the slaves from their cabins. He skitted to the hog pen with a heavy mallet in his hand. When he tapped Mister Hog 'tween the eyes with that mallet, 'malitis' set in mighty quick, but it was a uncommon 'disease,' even with hungry Negroes around all the time."

THE BOOTS THAT WOULDN'T COME OFF

One time a houseboy from another plantation wanted to come to one of our Saturday night dances, so his master told him to shine his boots for Sunday and fix his horse for the night and then he could git off for the frolic. Abraham shined his master's boots till he could see hisself in them, and they looked so grand he was tempted to try 'em on. They was a little tight but he thought he could wear 'em, and he wanted to show hisself off in 'em at the dance. They wa'n't so easy to walk in, and he was 'fraid he might git 'em scratched up walking through the fields, so he snuck his master's horse out and rode to the dance. When Abraham rid up there in them shiny boots, he got all the gals' 'tention. None of 'em wanted to dance with the other niggers. That Abraham was sure strutting till somebody run in and told him his horse had done broke its neck. He had tied it to a limb and sure enough, some way, that horse had done got tangled up and hung its own self. Abraham begged the other nigger boys to help him take the dead horse home, but he had done took their gals and he didn't get no help. He had to walk twelve miles home in them tight shoes. The sun had done riz up when he got there and it wa'n't long 'fore his master was calling: "Abraham, bring me my boots." That nigger would holler out, "Yes, sir, I's a-coming." But them boots wouldn't come off 'cause his foots had done swelled up in 'em. His master kept on calling and when Abraham seed he couldn't put it off no longer, he just cut them boots off his foots and went in and told what he had done. His master was awful mad and said he was a good mind to take the hide off Abraham's back. "Go git my horse quick, nigger, 'fore I most kills you," he yelled. Then Abraham told him: "Master, I knows you is going to kill me now, but your horse is done dead." Then poor Abraham had to out and tell the whole story, and his master got to laughing so 'bout how he took all the gals away from the other boys and how them boots hurt him that it looked like he never could stop. When he finally did stop laughing and shaking his sides, he said: "That's all right, Abraham. Don't never let nobody beat your time with the gals." And that's all he ever said to Abraham 'bout it.

I COME TO TELL THEM I COULDN'T COME

See, I wa'n't so old, just a young boy in slavery time, but I recall Young Master told Tom, a young nigger there, one time not to go to the frolic.

"Clean up them dishes and go to bed," he say. And Tom said, "Yes, sir," but Marse Nep watch Tom through the door and after a while Tom slip out and away he went, with Young Master right behind him. He got there and found Tom cutting a ground shuffle big as anybody. Young Master called him. "Tom," he say, "Tom, didn't I tell you you couldn't come to this frolic?" "Yes, sir," says Tom, "you sure did, and I just come to tell 'em I couldn't come."

Young Master didn't hurt Tom none, but I is seed 'em strip 'em plumb naked and nigh about kill 'em.

MASTER PUMPKIN

Master didn't whip, only once. That 'cause a nigger steal he favorite pumpkin. He am saving that for to get the seed, and it am big as the ten-gallon jug. The corn field am full of pumpkins, but that nigger done took Master's choice one. That pumpkin am so big he have to tussle with it 'fore he get it to he cabin. It like stealing a elephant, you can't hide it in the watch pocket. Course, lots of niggers seed that colored gentleman with that pumpkin, and 'fore long Master know it.

Well, sir, it am the funny sight to see him punish that nigger. First, Master sot him down on the ground front the quarters, where us all see him. Then he make that nigger set down and give him the big bowl pumpkin sauce and make him eat it. Him eat and eat and get so full him can't hardly swallow, and Master say, "Eat some more, it am awful good." That nigger try, but him can't eat no more. Master give him the light brushing, and it am funny to see that colored gentleman with pumpkin smear on he face and tears running down he face. After that, us children call him Master Pumpkin, and Master never have no more trouble with stealing he seed pumpkins.

WHAT THE PASS SAID

I

They had what you call patrollers who would catch you from home and wear you out and send you back to your master. If a master had slaves he just could not rule (some of 'em was hard and just would not mind the boss), he would ask him if he wanted to go to another plantation and if he said he did, then he would give him a pass, and that pass would read: "Give this nigger hell." Of course, when the patrollers or other plantation boss would read the pass, he would beat him nearly to death and send him back. Of course, the nigger could not read and did not know what the pass said. You see, they did not 'low no nigger to have a book or piece of paper of any kind, and you know they was not going to teach any of 'em to read.

II

. . . There was one woman owns some slaves and one of 'em asks her for a pass, and she give him the piece of paper supposed to be the pass, but she writes on it:

> His shirt am rough and his back am tough,
> Do, pray, Mr. Paddleroller, give him enough.

The paddlerollers beat him nearly to death, 'cause that's what's wrote on the paper he give 'em.

POLLY PARROT

The mistress had an old parrot, and one day I was in the kitchen making cookies, and I decided I wanted some of them, so I tooks me out some and put them on a chair; and when I did this the mistress entered the door. I picks up a cushion and throws over the pile of cookies on the chair, and Mistress came near the chair and the old parrot cries out, "Mistress burn, Mistress burn." Then the mistress looks under the cushion, and she had me whupped, but the next day I killed the parrot, and she often wondered who or what killed the bird.

THE TERRAPIN THAT COULD TALK

This nigger went down to the spring and found a terrapin, and he say, "What brung you here?" Just imagine how he felt when it say to him, "Teeth and tongue bring me here, and teeth and tongue will bring you here." He run to the house and told his master that he found a terrapin that could talk. They went back, and he asked the terrapin what bring him here and it wouldn't say a word. Old Master didn't like it 'cause he went down there just to see a common ordinary terrapin, and he told the nigger he was going to get into trouble for telling him a lie. Next day the nigger seen the terrapin and it say the same thing again. Soon after that this nigger was lynched right close to the place he saw the terrapin.

TURN THE TRAY AROUND

Just 'fore the war, a white preacher he come to us slaves and says: "Do you want to keep your homes where you get all to eat, and raise your children, or do you want to be free to roam around without a home, like the wild animals? If you want to keep your homes you better pray for the South to win. All they wants to pray for the South to win, raise the hand." We all raised our hands 'cause we was scared not to, but we sure didn't want the South to win.

That night all the slaves had a meeting down in the hollow. Old Uncle Mack, he gets up and says: "One time over in Virginia there was two old niggers, Uncle Bob and Uncle Tom. They was mad at one another, and one day they decided to have a dinner and bury the hatchet. So they sat down, and when Uncle Bob wasn't looking Uncle Tom put some poison in Uncle Bob's food, but he saw it and when Uncle Tom wasn't looking Uncle Bob he turned the tray around on Uncle Tom, and he gets the poison food." Uncle Mack, he says: "That's what we slaves is gwine do, just turn the tray around and pray for the North to win."

I COME FROM ABOVE, WHERE ALL IS LOVE

The slaves would get tired of the way they was treated and try to run away to the North. I had a cousin to run away one time. Him and another fellow had got 'way up in Virginia 'fore Master Jim found out where they was. Soon as Master Jim found the whereabouts of George, he went after him. When Master Jim gets to George and 'em, George pretended like he didn't know Master Jim. Master Jim asks him, "George, don't you know me?" George he say, "I never seed you 'fore in my life." Then they ask George and 'em where did they come from. George and this other fellow look up in the sky and say, "I come from above, where all is love." If they had owned they knowed Master Jim, he could have brung 'em back home.

LAYING DOWN AND GETTING UP

After Old Ned got such a terrible beating for praying for freedom, he slipped off and went to the North to jine the Union army. After he got in the army he wrote to Master Tom. In his letter he had those words:

"I am laying down, Master, and gitting up, Master," meaning that he went to bed when he felt like it and got up when he pleased to.

CUSSING MASTER

. . . Well, all Master Ed Mobley's niggers like to stay with him after freedom. They just stay on without the whippings. Instead of whippings they just got cussings, good ones too. There was two old men, Joe Raines and Joe Murray, that he was particular fond of. Maybe he more love Joe Raines the bestest. One day Joe Murray let the cows get away in the corn field. At dinnertime Master Ed cuss him before the whole crowd of hands, laying around before dinner; and he cuss him powerful. After dinner Joe Murray grieve and complain much about it to the crowd. Joe Raines up and allow: "Next time he cuss you, do like I do, just cuss him back. This is a free country, yes sir. Just give him as good a cussing as he gives you."

Not long after that, the boar hog get out the lot gate, when Joe Murray was leading his mule out. Master Ed lit out on Joe Murray a-cussing, and Joe Murray lit out on Master Ed a-cussing, and then Master Ed catch Joe and give him a slavery-time whipping and turn him loose. Joe Murray take his mule on to the field, where he glum with Joe Raines. Joe Murray tell about the boar hog getting out and the cussings and the whippings. Joe Raines allow: "You didn't cuss him right. You never cuss him like I cuss him, or you'd-a never got a whipping." Joe Murray allow: "How you cuss him then, Joe?" Say Joe Raines very slow: "Well, when I cuss Master Ed, I goes 'way down in the bottoms where the corn grow high and got a black color. I looks east and west and north and south. I see no Master Ed. Then I pitches into him and gives him the worst cussing a man ever give another man. Then when I goes back to the house, my feelings is satisfied from the cussing I have give him, and he is sure to make up with me, for Master Ed don't bear anger in his bosom long. The next time cuss him, but be sure to go 'way off somewhere so he can't hear you, nigger."

JOKE: PUTTING HAND UNDER OLD MISTRESS' DRESS

I'll tell you 'nother funny joke 'bout Henry Johnson. He had to clean up most of the time. So Mrs. Newton's dress was hanging in the room up on the wall, and when he come out he said to old Uncle Jerry, he said: "Jerry, guess what I done." And Jerry said: "What?" And Uncle Henry said: "I put my hand under Old Mistress' dress." Uncle Jerry said: "What did she say?" Uncle Henry say: "She didn't say nothing." So Uncle Jerry 'cided he'd try it. So he went dragging on in the house. Set down on the floor by Old Mistress. After while he run his hand up under her dress, and Old Master jumped up and jumped on Jerry and like to beat him to death. Jerry went out crying and got out and called Henry. He said: "Henry, I thought you said you put your hand under Old Mistress' dress and she didn't say nothing." Uncle Henry said: "I did and she didn't say nothing." Jerry said: "I put my hand under her dress, and Old Master like to beat me to death." Uncle Henry said: "You crazy thing, her dress was hanging up on the wall when I put my hand up under it."

Tall Tales and Tall Talk

His master hired a new overseer, who hung around for a bit, watching my father. Finally, my father asked him, "Now what are you able to do?" The overseer answered, "Why, I can see all over and whip all over, and that's as much as any damn man can do."

THE PROMISED LAND

Yes, sir, Boss Man, the niggers is easy fooled. They always is been that way, and we was fooled away from Alabama to Arkansas by them two Yankee mens, Mr. Van Fleet and Mr. Bill Bowman, what I told you about, that brung that hundred head of folks the time us come. They told us that in Arkansas the hogs just laying around already baked with the knives and the forks sticking in them ready for to be et, and that there was fritter ponds everywhere with the fritters a-frying in them ponds of grease, and that there was money trees where all you had to do was to pick the money offen 'em like picking cotton offen the stalk, and us was sure put out when us git here and find that the onliest meat to be had was that what was in the store, and them fritters had to be fried in the pans, and that there wa'n't no money trees a-tall.

BIG CORN

There happen to be a young nigger there, back from the West for a visit, and he was a great bragger. He was telling 'bout corn in Texas. "There," he said, "corn grow twenty feet high, with stalks as big as the arm of John L. Sullivan, when he whupped Kilrain, and half a dozen big ears on each stalk." The crowd was thunderstruck.

My daddy cleared his throat and say: "That am nothing in the way of corn. One day I was walking past a forty-acre patch of corn, on the Governor Heyward plantation by the Combahee River, and the corn was so high and thick, I decide to ramble through it. 'Bout halfway over, I hears a commotion. I walks on and peeps. There stands a four-ox wagon backed up to the edge of the field, and two niggers was sawing down a stalk. Finally they drag it on the wagon and drive off. I seen one of them, in a day or two, and asks 'bout it. He say: "We shelled 356 bushels of corn from that one ear, and then we saw 800 feet of lumber from the cob."

That young man soon slip out from the crowd and has never been seen here since.

THEY WERE MEN IN THOSE DAYS

Old John Drayton was the smartest of all the niggers on the master's place. He work so hard sometime that Master just got to stop him, or he kill heself. I never see such a man for work in all my life. Master think a lot of him, 'cause he been a good field hand, beside know lot 'bout cutting wood and building fence. What been more, Old John play for all the dances on the plantation. He fair make fiddle talk. When Master give a dance he always call 'pon John.

Yes, sir, that man sure could play. When he saw down on the fiddle and pull out that tune, "Oh, the Monkey Marry to the Baboon' Sister," he make a parson dance.

One day more than all, Master Murray send word to John that the cow done break out of the pasture, and he got to mend the fence quick. But John done promise some nigger on Fenwick Island to play for a dance, and he steal path and go [went by stealth]. That been Friday night, and Master say John got to finish the fence by sundown the next day.

When Old John ain't up Saturday morning, Master ax everybody where he been, and the niggers all band together and tell Master that they see him leave in a boat to go fish and he ain't seen since. Master been worry sure 'nough then 'cause he think John might be drown. He 'gage four men to shoot gun all over creek to make John' body rise. After that they drag all 'bout in the gutter.

Master gone bed with heavy heart 'cause he been very fond of Old John.

John come back from Fenwick Island early Monday morning and 'fore day clear he in the wood cutting fence rail. Now, one hundred rail been call a good day' work, but Old John decide he going to do better than that. He find five tree grow close together, and he cut piece out of every one. Then he chop at the biggest tree till he fall, and that tree knock all the rest over with him.

When all them tree fall together, it made such a noise that Old Master hear um in he bed, and hasten to dress so he can see what done go on in the woods.

Master saddle the horse and ride till he git to the center of the noise, and there he see Old John cutting 'way like he crazy. Master been mad sure 'nough, but then he glad to see John ain't drown. He start to say something, but Old John interrupt, and sing out: "Go 'way, Master, I ain't got time to talk with you now."

Old John then gather up five ax, and go to the five tree laying down on the ground. He drive a ax in every tree and then grab a heavy maul. When Master look on, he take the maul and run from one tree to the other and quick as he hit the ax, the tree split wide open. Master start to say something 'gain, but John ain't let him talk. He say: "Go on home to Missus, Master, I too shame, great God, I too shame! Go on home."

Master turn round in he track and go home without a word, 'cause he see the old nigger ain't going to give him any satisfaction 'bout Saturday. When he go back in the wood that evening, he check up and find that Old John done cut five hundred rail. Oh, them been man in those day, I tell you.

SET-DOWN HOGS

Sometimes I wishes that I could be back to the old place, 'cause us did have plenty to eat, and at hog-killing time us had more'n a plenty. Old Master kill eight or ten set-down hogs at one time, and the meat and the lard and the hogjowl and the chitlins—mmm, I can see 'em now.

What a set-down hog? It's a hog what done et so much corn he got so fat that he feets can't hold him up, and he just set on he hind quarters and grunts and eats, and eats and grunts, till they knock him in the head.

BAD MAN YELL

He had a overseer, J. B. Mullinax. I 'member him, and he was big and tough. He whipped a nigger man to death. He would come out of a morning, and give a long, keen yell, and say, "I'm J. B. Mullinax, just back from a week in Hell, where I got two new eyes, one named Snap and Jack, and t'other Take Hold. I'm going to whip two or three niggers to death today." He lived a long time, but long 'fore he died his eyes turned backward in his head. I seen 'em thataway. . . .

How Come

Why, woman, I was twelve years old 'fore I knowed babies didn't come out a holler log. I used to go round looking in logs for a baby.

WHY THE BOLL WEEVIL CAME

I knows why that boll weevil done come. They say he come from Mexico, but I think he always been here. Away back yonder a spider live in the country, 'specially in the bottoms. He live on the cotton leaves and stalks, but he don't hurt it. These spiders kept the insects eat up. They don't plow deep then, and plants cotton in February, so it made 'fore the insects git bad.

Then they gits to plowing deep, and it am colder 'cause the trees all cut, and they plows up all the spiders and the cold kill them. They plants later, and there ain't no spiders left to eat up the boll weevil.

THE BROWN BEAR AND THE PICKANINNY

There a big old brown bear what live in the woods, and she have lots of little cub bears and they still nursing at the breast. Old mama bear she out hunting one day, and she come by the field where lots of darkies working, and there on a pallet she see fat little pickaninny baby. Mama bear she up and stole that little pickaninny baby and takes it home. It hongry, but after she git all the cub bears fed, there ain't no milk left for the nigger baby. Mama bear git so exasperated she say to her babies, "Go 'long, you go 'way and play." Then she feed the little pickaninny baby and that how she raise that nigger baby.

Now, every time Old Missy come to that place in the story, she start laughing; 'cause I always used to ask her, "How come they didn't no hair grow on that baby?"

NICODEMUS AND THE SYCAMORE TREE

In the days of the disciples there was a small colored man name Niggerdemos [Nicodemus], that was a Republican and run a eating-house in Jerusalem. He done his own cooking and serving at the tables. He heard the tramp, tramp, tramp of the multitude a-coming, and he asked: "What that going on outside?" They told him the disciples done borrowed a colt and was having a parade over the city. Niggerdemos thought the good Lord would cure him of the lumbago in his back. Hearing folks a-shouting, he throwed down his dishrag, jerked off his apron, and run for to see all that was gwine on, but having short legs he couldn't see nothing. A big sycamore tree stood in the line of the parade, so Niggerdemos climbed up it, going high enough for to see all. The Savior tell him: "Come down; we gwine to eat at your house, Niggerdemos." Niggerdemos come down so fast, when he hear that, he scrape the bark off the tree in many places. Niggerdemos was sure cured of the lumbago, but sycamores been blistered ever since. Next time you pass a sycamore tree, look how it is blistered!

WHY PARTRIDGES CAN'T FLY OVER TREES

. . . My pappy allowed the reason partridges couldn't fly over trees was: One day the Savior was a-riding 'long on a colt to the Mount of Olive Trees, and the drove flewed up, make such a fuss they scared the colt and he run away with Him. The Master put a curse on the partridges for that, and ever since, they can't fly over tree tops.

THE SHEEP AND THE GOATS

The niggers kept talking about being free, but they wasn't free then and they ain't now.

Putting them free just like putting goat hair on a sheep. When it rain the goat come a-running and git in the shelter, 'cause his hair won't shed the rain and he git cold, but the sheep ain't got sense enough to git in the shelter but just stand out and let it rain on him all day.

But the good Lord fix the sheep up with a woolly jacket that turn the water off, and he don't git cold, so he don't have to have no brains.

The nigger during slavery was like the sheep. He couldn't take care of hisself, but his master looked out for him, and he didn't have to use his brains. The master's protection was like the woolly coat.

But the 'mancipation come and take off the woolly coat and leave the nigger with no protection and he can't take care of hisself either.

THE COON AND THE DOG

Every time I think of slavery and if it done the race any good, I think of the story of the coon and dog who met. The coon said to the dog, "Why is it you're so fat and I am so poor, and we is both animals?" The dog said: "I lay round Master's house and let him kick me and he gives me a piece of bread right on." Said the coon to the dog: "Better, then, that I stay poor." Them's my sentiment. I'm like the coon, I don't believe in 'buse.

YOU JUST CAN'T GET AWAY FROM WHAT THE LORD SAID

God gave it [religion] to Adam and took it away from Adam and gave it to Noah, and you know, Miss, Noah had three sons, and when Noah got drunk on wine, one of his sons laughed at him, and the other two took a sheet and walked backwards and threw it over Noah. Noah told the one who laughed, "You children will be hewers of wood and drawers of water for the other two children, and they will be known by their hair and their skin being dark." So, Miss, there we are, and that is the way God meant us to be. We have always had to follow the white folks and do what we saw them do, and that's all there is to it. You just can't get away from what the Lord said.

Lincoln and Others

The children of Israel was in bondage one time, and God sent Moses to 'liver them. Well, I s'pose that God sent Abe Lincoln to 'liver us.

WHERE LINCOLN WROTE HIS NAME

I

I think Abe Lincoln was next to the Lord. He done all he could for the slaves; he set 'em free. People in the South knowed they'd lose their slaves when he was elected president. 'Fore the election he traveled all over the South, and he come to our house and slept in Old Mistress' bed. Didn't nobody know who he was. It was a custom to take strangers in and put them up for one night or longer, so he come to our house and he watched close. He seen how the niggers come in on Saturday and drawed four pounds of meat and a peck of meal for a week's rations. He also saw 'em whipped and sold. When he got back up North he writ Old Master a letter and told him he was going to have to free his slaves, that everybody was going to have to, that the North was going to see to it. He also told him that he had visited at his house and if he doubted it to go in the room he slept in and look on the bedstead at the head and he'd see where he'd writ his name. Sure enough, there was his name: A. Lincoln.

II

Abraham Lincoln gits too much praise. I say, shucks, give God the praise. Lincoln come through Gallitan, Tennessee, and stopped at Hotel Tavern with his wife. They was dressed just like tramps, and nobody knowed it was him and his wife till he got to the White House and writ back and told 'em to look 'twixt .the leaves in the table where he had set and they sure enough found out it was him.

WHEN LINCOLN CAME DOWN TO FREE US

I

Oooh, child, you ought to been there when Mr. Linktum come down to free us. Policemen ain't in it. You ought to seen them big black bucks. Their suits was so fine trimmed with them eagle buttons and they was gold too. And their shoes shined so they hurt your eyes. I tell you I can't remember my age but it's been a long time ago.

I wouldn't take $100 for living in slavery days, and I 'member when they all parted out. Mr. Linktum come down. Yes'm, Mr. Abe Linktum and his partner, Horace Greeley, comed down. Lieutenants and Sarges all comed. And some big yellow buck niggers all dressed up fine. I served Mr. Linktum myself with my own hands. Yes'm, I did. I fotched cold water from the spring on a waiter, and I stood straight and held it out just like this in front of me. Yes'm, and his partner, Mr. Horace Greeley, too. And them big yellow buck niggers went in the kitchen where my mammy was cooking and told her: "Git outa here, nigger. You don't have to wait on these white folks no more." Yes'm, they did. And they done said: "You ain't got no more master and no more missus. You don't have to work here no more." But my mother said: "I's putting Old Master's victuals on to cook. Wait till I gets 'em on." And they told her again that she didn't have no more master and no more missus. I told my mammy to kick him down the step, but she said she was afeared he would shoot her. All I hates about them Sarges and Lieutenants is they never did shave. Them days all wore whiskers. . . .

II

I knowed the time when Abram Linkum come to the plantation. He come through there on the train and stopped over night oncet. He was known by Dr. Jameson, and he came to Perry to see about the food for the soldiers.

We all had part in entertaining him. Some shined his shoes, some cooked for him, and I waited on the table, I can't forget that. We had chicken hash and batter cakes and dried venison that day. You be sure we knowed he was our friend, and we catched what he had to say. Now, he said this (I never forget that so long as I live): "If you free the people, I'll bring you back into the Union. [To Dr. Jameson.] If you don't free your slaves, I'll whip you back into the Union. Before I'd allow my wife and children to be sold as slaves, I'll wade in blood and water up to my neck."

Now he said all that. If my mother and father were living, they'd tell you the same thing. That's what Linkum said.

He came through after freedom and went to the Sheds' first. I couldn't 'magine what was going on, but they came running to tell me, and what a time we had.

Linkum went to the smokehouse and opened the door and said, "Help yourselves; take what you need; cook yourselves a good meal!" and we sure had a celebration.

III

When Fillmore, Buchanan, and Lincoln ran for President, one of my old bosses said, "Hurrah for Buchanan," and I said, "Hurrah for Lincoln." One of my mistresses said, "Why do you say, 'Hurrah for Lincoln'?" And I said, "Because he's going to set me free."

During that campaign, Lincoln came to North Carolina and ate breakfast with my master. In those days the kitchen was off from the house. They had for breakfast ham with cream gravy made out of sweet milk, and they had biscuits, poached eggs on toast, coffee and tea, and grits. They had waffles and honey and maple syrup. That was what they had for breakfast.

He told my old boss that our sons are conceiving children by slaves and buying and selling our own blood, and it will have to be stopped. And that is what I know about that.

IV

I was looking right in Lincoln's mouth when he said, "The colored man is turned loose without anything. I am going to give a dollar a day to every Negro born before Emancipation until his death—a pension of a dollar a day." That's the reason they killed him. But they sure didn't get it. It's going to be an awful thing up yonder when they hold a judgment over the way that things was done down here.

When the war was declared over, Abraham Lincoln came South and went to the capitol [in Atlanta], and there was so many people to meet him he went up to the tower instead of in the State House. He said, "I did everything I could to keep out of war. Many of you agreed to turn the Negroes loose, but Jeff Davis said that he would wade in blood up to his neck before he would do it."

He asked for all of the Confederate money to be brought up there. And when it was brought, he called for the oldest colored man around. He said, "Now, is you the oldest?" The man said, "Yes, sir." Then he threw him one of those little boxes of matches and told him to set fire to it and burn it up.

Then he said, "I am going to disfranchise every one of you [the white folks], and it will be ten years before you can even vote or get back into the Union."

MAYBE MR. LINCOLN AIN'T SO BAD

In them days they was peddlers gwine round the country selling things. They toted big packs on they backs filled with everything from needles and thimbles to bedspreads and frying pans. One day a peddler stopped at Miss Fanny's house. He was the ugliest man I ever seed. He was tall and bony with black whiskers and black bushy hair and curious eyes that set 'way back in his head. They was dark and look like a dog's eyes after you done hit him. He set down on the porch and opened his pack, and it was so hot and he looked so tired that Miss Fanny give him a cool drink of milk that had done been setting in the springhouse. All the time Miss Fanny was looking at the things in the pack and buying, the man kept up a running talk. He ask her how many niggers they had, how many men they had fighting on the 'Federate side, and what was she gwine do if the niggers was set free. Then he ask her if she knowed Mr. Abraham Lincoln.

'Bout that time Miss Virginia come to the door and heard what he said. She blaze up like a lightwood fire and told that peddler that they didn't want to know nothing 'bout Mr. Lincoln, that they knowed too much already, and that his name wasn't 'lowed called in her house. Then she say he wasn't nothing but a black devil messing in other folks' business, and that she'd shoot him on sight if she had half a chance.

The man laughed. "Maybe Mr. Lincoln ain't so bad," he told her. Then he packed his pack and went off down the road, and Miss Virginia watched him till he went out of sight round the bend.

Two or three weeks later Miss Fanny got a letter. The letter was from that peddler. He told her that he was Abraham Lincoln heself, that he was peddling over the country as a spy, and he thanked her for the rest on her shady porch and the cool glass of milk she give him.

When that letter come, Miss Virginia got so hopping mad that she took all the stuff Miss Fanny done bought from Mr. Lincoln and made us niggers burn it on the ash pile. Then she made Pappy rake up the ashes and throw them in the creek.

WHAT FREDERICK DOUGLASS SAID

I knowed Fred Douglass. I shook hands with him and talked with him here in Little Rock. They give him the opera house. We had the first floor. The white folks had the gallery. That was when the Republicans were in power.

He said: "They all seem to be amazed and dumfounded over me having a white woman for a wife." He said: "You all don't know that my father was my mother's master and she was as black as a crow. Don't it seem natural that history should repeat itself? I have often wondered why he liked such a black woman as my mother. I was just a chip off the old block."

STEVE RENFROE

Us lived in the third house from the big house in the quarter, and when I was a boy it was my job to set out shade trees. And one day the Ku Klux come riding by, and they leader was Mr. Steve Renfroe.[1] He wore long hair, and he call my pappy out and ax him a heap of questions. While he sitting there, his horse pull up nigh 'bout all the trees I done sot out.

After talking to my pappy, he rode on 'cross Horn's bridge, 'bout two miles south of here, and there he met Old Man Enoch Sledge and Frank Sledge. They was darkies what belonged to Master Simmy Sledge's father, Old Doctor Sledge. Slaves on that plantation was 'lowed pretty good privilege after the surrender and was working on halvens. Uncle Enoch and Frank was in town trading some, and Mr. Renfroe didn't want 'em to have anything. When they left town, they pass the Ku Kluxes right on the slough bridge. Mr. Renfroe ax Enoch to give him a piece of string to fix his saddle with; then shot him. Frank run to the river, but the Ku Kluxes cotched him and shot him, too.

The niggers went down to the river that night and got the bodies and buried 'em in the old Travis graveyard. My mammy and daddy is buried there, too.

Didn't nobody do nothing 'bout Mr. Renfroe till he went on and got to messing with Master Simmy Sledge's things; stole a pair of mules, and the white folks rambled after him till they found him in Linden. They got so hot after him that he went to his camp in the flat woods down on Bear Creek. Them was scary times, 'cause that man never had no mercy for nobody.

SAM BASS

I don't 'member much 'bout the war, but I was born in slavery near the line of Tarrant County, in 1861. My master was named Wolf, but 'bout the end of the war he sells me to Dr. Barkswell, who owns my mammy.

When the war is over, we gits out and comes to Birdville, and after three years Master Moser gives my mammy seventeen acres of land. He owned lots of slaves and gives 'em all some land for a home.

For ten-twelve years after the war, the Klux gits after the niggers who is

---

[1] Sumter County's "Outlaw Sheriff" of Reconstruction days.

gitting into devilment. The colored folks sure quavered when they thought the Klan was after them. One nigger crawls up the chimney of the fireplace, and that nigger soon gits powerful hot and has to come out. You should of seen that nigger. He wa'n't human-looking. He is all soot, fussed up, choked, and scared. They wa'n't after him but wants to ask him if he knows where other niggers is hiding. I was too young to git in no picklement with the Klux.

Years after that, I's married and have four-five children, and I's coming home. I's stopped by seven men on hosses, and they all has rifles and pistols. I says to myself, "The Klux sure have come back and they is gwine to git me. It sure looks like troublement."

One of them weighs 'bout 135 pounds and has dark hair and complexium, and he says to me, "Nigger, where's the lower Dalton crossing?" There was two crossings of the Trinity River, the upper and the lower. I says, "The upper crossing is back yonder."

He says, "I knows where the upper crossing is, I's asking you where the lower one is. Don't fool with us, nigger."

There was a big fellow, 'bout 250, setting in the saddle and sorta antigogglin, with his gun pointing at me. The hole in the end of that gun looked big as a cannon. He was mean-looking and chewing a quid of t'baccy. He says, "You is going with us to the crossing. Lead the way." Then I gits the quaverment powerful bad. I knows I's a gone nigger.

I says to them, "I done nothing," and the big fellow raises his gun and says, "Git going, nigger, to that lower crossing, or you'll be a dead nigger."

On the way I never says a word, but I's praying the good Lord to save this nigger. When we reached the crossing, I says to myself, "This am the end."

The little fellow says, "Do you know who I is?" I says, "No."

He says, "I's Sam Bass."

I's heard of Sam Bass. Everybody had in them days. He was leader of a band.

He says, "We don't want nobody to know we been here. Which you rather be, a dead nigger before or after telling?"

The big fellow says, "Make a sure job. A dead nigger can't talk," and then starts raising the gun.

I wants to talk, but I's so scared I can't say one word.

Then Sam Bass says, "No, no! Let him go," and then I knows the Lord has heared this nigger's prayers.

They tells me they's coming back if I tells, and I promised not to tell. I's scared for a week after that.

In a few weeks, I hears that Sam Bass is killed at Round Rock. Then I tells.

Birds and Beasts

Yes, sir, they talk just like we do, but 'tain't everybody can understand 'em.

I'M BEING TOOK

You never drive the ox, did you? The mule ain't stubborn 'side of the ox. The ox am stubborn and then some more. One time I's hauling fence rails, and the oxen starts to turn gee when I wants them to go ahead. I calls for haw, but they pays this nigger no mind and keeps agwine gee. Then they starts to run, and the overseer hollers and asks me, "Where you gwine?" I hollers back, "I's not gwine, I's being took." Them oxen takes me to the well for the water, 'cause if they gits dry and is near water, they goes in spite of the devil.

BREAKING THE BALK

I druv the ox, and driving that ox am agitation work in the summer time when it am hot, 'cause they runs for water every time. But the worst trouble I ever has is with one hoss. I fotches the dinner to the workers out in the field, and I use that hoss, hitched to the two-wheel cart. One day him am halfway and that hoss stop. He look back at me, a-rolling the eye, and I knows what that mean— "Here I stays, nigger." But I heared to tie the rope on the balky hoss's tail and run it 'twixt he legs and tie to the shaft. I done that and puts some cockleburs on the rope, too. Then I touch him with the whip and he gives the rear backwards. That he best rear. When he do that, it pull the rope and the rope pull the tail and the burs gits busy. That hoss moves forward faster and harder than what he ever done 'fore, and he keep on gwine. You see, he am trying git 'way from he tail, but the tail am too fast. Course, it stay right behind him. Then I's in the picklement. That hoss am running away, and I can't stop him. The workers lines up to stop him, but the cart give the shove and that pull he tail and, Lordy whoo! that hoss jump forward like the jackrabbit and go through that line of workers. So I steers him into the fencerow, and there's no more running but an awful mix-up with the hoss and the cart and the rations. That hoss so scared him have the quavers. Master say, "What you doing?" I says,

"Break the balk." He say, "Well, you's got everything else broke. We'll see 'bout the balk later."

THE PARTRIDGE AND THE FOX

. . . A partridge and a fox 'greed to kill a beef. They kilt and skinned it. Before they divide it, the fox said, "My wife says send her some beef for soup." So he took a piece of it and carried it down the hill, then come back and said, "My wife wants more beef for soup." He kept this up till all the beef was gone 'cept the liver. The fox come back, and the partridge says, "Now let's cook this liver and both of us eat it." The partridge cooked the liver, et its parts right quick, and then fell over like it was sick. The fox got scared and said that beef is pizen, and he ran down the hill and started bringing the beef back. And when he brought it all back, he left, and the partridge had all the beef.

THE TORTOISE AND THE RABBIT

I want to tell you one story 'bout the rabbit. The rabbit and the tortoise had a race. The tortoise git a lot of tortoises and put 'em 'long the way. Ever' now and then a tortoise crawl 'long the way, and the rabbit say, "How you now, Br'er Tortoise?" And he say, "Slow and sure, but my legs very short." When they git tired, the tortoise win 'cause he there, but he never run the race, 'cause he had tortoises strowed out all 'long the way. The tortoise had other tortoises help him.

FATAL IMITATION

I 'members the story 'bout the man what owned the monkey. That monkey, he watch and try to do everything a man do. One time a nigger make up he mind scare 'nother nigger, and when nighttime come, he put a white sheet over him and sot out for the place that nigger pass. The monkey he seed that nigger with the sheet, and he grab the nice white tablecloth and throw it over him and he follow the nigger. That nigger, he hear something behind him and look round and see something white following him, and he think it a real ghostie. Then he took out and run fitten to kill hisself. The monkey he took out after that nigger, and when he fall exhausted in he doorway he find out that a monkey chasing him, and he want to kill that monkey, but he can't do that, 'cause the monkey the master's pet.

So one day that nigger shaving and the monkey watching him. He know right then the monkey try the same thing, so when he gits through shaving he turn the razor quick in he hand, so the monkey ain't seeing him, and draw the back of the razor quick 'cross the throat. Sure enough, when he gone, the monkey git the bresh and rub the lather all over he face, and the nigger he watching through the crack. When that monkey through shaving he draw the razor quick 'cross he throat, but he ain't know for to turn it, and he cut he own throat and kill hisself. That what the nigger want him to do, and he feel satisfy that the monkey done dead and he have he revengeance.

BARNYARD TALK

Sure—roosters and gobblers can talk. One day there was a turkey hen and a lots of little turkeys scratching around a certain place on a hill. The little turkeys were heard to say, "Please mam, please mam." An old gobbler, standing and strutting near, cried out, "Get the hell out of here." The turkey hen then moved to another place to feed.

.   .   .   .

The rooster will say something, and the hens will listen; then answer him back, "Yes." One day I heard a turkey hen say, "We are poor, we are poor." The old turkey gobbler said, "Well, who in hell can help it." Yes, sir, they talk just like we do, but 'tain't everybody can understand 'em.

WHAT THE FOWL SAID

Us didn't see no Yankees till they come along after the war was gone, and they took Old Mistis' good hosses and left some poor old mules, and they took all us's corn and didn't left us nothing to eat in the smokehouse. They runned off all the chickens they couldn't catch, and just 'fore they left, the old rooster flewed up on the fence 'hind the orchard and crow: "IS THE YANKEES G-O-O-O-N-E?" And the guinea setting on the lot fence say: "Not yit, not yit," and the old drake what was hid under the house, he say: "Hush-h-h, hush-h-h."

WHAT THE BIRDS SAID

Old lady Abbie looked out for our rations. The mens eat on one side, and the gals on t'other side the trough. We eat breakfast when the birds first commence singing offen the roost. Jay birds'd always call the slaves. They 'lowed: "It's day, it's day," and you had to git up. There wasn't no waiting 'bout it. The whip-poorwill say, "Cut the chip out the whiteoak; you better git up to keep from gitting a whipping." Doves say, "Who you is? Who you is?" That's a great sign in a dove. Once people wouldn't kill doves. Old Marse sure would whip you if you did. Dove was first thing that bring something back to Noah when the flood done gone from over the land. When freedom come, birds change song. One say, "Don't know what you gwine to do now." Another one 'low, "Take a lien, take a lien."

WHAT THE HOUNDS SAID

. . . You could hear the hounds all hours of the night. . . . . I used to mock them hounds. The first hound would say, "Oo-oo-oo, he-e-e-e-ere he-e-e-e-e go-o-o-o-oes." The others would say, "Put 'im up. Put 'im up. Put 'im up. Put 'im up. Put 'im up."

Pastor and Flock

They'd pray, "Lord, deliver us from under bondage."

WHAT THE PREACHER SAID

I

We went to the white folks' church, so we sit in the back on the floor. They allowed us to join their church whenever one got ready to join or felt that the Lord had forgiven them of their sins. We told our determination; this is what we said: "I feel that the Lord have forgiven me for my sins. I have prayed and I feel that I am a better girl. I belong to Master So and So and I am so old." The white preacher would then ask our miss and master what they thought about it and if they could see any change. They would get up and say: "I notice she don't steal and I notice she don't lie as much and I notice she works better." Then they let us join. We served our mistress and master in slavery time and not God.

II

They had preaching one Sunday for white folks and one Sunday for black folks. They used the same preacher there, but some colored preachers would come on the place at times and preach under the trees down at the quarters. They said the white preacher would say, "You may get to the kitchen of heaven if you obey your master, if you don't steal, if you tell no stories," etc.

III

The niggers didn't go to the church building; the preacher came and preached to them in their quarters. He'd just say, "Serve your masters. Don't steal your master's turkey. Don't steal your master's chickens. Don't steal your master's hogs. Don't steal your master's meat. Do whatsomever your master tells you to do." Same old thing all the time.

IV

When Grandma was fourteen or fifteen years old, they locked her up in the seedhouse once or twice for not going to church. You see, they let the white folks go to the church in the morning and the colored folks in the evening, and my grandma didn't always want to go. She would be locked up in the seed bin, and she would cuss the preacher out so he could hear her. She would say, "Master, let us out." And he would say, "You want to go to church?" And she would say, "No, I don't want to hear that same old sermon: 'Stay out of your missus' and master's henhouse. Don't steal your missus' and master's chickens. Stay out of your missus' and master's smokehouse. Don't steal your missus' and master's hams.' I don't steal nothing. Don't need to tell me not to."

She was telling the truth, too. She didn't steal because she didn't have to. She had plenty without stealing. She got plenty to eat in the house. But the other slaves didn't git nothing but fat meat and corn bread and molasses. And they got tired of that same old thing. They wanted something else sometimes. They'd go to the henhouse and get chickens. They would go to the smokehouse and get hams and lard. And they would get flour and anything else they wanted, and they would eat something they wanted. There wasn't no way to keep them from it.

V

One time when an old white man came along who wanted to preach, the white people gave him a chance to preach to the niggers. The substance of his sermon was this:

"Now when you servants are working for your masters, you must be honest. When you go to the mill, don't carry along an extra sack and put some of the meal or the flour in for yourself. And when you women are cooking in the big house, don't make a big pocket under your dress and put a sack of coffee and a sack of sugar and other things you want in it."

They took him out and hanged him for corrupting the morals of the slaves.

GOD GOT A CLEAN KITCHEN TO PUT YOU IN

There wasn't no church on the plantation where I stay. Had preaching in Mr. Ford's yard sometimes, and then another time the slaves went to white people's church at Bear Swamp. Boss tell slaves to go to meeting 'cause he say he pay the preacher. Dean Ears, white man, gave out speech to the slaves one day there to Nichols. Slaves sat in gallery when they go there. He tell them to obey they master and missus. Then he say, "God got a clean kitchen to put you in. You think you gwine be free, but you ain't gwine be free long as there an ash in Ashpole Swamp." White folks complain 'bout the slaves getting two sermons and they get one. After that, they tell old slaves not to come to church till after the white folks had left. That never happen till after the war was over.

TWO WAYS OF PREACHING THE GOSPEL

I been preaching the gospel and farming since slavery time. I jined the church 'most 83 years ago when I was Major Gaud's slave, and they baptizes me in the spring branch close to where I finds the Lord. When I starts preaching I couldn't read or write and had to preach what Master told me, and he say tell them niggers iffen they obeys the master they goes to Heaven; but I knowed there's something better for them, but daren't tell them 'cept on the sly. That I done lots. I tells 'em iffen they keeps praying, the Lord will set 'em free.

EVERY KIND OF FISH IS CAUGHT IN A NET

Sunday morning he preached "Every kind of fish is caught in a net." . . . Parson sure told 'em 'bout it. He say, "First, they catch the crawfish, and that fish ain't worth much; anybody that gets back from duty or one which says I will and then won't is a crawfish Christian." Then he say, "The next is a mudcat; this kind of a fish likes dark trashy places. When you catch 'em, you won't do it in front water; it likes back water and wants to stay in mud. That's the way with some people in church. You can't never get them to the front for nothing. You has to fish deep for them. The next one is the jellyfish. It ain't got no backbone to face the right thing. That the trouble with our churches today. Too many jellyfishes in 'em. Next," he say, "is the goldfish—good for nothing but to look at. They is pretty. That the way folks is. Some of them go to church just to sit up and look pretty to everybody. Too pretty to sing; too pretty to say Amen!" That what the parson preached Sunday. Well, I'm a full-grown man and a full-grown Christian, praise the Lord. Yes'm, parson is a real preacher.

THEY'D PRAY

My master used to ask us children, "Do your folks pray at night?" We said "No," 'cause our folks had told us what to say. But the Lord have mercy, there was plenty of that going on. They'd pray, "Lord, deliver us from under bondage."

MASTER FRANK HAS COME THROUGH

We went to church all the time. We had both white and colored preachers. Master Frank wasn't a Christian, but he would help build brush-arbors for us to have church under, and we sure would have big meetings, I'll tell you.

One day Master Frank was going through the woods close to where niggers was having church. All on a sudden he started running and beating hisself and hollering, and the niggers all went to shouting and saying, "Thank the Lord, Master Frank has done come through!" Master Frank after a minute say, "Yes, through the worst of 'em." He had run into a yellow jackets' nest.

DAMN POOR PREACHER

I never went to school a day in my life. I learned my ABC's after I was nineteen years old. I went to night school, then to a teacher by the name of Nelse Otom. I was the first nigger to join the church on this side of the Mason and Dixie line. During slavery we all joined the white folks' church, set in the back. After slavery in 1866 they met in conference and motioned to turn all of the black sheep out then. There was four or five they turned out here and four or five there, so we called our preacher, and I was the first one to join. Old Master asked our preacher what we paid him to preach to us. We told him old shoes and clothes. Old Master says, "Well, that's damn poor pay." Our preacher says, "And they got a damn poor preacher."

BOOTS OR NO BOOTS

Once when Master Gilliam took one of his slaves to church at old Tranquil, he told him that he mustn't shout that day—said he would give him a pair of new boots if he didn't shout. About the middle of services, the old nigger couldn't stand it no longer. He jumped up and hollered: "Boots or no boots, I gwine to shout today."

METHODIST DOGS AND BAPTIST DOGS

Master John had a big fine bird dog. She was a mammy dog, and one day he found six puppies out in the harness-house. They was 'most all girl puppies, so Master gwine drown 'em. I axed him to give 'em to me, and pretty soon the missus sent me to the postoffice, so I put the puppies in a basket and took 'em with me. Dr. Lyles come by where I was setting, and he say, "Want to sell them pups, Siney?" I tell him, "Uh-huh." Then he say, "What 'nomination is they?" I tell him, "They's Methodist dogs." He didn't say no more. 'Bout a week after that Old Missus sent me to the postoffice again, so I took my basket of puppies. Sure 'nough, 'long come Dr. Lyles, and he say, "Siney, see you still ain't sold them pups." I say, "No, sir." Then he axed me again what 'nomination they belong to. I told him they was Baptist dogs. He say, "How come? You told me last week them was Methodist pups." Ha! Ha! Bless God! Look like he had me. But I say, "Yes, sir, but you see, Doctor, they got their eyes open since then." He laugh and go on down to his newspaper office.

The Power

There is some born under the power of the Devil and have the power to put injury and misery on people, and some born under the power of the Lord for to do good and overcome the evil power.

A POCKET FULL OF CONJURE THINGS

Us children hang round close to the big house, and us have a old man that went round with us and look after us, white children and black children, and that old man was my great grand-daddy. Us sure have to mind him, 'cause iffen we didn't, us sure have bad luck. He always have the pocket full of things to conjure with. That rabbit foot, he took it out, and he work that on you till you take the creeps and git shaking all over. Then there's a pocket full of fish scales, and he kind of squeak and rattle them in the hand, and right then you wish you was dead and promise to do anything. Another thing he always have in the pocket was a little old dry-up turtle, just a mud turtle 'bout the size of a man's thumb, the whole thing just dry up and dead. With that thing he say he could do 'most anything, but he never use it iffen he ain't have to. A few times I seed him git all tangle up and bothered, and he go off by hisself and sot down in a quiet place, take out this very turtle and put it in the palm of the hand and turn it round and round and say something all the time. After while he git everything untwisted, and he come back with a smile on he face and maybe whistling.

OLD BAB, THE CONJURE MAN

Little pinch o' pepper,
Little bunch o' wool.

Mumbledy—mumbledy.

Two, three Pammy Christy beans,
Little piece o' rusty iron.

Mumbledy—mumbledy.

Wrop it in a rag and tie it with hair,
Two from a hoss and one from a mare.

Mumbledy, mumbledy, mumbledy.

Wet it in whiskey
Boughten with silver;
That make you wash so hard your sweat pop out,
And he come to pass, sure!

That's how the niggers say Old Bab Russ used to make the hoodoo hands he made for the young bucks and wenches, but I don't know, 'cause I was too trusting to look inside the one he make for me, and anyways I lose it, and it no good nohow!

Old Bab Russ live about two mile from me, and I went to him one night at midnight and ask him to make me the hand. I was a young strapper about sixteen years old, and thinking about wenches pretty hard and wanting something to help me out with the one I liked best.

Old Bab Russ charge me four bits for that hand, and I had to give four bits more for a pint of whiskey to wet it with, and it wasn't no good nohow!

Course that was five-six years after the war. I wasn't yet quite eleven when the war close. Most all the niggers was farming on the shares, and whole lots of them was still working for their old master yet. Old Bab come in there from deep South Carolina two-three years before, and live all by himself. The gal I was worrying about had come with her old pappy and mammy to pick cotton on the place, and they was staying in one of the cabins in the settlement, but they didn't live there all the time.

I don't know whether I believed in conjure much or not in them days, but anyways I tried it that once, and it stirred up such a rumpus everybody called me "Hand" after that until after I was married and had a pack of children.

Old Bab Russ was coal black, and he could talk African or some other unknown tongue, and all the young bucks and wenches was mortal 'fraid of him!

Well sir, I took that hand he made for me and set out to try it on that gal. She never had give me a friendly look even, and when I would speak to her polite she just hang her head and say nothing!

We was all picking cotton, and I come along up behind her and decided to use my hand. I had bought me a pint of whiskey to wet the hand with but I was scared to take it out of my pocket and let the other niggers see it, so I just set down in the cotton row and taken a big mouthful. I figured to hold it in my mouth until I catched up with that gal and then blow it on the hand just before I tech her on the arm and speak to her.

Well, I take me a big mouthful, but it was so hot and scaldy it just slip right on down my throat! Then I had to take another, and when I was gitting up I kind of stumbled and it slip down, too!

Then I see all the other get 'way on ahead, and I took another big mouthful—the last in the bottle—and drap the bottle under a big stalk and start picking fast and holding the whiskey in my mouth this time. I missed about half the cotton I guess, but at last I catch up with the rest and git close up behind that purty gal. Then I started to speak to her, but forgot I had the whiskey in my mouth and I lost most of it down my neck and all over my chin, and then I strangles a little on the rest, so as when I went to squirt it on the hand I didn't have nothing left to squirt but a little spit.

That make me a little nervous right then, but anyways I step up behind that gal and lay my hand on her arm and speak polite and start to say something, but I finish up what I start to say laying on my neck with my nose shoved up under a cotton stalk about four rows away!

The way that gal lam me across the head was a caution! We was in new ground, and she just pick up a piece of old root and whopped me right in the neck with it!

That raise such a laugh on me that I never say nothing to her for three-four days, but after while I gets myself wound up to go see her at her home. I didn't know how she going to act, but I just took my foot in my hand and went on over.

Her old pappy and mammy was asleep in the back of the room on a pallet, and we set in front of the fireplace on our haunches and just looked at the fire and punched it up a little. It wasn't cold, but the malary fog was thick all through the bottoms.

After while I could smell the whiskey soaked up in that hand I had in my pocket, and I was scared she could smell it too. So I just reached in my pocket and teched it for luck, then I reached over and teched her arm. She jerked it back so quick she knocked over the churn and spilled buttermilk all over the floor! That make the old folks mad, and they grumble and holler and told the gal, "Send that black rapscallion on out of here!" But I didn't go.

I kept on moving over closer and she kept on backing away, but after while I reach over and put my hand on her knee. All I was going to do was say something, but I sure forgot what it was the next minute, 'cause she just whinnied like a scared hoss and give me a big push. I was setting straddledy-legged on the floor, and that push sent me on my head in the hot ashes in the far corner of the chimney!

Then the old man jump up and make for me and I make for the door! It was dark, all 'cepting the light from the chimney, and I fumble all up and down the door jamb before I find the latch pin. The old man surely git me if he hadn't stumble over the eating table and whop his hand right down in the dish of fresh-made butter. That make him so mad he just stand and holler and cuss.

I git the pin loose and jerk the door open so quick and hard I knock the powder gourd down what was hanging over it, and my feet git caught in the string. The stopper gits knocked out, and when I untangle it from my feet and throw it back in the house it fall in the fireplace.

I was running all the time, but I hear that gourd go "Blammity blam!" and then all the yelling, but I didn't go back to see how they git the hot coals all put out what was scattered all over the cabin!

I done drap that hand, and I never did see it again. Never did see the gal but two-three times after that, and we never mention about that night. Her old pappy was too old to work, so I never did see him neither, but she must of told about it because all the young bucks called me "Hand" after that for a long time.

Old Bab kept on trying to work his conjure with the old niggers, but the young ones didn't pay him much mind 'cause they was hearing about the Gospel and the Lord Jesus Christ. We was all free then, and we could go and come without a pass, and they was always some kind of church meeting going on close enough to go to. Our niggers never did hear about the Lord Jesus until after we was free, but lots of niggers on the other plantations had masters that told them all about Him, and some of them niggers was pretty good at preaching. Then the good church people in the North was sending white preachers amongst us all the time too. Most of the young niggers was Christians by that time.

One day Old Bab was hoeing in a field and got in a squabble about something with a young gal name Polly, same name as his wife. After while he git so mad he reach up with his fingers and wet them on his tongue and point straight up and say, "Now you got a trick on you! There's a heavy trick on you now! Iffen you don't change your mind you going pass on before the sun go down!"

All the young niggers looked like they want to giggle but afraid to, and the old ones start begging Old Bab to take the trick off, but that Polly git her dander up and take in after him with a hoe!

She knocked him down, and he just laid there kicking his feet in the air and trying to keep her from hitting him in the head!

Well, that kind of broke up Bab's charm, so he set out to be a preacher. The Northern whites was paying some of the Negro preachers, so he tried to be one too. He didn't know nothing about the Bible but to shout loud, so the preacher board at Red Mound never would give him a paper to preach. Then he had to go back to tricking and trancing again.

One day he come in at dinner and told his wife to git him something to eat. She told him they ain't nothing but some buttermilk, and he says give me some of that. He hollered around till she fix him a big ash cake, and he ate that and she made him another and he ate that. Then he drunk the rest of the gallon of buttermilk and went out and laid down on a tobacco scaffold in the yard and nearly died.

After while he just stiffened out and looked like he was dead, and nobody couldn't wake him up. 'Bout forty niggers gathered round and tried, but it done no good. Old Mammy Polly got scared and sent after the white judge, old Squire Wilson, and he tried, and then the white preacher, Reverend Dennison, tried, and old man Gorman tried. He was a infidel, but that didn't do no good.

By that time it was getting dark, and every nigger in a square mile was there, looking on and acting scared. Me and my partner who was a little bit cripple but mighty smart come up to see what all the rumpus was about, and we was just the age to do anything.

He whispered to me to let him start it off and then me finish it while he got a head running start. I ast him what he talking about.

Then he fooled round the house and got a little ball of cotton and soaked it in kerosene from a lamp. It was a brass lamp with a hole and a stopper in the side of the bowl. Wonder he didn't burn his fool head off! Then he sidle up close and stuck that cotton 'tween Old Bab's toes. Old Bab had the biggest feet I ever see, too.

'Bout that time I lit a corn shuck in the lamp and run out in the yard and stuck it to the cotton and just kept right on running!

My partner had a big start, but I catch up with him and we lay down in the bresh and listened to everybody hollering and Old Bab hollering louder than anybody. Old Bab moved away after that.

HOODOO

My wife was sick, down, couldn't do nothing. Someone got to telling her about Cain Robertson. Cain Robertson was a hoodoo doctor in Georgia. They [say] there wasn't nothing Cain couldn't do. She says, "Go and see Cain and have him come up here."

I says, "There ain't no use to send for Cain. Cain ain't coming up here because they say he is a 'two-head' nigger." (They called all them hoodoo men 'two-head' niggers; I don't know why they called them two-head). "And you know he knows the white folks will put him in jail if he comes to town."

But she says, "You go and get him."

So I went.

I left him at the house, and when I came back in, he said, "I looked at your wife and she had one of them spells while I was there. I'm afraid to tackle this thing because she has been poisoned, and it's been going on a long time. And if she dies, they'll say I killed her, and they already don't like me and looking for an excuse to do something to me."

My wife overheard him and says, "You go on, you got to do something."

So he made me go to town and get a pint of corn whiskey. When I brought it back he drunk a half of it at one gulp, and I started to knock him down. I'd thought he'd get drunk with my wife lying there sick.

Then he said, "I'll have to see your wife's stomach." Then he scratched it, and put three little horns on the place he scratched. Then he took another drink of whiskey and waited about ten minutes. When he took them off her stomach, they were full of blood. He put them in the basin in some water and sprinkled some powder on them, and in about ten minutes more he made me get them and they were full of clear water and there was a lot of little things that looked like wiggle tails swimming around in it.

He told me when my wife got well to walk in a certain direction a certain distance, and the woman that caused all the trouble would come to my house and start a fuss with me.

I said, "Can't you put this same thing back on her?"

He said, "Yes, but it would kill my hand." He meant that he had a curing hand and that if he made anybody sick or killed them, all his power to cure would go from him.

I showed the stuff he took out of my wife's stomach to old Doc Matthews, and he said, "You can get anything into a person by putting it in them." He asked me how I found out about it, and how it was taken out, and who did it.

I told him all about it, and he said, "I'm going to see that that nigger practices anywhere in this town he wants to and nobody bothers him." And he did.

THE CONJURE THAT DIDN'T WORK

They was pretty good to us, but old Mr. Buck Brasefield, what had a planta- tion 'jining us'n, was so mean to his'n that 'twa'n't nothing for 'em to run away. One nigger, Rich Parker, runned off one time, and whilst he gone he seed a hoodoo man, so when he got back Mr. Brasefield took sick and stayed sick two or three weeks. Some of the darkies told him, "Rich been to the hoodoo doctor." So Mr. Brasefield got up outen that bed and come a-yelling in the field, "You thought you had old Buck, but by God he rose again." Them niggers was so scared they squatted in the field just like partridges, and some of 'em whispered, "I wish to God he had-a died."

CURED BY PRAYER

I'm puny and no 'count. Ain't able to do much. But I was crippled. I had a hurting in my leg, and I couldn't walk without a stick. Finally, one day I went to go out and pick some turnips. I was visiting my son in Palestine. My leg hurt so bad that I talked to the Lord about it. And it seemed to me, He said, "Put down your stick." I put it down, and I ain't used it since. I put it down right there, and I ain't used it since. God is a momentary God. God knowed what I wanted and He said, "Put down that stick," and I ain't been crippled since. It done me so much good. Looks like to me when I get to talking about the Lord, ain't nobody a stranger to me.

I KNOW IT WAS A SIGN

Mama had done sent me out to feed the chickens soon of a morning. Here was the smokehouse, and there was a turkey in a coop. And when I throwed it the feed, I heard something sounded just like you was dragging a brush over leaves. It come around the corner of the smokehouse and look like a tall woman. It kept on going toward the house till it got to the hickory nut tree and still sound like dragging a brush. When it got to the hickory nut tree, it changed and look like a man. I looked and I said, "It's Old Master." And the next day he got killed. I run to the house and told Mama, "Look at that man." She said, "Shut your mouth, you don't see no man." Old Miss heard and said, "Who do you suppose it could be?" But Mama wouldn't let me talk.

But I know it was a sign that Old Master was going to die.

HE IS A GOOD GOD

My folks lived in South Carolina and belonged to Colonel Bob Beatty and his family.

If I should lay down tonight I could tell when my folks were going to die, because the Lord would tell me in a vision.

Just before my grandmother died, I got up one morning and told my aunt that Gran'ma was dead. Aunt said she did not want me telling lies.

Then I saw another aunt laying on the bed, and she had her hand under her jaw. She was smiling. The house was full of people. After awhile they heard that my aunt was dead too, and after that they paid attention to me when I told them somebody was going to die.

I's a member of the Holiness Church. I believes step up right and keep the faith.

I seen my aunt walking up and down on a glass. The Lord tells me in a vision to step right up and see the faith.

I am living in Jesus. He is coming to Pine Bluff soon. He is going to separate the lions from the sheep.

I was born in slavery times. I 'member folks riding around on horses.

Them days I used to wash my mistis' feet and legs, and sometimes I would fall asleep against my mistis' knees. I tells the young fry to give honor to the white folks, and my preacher tell 'em to obey the white folks, that they are our best friends, they is our dependence, and it would be hard getting on if we didn't have 'em to help us.

Me and my husband moved into a house that a man, Uncle Bill Hearn, died in, and we wanted that house so bad we moved right in as soon as he was taken out. We ate supper and went to bed.

By the time we got to sleep we heard sounds like someone was emptying shelled corn, and I hunched up under my husband scared to death and then moved out the next day. The dead haven't gone to Heaven. When death comes, he comes to your heart. He has your number and knows where to find you. He won't let you off, he has the key.

Death comes and unlocks the heart and twists the breath out of that heart and carries it back to God.

Nobody has gone to Heaven, no one can get past Jesus until the day of His redemption, which is Judgment Day.

We can't pass the door without being judged. On the day of resurrection the trumpet will sound, and us will wake up out of the graveyard and come forth to be judged. The sea shall give up its dead. Every nation will have to appear before God and be judged in a twinkling of an eye. If you aren't prepared before Jesus comes, it will be too late. God is everywhere, He is the almighty. God is a nice God, He is a clean God, He is a good God. I would be afraid to tell you a lie for God would strike me down.

Eight years ago I couldn't see. I wore specs three years. I forgot my specs one morning. I prayed for my eyesight, and it was restored that morning.

Our master was a good man. The overseers sometimes was bad, but they did not let masters know how they treated their girl slaves. My grandmother was whipped by the overseers one time, it made welts on her back. My sister Mary had a child by a white man.

To get joy in the morning, get up and pray and ask Him to bless you. God will feed all alike, He is no respecter of persons. He shows no extra favors 'twixt the rich and the poor.

THE POWER

I's born a slave, 93 years ago, so of course I 'members the war period. Like all the other slaves I has no chance for education. Three months am the total time I's spent going to school. I teached myself to read and write. I's anxious to larn to read so I could study and find out about many things. That I has done.

There am lots of folks, and educated ones, too, what says we-uns believes in superstition. Well, it's 'cause they don't understand. 'Member the Lord, in some of His ways, can be mysterious. The Bible says so. There am some things the

Lord wants all folks to know, some things just the chosen few to know, and some things no one should know. Now, just 'cause you don't know 'bout some of the Lord's laws, 'tain't superstition if some other person understands and believes in such.

There is some born to sing, some born to preach, and some born to know the signs. There is some born under the power of the devil and have the power to put injury and misery on people, and some born under the power of the Lord for to do good and overcome the evil power. Now, that produce two forces, like fire and water. The evil forces starts the fire, and I has the water force to put the fire out.

How I larnt such? Well, I's done larn it. It come to me. When the Lord gives such power to a person, it just comes to 'em. It am 40 years ago now when I's first fully realize that I has the power. However, I's always interested in the working of the signs. When I's a little pickaninny, my mammy and other folks used to talk about the signs. I hears them talk about what happens to folks 'cause a spell was put on them. The old folks in them days knows more about the signs that the Lord uses to reveal His laws than the folks of today. It am also true of the colored folks in Africa, they native land. Some of the folks laughs at their beliefs and says it am superstition, but it am knowing how the Lord reveals His laws.

Now, let me tell you of something I's seen. What am seen, can't be doubted. It happens when I's a young man and before I's realize that I's one that am chosen for to show the power. A mule had cut his leg so bad that him am bleeding to death, and they couldn't stop it. An old colored man live near there that they turns to. He comes over and passes his hand over the cut. Before long the bleeding stop and that's the power of the Lord working through that nigger, that's all it am.

I knows about a woman that had lost her mind. The doctor say it was caused from a tumor in the head. They took an X-ray picture, but there's no tumor. They gives up and says it's a peculiar case. That woman was took to one with the power of the good spirit, and he say it's a peculiar case for them that don't understand. This am a case of the evil spell. Two days after, the woman had her mind back.

They's lot of those kind of cases the ord'nary person never hear about. You hear of the case the doctors can't understand, nor will they 'spond to treatment. That am 'cause of the evil spell that am on the persons.

'Bout special persons being chosen for to show the power, read your Bible. It says in the book of Mark, third chapter, "And He ordained twelve, that they should be with Him, that He might send them forth to preach and to have the power to heal the sick and to cast out devils." If it wasn't no evil in people, why does the Lord say, "Cast out such"? And in the fifth chapter of James, it further say, "If any am sick, let him call the elders. Let them pray over him. The prayers of faith shall save him." There 'tis again. Faith, that am what counts.

When I tells that I seen many persons given up to die, and then a man with the power comes and saves such person, then it's not for people to say it am superstition to believe in the power.

Don't forgit—the agents of the devil have the power of evil. They can put misery of every kind on people. They can make trouble with the work and with the business, with the family and with the health. So folks must be on the watch all the time. Folks has business trouble 'cause the evil power have control of 'em. They has the evil power cast out and save the business. There am a man in Waco that come to see me 'bout that. He say to me everything he try to do in the last six months turned out wrong. It starts with him losing his pocketbook with $50 in it. He buys a carload of hay, and it catch fire, and he lost all of it. He spends $200 advertising the three-day sale, and it begin to rain, so he lost money. It sure am the evil power.

"Well," he say, "that am the way it go, so I comes to you."

I says to him, "It's the evil power that have you control and we-uns shall cause it to be cast out." It's done, and he has no more trouble.

You wants to know if persons with the power for good can be successful in casting out devils in all cases? Well, I answers that, yes and no. They can in every case if the affected person have the faith; if the party not have enough faith, then it am a failure.

Wearing the coin for protection 'gainst the evil power? That am simple. Lots of folks wears such, and they uses mixtures that am sprinkled in the house, and such. That am a question of faith. If they has the true faith in such, it works. Otherwise, it won't.

Hants

I don't know whether there's hants or not, but I's sure heard things I couldn't see.

BLOW, GABRIEL, BLOW

But I'm a believer, and this here voodoo and hoodoo and spirits ain't nothing but a lot of folks outen Christ. Hants ain't nothing but somebody died outen Christ and his spirit ain't at rest, just in a wandering condition in the world.

This is the evil spirit what the Bible tells about when it say a person has got two spirits, a good one and a evil one. The good spirit goes to a place of happiness and rest, and you don't see it no more, but the evil spirit ain't got no place to go. Its dwelling place done tore down when the body died, and it's just a-wandering and a-waiting for Gabriel to blow his trump, then the world gwine to come to an end. But when God say, "Take down the silver mouth trump and blow, Gabriel," and Gabriel say, "Lord, how loud shall I blow?" then the Lord say, "Blow easy, Gabriel, and calm, not to 'larm my lilies." The second time Gabriel say, "How loud must I blow, Lord?" Then the Lord say, "Blow it as loud as seven claps of thunder all added into one echo, so as to wake up them damnable spirits sleeping in the graveyards what ain't never made no peace with they God, just a-laying there in they sins."

But the Christian Army, it gits up with the first trump, and them what is deef is the evil ones what anybody can see any time. I ain't scared of 'em, though. I passes 'em and goes right on plowing, but iffen you wants 'em to git outen your way, all you got to do is just turn your head least bit and look back. They gone just like that! When my first wife died 'bout thirty years ago, I was going up to Gaston to see Sara Drayden, old Scot Drayden's wife, and I took out through Kennedy Bottom 'bout sundown right after a rain. I seed something a-coming down the road 'bout that high, 'bout size a little black shaggy dog, and I says, "What's that I sees coming down the road? Ain't nobody round here got no black shaggy dog." It kept a-coming and kept a-gitting bigger and bigger and closer and closer, and time it got right to me 'twas as big as a half-growed yearling, black as a crow. It had four feet and drop ears, just like a dog, but 'twa'n't no dog. I knows that. Then he shy out in the bushes, and he come right back in the road, and it went on the way I was coming from, so I went on the way it was coming from. I ain't never seed that thing no more. But I's got a pretty good notion 'bout who it 'twas.

JOSH AND THE LORD

A old man named Josh, he pretty old and notionate. Every evening he squat down under a oak tree. Marse Smith, he slip up and hear Josh praying, "Oh, God, please take poor old Josh home with you." Next day, Marse Smith wrop heself in a sheet and git in the oak tree. Old Josh come 'long and pray, "Oh, God, please come take poor old Josh home with you." Marse say from top the tree, "Poor Josh, I's come to take you home with me." Old Josh, he riz up and seed that white shape in the tree, and he yell, "Oh, Lord, not right now. I hasn't git forgive for all my sins." Old Josh, he just shaking and he dusts out there faster than a wink. That broke up he praying under that tree.

BUT IT WAS A FAST MULE

Green Hale and Isham Mathews belonged to New Hope Church, and the Rev. Bird Hall pastored there. They axed me down to hear him preach one night, and us three, me and Green and Isham, was riding along side and side. I's riding a mule, but it was a fast mule, and Green couldn't keep up, and Isham said: "Somebody been hunting." I looked up and 'twas a sapling right 'cross the road. He said, "Fellow oughten leave nothing like that. When the moon git low, it him him in the face." The moon was straight up and down then, and I said: "That's right," and I's telling you the truth, that sapling just riz up, turned around in the air, and the brush part tickled my mule and Isham's horse in the face. If you ever seed 'em buck and rare and jump up, they sure did. Then they took off down the road, and we didn't hold 'em back, and here come Green. We left him behind, 'cause his mule couldn't keep up. If you ever heard a man pray more earnester than old Green, I ain't! He come down the road a-yelling: "Lord, us live together, let us die together." He meant for us to wait on him, but I couldn't hold that mule, and I wa'n't trying to hold him! I was gitting away from there!

When us come together, us was a mile from where us done been, then us had to decide what to do. Isham said for us to go with him, and Green said no, us nearer to his house; but us wa'n't near to nobody and I was so scared, hadn't been for Alice, I'd-a just stayed right where us was till sun-up. I said, "No, every man better take care his own self," and us did. When I got home, I didn't take nothing off that mule but myself. I just left him standing at the door with the saddle on. What scared Green so was a man, he said, what was riding right 'side him and didn't have no head! 'Twas a good thing he didn't tell me that then. I'd just naturally drop dead!

THE PHANTOM RIDER

No'm, I don't exactly believes in ghosties, but I heared Mr. Marshall Lee say he was riding on home one night and a woman stepped out in the road and say: "Marshall, let me ride." He say: "My hoss won't tote double." She say: "Yes, it will," and she jump up behind him, and that hoss bucked and jumped nigh 'bout from under him, but when he got home, she wa'n't there. He say his sister had just died and it mought been her.

JOSH, BLOW YOUR HORN

And I can tell you something else. It's just like I say, I's always been a hunter, and one night I went down in the post oak woods hunting by myself. This is a fact; 'tain't no lie. It's what I done. I had a mighty good dog, and I just kept walking and walking, and I got mighty nigh to Mr. Redhead Jim Lee's place, and I walked on and after a while I seed I'd lost my dog. I couldn't see him nowhere, and I couldn't hear him nowheres; and then something say to me, just like this: "Josh, blow your horn!" Just like that, like somebody talking to me. Well, I give three loud, long blows and set there awhile longer, but that dog didn't come. Course I knowed he'd come sometime, and so I just set there on that log, and I just turned a fool, I reckon, but 'twas just like somebody talking to me, like it 'peared to me was whispering: "Josh, you out here in these woods by yourself. You blowed that horn and your enemy heard you. You's a fool, you is." And I whispered back: "That's a fact." I couldn't hear what it was a-whispering to me, but us just talk back to one another, and 'bout that time I look up and here come three men riding on new saddles with shiny buckles gwine "squeechy, squeechy," just like that. I hear the horses' feet just as natural as could be. I thought sure I seed 'em, and it 'pears to look clean out of reason, but them men come riding on up to me, and I jump over that log and lay down flat on the other side, and it look like I could see right through that log and heared 'em say: "There he is, there he is," and I seed 'em pointing they finger right where I was. I knowed them horses gwine to step over the log on top me, and I's telling you the truth, I jump up from 'hind that log and run 'bout two miles, and if it hadn't been for that slough, I don't know where I'd-a went. I come to myself in the middle of that water, up to here, waist high, and there was my dog, old Cuba, done treed a possum.

OLD JOE IS OVER THERE GETTING 'SIMMONS AND CHOPPING WOOD

There was another hant on the plantation, too. Marse Jim had some trouble with a big double-jinted nigger named Joe. One day he turn on Marse Jim with a fence rail, and Marse Jim had to pull his gun and kill him. Well, that happen in a skirt of woods where I get my lightwood what I use to start a fire. One day I went to them same woods to get some 'simmons. Another nigger went with me, and he clumb the tree to shake the 'simmons down whilst I be picking 'em up. 'Fore long I heared another tree shaking; every time us shake our tree, that other tree shake too, and down come the 'simmons from it. I say to myself, "That's Joe, 'cause he likes 'simmons too." Then I grab up my basket and holler to the boy in the tree, "Nigger, turn loose and drap down from there, and catch up with me if you can. I's leaving here right now, 'cause Old Joe is over there getting 'simmons too."

Then another time I was in the woods chopping lightwood. It was 'bout sundown, and every time my ax go "whack" on the lightwood knot, I hear another whack 'sides mine. I stops and listens and don't hear nothing. Then I starts chopping again—I hears the other whacks. By that time my hound dog was crouching at my feets, with the hair standing up on his back, and I couldn't make him git up nor budge.

This time I didn't stop for nothing. I just drap my ax right there, and me and that hound dog tore out for home lickety split. When us got there Marse Jim was setting on the porch, and he say: "Nigger, you been up to something you got no business. You is all outen breath. Who you running from?" Then I say: "Marse Jim, somebody 'sides me is chopping in your woods, and I can't see him." And Marse Jim, he say: "Ah, that ain't nobody but Old Joe. Did he owe you anything?" And I say: "Yes, sir, he owe me two bits for helping him shuck corn." "Well," Marse Jim say, "don't pay him no mind; it just Old Joe come back to pay you."

Anyhow, I didn't go back to them woods no more. Old Joe can just have the two bits what he owe me, 'cause I don't want him follering round after me. When he do I can't keep my mind on my business.

RENFROE'S TREE

I never heard many ghost yarns 'cept 'bout the chinaberry tree where they hung Mr. Steve Renfroe. He was 'lected High Sheriff that time they got all the niggers to go to the circus 'stead of going to the 'lection. He a fine-looking man and ride a big white horse and everybody like him a lot 'cept the carpetbaggers and bothersome niggers. No matter where, if he meet one of 'em, he look 'em square in the eye for a minute, then 'bout all he say would be, "Get to hell outen here!" And man, iffen they could fly, that would be too slow traveling for 'em, getting outen the country. But after while he got in trouble 'bout money matters. They say he got color blind, couldn't tell his money from the county's. So they 'rest him and put him in jail, but he bust right out and run off. After while he sneak back, and 'cause his Ku Klux friends wouldn't help him outen the trouble when he got back in jail, he give 'em away and tell what their name was. One night a gang took him outen the Livingston jail and go 'bout a mile outen town and hang him to a chinaberry tree. I's heard iffen you go to that tree today and kinda tap on it and say, "Renfroe, Renfroe, what did you do?" the tree say right back at you, "Nothing."

THE HANTS OF BASKIN LAKE

When the war began and my father went to war, my mother left Helena and came here. She run off from the Grissoms. They whipped her too much, those white folks did. She got tired of all that beating. She took all of us with her. All six of us children were born before the war. I was the fourth.

There is a place down here where the white folks used to whip and hang the niggers. Baskin Lake they call it. Mother got that far. I don't know how. I think that she came in a wagon. She stayed there a little while, and then she went to Churchill's place. Churchill's place and John Addison's place is close together down there. That is old time. Them folks is dead, dead, dead. Churchill's and Addison's places joined near Horse Shoe Lake. They had hung and burnt people —killed 'em and destroyed 'em at Baskin Lake. We stayed there about four days before we went on the Churchills' place. We couldn't stay there long.

The hants—the spirits—bothered us so we couldn't sleep. All them people that had been killed there used to come back. We could hear them tipping round in the house all the night long. They would blow out the light. You would cover up, and they would git on top of the cover. Mama couldn't stand it; so she come down to General Churchill's place and made arrangements to stay there. Then she came back and got us children. She had an old man to stay there with us until she come back and got us. We couldn't stay there with them hants dancing round and carrying us a merry gait.

ALEX COMES HOME

Do I 'member any hant stories? Well, we'd sit round the fire in the winter-time and tell ghost stories till us children 'fraid to go to bed at night. Iffen I can 'lect, I'll tell you one. This story am 'bout a old, haunted house, a big, old house with two front rooms down and two front rooms up and a hall running from back to front. In back am the little house where Alex, Master's boy what kept he horse, stay.

This big house face the river. Old Master go to war and never come back no more. Old Miss just wait and wait, till finally they all say she am weak in the head. Every day she tell the niggers to kill the pig, that Master be home today. Every day she fix up in the Sunday best and wait for him. It go on like that for years and years, till Old Miss am gone to be with Old Master, and the niggers all left, and there am just the old house left.

One day long time after freedom Alex come back, and he hair turned white. He go up the river to the old plantation to tell Old Miss that Old Master gone to he Heavenly Home, and won't be back to the old place. He come up to the old house, and the front gate am offen the hinges and the grass high as he head, and the blinds all hanging sideways and rattle with the wind. They ain't no lightning bug and no crickets on the fireplace, just the old house and the wind a-blowing through the window blinds and moaning through the trees.

Old Alex so broke up he just sot down on the steps and 'fore he knowed it he's asleep. He saw Old Master and hisself gwine to war, and Old Master am on he white horse and [wearing] he new gray uniform what the women make for him, and the band am playing Dixie. Old Alex seed hisself riding the little roan pony by Old Master's side. Then he dream of after the battle when he look for Old Master and finds him and he horse lying side by side, done gone to where there ain't no more war. He buries him, and—then the thunder and lightning make Alex wake up and he look in Old Miss's room and there she am, just sitting in her chair, waiting for Old Master. Old Alex go to talk with her, and she fade 'way. Alex stay in he little old cabin and waiting to tell Old Miss, and every time it come rain and lightning she always sot in her chair and go 'way 'fore he git in her room. So Old Alex finally goes to sleep forever, but he never left he place of watching for Old Miss.

The white folks and niggers what live in them days wouldn't live in that big old house, so it am call the "hanted house by the river." It stands all 'lone for years and years, till the new folks from up North come and tore it down.

BUT SHE WAS AFRAID

Yes'm, I believes in hants. Let me tell you something. My mama seen my daddy after he been dead a long time. He come right up through the crack by the fireplace and he said, "Don't you be afraid, Emmaline"; but she was a-going. They had to sing and pray in the house 'fore my mama would go back, but she never seen him again.

GHOST TALK

I

I was out in the hills west of town, walking along the banks of a little creek, when I heard a voice. Queer like. I called out, "Who is that talking?" and I hears it again.

"Go to the white oak tree and you will find ninety thousand dollars!" That's what I hear. I look around, nobody in sight, but I see the tree. A big white oak tree standing taller than all the rest roundabout.

Under the tree was a grave. An old grave. I scratch around but finds no money and thinks of getting some help.

I done some work for a white man in town and told him about the voice. He promised to go with me, but the next day he took two white mens and dug around the tree. Then he says they was nothing to find.

To this day I know better. I know wherever they's a ghost, money is around some place! That's what the ghost comes back for.

Somebody dies and leaves buried money. The ghost watches over it till it sees somebody it likes. Then the ghost shows himself—lets know he's around. Sometimes the ghost tells where is the money buried, like that time at Russelville.

That ain't the only ghost I've seen or heard. I see one around the yard where I is living now. A woman. Some of these times she'll tell me where the buried money is.

Maybe the ghost woman thinks I is too old to dig. But I been a-digging all these long years. For a bite to eat and a sleep-under cover.

I reckon pretty soon she's going to tell where to dig. When she does, then old Uncle John won't have to dig for the eats no more!

II

There am only one way to best the ghost, and it am call the Lord and He will banish 'em. Some folks don't know how to best 'em, so they gits tantalized bad. There a man call Everson, and he been the slave. The ghost come and tell him to go dig in the graveyard for the pot of gold, and to go by himself. But he am 'fraid of the graveyard and didn't go. So the ghost 'pears 'gain, but that man don't go till the ghost come the third time. So he goes, but he takes two other men with him.

Everson digs 'bout five feet, where the ghost tolt him to, and he spade hit the iron box. He prises the cover off and that box am full of the gold coins, fives and tens and twenties, gold money, a whole bushel in that box. He hollers to the two men, and they comes running, but by the time they gits there, the box am sunk and all they can see is the hole where it go down. They digs and digs, but it ain't no use. If him hadn't taken the men with him, him be rich, but the ghost didn't want them other men there.

MARSE GLENN'S MONEY

Marse Glenn had sixty-four slaves. On Saturday night, the darkies would have a little fun on the side. A way off from the big house, down in the pasture, there was about the biggest gully what I is ever seed. That was the place where us collected 'most every Saturday night for our little mite of fun from the white folks' hearing. Sometime it was so dark that you could not see the fingers on your hand when you would raise it 'fore your face. Them was sure screech nights, the screechiest what I is ever witnessed in all of my born natural days. Then, of course, there was the moonlight nights when a darky could see; then he see too much. The pasture was big, and the trees made dark spots in it on the brightest nights. All kind of varmints took and hollered at you as you be gwine along to reach that gully. Course us would go in droves sometime, and then us would go alone to the gully sometime. When us started together, look like us would git parted 'fore we reach the gully all together. One of us see something and take to running. Maybe the other darkies in the drove, they wouldn't see nothing just then. That's exactly how it is with the spirits. They mought show theyself to you and not to me. They acts real queer all the way round. They can take a notion to scare the daylights outen you when you is with a gang, or they can scare the whole gang; then, on the other hand, they can show theyself off to just two or three. It ain't never no knowing as to how and when them things is gwine to come in your path right 'fore your very eyes; specially when you is partaking in some real dark secret where you is planned to act real soft and quiet-like all the way through.

Them things be's light on dark nights; they shines theyself just like these electric lights does out there in that street every night, 'cept they is a scared weary light that they shines with. On light nights, I is seed them look, first dark like a tree shadow; then they gits real scary white. 'Taint no use for white folks to 'low that it ain't no hants and grievements that follows ye all around, 'cause I is done had too many 'speriences with them. Then there is these young niggers what ain't fit to be called darkies, that tries to act educated, and says that it ain't any spirits that walks the earth. When they 'lows that to me, I rolls my old eyes at them and axes them how comes they runs so fast through the woods at night. Yessirree, them fool niggers sees them just as I does. Really, the white folks doesn't have eyes for such as we darkies does; but they be's there just the same.

Never minding all of that, we used to steal our hog every Saturday night and take off to the gully where us'd git him dressed and barbecued. Niggers has the mostest fun at a barbecue that there is to be had. As none of our gang didn't have no 'ligion, us never felt no scruples 'bout not getting the 'cue ready 'fore Sunday. Us'd git back to the big house along in the evening of Sunday. Then Marse, he come out in the yard and 'low, "Where was you niggers this morning? How come the children had to do the work round here?" Us would tell some lie 'bout gwine to a church 'ciety meeting. But we got real scared and 'most 'cided that the best plan was to do away with the barbecue in the holler. Conjuring Doc say that he done put a spell on Old Marse so that he was believing everything that us told him 'bout Saturday night and Sunday morning. That give our minds 'lief; but it turned out that in a few weeks the marse come out from under the spell. Doc never even knowed nothing 'bout it. Marse had done got to counting his hogs every week. When he cotch us, us was all punished with a hard long task. That cured me of believing in any conjuring and charming, but I still knows that there is hants; 'cause every time you goes to that gully at night, up to this very day, you can hear hogs still grunting in it, but you can't see nothing.

After Marse Glenn took and died, all of the white folks went off and left the plantation. Some more folks that was not of quality come to live there and run the plantation. It was done freedom then. Wa'n't long 'fore them folks pull up and left real unexpected-like. I doesn't recollect what they went by, that is done slipped my mind; but I must have knowed. But they 'lowed that the house was too drafty and that they couldn't keep the smoke in the chimney and that the doors would not stay shut. Also they 'lowed that folks prowled around in the yard in the nighttime a-keeping them awake.

Then Marse Glenn's boys put Mammy in the house to keep it for 'em. But Lord God! Mammy said that the first night she stayed there the hants never let her git not nary mite of sleep. Us all had 'lowed that was the real reason them white folks left out so fast. When Mammy could not live in that big house where she had stayed for years, it wa'n't no use for nobody else to try. Mammy 'low that it the Marse a-looking for his money what he done took and buried and the boys couldn't find no sign of it. After that, the sons took and tacked a sign on the front gate, offering $200 to the man, white or black, that would stay there and find out where that money was buried. Our preacher, the Reverend Wallace, 'lowed that he would stay there and find out where that money was from the spirits. He knowed that they was trying to show the spot where that money was.

He went to bed. A dog began running down them steps; and a black cat run across the room that turned to white before it run into the wall. Then a pair of white horses come down the stairway a-rattling chains for harness. Next a woman dressed in white come in that room. Brother Wallace up and lit out that house, and he never went back no more.

Another preacher tried staying there. He said he gwine to keep his head covered plumb up. Something uncovered it, and he seed a white goat agrinning at him. But as he was a brave man and trust the Lord, he 'lowed, "What you want with me nohow?" The goat said, "What is you doing here? Raise, I knows that you ain't 'sleep." The preacher say, "I wants you to tell me where Old Marse done took and hid that money." The goat grin and 'low, "How come you don't look under your pillar, sometime?" Then he run away. The preacher hopped up and looked under the pillar, and there was the money sure 'nough. 'Pears like it was the one on the left end of the back porch, but I disremembers 'bout that.

THE SHINING SHOVEL

Me and Wade Carlisle was possum hunting one night in the fall when the dogs bedded a possum in a grave. We dug down and got the possum. He was that big and fat and his hair was so shiny and pretty that we 'lowed that he the finest possum we had cotch that fall.

Just then, Wade struck the box that the dead man was a-lying in. Just as he did that, a light jumped outen that grave right in front of us and all over Wade's shovel. Our two dogs took and run and holler and stick they tails betwixt they legs like somebody a-whipping them. Them dogs never stopped running and howling till they reached home, me and Wade right behind them. Wade had that possum in his hand. That light now and then jump right in front of us. I hollered, "Wade, for the Lord in Heaven' sake, drap that possum." He drapped it, and we run till we got home. Wade still had that shovel—or was it a axe—I just don't recollects which. Anyway, he still had it in his hand; and when I looked at it, it was still shining. I pinted my finger at it, 'cause I was that scared that no words wouldn't come from my mouth. Wade throwed it in the wood pile, and we run in the house with it still shining at us.

I stayed there all night, and I ain't never been hunting in no graveyard at night since that; and if the good Lord give me the sense I is got now, I ain't never gwine to do it no more.

It ain't no good a-'sturbing dead folks. All before that I is heard it gits you in bad, and now since then I knows it.

THE PETRIFIED MAN

There's one thing I wants to tell you 'bout old Marse John. Him was 'suaded by the Hamptons to buy a big plantation in Mississippi. Him go out there to raise cattle, race horses, cotton, sugar cane, and niggers. When him die, after so long a time they take him out of his grave. The Harrisons done built a long, big, rock family vault in the graveyard here to put all the dead of the family name in. Well, what you reckon? Why, when that coffin reach Ridgeway, and they find it mighty heavy for just one man's body, they open it and find Marse John's body done turned to solid rock. What you think of that? And what you think of this? They put him in the vault in the summertime. That fall a side show was going on in Columbia, showing a petrified man. You had to pay twenty-five cents to go in and see it. The show leave and go up North. 'Bout Christmas, the family go together to the vault, open it, and bless God, that rock body done got up and left that vault. What you think 'bout that? What people say? Some say one thing, some say another. Niggers all 'low, "Marse John done rose from the dead." White folks say: "Somebody done stole that body of Marse John and making a fortune out of it, in the side show line."

Anecdotes

Uncle Joshua was once asked a great question. It was: "If you had to be blown up, which would you choose, to be blown up on the railroad or on the steamboat?" "Well," said Uncle Joshua, "I don't want to be blowed up no way; but if I had to be blowed up I would rather be blowed up on the railroad, because, you see, if you is blowed up on the railroad, there you is, but if you is blowed up on the steamboat, where is you?"

THE ROOSTER TEST

One time Master missed some of his money, and he didn't want to 'cuse nobody, so he 'cided he would find out who had done the devilment. He put a big rooster in a coop with his head sticking out. Then he called all the niggers up to the yard and told 'em somebody had been stealing his money, and that everybody must get in line and march round that coop and touch it. He said that when the guilty ones touched it the old rooster would crow. Everybody touched it 'cept one old man and his wife; they just wouldn't come nigh that coop where that rooster was a-looking at everybody out of his little red eyes. Master had that old man and woman searched and found all the money what had been stole.

THE STOLEN COLT

I know that some people can tell things that are going to happen. Old man Julks lived at Pumpkin Bend. He had a colt that disappeared. He went to Aunt Caroline—that's Caroline Dye. She told him just where the colt was and who had it and how he had to get it back. She described the colt and told him that was what he come to find out about before he had a chance to ask her anything. She told him that white people had it and told him where they lived and told him he would have to have a white man go and git it for him. He was working for a good man, and he told him about it. He advertised for the colt, and the next day the man that stole it came and told him that a colt had been found over on his place and for him to come over and arrange to git it. But he said, "No,

I've placed that matter in the hands of my boss." He told his boss about it, but the fellow brought the horse and give it to the boss without any argument.

THE PEDDLER AND THE PONY

One time a peddler come to our house, and after supper he goes to see 'bout his pony. Pa done feed that pony fifteen ears of corn. The peddler tell Master his pony ain't been fed nothing, and Master git mad and say, "Be on your way iffen you gwine 'cuse my niggers of lying."

HOPPING JOHN

My father belonged to Judge Prioleau and was trained to wait on the table from the time he was a boy; and this is how he nearly got a whipping. His master like hopping John,[1] and there was some cold on the table—you know hopping John? His master told him to "heat it"; he thought his master said "eat it," so he took it out and sat down and eat it. When he went back, his master asked him where was the hopping John. Paris say he eat it. His master was mad after waiting all that time—and say he should have a whipping. But Mistress say, "Oh, no, he is young and didn't understand"; so he never got the whipping.

THE LORD HAD CALLED HIM TO PREACH

We all went to church every Sunday. We would go to the white folks' church in the morning and to our church in the evening. Bill McWilliams, Old Master's oldest boy, didn't take much stock in church. He owned a nigger named Bird, who preached for us. Bill said, "Bird, you can't preach, you can't read. How on earth can you get a text out of the Bible when you can't even read? How'n hell can a man preach that don't know nothing?" Bird told him the Lord had called him to preach and He'd put the things in his mouth that he ought to say. One night Bill went to church, and Bird preached the hair-raisingest sermon you ever heard. Bill told him all right to go and preach, and he gave Bird a horse and set him free to go anywhere he wanted to and preach.

---

[1] Cowpeas, with or without rice, boiled with bacon or pork.

THE LORD TELLS ME WHEN IT'S RIGHT

Us house servants was taught to read by the white folks, but my grandmammy, Alvain Hunter, that didn't have no learning but that knowed the Bible backwards and forwards, made us study. When me and my brother was learning outen the blue-black speller she say:

"How's that? Go over it."

Then we would laugh and answer, "How you know? You can't read."

"Just don't sound right. The Lord tell me when it's right. You-all can't fool me, so don't try."

IF YOU DO, THEY WILL KILL ME

There was an old white man used to come out and teach Papa to read the Bible.

Papa said, "Ain't you 'fraid they'll kill you if they see you?"

The old man said, "No, they don't know what I'm doing, and don't you tell 'em. If you do, they will kill me."

BOSOM AND NO SHIRT

In slavery, when the patrollers rode up and down the roads, once a nigger boy stole out to see his gal, all dressed up to kill. The patrollers found him at his gal's house and started to take off his coat so they could whip him; but he said, "Please don't let my gal see under my coat, 'cause I got on a bosom and no shirt."[1]

MASTER SURE MADE A MESS OF THINGS THAT TIME

. . . Tom Mitchell, a slave, sassed Master. Master told him he would not whup him, but he would sell him. Tom's brother, Henry, told him if he was left

[1] The custom was to wear a stiff white bosom held up around the neck when no shirt was on. This gave the appearance of a shirt.

he would run away, so Master sold both. He carried 'em to Richmond to sell 'em. He sold 'em on the auction block there, 'way down on Broad Street. When they put Tom on the auction block, they found Tom had a broken leg, and Master didn't git much for him. He wanted to git enough for these two grown settled men to buy two young men. Tom was married. He was sold from his wife and children. Master did not git enough for 'em to pay for these two young boys. He had to pay the difference in money. The boys were 'bout twenty-one or twenty-two years old. When Master got back with 'em, the overseer told him he had ruined his plantation. The boys soon become sick with yellow fever, and both died. They strowed it round, and many died. Master sure made a mess of things that time.

NO MORE HANGINGS

Me and Old Man Zack went to a hanging one time. Both of us clambed up into a tree so that we could look down on the transaction from a better angle. The man, I means the sheriff, let us go up there. He let some more niggers clamb up in the same tree with us. The man that was being hung was called Alf Walker. He was a mulatto, and he had done kilt a preacher, so you see they was hanging him for his wickedness, sure as you born they was.

While me and Zack up in that tree a-witnessing that transaction, 'pears like we become more acquainted with one another than we had ever been since us knowed one another.

Sheriff 'lowed, "You is got only fifteen minutes to live in. What has you got to say?" Alf got up and talked by giving a lecture to folks about being lawful citizens. He give a lecture also to young folks who he 'lowed that was not in such condition as he was. He talking to them 'bout obeying the parents and staying at home. Me and Zack exchange glances and Zack 'low, "Alf ain't never stayed at home none since he been big enough to tramp over the country, and he up there fixing to git his neck broke for his wariness, and trying to tell us good folks young and old how us should act. Now ain't he something to be a-telling us what to do!"

Finally, Alf had done talked his time out, and the sheriff 'low, "Now you is only got two minutes, what does you want?"

Alf hollered, "Mr. Sheriff, lemme shake hands with somebody." Sheriff say everybody that wishes to may shake his hand. Me and Zack stayed up in that tree, but some of the niggers went up and shaked hands with Alf.

Time out! You coulda heard a pin drap. I could hear my breath a-coming. I got scared. Zack looked real ashy. Nobody on the ground moved, just stayed real quiet and still. Noose drapped over the man's neck and tightened. Someone moved the block from under his foots. That jerked him down. Whoop! All them in the tree fell out 'cept me and Zack, they was so scared. Alf Walker wasn't no more. Me and Zack sot up in that tree as if it hadn't took no 'fect on us a-tall. All the other folks got 'fected. Zack tickled me when he saw me studying. He 'low, "You act awful hard-hearted." I 'low, "That man telling us how to do just now. And there he is hanged. Us still a-setting in this tree, ain't we? We ain't never wanting to see no more hangings, is we, Zack?" Zack 'low that we ain't.

LOSING THE BABY

The funniest thing that ever happened to me was when I was a real young gal. Master and Miss Julie was going to see one of his sisters that was sick. I went along to take care of the baby for Miss Julie. The baby was about a year old. I had a bag of clothes and the baby to carry. I was riding a pacing mule, and it was plumb gentle. I was riding along behind Master Frank and Miss Julie, and I went to sleep. I lost the bag of clothes and never missed it. Pretty soon I let the baby slip out of my lap, and I don't know how far I went before I nearly fell off myself, and just think how I felt when I missed that baby! I turned around and went back and found the baby setting in the trail sort of crying. He wasn't hurt a mite as he fell in the grass. I got off the mule and picked him up and had to look for a log so I could get back on again.

Just as I got back on Master Frank rode up. He had missed me and come back to see what was wrong. I told him that I had lost the bag of clothes, but I didn't say anything about losing the baby. We never did find the clothes and I sure kept awake the rest of the way. I wasn't going to risk losing that precious baby again! I guess the reason he didn't cry much was because he was a Indian baby. He was sure a sweet baby though.

JUST LIKE IT WAS HER OWN

. . . One of the babies had to take goat's milk. When she cry, my mistress say, "Cheney, go on and git that goat." Yes, Lord! And that goat sure did talk sweet to that baby! Just like it was her own. She look at it and wag her tail so fast and say: "Ma-a-a-a." Then she lay down on the floor whilst us holds her feets and let the baby suck the milk. All the time that goat be's talkin', "Ma-a-a-a," till that baby got satisfied.

COLDY

My mother had eight children to feed. After the Emancipation she had to hustle for all of them. She would go up to work—pick cotton, pull corn, or whatnot—and when she came home at night she had an old dog she called "Coldy." She would go out and say, "Coldy, Coldy, put him up." And a little later, we would hear Coldy bark, and she would go out and Coldy would have something treed. And she would take whatever he had—possum, coon, or what-not—and she would cook it, and we would have it for breakfast the next morning.

Mother used to go out on neighboring farms, and they would give her the scraps when they killed hogs and so on. One night she was coming home with some meat when she was attacked by wolves. Old Coldy was along and a little yellow dog. The dogs fought the wolves, and while they were fighting, she slipped home. Next morning Old Coldy showed up cut almost in two where the wolves had bitten him. We bandaged him up and took care of him. And he lived for two or more years. The little yellow dog never did show up no more. Mother said that the wolves must have killed and eaten him.

THE QUILTS THAT PINCHED

Now I'll tell you another incident. This was in slave times. My mother was a great hand for nice quilts. There was a white lady had died, and they were going to have a sale. Now this is true stuff. They had the sale, and Mother went and bought two quilts. And let me tell you, we couldn't sleep under 'em. What happened? Well, they'd pinch your toes till you couldn't stand it. I was just a boy and I was sleeping with my mother when it happened. Now that's straight stuff. What do I think was the cause? Well, I think that white lady didn't want no nigger to have them quilts. I don't know what Mother did with 'em, but that white lady just wouldn't let her have 'em.

INDIANS DON'T TELL

Mother worked with a white woman. Mother was full-blood Indian herself. The woman's husband got to dealing with his daughter. She had three babies in all. They said they put them up in the ceiling, up in a loft. This old man got mad with Bob Young and burnt his gin. Mother seen him slipping around.

They ask her, but she wouldn't tell on him, for she didn't see him set it on fire. They measured the tracks. He got scared mother would tell on him. One night a colored man on the place come over. Her husband was gone somewhere and hadn't got home. She was cooking supper. They heard somebody but thought it was a pig come around. Hogs run out all time. The step was a big limestone rock. She opened the door and put the hot lid of the skillet on it to cool. Stood it up sideways. Then they heard a noise at that door. It was pegged. So she went along with the cooking. It wasn't late. He found a crack at the side of the stick and dirt chimney, put the muzzle of the gun in there and shot her through her heart. The man flew. She struggled to the edge of the bed and fell. The children was asleep, and I was afraid to move. The moon come up. I couldn't get her on the bed. I put a pillow under her head and a quilt over her, but I didn't think she was dead. The baby cried in the night. I was so scared I put the 8-months-old baby down under there to nurse. It nursed. She was dead then, I think now. When 4 o'clock come it was daylight. The little brother said, "I know what's the matter, our mama's dead." I went up to Mr. Bob Young's. He brought the coroners. I was so young I was afraid they was going to take us to jail. I asked little brother what they said they was going to do. He said, "They are going to bury mama in a heep [deep] hole." They set out after her husband and chased him clear off. They thought he shot her by him not coming home that night and her cooking supper for him.

This white man left and went to Texas. His wife said the best woman in Decatur had been killed. They put him on the gallows for killing his daughter's babies, three of them, and putting them in the loft. He told how he killed mother. He had murdered four. He was afraid mother would tell about him. She knowed so much. She didn't tell. Indians don't tell. She was with his girl when the first baby was born, but she thought it died and she thought the girl come home visiting, so his wife said she had told her to keep her from telling. It was a bad disgrace. His wife was a good, humble, kind woman.

SHE PRAYED FOR FREEDOM

Aunt Jane Peterson, old friend of mine, come to visit me nearly every year after she got so old. She told me things took place in slavery times. She was in Virginia till after freedom. She had two girls and a boy with a white daddy. She told me all about how that come. She said no chance to run off or ever get off, you had to stay and take what come. She never got to marry till after freedom. Then she had three more black children by her husband. She said she was the cook. Old Master say, "Jane, go to the lot and get the eggs." She was scared to go and scared not to go. He'd beat her out there, put her head between the slip gap where they let the hogs into the pasture from the lot down back of the barn.

She say, "Old Missus whip me. This ain't right." He'd laugh. Said she bore three of his children in a room in the same house his family lived in. She lived in the same house. She had a room so as she could build fires and cook breakfast by four o'clock sometimes, she said. She was so glad freedom come on and soon as she heard it she took her children and was gone, she said. She had no use for him. She was scared to death of him. She learned to pray and prayed for freedom. She died in Cold Water, Mississippi. She was so glad freedom come on before her children come on old enough to sell. Part white children sold for more than black children. They used them for house girls.

THE SON WHO MARRIED HIS MOTHER

A man once married his ma and didn't know it. He was sell from her when 'bout eight years old. When he grow to a young man, slavery then was over, he met this woman who he like and so they were married. They was married a month when one night they started to tell of their experiences and how many times they was sold. The husband told how he was sold from his mother who liked him dearly. He told how his ma faint when they took him away and how his master then use to brand his baby slaves at a year old. When he showed her the brand she faint 'cause she then realize that she had married her son.

BUT I CAN KILL YOU

My papa was strong. He never had a licking in his life. He helped the master, but one day the master says, "Si, you got to have a whopping," and my poppa says, "I never had a whopping and you can't whop me." And the master says, "But I can kill you," and he shot my papa down. My mama took him in the cabin and put him on a pallet. He died.

A BARREL OF MOLASSES

Green my brother, took me to Miss Mary Ann Roscoe when Mama died. She was my ma's owner. I stayed there till Green died. A whole lot of boys was standing around and bet Green he couldn't tote that barrel of molasses a certain piece. They helped it up and was to help him put it down and give him five dollars. That was late in the evening. He let the barrel down, and a ball as big as a goose egg of blood come out of his mouth. The next day he died. Master got Dr. Blevins quick as he could ride there. He was mad as he could be. Dr. Blevins said it weighed eight hundred pounds. It was a hogshead of molasses. Green was much of a man. He was a giant. Dr. Blevins said they had killed a good man. Green was good and so strong. I never could forget it. Green was my standby.

BUZZARD ROOST

Dr. Bell's calves got out and did not come back for a long time. Mrs. Bell feared that they was gitting wild, so she sent the milk girl down on the creek to git them calves. That girl had a time, but she found 'em and drove 'em back to the lot. The calves give her a big chase and jumped the creek near a big raft of logs that had done washed up from freshets. All over them logs she saw possums, muskrats and buzzards a-setting around. She took her stick and drove them all away, with them buzzards puking at her. When they had left, she seed Uncle Alex laying up there half et up by all them varmints.

She knowed that it must be him. When she left, them buzzards went back to their perch. First thing they done was to lap up their own puke before they started on Uncle Alex again. Yes sir, that's the way turkey buzzards does. They pukes on folks to keep them away, and you can't go near 'cause it be's so nasty; but them buzzards don't waste nothing. Little young buzzards looks like down till they gits over three days old. You can go to a buzzard roost and see for yourself, but you sure better stay outen the way of the old buzzard's puke. They sets around the little ones and keeps everything off by puking.

Pacolet used to be called Buzzard Roost, 'cause in the old days they had a rail outside the barroom that the drunks used to hang over and puke in a gully. The buzzards would stay in that gully and lap up them drunkards' puke. One night a old man went in a drunkard's sleep in the barroom. The bartender shoved him out when he got ready to close, and he rolled up against this here rail that I am telling you about. He 'lowed that next morning when he woke up, two buzzards was setting on his shirt front eating up his puke. He said, "You is too soon," and grabbed one by the leg and wrung his head off. But before he could get his head wrung off it had done puked his own puke back on him. He said that was the nastiest thing he ever got into, and that he never drunk no more liquor. Them days is done past and gone, and it ain't nobody hardly knows Pacolet used to be called Buzzard Roost.

JIGGING CONTEST

Master always wanted to help his colored folks live right, and my folks always said the best time of they lives was on the old plantation. He always 'ranged for parties and such. Yes, sir, he wanted them to have a good time, but no foolishment, just good, clean fun. There am dancing and singing mostest every Saturday night. He had a little platform built for the jigging contests. Colored folks comes from all around, to see who could jig the best. Sometimes two niggers each put a cup of water on the head and see who could jig the hardest without spilling any. It was lots of fun.

I must tell you 'bout the best contest we ever had. One nigger on our place was the jigginest fellow ever was. Everyone round tries to git somebody to best him. He could put the glass of water on his head and make his feet go like triphammers and sound like the snaredrum. He could whirl round and such, all the movement from his hips down. Now it gits noised round a fellow been found to beat Tom and a contest am 'ranged for Saturday evening. There was a big crowd and money am bet, but Master bets on Tom, of course.

So they starts jigging. Tom starts easy and a little faster and faster. The other fellow doing the same. They gits faster and faster, and that crowd am a-yelling. Gosh! There am 'citement. They just keep a-gwine. It look like Tom done found his match, but there am one thing yet he ain't done—he ain't made a whirl. Now he does it. Everybody holds he breath, and the other fellow starts to make the whirl and he makes it, but just a spoonful of water sloughs out his cup, so Tom am the winner.

SNIPE HUNTING

Grown boys didn't want us children going 'long possum hunting with 'em, so all right, they took us way off 'crost the fields till they found a good thick clump of bushes, and then they would holler out that there was some moughty fine snipes round there. They made us hold the poke open so the snipes could run in. Then they blowed out their lightwood knot torches, and left us children holding the poke whilst they went on hunting possums.

RED FLANNEL

Granny Judith said that in Africa they had very few pretty things, and that they had no red colors in cloth, in fact they had no cloth at all. Some strangers with pale faces come one day and drapped a small piece of red flannel down on the ground. All the black folks grabbed for it. Then a larger piece was drapped a little further on, and on until the river was reached. Then a large piece was drapped in the river and on the other side. They was led on, each one trying to git a piece as it was drapped. Finally, when the ship was reached, they drapped large pieces on the plank and up into the ship till they got as many blacks on board as they wanted. Then the gate was chained up, and they could not get back. That is the way Granny Judith say they got her to America. Of course, she did not even know that the pieces was red flannel or that she was being enticed away. They just drapped red flannel to them like us draps corn to chickens to git them on the roost at night.

When they got on board the ship, they were tied until the ship got to sea; then they was let loose to walk about 'cause they couldn't jump overboard. On the ship they had many strange things to eat, and they liked that. They was give enough red flannel to wrap around themselves. She liked it on the boat. Granny Judith born Millie, and Millie born me. No, I ain't never had no desire to go to Africa, 'cause I gwine to stay where I is.

TRAIN GOING TO AFRICA

How come I here? When I was fourteen years old my family heard how fine this state was and moved to Helena. I lived at Moro and Cotton Plant. Then, the way I come here was funny. A man come up there and say a free train was coming to go back to Africa. All who wanted to go could go. My pa sold out 'bout all we had, and we come here like they say. No train come yet going to Africa as I seed. My pa give the white man $5 to pay for the train. Tom Watson was one of 'em too. He was a sorta leader 'mong 'em wanting to go back. Well, when the day come that the train due to start everybody come to the depot where the train going to stop. There was a big crowd. Yes, mam, dressed up, and a little provisions and clothes fixed up. Just could take along a little. They say it would be crowded so. We stayed around here a week or two waiting to hear something or be ready to go. 'Most everybody stayed pretty close to the depot for two or three days. yes, mam, there sure was a crowd—a whole big train full from here, 'sides the other places. I just stayed here and been here ever since. The depot agent, he told 'em he didn't know 'bout no train going to Africa. The tickets was no good on his trains.

ASKING OUR AGE

I think I was 'bout twelve years old when freedom come. We used to ask Old Missus how old we was. She'd say, "Go on, if I tell you how old you is, your parents couldn't do nothing with you. Just tell folks you was born in slavery times!" Gramma wouldn't tell me neither. She'd say, "You hush, you wouldn't work if you knowed how old you is."

TELLING THEM OFF

. . . White folks come to me sometimes about all that.

You just ought to hear me answer them. I tells them about it just like I would colored folks.

"Them your teeth in your mouth?"

"Whose you think they is? Certainly they're my teeth."

"Ain't you sorry you free?"

"What I'm going to be sorry for? I ain't no fool."

"How old is you?"

I tells them. Some of 'em want to argue with me and say I ain't that old. Some of 'em say, "Well, the Lord sure has blessed you." Sure He's blessed me. Don't I know that?

PART TWO

Long Remembrance

I's sure glad to tell you all I 'members, but that am a long 'membrance.

Like most old people, the ex-slave lives in the past and takes a peculiar pleasure in recapturing the sights and sounds, the smells and tastes, of childhood. And like all untutored and unlettered folk, he lives in a restricted world, akin to that of the child and also that of the primitive, for whom, as Goldenweiser says, "the past comes to the present as things or words; what is neither seen nor said nor remembered vanishes beyond recovery." In the bookless world, memory—thinking and talking about old times—thus takes the place of history and biography. That does not mean, however, that the reminiscences of aged survivors of slavery (which Ulrich B. Phillips regarded as "unsafe even in supplement" because the "lapse of decades has impaired inevitably the memories of men") are history or true life-history. Rather, they are a kind of legendary history of one's life and times, which furnishes "unconscious evidence" for the historian and the student of culture and personality.

The narrators testify repeatedly to the freshness, vividness, and concreteness of their memories. "Does I 'member much 'bout slavery times? Well, there is no way for me to disremember unless I die." "I got 'membrance like they don't have nowadays. That 'cause things is going round and round too fast without no setting and talking things over." "I 'members now clear as yesterday things I forgot for a long time." "I remember that day just as good as it had been this day right here." "I recollects just as bright as the stars be shining."

When there are fewer things to remember, as is the case in a restricted world, one remembers things more vividly, especially little things. And it is the little things—associations of events with objects, images, and sensations—that, in the absence of written records, help one to remember.

I know my mama told me years ago that I was born in watermelon time. She said she ate the first watermelon that got ripe on the place that year, and it made her sick. She thought she had the colic. Said she went and ate a piece of calamus root for the pain and after eating the root for the pain, behold I was born. So if I live and nothing happens to me in watermelon

— 71

time, I will be eighty this year. I was a boy at surrender about the age of fourteen or fifteen.

When the day begin to crack, the whole plantation break out with all kinds of noises, and you could tell what going on by the kind of noise you hear.

They's a old sugar boat in the bayou with blood and sugar running 'longside the busted barrels. 'Lasses run in the bayou, and blood run in the ditches.

When the ex-slave speaks of what he has seen and heard and felt and experienced, he is telling the truth as he knows it. And he insists that it is the truth: "Every word that I tells you is the truth, and I is got to meet that word somewheres else; and for that reason the truth is all this old man ever tells." "I'll tell you all I can, but I won't tell you nothing but the truth."

In some cases, as in the narratives of Millie Evans and Cato ————, the ex-slave subordinates personal history to social history and tells what is true for all or most slaves. In other cases, like that of Katie Rowe, the ex-slave tells what is true of the individual life. And by putting the two together one gets what a true life-history should give—not only the "organic reality of the person" but also a sense of the "growth of a person in a cultural milieu."[1]

In still other cases (notably, Allen V. Manning, Joanna Draper, and Mary Reynolds) the narrator transcends both personal and social history and raises the art of casual narrative to a high point. This art is more than simply the love of telling a good story. It is a faculty for sustaining interest and projecting character through dramatic conflict and the interaction of personality and environment. Here the ex-slave not only sees and feels and remembers vividly but interprets clearly.

. . . Some folks been taught one way, and some been taught another, and folks always thinks the way they has been taught.

I never will forgive that white man for not telling me I was free, and not helping me to git back to my mammy and pappy! Lots of white people done that.

We prays for the end of tribulation and the end of beatings and for shoes that fit our feet. We prayed that us niggers could have all we wanted to eat and special for fresh meat. Some the old ones say we have to bear all, 'cause that all we can do. Some say they was glad to the time they's dead, 'cause they'd rather rot in the ground than have the beatings. What I hated most

[1] See John Dollard, *Criteria for the Life History* (New Haven: Yale University Press, 1935).

was when they'd beat me and I didn't know what they beat me for, and I hated them stripping me naked as the day I was born.

MILLIE EVANS: NORTH CAROLINA

Was born in 1849, but I don't know just when. My birthday comes in fodder-pulling time 'cause my ma said she was pulling up till 'bout a hour 'fore I was born. Was born in North Carolina and was a young lady at the time of surrender.

I don't 'member Old Master's name; all I 'member is that we call 'em Old Master and Old Mistress. They had 'bout a hundred niggers, and they was rich. Master always tended the men, and Mistress tended to us.

Every morning 'bout four 'clock Old Master would ring the bell for us to git up by, and you could hear that bell ringing all over the plantation. I can hear it now. It would go ting-a-ling, ting-a-ling, and I can see 'em now stirring in Carolina. I git so lonesome when I think 'bout times we used to have. 'Twas better living back yonder than now.

I stayed with my ma every night, but my mistress raised me. My ma had to work hard, so every time Old Mistress thought we little black children was hungry 'tween meals she would call us up to the house to eat. Sometime she would give us johnnycake and plenty of buttermilk to drink with it. They had a long trough for us that they would keep so clean. They would fill this trough with buttermilk, and all us children would git round the trough and drink with our mouths and hold our johnnycake with our hands. I can just see myself drinking now. It was so good. There was so many black folks to cook for that the cooking was done outdoors. Greens was cooked in a big black washpot just like you boils clothes in now. And sometimes they would crumble bread in the potlicker and give us spoons, and we would stand round the pot and eat. When we et our regular meals, the table was set under a chinaberry tree with a oilcloth tablecloth, and when they called us to the table they would ring the bell. But we didn't eat out of plates. We et out of gourds and had homemade wood spoons. And we had plenty to eat. Whooo-eee! Just plenty to eat. Old Master's folks raised plenty of meat, and they raise their sugar, rice, peas, chickens, eggs, cows, and just everything good to eat.

Every evening at three 'clock Old Mistress would call all us litsy bitsy children in, and we would lay down on pallets and have to go to sleep. I can hear her now singing to us pickaninnies. . . .

When I got big 'nough I nursed my mistress' baby. When the baby go to sleep in the evening, I would put it in the cradle and lay down by the cradle and go to sleep. I played a heap when I was little. We played Susanna Gal, jump rope, calling cows, running, jumping, skipping, and just everything we could think of. When I got big 'nough to cook, I cooked then.

The kitchen of the big house was built 'way off from the house, and we cooked on a great big old fireplace. We had swing pots and would swing 'em over the fire and cook and had a big old skillet with legs on it. We call it a oven and cooked bread and cakes in it.

We had the best mistress and master in the world, and they was Christian folks, and they taught us to be Christian-like too. Every Sunday morning Old Master would have all us niggers to the house while he would sing and pray and read the Bible to us all. Old Master taught us not to be bad; he taught us to be good; he told us to never steal nor to tell false tales and not to do anything that was bad. He said: "You will reap what you sow, that you sow it single and reap double." I learnt that when I was a little child, and I ain't forgot it yet. When I got grown I went the Baptist way. God called my pa to preach and Old Master let him preach in the kitchen and in the back yard under the trees. On preaching day Old Master took his whole family and all the slaves to church with him.

We had log schoolhouses in them days, and folks learnt more than they does in the bricks today.

Down in the quarters every black family had a one- or two-room log cabin. We didn't have no floors in them cabins. Nice dirt floors was the style then, and we used sage brooms. Took a string and tied the sage together and had a nice broom outen that. We would gather broom sage for our winter brooms just like we gathered our other winter stuff. We kept our dirt floors swept as clean and white. And our bed was big and tall and had little beds to push under there. They was all little enough to go under the other and in the daytime we would push 'em all under the big one and make heaps of room. Our beds was stuffed with hay and straw and shucks, and, believe me, child, they sure slept good.

When the boys would start to the quarters from the field, they would get a turn of lider [lightwood] knots. I 'specks you knows 'em as pine knots. That was what we use for light. When our fire went out, we had no fire. Didn't know nothing 'bout no matches. To start a fire we would take a skillet lid and a piece of cotton and a flint rock. Lay the cotton on the skillet lid and take a piece of iron and beat the flint rock till the fire would come. Sometime we would beat for thirty minutes before the fire would come and start the cotton, then we would light our pine.

Up at the big house we didn't use lider knots but used tallow candles for lights. We made the candles from tallow that we took from cows. We had molds and would put string in there and leave the end sticking out to light and melt the tallow and pour it down around the string in the mold.

We use to play at night by moonlight, and I can recollect singing with the fiddle. Oh, Lord, that fiddle could almost talk, and I can hear it ringing now. Sometime we would dance in the moonlight too.

Old Master raised lots of cotton, and the womenfolks carded and spun and wove cloth, then they dyed it and made clothes. And we knit all the stockings we wore. They made their dye too, from different kinds of bark and leaves and things. They would take the bark and boil it and strain it up and let it stand a day, then wet the 'terial in cold water and shake it out and drop in the boiling dye and let it set 'bout twenty minutes, then take it out and hang it up and let it dry right out of that dye. Then rinse it in cold water and let it dry, then it would be ready to make.

I'll tell you how to dye. A little beech bark dyes slate color, set with copperas. Hickory bark and bay leaves dye yellow, set with chamber lye; bamboo dyes turkey red, set color with copperas. Pine straw dyes purple, set color with chamber lye. To dye cloth brown we would take the cloth and put it in the water where leather had been tanned and let it soak, then set the color with apple vinegar. And we dyed blue with indigo and set the color with alum.

We wore drawers made out of domestic that come down longer than our dresses, and we wore seven petticoats with sleeves in them petticoats in the winter, and the boys wore big old long shirts. They didn't know nothing 'bout no britches till they was great big, just went round in they shirttails. And we all wore shoes 'cause my pa made shoes.

Master taught Pa to make shoes, and the way he done, they killed a cow and took the hide and tanned it. The way they tanned it was to take red oak bark and put in vats made something like troughs that held water. First he would put in a layer of leather and a layer of oak ashes and a layer of leather and a layer of oak ashes till he got it all in and cover with water. After that he let it soak till the hair come off the hide. Then he would take the hide out, and it was ready for tanning. Then the hide was put to soak in with the red oak bark. It stayed in the water till the hide turned tan, then Pa took the hide out of the red oak dye, and it was a pretty tan. It didn't have to soak long. Then he would get his pattern and cut and make tan shoes outen the tanned hides. We called 'em brogans.

They planted indigo, and it growed just like wheat. When it got ripe, they gathered it, and we would put it in a barrel and let it soak 'bout a week, then we would take the indigo stems out and squeeze all the juice out of 'em and put the juice back in the barrel and let it stand 'bout 'nother week, then we just stirred and stirred one whole day. We let it set three or four days, then drained the water off and left the settlings, and the settlings was blueing just like we have these days. We cut ours in little blocks, and we dyed clothes with it too.

We made vinegar out of apples. Took overripe apples and ground 'em up and put 'em in a sack and let drip. Didn't add no water, and when it got through dripping we let it sour and strained and let it stand for six months and had some of the best vinegar ever made.

We had homemade tubs and didn't have no washboards. We had a block and battling stick. We put our clothes in soak, then took 'em out of soak and lay them on the block and take the battling stick and battle the dirt out of 'em. We mostly used rattan vines for clotheslines, and they made the best clotheslines they was.

Old Master raised big patches of t'baccy, and when they gather it they let it dry and then put it in 'lasses. After the 'lasses dripped off, then they roll it up and twisted it and let it dry in the sun ten or twelve days. It sure was ready for some grand chewing and it was sweet and stuck together so you could chew and spit and 'joy it.

The way we got our perfume we took rose leaves, Cape jasmines, and sweet basil and laid 'em with our clothes and let 'em stay three or four days, then we had good-smelling clothes that would last too.

When there was distressful news Master would ring the bell. When the niggers in the field would hear the bell, everyone would listen and wonder what the trouble was. You'd see 'em stirring too. They would always ring the bell at twelve 'clock. Sometime then they would think it was something serious and they would stand up straight, but if they could see they shadow right under 'em they would know it was time for dinner.

The reason so many white folks was rich was they made money and didn't have nothing to do but save it. They made money and raised everything they used, and just didn't have no use for money. Didn't have no banks in them days, and Master buried his money.

The floors in the big house was so pretty and white. We always kept them scoured good. We didn't know what it was to use soap. We just took oak ashes out of the fireplace and sprinkled them on the floor and scoured with a corn-shuck mop. Then we would sweep the ashes off and rinse two times and let it dry. When it dried it was the cleanest floor they was. To make it white, clean sand was sprinkled on the floor, and we let it stay a couple of days, then the floor would be too clean to walk on. The way we dried the floor was with a sack and a rag. We would get down on our knees and dry it so dry.

I 'member one night one of Old Master's girls was going to get married. That was after I was big 'nough to cook, and we was sure doing some cooking. Some of the niggers of the place just naturally would steal, so we cook a big cake of corn bread and iced it all pretty and put it out to cool, and some of 'em stole it. This way Old Master found out who was doing the stealing 'cause it was such a joke on 'em they had to tell.

All Old Master's niggers was married by the white preacher, but he had a neighbor who would marry his niggers hisself. He would say to the man: "Do you want this woman?" and to the girl, "Do you want this boy?" Then he would call the Old Mistress to fetch the broom, and Old Master would hold one end and Old Mistress the other and tell the boy and girl to jump this broom, and he would say: "That's your wife." They called marrying like that jumping the broom.

Now, child, I can't 'member everything I done in them days, but we didn't have to worry 'bout nothing. Old Mistress was the one to worry. 'Twasn't then like it is now, no 'twasn't. We had such a good time, and everybody cried when the Yankees cried out: "Free." T'other niggers say they had a hard time 'fore they was free, but 'twas then like 'tis now. If you had a hard time, we done it ourselves.

Old Master didn't want to part with his niggers, and the niggers didn't want to part with Old Master, so they thought by coming to Arkansas they would have a chance to keep 'em. So they got on their way. We loaded up our wagons and put up our wagon sheet, and we had plenty to eat and plenty of horse feed. We traveled 'bout fifteen or twenty miles a day and would stop and camp at night. We would cook enough in the morning to last all day. The cows was drove together. Some was gentle and some was not, and did they have a time. I mean, they *had* a time. While we was on our way, Old Master died, and three of the slaves died too. We buried the slaves there, but we camped while Old Master was carried back to North Carolina. When Old Mistress come back, we started on to Arkansas and reached here safe, but when we got here we found freedom here too. Old Mistress begged us to stay with her, and we stayed till she died, then they took her back to Carolina. There wasn't nobody left but Miss Nancy, and she soon married and left, and I lost track of her and Mr. Tom.

LEE GUIDON: SOUTH CAROLINA

Yes, ma'am, I sure was in the Civil War. I plowed all day, and me and my sister helped take care of the baby at night. It would cry, and me bumping it [in a straight chair, rocking]. Time I git it to the bed where its mama was, it wake up and start crying all over again. I be so sleepy. It was a puny sort of baby. Its papa was off at war. His name was Jim Cowan, and his wife Miss Margaret Brown 'fore she married him. Miss Lucy Smith give me and my sister to them. Then she married Mr. Abe Moore. Jim Smith was Miss Lucy's boy. He lay out in the woods all time. He say no need in him gitting shot up and killed. He say let the slaves be free. We lived, seemed like, on 'bout the line of York and Union counties. He lay out in the woods over in York County. Mr. Jim say all they fighting 'bout was jealousy. They caught him several times, but every time he got away from 'em. After they come home Mr. Jim say they never win no war. They stole and starved out the South.

They didn't want the slaves talking 'bout things. One time I got ruffed up, and I say I was going to freedom—the wood where Mr. Jim be—and I recollect we was crossing over a railing fence. My ma put her hand over my mouth like this and say, "You don't know anything 'bout what you saying, boy."

I never will forgit Mr. Neel. He was all our overseer. He say, "Lee Good Boy plows so good." He never spoke an unkind word in his life to me. When I have to go to his house, he call me in and give me hot biscuits or maybe a potato [sweet potatoes]. I sure love potato. He was a good old Christian man. The church we all went to was made outa hand-hewed logs—great big things. My pa lived in Union County on the other side the church.

He lived to be 103 years old. Ma lost her mind. They both died right here with me—a piece outa town. He was named Pompey and Ma Fannie. Her name 'fore freedom was Fannie Smith, then she took the name Guidon.

After freedom a heap of people say they was going to name theirselves over. They named theirselves big names, then went roaming round like wild, hunting cities. They changed up so it was hard to tell who or where anybody was. Heap of 'em died, and you didn't know when you hear about it if he was your folks hardly. Some of the names was Abraham, and some called theirselves Lincum. Any big name 'cepting their master's name. It was the fashion. I heard 'em talking 'bout it one evening, and my pa say, "Fine folks raise us and we gonna hold to our own names." That settled it with all of us.

Ma was a sickly woman all her life. They kept her round the house to help cook and sweep the yards. Not a speck of grass, not a weed growed on her yard. She swept it 'bout two times a week. It was pretty and white. The sand just shined in the sun. Had tall trees in the yard.

I can't recollect 'bout my papa's master 'cause I was raised at my mama's master's place. He said many and many a time Joe Guidon never had to whup him. After he growed up, he never got no whuppings a-tall. Joe Guidon learned him to plow, and he was boss of the plow hands. His wife was named Maria Guidon. He say she was a mighty good easy woman too.

Saturday was ration day and Sunday visiting day. But you must have your pass if you leave the farm and go over to somebody else's farm.

When I was a boy one thing I love to do was go to Stingy Tom's stillhouse. His name was Tom Whiteside. He sure was stingy and the meanest white man I ever seed. I went to the stillhouse to beat peaches to make brandy. It was four miles over there, and I rode. We always made least one barrel of peach brandy and one of cider. That would be vinegar 'nough by spring. 'Simmon beer was good in the cold freezing weather too. We make much as we have barrels if we could get the persimmons. . . .

Once an old slave woman lost her mind. Stingy Tom sent her to get a bull tongue [a plow], and she chased after one of the bulls down at the lot trying to catch it. She set his barn fire and burned thirteen head of horses and mules together. Stingy Tom had the sheriff try to get her tell what white folks put her up to do it. He knowed they all hated him 'cause he just so mean. The old woman never did tell, but they hung her anyhow. There was a big crowd to see it. Miss Lucy just cried and cried. She say Satan got no use for Stingy Tom he so mean. That the first person I ever seed hung. They used to hang folks a heap. The biggest crowds turned out to see it.

The old woman's son he went to the woods, he so hurt 'cause they going to hang his ma.

The Missouri soldiers were worse than the Yankees. They waste and steal your corn and take your horses. They brought a little girl they stole and let Stingy Tom have her. He kept her and treated her so mean. They thrash out wheat and put it on big heavy sheets to dry. The little girl had to sit out in the sun and keep the chickens offen it. I seed him find her 'sleep and hit hard as he could in the face with big old brush. It was old dogwood brush with no leaves on it. He wouldn't let that little girl have no biscuit on Sunday morning. Everybody had all the hot biscuit they could eat on Sunday morning. Well, after freedom, long time, her aunt heard she was down there and come and got her. She grow up to be a nice woman. Them same Missouri soldiers took Henry Guidon [younger brother of Lee Guidon] off. Stole him from the master—stole his mule. They was so mean. They found out when they shoot, the mule so scared it would throw Henry. They kept it up and laughed. Course it hurt Henry. Liable to kill him. They say they making a Yankee soldier outen him that way. One night before they got too far gone, he rode off home. They burn whole cribs corn. Could smell it a long ways off. They was mean to everybody.

I reckon I do know 'bout the Ku Kluck. I knowed a man named Alfred Owens. He seemed all right, but he was a Republican. He said he was not afraid. He run a tanyard and kept a heap of guns in a big room. They all loaded. He married a Southern woman. Her husband either died or was killed. She had a son living with them. The Ku Kluck was called Upper League. They get this boy to unload all the guns. Then the white men went there. The white man give up and said, "I ain't got no gun to defend myself with. The guns all unloaded, and I ain't got no powder and shot." But the Ku Kluck shot in the houses and shot him up like lacework. He sold fine harness, saddles, bridles—all sorts of leather things. The Ku Kluck sure run them outen their country. They say they not going to have them round, and they sure run them out, back where they came from.

Charles Good had a blacksmith. The Missouri soldiers opened a fence gap when they came through. They took him, tied him to a tree, and shot him in the face with little shot. He suffered there till Wednesday, when he was still living. They tied him to the tree with his own galluses. They was doubled and strong. Then some of them went down there and finished up the job beating him over the head with the guns till he was dead. The Ku Kluck broke up every gun they could find. They sure better not catch a gun at the quarters of colored folks. They whup him and break up the gun. Ask him where he got that gun and start more bad trouble.

They packed a two-story jail so full of men they had orders to turn 'em out. Then they built a high fence 'bout eight foot tall and put 'em in it. They had lights and guards all around it. They kept 'em right out in the hot sun in that pen. That's where the Yankees put the Ku Kluck. Then they had trials, and some was sent to Albany for three years and eight years and the like. They made glass at Albany. Them Yankees wouldn't let 'em have no bonds. Then the white folks told them they needn't settle among them. They owned all the land and wouldn't sell them a foot for nothing. A heap of lawyers and doctors got in it. That fence was iron and bob wire. The Ku Kluck killed good men, but Republicans.

We stayed on like we were 'cause we done put in the crop and the Ku Kluck never did bother us. We made a pretty good crop. Then we took our freedom. Started working for money and part of the crop.

I married in 1871. Me and Emma went to bed. Somebody lam on the door. Emma say, "You run, they won't hurt me." I say, "They kill me sure." We stayed and opened the door. They pull the cover offen her, looking. They lifted up a cloth from over a barrel behind the bed in the corner. I say, "That are a hog." He say, "We right from hell, we ain't seen no meat." Then they soon gone. The moon shining so bright that night. They were looking for my wife's brother, I heard 'em say. They say he done something or another. . . .

One man I heard 'em talk a heap about had the guns and powder. They shot holes in the walls. He climbed up in the fireplace chimney and stood up there close to the brick. It was dark, and they couldn't see him. They looked up the chimney but didn't see him. It was a two-story chimney. Lady, if you ain't never seen one I can't tell you just how it was. But they shot the house full of holes and never harmed him.

For them what stayed on like they were, Reconstruction times 'bout like times before that 'cepting the Yankee stole out and tore up a scandalous heap. They tell the black folks to do something, and then come white folks you live with and say Ku Kluck whup you. They say leave, and white folks say better not listen to them old Yankees. They'll git you too far off to come back, and you freeze. They done give you all the use they got for you. How they do? All sorts of ways. Some stayed at their cabins glad to have one to live in and farmed on. Some running round begging, some hunting work for money, and nobody had no money 'cepting the Yankees, and they had no homes or land and mighty little work for you to do. No work to live on. Some going every day to the city. That winter I heard 'bout them starving and freezing by the wagon loads.

I never heard nothing 'bout voting till freedom. I don't think I ever voted till I come to Mississippi. I votes Republican. That's the party of my color, and I stick to them long as they do right. I don't dabble in white folks' business, and that white folks' voting is their business. If I vote, I go do it and go on home.

I been plowing all my life, and in the hot days I cuts and saws wood. Then when I gets outa cotton-picking, I put each boy on a load of wood and we sell wood. The last years we got $3 a cord. Then we clear land till next spring. I don't find no time to be loafing. I never missed a year farming till I got the Bright's disease and it hurt me to do hard work. Farming is the best life there is when you are able.

I come to Holly Springs in 1880, stopped to visit. I had six children and $90 in money. We come on the train. My parents done come on from South Carolina to Arkansas. Man say this ain't no richer land than you come from. I tried it seven years. Then I drove from there, ferried the rivers. It took a long time. We made the best crop I ever seed in 1888. I had eight children, my wife. I cut and hauled wood all winter. I soon had three teams hauling wood to Clarendon. Some old men [white men], mean things, learned one of my boys to play craps. They done it to git his money.

When I owned most, I had six head mules and five head horses. I rented 140 acres of land. I bought this house and some other land about. The anthrax killed nearly all my horses and mules. I got one big fine mule yet. Its mate died. I lost my house. My son give me one room, and he paying the debt off now. It's hard for colored folks to keep anything. Somebody gets it from 'em if they don't mind.

The present times is hard. Timber is scarce. Game is about all gone. Prices higher. Old folks cannot work. Times is hard for younger folks too. They go to town too much and go to shows. They going to a tent show now. Circus coming, they say. They spending too much money for foolishness. It's a fast time. Folks too restless. Some of the colored folks work hard as folks ever did. They spends too much. Some folks is lazy. Always been that way.

I signed up to the government, but they ain't give me nothing 'cepting powdered milk and rice what wasn't fit to eat. It cracked up and had black something in it. A lady said she would give me some shirts that was her husband's. I went to get them, but she wasn't home. These heavy shirts give me heat. They won't give me the pension, and I don't know why. It would help me buy my salts and pills and the other medicines like Swamp Root. They won't give it to me.

TINES KENDRICKS: GEORGIA

My name is Tines Kendricks. I was borned in Crawford County, Georgia. You see, boss, I is a little nigger, and I really is more smaller now than I used to be when I was young 'cause I so old and stooped over. I mighty nigh wore out from all these hard years of work and serving the Lord. My actual name what was give to me by my white folks, the Kendricks, was "Tiny." They called me that 'cause I never was no size much. After us all sot free I just changed my name to "Tines," and that's what I been going by for nigh on to ninety years.

'Cording to what I 'member 'bout it, boss, I is now past a hundred and four year old this past July the fourth, two hours before day. What I means is what I 'member 'bout what the old marse told me that time I comed back to the home place after the war quit, and he say that I past thirty then. My mammy, she said I born two hours before day on the Fourth of July. That what they told me, boss. I is been in good health all my days. I ain't never been sick any in my life 'scusing these last years when I git so old and feeble and stiff in the joints, and my teeth 'gin to cave, and my old bones, they 'gin to ache. But I just keep on living and trusting in the Lord 'cause the Good Book say, "Wherefore the evil days come and the darkness of the night draw nigh, your strength, it shall not perish. I will lift you up 'mongst them what 'bides with me." That is the Gospel, boss.

My old marse, he was named Arch Kendricks, and us lived on the plantation what the Kendricks had not far from Macon in Crawford County, Georgia. You can see, boss, that I is a little bright and got some white blood in me. That is 'counted for on my mammy's side of the family. Her pappy, he was a white man. He wasn't no Kendrick though. He was a overseer. That what my mammy she say, and then I know that wasn't no Kendrick mixed up in nothing like that. They didn't believe in that kind of business. My old marse, Arch Kendricks, I will say this, he certainly was a good fair man. Old Miss and the young marse, Sam, they was strictly tough and, boss, I is telling you the truth, they was cruel. The young marse, Sam, he never taken at all after he pa. He got all he meanness from Old Miss, and he sure got plenty of it, too. Old Miss, she cuss and rare worse'n a man. 'Way 'fore day she be up hollering loud enough for to be heared two miles, 'rousing the niggers out for to git in the fields ever 'fore light. Marse Sam, he stand by the pots handing out the grub and giving out the bread, and he cuss loud and say: "Take a sop of that grease on your hoecake and move along fast 'fore I lashes you." Marse Sam, he was a big man too, that he was. He was nigh on to six and a half feet tall. Boss, he certainly was a child of the devil. All the cooking in them days was done in pots hanging on the pot racks. They never had no stoves enduring the times what I is telling you 'bout. At times they would give us enough to eat. At times they wouldn't—just 'cording to how they feeling when they dishing out the grub. The biggest what they would give the field hands to eat would be the truck what us had on the place, like greens, turnips, peas, side meat, and they sure would cut the side meat awful thin too, boss. Us always had a heap of corn-meal dumplings and hoecakes. Old Miss, her and Marse Sam, they real stingy. You better not leave no grub on your plate for to throw away. You sure better eat it all iffen you like it or no. Old Miss and Marse Sam, they the real bosses, and they was wicked. I's telling you the truth, they was. Old Marse, he didn't have much to say 'bout the running of the place or the handling of the niggers. You know, all the property and all the niggers belonged to Old Miss. She got all that from her peoples. That what they left to her on their death. She the real owner of everything.

Just to show you, boss, how 'twas with Marse Sam and how contrary and fractious and wicked that young white man was, I wants to tell you 'bout the time that Aunt Hannah's little boy Mose died. Mose, he sick 'bout a week. Aunt Hannah, she try to doctor on him and git him well, and she tell Old Miss that she think Mose bad off and ought to have the doctor. Old Miss she wouldn't git the doctor. She say Mose ain't sick much, and, bless my soul, Aunt Hannah she right. In a few days from then Mose is dead. Marse Sam, he come cussing and told Gabe to get some planks and make the coffin and sont some of them to dig the grave over there on the far side of the place where they had a burying-ground for the niggers. Us toted the coffin over to where the grave was dug and gwine bury little Mose there, and Uncle Billy Jordan, he was there and begun to sing and pray and have a kind of funeral at the burying. Everyone was moaning and singing and praying, and Marse Sam heard 'em and come sailing over there on he hoss and lit right in to cussing and raring and say that if they don't hurry and bury that nigger and shut up that singing and carrying on, he gwine lash every one of them, and then he went to cussing worser and 'busing Uncle Billy Jordan. He say iffen he ever hear of him doing any more preaching or praying round 'mongst the niggers at the graveyard or anywheres else, he gwine lash him to death. No, sir, boss, Marse Sam wouldn't even 'low no preaching or singing or nothing like that. He was wicked. I tell you he was.

Old Miss, she generally looked after the niggers when they sick and give them the medicine. And, too, she would get the doctor iffen she think they real bad off 'cause like I said, Old Miss, she mighty stingy, and she never want to lose no nigger by them dying. Howsomever, it was hard sometime to get her to believe you sick when you tell her that you was, and she would think you just playing off from work. I have seen niggers what would be mighty near dead before Old Miss would believe them sick at all.

Before the war broke out, I can 'member there was some few of the white folks what said that niggers ought to be sot free, but there was just one now and then that took that stand. One of them that I 'member was the Rev. Dickey what was the parson for a big crowd of the white peoples in that part of the county. Rev. Dickey, he preached freedom for the niggers and say that they all should be sot free and gived a home and a mule. That preaching the Rev. Dickey done sure did rile up the folks—that is, the most of them, like the Kendricks and Mr. Eldredge and Dr. Murcheson and Nat Walker and such as them what was the biggest of the slaveowners. Right away after Rev. Dickey done such preaching, they fired him from the church and 'bused him, and some of them say they gwine hang him to a limb or either gwine ride him on a rail out of the country. Sure enough, they made it so hot on that man he have to leave clean out of the state, so I heared. No, sir, boss, they say they ain't gwine divide up no land with the niggers or give them no home or mule or their freedom or nothing. They say they will wade knee deep in blood and die first.

When the war start to break out, Marse Sam 'listed in the troops and was sent to Virginny. There he stay for the longest. I hear Old Miss telling 'bout the letters she got from him, and how he wishing they hurry and start the battle so's he can get through killing the Yankees and get the war over and come home. Bless my soul, it wasn't long before they had the battle what Marse Sam was shot in. He writ the letter from the hospital where they had took him. He say they had a hard fight, that a ball busted his gun, and another ball shoot his cooterments [accouterments] off him; the third shot tear a big hole right through the side of his neck. The doctor done sew the wound up; he not hurt so bad. He soon be back with his company.

But it wasn't long 'fore they writ some more letters to Old Miss and say that Marse Sam's wound not getting no better; it wasn't healing to do no good; every time that they sew the gash up in his neck, it broke loose again. The Yankees had been putting poison grease on the bullets. That was the reason the wound wouldn't get well. They feared Marse Sam going to die, and a short time after that letter come I sure knowed it was so. One night just about dusk dark, the screech owls, they come in a swarm and lit in the big trees in the front of the house. A mist of dust come up, and the owls, they holler and carry on so that Old Marse get he gun and shot it off to scare them away. That was a sign, boss, that somebody gwine to die. I just knowed it was Marse Sam.

Sure enough, the next day they got the message that Marse Sam dead. They brung him home all the way from Virginny and buried him in the graveyard on the other side of the garden with his gray clothes on him and the flag on the coffin. That's what I's telling you, boss, 'cause they called all the niggers in and 'lowed them to look at Marse Sam. I seen him, and he sure looked like he peaceful in he coffin with his soldier clothes on. I heared afterwards that Marse Sam bucked and rared just 'fore he died and tried to get outen the bed, and that he cussed to the last.

It was this way, boss, how come me to be in the war. You see, they 'quired all of the slaveowners to send so many niggers to the army to work digging the trenches and throwing up the breastworks and repairing the railroads what the Yankees done 'stroyed. Every marse was 'quired to send one nigger for every ten that he had. Iffen you had a hundred niggers, you had to send ten of them to the army. I was one of them that my marse 'quired to send. That was the worst times that this here nigger ever seen, and the way them white men drive us niggers, it was something awful. The strap, it was going from 'fore day till 'way after night. The niggers, heaps of 'em, just fall in they tracks—give out—and them white men laying the strap on they backs without ceasting. That was 'zackly way it was with them niggers like me what was in the army work. I had to stand it, boss, till the war was over.

That sure was a bad war that went on in Georgia. That it was. Did you ever hear 'bout the Andersonville prison in Georgia? I tell you, boss, that was 'bout the worstest place that ever I seen. That was where they keep all the Yankees that they capture, and they had so many there they couldn't nigh take care of them. They had them fenced up with a tall wire fence and never had enough houseroom for all them Yankees. They would just throw the grub to 'em. The mostest that they had for 'em to eat was peas, and the filth, it was terrible. The sickness, it broke out 'mongst 'em all the while, and they just die like rats what been pizened. The first thing that the Yankees do when they take the state 'way from the Confederates was to free all them what in the prison at Andersonville.

Slavery time was tough, boss. You just don't know how tough it was. I can't 'splain to you just how bad all the niggers want to get they freedom. With the free niggers it was just the same as it was with them that was in bondage. You know there was some few free niggers in that time even 'fore the slaves taken outen bondage. It was really worse on them than it was with them what wasn't free. The slaveowners, they just despised them free niggers and make it just as hard on them as they can. They couldn't get no work from nobody. Wouldn't ary man hire 'em or give 'em any work at all. So because they was up against it and never had any money or nothing, the white folks make these free niggers 'sess the taxes. And 'cause they never had no money for to pay the tax with, they was put up on the block by the court man or the sheriff and sold out to somebody for enough to pay the tax what they say they owe. So they keep these free niggers hired out all the time 'most, working for to pay the taxes. I 'member one of them free niggers mighty well. He was called Free Sol. He had him a little home and a old woman and some boys. They was kept bounded out nigh 'bout all the time working for to pay they tax. Yes, sir, boss, it was heap more better to be a slave nigger than a free one. And it was really a heavenly day when the freedom come for the race.

In the time of slavery another thing what make it tough on the niggers was them times when a man and he wife and their children had to be taken 'way from one another. This separation might be brung 'bout 'most any time for one thing or another, such as one or t'other, the man or the wife, be sold off or taken 'way to some other state like Louisiana or Mississippi. Then when a marse die what had a heap of slaves, these slave niggers be divided up 'mongst the marse's children or sold off for to pay the marse's debts. Then at times when a man married to a woman that don't belong to the same marse what he do, then they is liable to git divided up and separated 'most any day. They was heaps of nigger families that I know what was separated in the time of bondage that tried to find they folkses what was gone. But the mostest of 'em never git together again even after they sot free 'cause they don't know where one or the other is.

After the war over and the slaves taken out of they bondage, some of the very few white folks give them niggers what they liked the best, a small piece of land for to work. But the mostest of them never give 'em nothing, and they sure despise them niggers what left 'em. Us old marse say he want to 'range with all his niggers to stay on with him, that he gwine give 'em a mule and a piece-a ground. But us know that Old Miss ain't gwine agree to that. And sure enough she wouldn't. I's telling you the truth, every nigger on that place left. They sure done that; and Old Marse and Old Miss, they never had a hand left there on that great big place, and all that ground laying out.

The government seen to it that all of the white folks had to make contracts with the niggers that stuck with 'em, and they was sure strict 'bout that too. The white folks at first didn't want to make the contracts and say they wasn't gwine to. So the government filled the jail with 'em, and after that everyone make the contract.

When my race first got they freedom and begin to leave they marses, a heap of the marses got raging mad and just tore up truck. They say they gwine kill every nigger they find. Some of them did do that very thing, boss, sure enough. I's telling you the truth. They shot niggers down by the hundreds. They just wasn't gwine let 'em enjoy their freedom. That is the truth, boss.

After I come back to the old home place from working for the army, it wasn't long 'fore I left there and git me a job with a sawmill and worked for the sawmill peoples for 'bout five years. One day I heared some niggers telling 'bout a white man what done come in there gitting up a big lot of niggers to take to

Arkansas. They was telling 'bout what a fine place it was in Arkansas and how rich the land is and that the crops grow without working, and that the 'taters grow big as a watermelon and you never have to plant 'em but the one time, and all such as that. Well, I 'cided to come. I joined up with the man and come to Phillips County in 1875. A heap-a niggers come from Georgia at the same time that me and Callie come. You know Callie, that's my old woman what's in the shack there right now. Us first lived on Mr. Jim Bush's place over close to Barton. Us ain't been far off from there ever since us first landed in this county. Fact is, boss, us ain't been outen the county since us first come here, and us gwine be here now, I know, till the Lord call for us to come on home.

BEN SIMPSON: GEORGIA AND TEXAS

Boss, I's born in Georgia, in Norcross, and I's ninety years old. My father's name was Roger Stielszen, and my mother's name was Betty. Massa Earl Stielszen captures them in Africa and brung them to Georgia. He got kilt, and my sister and me went to his son. His son was a killer. He got in trouble there in Georgia and got him two good-stepping hosses and the covered wagon. Then he chains all he slaves round the necks and fastens the chains to the hosses and makes them walk all the way to Texas. My mother and my sister had to walk. Emma was my sister. Somewhere on the road it went to snowing, and Massa wouldn't let us wrap anything round our feet. We had to sleep on the ground, too, in all that snow.

Massa have a great, long whip platted out of rawhide, and when one the niggers fall behind or give out, he hit him with that whip. It take the hide every time he hit a nigger. Mother, she give out on the way, 'bout the line of Texas. Her feet got raw and bleeding, and her legs swoll plumb out of shape. Then Massa, he just take out he gun and shot her, and whilst she lay dying he kicks her two-three times and say, "Damn a nigger what can't stand nothing." Boss, you know that man, he wouldn't bury mother, just leave her laying where he shot her at. You know, then there wasn't no law 'gainst killing nigger slaves.

He come plumb to Austin through that snow. He taken up farming and changes he name to Alex Simpson and changes our names, too. He cut logs and builded he home on the side of them mountains. We never had no quarters. When nighttime come, he locks the chain round our necks and then locks it round a tree. Boss, our bed were the ground. All he feed us was raw meat and green corn. Boss, I et many a green weed. I was hungry. He never let us eat at noon, he worked us all day without stopping. We went naked, that the way he worked us. We never had any clothes.

He brands us. He brand my mother before us left Georgia. Boss, that nearly kilt her. He brand her in the breast, then between the shoulders. He brand all us.

My sister, Emma, was the only woman he have till he marries. Emma was wife of all seven Negro slaves. He sold her when she's 'bout fifteen, just before her baby was born. I never seen her since.

Boss, Massa was a outlaw. He come to Texas and deal in stolen hosses. Just before he's hung for stealing hosses, he marries a young Spanish gal. He sure mean to her. Whips her 'cause she want him to leave he slaves alone and live right. Bless her heart, she's the best gal in the world. She was the best thing God ever put life in, in the world. She cry and cry every time Massa go off. She let us a-loose, and she feed us good one time while he's gone. Missy Selena, she turns us a-loose, and we wash in the creek clost by. She just fasten the chain on us and give us great big pot cooked meat and corn, and up he rides. Never says a word but come to see what us eating. He pick up he whip and whip her till she falls. If I could have got a-loose I'd kilt him. I swore if I ever got a-loose I'd kill him. But before long after that he fails to come home, and some people finds him hanging to a tree. Boss, that long after war time he got hung. He didn't let us free. We wore chains all the time. When we work, we drug them chains with us. At night he lock us to a tree to keep us from running off. He didn't have to do that. We were 'fraid to run. We knew he'd kill us. Besides, he brands us, and they no way to git it off. It's put there with a hot iron. You can't git it off.

If a slave die, Massa made the rest of us tie a rope round he feet and drag him off. Never buried one, it was too much trouble.

Massa always say he be rich after the war. He stealing all the time. He have a whole mountainside where he keep he stock. Missy Selena tell us one day we s'posed to be free, but he didn't turn us a-loose. It was 'bout three years after the war they hung him. Missy turned us a-loose.

I had a hard time then. All I had to eat was what I could find and steal. I was 'fraid of everybody. I just went wild and to the woods, but, thank God, a bunch of men taken they dogs and run me down. They carry me to they place. General Houston had some niggers, and he made them feed me. He made them keep me till I git well and able to work. Then he give me a job. I marry one the gals before I leaves them. I'm plumb out of place there at my own wedding. Yes, sir, boss, it wasn't one year before that I'm the wild nigger. We had thirteen children.

I farms all my life after that. I didn't know nothing else to do. I made plenty cotton, but now I'm too old. Me and my wife is alone now. This old nigger gits the little pension from the government. I not got much longer to stay here. I's ready to see God, but I hope my old massa ain't there to torment me again.

MARIAH ROBINSON: GEORGIA AND TEXAS

I's borned over in Georgia, in that place call Monroe, and Mammy was Lizzie Hill, 'cause her massa Judge Hill. I's honest, I don't know the 'zact date I's borned. Missy Jo, my missy, put the record of all ages in the courthouse for safekeeping, to keep the Indians from burning them up, and they's burnt up when the courthouse burns. All I knows is my youngest sister, what live in Georgia, writ me 'bout a year ago and say, "Last Thursday I's 81 year old." There is five children 'twixt my and her age, and there is six children younger'n me. That the best I can give of my age.

Judge Hill's daughter, Miss Josephine, married Dr. Young's son, what lived in Cartersville, in Georgia, but had done moved to Texas. Then my missy give me to Miss Josephine to come to Texas with her to keep her from the lonely hours and being sad so far 'way from home. We come by rail from Monroe to Social Circle and there boards the boat "Sweet Home." There was just two boats on the line, the "Sweet Home" and the "Katie Darling."

Us sails down the Atlantic Ocean to New Orleans, myself and my Aunt Lonnie and Uncle Johns, all with Miss Josephine. When us gits to New Orleans us 'rested and put in the trader's office. Us slaves, I mean. This the way of that. Our massa, Massa Bob Young, he a cotton buyer, and he done left Georgia without paying a cotton debt, and they holds us for that.

Miss Josephine wires back to Georgia to Dr. Young, and he come and git us out. He come walking down the street with the goldheaded walking cane. Us upstairs in the trader's office. I seed him coming and cries out, "Oh, yonder comes Massa Young." He looks up and shooked he goldheaded walking stick at me and says, "Never mind, Old Boss have you out in a few minutes." Then he gits the hack soon as us out and sends us to the port, for to catch the boat. Us gits on that boat and leaves that evening. Coming down the Mississippi 'cross the Gulf, us seed no land for days and days, and us go through the Gulf of Mexico and lands at the port, Galveston, and us come to Waco on the stage-coach.

Us live four year on Austin Street in Waco, that four year 'fore the war of 1861. Us boarded with Dr. Tinsley, and he and General Ross was good friends. I worked in a sewing-room, doing work such as whipping on laces and ruffling and tucking. Then us come to Bosque County right near Meridian, 'cause Massa Bob have the ranch there, and the time of the Freedom War us lives there.

Us be in the house at night, peeping out the window or pigeonhole and see Indians coming. The chief lead in front. They wild Comanches. Sometime there fifty or sixty in a bunch, and they did raiding at night. But I's pretty brave and goes three mile to Walnut Spring every day to git vegetables. I rid the donkey. Miss Josephine boards all the Bosque County school children, and us have to git the food. I seed droves of wild turkey and buffaloes and antelopes and deers. I seed wildcats and coons and bunches of wolves and heared the panthers scream like the woman.

Us lived in a log cabin with two chimneys and a long shedroom and cooked in the kitchen fireplace in the skillet and over the pot racks. Us made meal on the steel mill and hominy and cheese. I got the prize for spinning and weaving. I knitted the stockings, but Miss Jo had to drap the stitch for me to turn the heels and toes.

During the Freedom War Massa General Bob Young git kilt at the last battle. That the Bull Run battle, and he fit under General Lee. That left my missy the war widow, and she mammy come live with her and she teached in the school. I stays with them four year after freedom, and I's one of the family for the board and the clothes. They's good to me and likes to make me the best-looking and neatest slave in that place. I had such as pretty starched dresses, and they holp me fix the hair nice.

Us used the soft, dim candlelight, and I make the candlesticks. Us have gourd dippers and oak buckets to dip water out the well, and us make wooden tubs out of stumps and battling sticks to clean the clothes.

I done already met up with Peter Robinson. He's the slave of Massa Ridley Robinson what was gwine to California from Alabama, with all he slaves. Massa Robinson git kilt by the Mexicans, and a white man name Gibb Smith gits to own Peter. He hires him out to a farmer clost by us ranch, and I gits to meet him, and us have the courtship and gits married. That 'fore freedom. Us married by Caesar Berry, the slave of Massa Buck Berry. Caesar am the colored preacher. Pete was 'telligent and 'liable and the good man. He played the fiddle all over the country, and I rid horseback with him miles and miles to them dances.

Peter could write the plain hand, and he gits to haul lumber from Waco to make the Bosque County courthouse. He larns more and gits to be the county's first colored trustee and the first colored teacher. He gits 'pinted to see after the widows in time of war and in the 'construction days. Finally, he is sont to Austin, the capital of Texas, to be representative.

Pete and me begot ten children. My first child am borned two months 'fore freedom. After us slaves is freed, us hired out for one year to git means to go free on. Us held by the committee call "Free Committee Men." The wages is ten dollars the month to the family. After us ready to go for ourselves, my missy am the poor widow, and she have only three cows and three calves, but she give one of each of them to Pete and me.

After leaving Miss Jo, us move here and yonder till I gits tired of such. By then us have several children, and I changes from the frivolity of life to the sincereness, to shape the destiny of the children's life. I tells Pete, when he comes back from fiddling one night, to buy me the home or hitch up and carry me back to Missy Jo. That lead him to buy a strip of land in Meridian. He pays ten dollar the acre. We has a team of oxen, call Broad and Buck, and we done our farming with them. Pete builds me a house, hauls the lumber from Waco. Twicet us gits burnt out, but builds it 'gain. Us makes the orchard and sells the fruit. Us raises bees and sells the honey and gits cows and chickens and turkeys. Pete works good, and I puts on my bonnet and walks behind him and draps the corn.

He gits in organizing the first colored church in Meridian, the colored Cumberland Presbyterian Church. Us has ever lived the useful life. I works at cooking and washing and ironing. I helps the doctors with the babies.

But the disability of age have to come, and now I is 'most disabled and feels stunted and poverty-stricken. I'd like to work now, but I isn't able.

NICEY KINNEY: GEORGIA

Marse Gerald Sharp and his wife, Miss Annie, owned us and, child, they was grand folks. Their old home was 'way up in Jackson County, 'twixt Athens and Jefferson. That big old plantation run plumb back down to the Oconee River. Yes, ma'am, all them rich river bottoms was Marse Gerald's.

Mammy's name was Caroline, and she belonged to Marse Gerald, but Marse Hatton David owned my daddy—his name was Phineas. The David place wa'n't but 'bout a mile from our plantation and Daddy was 'lowed to stay with his family 'most every night; he was always with us on Sundays. Marse Gerald didn't have no slaves but my mammy and her children, and he was sure mighty good to us.

Marse Gerald had a nice four-room house with a hall all the way through it. It even had two big old fireplaces on one chimney. No, ma'am, it wa'n't a rock chimney; that chimney was made out of homemade bricks. Master's family had their cooking done in a open fireplace like everybody else for a long time, and then just 'fore the big war he bought a stove. Yes, ma'am, Marse Gerald bought a cookstove, and us felt plumb rich 'cause there wa'n't many folks that had stoves back in them days.

Mammy lived in the old kitchen close by the big house till there got to be too many of us; then Marse Gerald built us a house just a little piece off from the big house. It was just a log house, but Master had all them cracks chinked tight with red mud, and he even had one of them Franklin-back chimneys built to keep our little cabin nice and warm. Why, child, ain't you never seed none of them old chimneys? Their backs sloped out in the middle to throw out the heat into the room and keep too much of it from gwine straight up the flue. Our beds in our cabin was corded just like them up at the big house, but us slept on straw ticks and, let me tell you, they sure slept good after a hard day's work.

The bestest water that ever was come from a spring right nigh our cabin, and us had long-handled gourds to drink it out of. Some of them gourds hung by the spring all the time, and there was always one or two of 'em hanging by the side of our old cedar waterbucket. Sure, us had a cedar bucket, and it had brass hoops on it; that was some job to keep them hoops scrubbed with sand to make 'em bright and shiny, and they had to be clean and pretty all the time or Mammy would git right in behind us with a switch. Marse Gerald raised all them long-handled gourds that us used 'stead of the tin dippers folks has now, but them wa'n't the onliest kinds of gourds he growed on his place. There was gourds 'most as big as waterbuckets, and they had short handles that was bent whilst the gourds was green, so us could hang 'em on a limb of a tree in the shade to keep water cool for us when us was working in the field during hot weather.

I never done much field work till the war come on, 'cause Mistress was larning me to be a housemaid. Marse Gerald and Miss Annie never had no children 'cause she wa'n't no bearing woman, but they was both mighty fond of little folks. On Sunday mornings Mammy used to fix us all up nice and clean and take us up to the big house for Marse Gerald to play with. They was good Christian folks and took the mostest pains to larn us children how to live right. Master used to 'low as how he had done paid $500 for Caroline but he sure wouldn't sell her for no price.

Everything us needed was raised on that plantation 'cept cotton. Nary a stalk of cotton was growed there, but just the same our clothes was made out of cloth that Mistress and my mammy wove out of thread us children spun, and Mistress took a heap of pains making up our dresses. During the war everybody had to wear homespun, but there didn't nobody have no better or prettier dresses than ours, 'cause Mistress knowed more'n anybody 'bout dyeing cloth. When time come to make up a batch of clothes, Mistress would say, "Caroline, holp me git up my things for dyeing," and us would fetch dogwood bark, sumac, poison ivy, and sweet-gum bark. That poison ivy made the best black of anything us ever tried, and Mistress could dye the prettiest sort of purple with sweet-gum bark. Copperas was used to keep the colors from fading, and she knowed so well how to handle it that you could wash cloth what she had dyed all day long and it wouldn't fade a speck.

Master was too old to go to the war, so he had to stay home, and he sure seed that us done our work raising something to eat. He had us plant all our cleared ground, and I sure has done some hard work down in them old bottom lands, plowing, hoeing, pulling corn and fodder, and I's even cut cordwood and split rails. Them was hard times, and everybody had to work.

Sometimes Marse Gerald would be away a week at a time when he went to court at Jefferson, and the very last thing he said 'fore he driv off always was, "Caroline, you and the children take good care of Mistress." He 'most always fetched us new shoes when he come back, 'cause he never kept no shoemaker man on our place, and all our shoes was store-bought. They was just brogans with brass toes, but us felt powerful dressed up when us got 'em on, 'specially when they was new and the brass was bright and shiny. There was nine of us children, four boys and five gals. Us gals had plain cotton dresses made with long sleeves, and us wore big sunbonnets. What would gals say now if they had to wear them sort of clothes and do work like what us done? Little boys didn't wear nothing but long shirts in summertime, but come winter everybody had good warm clothes made out of wool off of Marse Gerald's own sheep, and boys, even little tiny boys, had britches in winter.

Did you ever see folks shear sheep, child? Well, it was a sight in them days. Master would tie a sheep on the scaffold, what he had done built for that job, and then he would have me set on the sheep's head whilst he cut off the wool. He sont it to the factory to have it carded into bats, and us children spun the thread at home and Mammy and Mistress wove it into cloth for our winter clothes. Nobody wa'n't fixed up better on church days than Master's niggers, and he was sure proud of that.

Us went to church with our white folks 'cause there wa'n't no colored churches them days. None of the churches round our part of the country had meeting every Sunday, so us went to three different meeting houses. On the first Sunday us went to Captain Crick Baptist Church, to Sandy Crick Presbyterian Church on second Sundays, and on third Sundays meeting was at Antioch Methodist Church where Master and Mistress was members. They put me under the watch-care of their church when I was a mighty little gal, 'cause my white folks sure believed in the church and in living for God; the larning that them two good old folks gimme is done stayed right with me all through life, so far, and I aims to live by it to the end. I didn't sure 'nough jine up with no church till I was done growed up and had left Marse Gerald; then I jined the Cedar Grove Baptist Church and was baptized there, and there's where I belongs yet.

Master was too old to work when they sot us free, so for a long time us just stayed there and run his place for him. I never seed none of them Yankee soldiers but one time. Master was off in Jefferson, and while I was down at the washplace I seed 'bout twelve men come riding over the hill. I was sure scared; and when I run and told Mistress, she made us all come inside her house and lock all the doors. Them Yankee mens· just rode on through our yard down to the river and stayed there a little while; then they turned around and rid back through our yard and on down the big road, and us never seed 'em no more.

Soon after they was sot free, niggers started up churches of they own, and it was some sight to see and hear 'em on meeting days. They would go in big crowds, and sometimes they would go to meetings a far piece off. They was all fixed up in their Sunday clothes, and they walked barefoots with their shoes acrost their shoulders to keep 'em from gitting dirty. Just 'fore they got to the church they stopped and put on their shoes, and then they was ready to git together to hear the preacher.

Folks don't know nothing 'bout hard times now, 'specially young folks; they is on the gravy train and don't know it, but they is headed straight for 'struction and perdition; they's gwine to land in that burning fire if they don't mind what they's about. Just trust in the Lord, honey, and cast your troubles on Him and He'll stay with you, but if you turns your back on Him, then you is lost, plumb gone, just as sure as shelled corn.

When us left Marse Gerald and moved nigh Athens, he got a old nigger named Egypt, what had a big family, to live on his place and do all the work. Old Master didn't last long after us was gone. One night he had done let his farm hands have a big corn-shucking and had seed that they had plenty of supper and liquor to go with it and, as was the custom them days, some of them niggers got Old Master up on their shoulders and toted him up to the big house, singing as they went along. He was just as gay as they was, and joked the boys. When they put him down on the big house porch he told Old Mistress he didn't want no supper 'cept a little coffee and bread, and he strangled on the first bite. Mistress sont for the doctor, but he was too nigh gone, and it wa'n't long 'fore he had done gone into the glory of the next world. He was 'bout ninety-five years old when he died, and he had sure been a good man. One of my nieces and her husband went there after Marse Gerald died and took care of Mistress till she went home to glory too.

Mammy followed Old Mistress to glory in 'bout three years. Us was living on the Johnson place then, and it wa'n't long 'fore me and George Kinney got married. A white preacher married us, but us didn't have no wedding celebration. Us moved to the Joe Langford place in Oconee County but didn't stay there but one year; then us moved 'crost the crick into Clarke County, and after us farmed there nine years, us moved on to this here place where us has been ever since. Plain old farming is the most us is ever done, but George used to make some mighty nice chairs to sell to the white folks. He made 'em out of hickory what he seasoned just right and put rye split bottoms in 'em. Them chairs lasted a lifetime; when they got dirty, you just washed 'em good and sot 'em in the sun to dry, and they was good as new. George sold a lot of rugs and mats that he made out of plaited shucks. Most everybody kept a shuck footmat 'fore their front doors. The sunhats made out of shucks and bulrushes was mighty fine to wear in the field when the sun was hot. Not long after all ten of our children was borned, George died out and left me with them five boys and five gals.

Some old witch-man conjured me into marrying Jordan Jackson. That's the blessed truth, honey; a fortuneteller is done told me how it was done. I didn't want to have nothing to do with Jordan 'cause I knowed he was just a no-'count old drinking man that just wanted my land and stuff. When he couldn't get me to pay him no heed hisself, he went to a old conjure man and got him to put a spell on me. Honey, didn't you know they could do that back in them days? I knows they could, 'cause I never woulda run round with no nigger and married him if I hadn't been witched by that conjure business. The good Lord sure punishes folks for their sins on this earth, and that old man what put that spell on me died and went down to burning hell, and it wa'n't long then 'fore the spell left me.

Right then I showed that no-'count Jordan Jackson that I was a good woman, a powerful sight above him, and that he wa'n't gwine to git none of this land what my children's daddy had done left 'em. When I just stood right up to him and showed him he wa'n't gwine to outwhack me, he up and left me, and I don't even use his name no more 'cause I don't want it in my business no way a-tall. Jordan's done paid his debt now since he died and went down in that big old burning hell 'long with the old witch-man that conjured me for him.

Yes, honey, the Lord done put it on record that there is sure a burning place for torment, and didn't my master and mistress larn me the same thing? I sure does thank 'em to this day for the pains they took with the little nigger gal that growed up to be me, trying to show her the right road to travel. Oh! if I could just see 'em one more time! But they can look down from the glory land and see that I's still trying to follow the road that leads to where they is, and when I gits to that good and better world I just knows the Good Lord will let this aged woman be with her dear master and mistress all through the time to come. . . .

CATO ———: ALABAMA

I'm home today 'cause my little old dog is lost, and I has to stay round to hunt for him. I been going every day on the truck to the cotton patches. I don't pick no more, 'count my hands git too tired and begin to cramp on me. But I go and set in the field and watch the lunches for the other hands.

I am a hundred one years old, 'cause I's twenty-eight, going on twenty-nine, a man growned, when the breaking-up come. I'm pretty old, but my folks live that way. My old black mammy lived to be a hundred twenty-five, and my white massa—which was the brother of my daddy—lived to be a hundred four. He ain't been so long died. My own daddy lived to be very ageable, but I don't know when he died.

Back in Alabama, Missy Angela took me when I was past my creeping days to live in the big house with the white folks. I had a room built on the big house, where I stayed, and they was always good to me, 'cause I's one of their blood. They never hit me a lick or slapped me once, and they told me they'd never sell me away from them. They was the best-quality white folks and lived in a big, two-story house with a big hall what run all the way through the house. They wasn't rough as some white folks on their niggers.

My mammy lived in a hewn-oak log cabin in the quarters. There was a long row of cabins, some bigger than t'others, 'count of family size. My massa had over eighty head of slaves. Them little old cabins was cozy, 'cause we chinked 'em with mud and they had stick chimneys daubed with mud, mixed with hog-hair.

The fixings was just plain things. The beds was draw-beds—wooden bedsteads helt together with ropes drawed tight, to hold them. We scalded moss and buried it awhile and stuffed it into ticking to make mattresses. Them beds slept good, better'n the ones nowadays.

There was a good fireplace for cooking, and Sundays Missy give us niggers a pint of flour and a chicken, for to cook a mess of victuals. Then there was plenty game to find. Many a time I've kilt seventy-five or eighty squirrels out of one big beech. There was lots of deer and bears and quails and every other kind of game, but when they run the Indians out of the country, the game just followed the Indians. I've seed the biggest herds of deer following the way the Indians drifted. Whenever the Indians left, the game all left with them, for some reason I dunno.

Talking 'bout victuals, our eating was good. Can't says the same for all places. Some of the plantations half-starved their niggers and 'lowanced out their eating till they wasn't fitting for work. They had to slip about to niggers on other places to piece out their meals. They had field calls and other kinds of whoops and hollers, what had a meaning to 'em.

Our place was fifteen hundred acres in one block, and 'sides the crops of cotton and corn and rice and ribbon cane we raised in the bottoms, we had vegetables and sheep and beef. We dried the beef on scaffolds we built, and I used to tend it. But best of anything to eat, I liked a big fat coon, and I always liked honey. Some the niggers had little garden patches they tended for themselves.

Everything I tells you am the truth, but they's plenty I can't tell you. I heard plenty things from my mammy and grandpappy. He was a fine diver and used to dive in the Alabama River for things what was wrecked out of boats, and the white folks would git him to go down for things they wanted. They'd let him down by a rope to find things on the bottom of the riverbed. He used to git a piece of money for doing it.

My grandmammy was a juksie, 'cause her mammy was a nigger and her daddy a Choctaw Indian. That's what makes me so mixed up with Indian and African and white blood. Sometimes it mattered to me, sometimes it didn't. It don't no more, 'cause I'm not too far from the end of my days.

I had one brother and one sister I helped raise. They was mostly nigger. My white folks told me never to worry 'bout them, though, 'cause my mammy was of their blood and all of us in our family would never be sold, and sometime they'd make free men and women of us. My brother and sister lived with the niggers, though.

I was trained for a houseboy and to tend the cows. The bears was so bad then, a 'sponsible person who could carry a gun had to look after them.

My massa used to give me a little money 'long, to buy what I wanted. I always bought fine clothes. In the summer when I was a little one, I wore lowerings, like the rest of the niggers. That was things made from cotton sacking. Most of the boys wore shirttails till they was big yearlings. When they bought me red russets from the town, I cried and cried. I didn't want to wear no rawhide shoes. So they took 'em back. They had a weakness for my crying. I did have plenty fine clothes, good woolen suits they spinned on the place, and doeskins and fine linens. I druv in the carriage with the white folks and was 'bout the most dudish nigger in them parts.

I used to tend the nursling thread. The reason they called it that was when the mammies was confined with babies having to suck, they had to spin. I'd take them the thread and bring it back to the house when it was spinned. If they didn't spin seven or eight cuts a day, they'd git a whupping. It was considerable hard on a woman when she had a fretting baby. But every morning them babies had to be took to the big house, so the white folks could see if they's dressed right. They was money tied up in little nigger young-uns.

They whupped the women and they whupped the mens. I used to work some in the tannery, and we made the whups. They'd tie them down to a stob, and give 'em the whupping. Some niggers, it taken four men to whup 'em, but they got it. The nigger driver was meaner than the white folks. They'd better not leave a blade of grass in the rows. I seed 'em beat a nigger half a day to make him 'fess up to stealing a sheep or a shoat. Or they'd whup 'em for running away, but not so hard if they come back of their own 'cordance when they got hungry and sick in the swamps. But when they had to run 'em down with the nigger dogs, they'd git in bad trouble.

My massa never did have any real 'corrigible niggers, but I heard of 'em plenty on other places. When they was real 'corrigible, the white folks said they was like mad dogs and didn't mind to kill them so much as killing a sheep. They'd take 'em to the graveyard and shoot 'em down and bury 'em face downward, with their shoes on. I never seed it done, but they made some the niggers go for a lesson to them that they could git the same.

But I didn't even have to carry a pass to leave my own place, like the other niggers. I had a cap with a sign on it: "Don't bother this nigger, or there will be hell to pay." I went after the mail, in the town. It come in coaches and they put on fresh hosses at Pineapple. The coachman run the hosses into Pineapple with a big to-do and blowing the bugle to git the fresh hosses ready. I got the mail. I was a trusty all my days and never been 'rested by the law to this day.

I never had no complaints for my treatment, but some the niggers hated syrup-making time, 'cause when they had to work till midnight making syrup, it's four o'clock up, just the same. Sunup to sundown was for field niggers.

Corn-shucking was fun. Them days no corn was put in the cribs with shucks on it. They shucked it in the field and shocked the fodder. They did it by sides and all hands out. A beef was kilt, and they'd have a regular picnic feasting. They was plenty whiskey for the niggers, just like Christmas.

Christmas was the big day. Presents for everybody, and the baking and preparing went on for days. The little ones and the big ones were glad, 'specially the nigger mens, 'count of plenty good whiskey. Massa Cal got the best whiskey for his niggers.

We used to have frolics, too. Some niggers had fiddles and played the reels, and niggers love to dance and sing and eat.

'Course niggers had their serious side, too. They loved to go to church and had a little log chapel for worship. But I went to the white folks' church. In the chapel some nigger mens preached from the Bible but couldn't read a line no more than a sheep could. My white folks didn't mind their niggers praying and singing hymns, but some places wouldn't 'low them to worship a-tall, and they had to put their heads in pots to sing or pray.

Most the niggers I know, who had their marriage put in the book, did it after the breaking-up, plenty after they had growed children. When they got married on the places, mostly they just jumped over a broom and that made 'em married. Sometimes one the white folks read a little out of the Scriptures to 'em, and they felt more married.

Take me, I was never one for sickness. But the slaves used to git sick. There was jaundice in them bottoms. First off they'd give some castor oil, and if that didn't cure, they'd give blue mass. Then if he was still sick they'd git a doctor.

They used to cry the niggers off just like so much cattle, and we didn't think no different of it. I seed them put them on the block and brag on them something big. Everybody liked to hear them cry off niggers. The crier was a clown and made funny talk and kept everybody laughing.

When Massa and the other mens on the place went off to war, he called me and said, "Cato, you's always been a 'sponsible man, and I leave you to look after the women and the place. If I don't come back, I want you to always stay by Missy Angela!" I said, "Fore God, I will, Massa Cal." He said, "Then I can go away peaceable."

We thought for a long time the soldiers had the Federals whupped to pieces, but there was plenty bad times to go through. I carried a gun and guarded the place at nighttime. The paddyrollers [night riders?] was bad. I cotched one and took him to the house more'n once. They wore black caps and put black rags over their faces and was always skullduggerying round at night. We didn't use torches any more when we went round at night, 'cause we was afeared. We put out all the fires round the house at nighttime.

The young mens in grey uniforms used to pass so gay and singing, in the big road. Their clothes was good, and we used to feed them the best we had on the place. Missy Angela would say, "Cato, they is our boys and give them the best this place 'fords." We taken out the hams and the wine and kilt chickens for them. That was at first.

Then the boys and mens in blue got to coming that way, and they was fine-looking men, too. Missy Angela would cry and say, "Cato, they is just mens and boys, and we got to feed them, too." We had a pavilion built in the yard, like they had at picnics, and we fed the Federals in that. Missy Angela set in to crying and says to the Yankees, "Don't take Cato. He is the only nigger man I got by me now. If you take Cato, I just don't know what I'll do." I tells them soldiers I got to stay by Missy Angela so long as I live. The Yankee mens say to her, "Don't 'sturb youself, we ain't gwine to take Cato or harm nothing of yours." The reason they's all right by us was 'cause we prepared for them, but with some folks they was rough something terrible. They taken off their hosses and corn.

I seed the trees bend low and shake all over and heard the roar and popping of cannon balls. There was springs not too far from our place, and the soldiers used to camp there and build a fire and cook a mule, 'cause they'd got down to starvation. When some of the guerrillas seed the fire they'd aim to it, and many a time they spoiled that dinner for them soldiers. The Yankees did it, and our boys did it, too. There was killing going on so terrible, like people was dogs.

Massa Cal come back, and he was all wore out and ragged. He soon called all the niggers to the front yard and says, "Mens and womens, you are today as free as I am. You are free to do as you like, 'cause the damned Yankees done 'creed you are. They ain't a nigger on my place what was born here or ever lived here who can't stay here and work and eat to the end of his days, as long as this old place will raise peas and goobers. Go if you wants, and stay if you wants." Some of the niggers stayed and some went, and some what had run away to the North come back. They always called, real humble-like, at the back gate to Missy Angela, and she always fixed it up with Massa Cal they could have a place.

Near the close of the war I seed some folks leaving for Texas. They said if the Federals won the war, they'd have to live in Texas to keep slaves. So plenty started drifting their slaves to the West. They'd pass with the womens riding in the wagons and the mens on foot. Some took slaves to Texas after the Federals done 'creed the breaking-up.

Long as I lived, I minded what my white folks told me, 'cept one time. They was a nigger working in the field, and he kept jerking the mules and Massa Cal got mad, and he give me a gun and said, "Go out there and kill that man." I said, "Massa Cal, please don't tell me that. I ain't never kilt nobody, and I don't want to." He said, "Cato, you do what I tell you." He meant it. I went out to the nigger and said, "You has got to leave this minute, and I is, too, 'cause I is 'spose to kill you, only I ain't, and Massa Cal will kill me." He drops the harness, and we run and crawled through the fence and ran away.

I hated to go, 'cause things was so bad, and flour sold for $25 a barrel, and pickled pork for $15 a barrel. You couldn't buy nothing lessen with gold. I had plenty of 'Federate money, only it wouldn't buy nothing.

But today I is a old man, and my hands ain't stained with no blood. I is always been glad I didn't kill that man.

Mules run to a terrible price then. A right puny pair of mules sold for $500. But the Yankees give me a mule, and I farmed a year for a white man and watched a herd of mules, too. I stayed with them mules till four o'clock even Sundays. So many scoundrels was going 'bout, stealing mules.

That year I was bound out by 'greement with the white man, and I made $360. The bureau come by that year looking at niggers' contracts, to see they didn't git skunt out their rightful wages. My white folks didn't stay mad at me, and every Sunday they come by to see me and brung me little delicate things to eat.

They said a hundred times they regretted they never larned me to read or write, and they said my daddy done put up $500 for me to go to the New Allison school for colored folks. Miss Benson, a Yankee, was the teacher. I was twenty-nine years old and just starting in the blue-back speller. I went to school a while, but one morning at ten o'clock my poor old mammy come by and called me out. She told me she got put out, 'cause she too old to work in the field. I told her not to worry, that I'm the family man now, and she didn't never need to git any more three-quarter hand wages no more.

So I left school and turnt my hand to anything I could find for years. I never had no trouble finding work, 'cause all the white folks knowed Cato was a good nigger. I left my mammy with some fine white folks, and she raised a whole family of children for them. Their name was Bryan, and they lived on a little bayou. Them younguns was crazy 'bout Mammy, and they'd send me word not to worry about her, 'cause she'd have the best of care and when she died they'd tend to her burying.

Finally I come to Texas, 'cause I thought there was money for the taking out here. I got a job splitting rails for two years, and from then on I farmed, mostly. I married a woman and lived with her forty-seven years, rain or shine. We had thirteen children, and eight of them is living today.

Enduring the big war I got worried 'bout my little black mammy, and I wanted to go back home and see her and the old places. I went, and she was shriveled up to not much of anything. That's the last time I saw her. But for forty-four years I didn't forget to send her things I thought she'd want. I saw Massa Cal, and he done married after I left and raised a family of children. I saw Missy Angela and she was a old woman. We went out and looked at the tombstones and the rock markers in the graveyard on the old place, and some of them done near melted away. I looked good at lots of things, 'cause I knowed I wouldn't be that way 'gain. So many had gone on since I'd been there before.

After my first wife died I married 'gain, and my wife is a good woman, but she's old and done lost her voice and has to be in Terrell most the time. But I git 'long all right, 'cept my hands cramps some.

. . . I lived through plenty and I lived a long time. . . .

JENNY PROCTOR: ALABAMA

I's hear tell of them good slave days, but I ain't never seen no good times then. My mother's name was Lisa, and when I was a very small child I hear that driver going from cabin to cabin as early as 3 o'clock in the morning, and when he comes to our cabin he say, "Lisa, Lisa, git up from there and git that breakfast." My mother, she was cook, and I don't recollect nothing 'bout my father. If I had any brothers and sisters I didn't know it. We had old ragged huts made out of poles and some of the cracks chinked up with mud and moss and some of them wasn't. We didn't have no good beds, just scaffolds nailed up to the wall out of poles and the old ragged bedding throwed on them. That sure was hard sleeping, but even that feel good to our weary bones after them long hard day's work in the field. I 'tended to the children when I was a little gal and tried to clean the house just like Old Miss tells me to. Then soon as I was ten years old, Old Master, he say, "Git this here nigger to that cotton patch."

I recollects once when I was trying to clean the house like Old Miss tell me, I finds a biscuit, and I's so hungry I et it, 'cause we never see such a thing as a biscuit only sometimes on Sunday morning. We just have corn bread and syrup and sometimes fat bacon, but when I et that biscuit and she comes in and say, "Where that biscuit?" I say, "Miss, I et it 'cause I's so hungry." Then she grab that broom and start to beating me over the head with it and calling me low-down nigger, and I guess I just clean lost my head 'cause I knowed better than to fight her if I knowed anything 't all, but I start to fight her, and the driver, he comes in and he grabs me and starts beating me with that cat-o'-nine-tails,[1] and he beats me till I fall to the floor nearly dead. He cut my back all to pieces, then they rubs salt in the cuts for more punishment. Lord, Lord, honey! Them was awful days. When Old Master come to the house, he say, "What you beat that nigger like that for?" And the driver tells him why, and he say, "She can't work now for a week. She pay for several biscuits in that time." He sure was mad, and he tell Old Miss she start the whole mess. I still got them scars on my old back right now, just like my grandmother have when she die, and I's a-carrying mine right on to the grave just like she did.

Our master, he wouldn't 'low us to go fishing—he say that too easy on a nigger and wouldn't 'low us to hunt none either—but sometime we slips off at night and catch possums. And when Old Master smells them possums cooking 'way in the night, he wraps up in a white sheet and gits in the chimney corner and scratch on the wall, and when the man in the cabin goes to the door and say, "Who's that?" he say, "It's me, what's ye cooking in there?" and the man say, "I's cooking possum." He say, "Cook him and bring me the hindquarters and you and the wife and the children eat the rest." We never had no chance to git any rabbits 'cept when we was a-clearing and grubbing the new ground. Then we catch some rabbits, and if they looks good to the white folks they takes them and if they no good the niggers git them. We never had no gardens. Sometimes the slaves git vegetables from the white folks' garden and sometimes they didn't.

Money? Uh-uh! We never seen no money. Guess we'd-a bought something to eat with it if we ever seen any. Fact is, we wouldn't-a knowed hardly how to bought anything, 'cause we didn't know nothing 'bout going to town.

They spinned the cloth what our clothes was made of, and we had straight dresses or slips made of lowell. Sometimes they dye 'em with sumac berries or sweet-gum bark, and sometimes they didn't. On Sunday they make all the children change, and what we wears till we gits our clothes washed was gunny sacks with holes cut for our head and arms. We didn't have no shoes 'cepting

---

[1] A big leather whip, branching into nine tails.

some homemade moccasins, and we didn't have them till we was big children. The little children they goes naked till they was big enough to work. They was soon big enough though, 'cording to our master. We had red flannel for winter underclothes. Old Miss she say a sick nigger cost more than the flannel.

Weddings? Uh-uh! We just steps over the broom and we's married. Ha! Ha! Ha!

Old Master he had a good house. The logs was all hewed off smooth-like, and the cracks all fixed with nice chinking, plumb 'spectable-looking even to the plank floors. That was something. He didn't have no big plantation, but he keeps 'bout three hundred slaves in them little huts with dirt floors. I thinks he calls it four farms what he had.

Sometimes he would sell some of the slaves off of that big auction block to the highest bidder when he could git enough for one.

When he go to sell a slave, he feed that one good for a few days, then when he goes to put 'em up on the auction block he takes a meat skin and greases all round that nigger's mouth and makes 'em look like they been eating plenty meat and such like and was good and strong and able to work. Sometimes he sell the babes from the breast, and then again he sell the mothers from the babes and the husbands and the wives, and so on. He wouldn't let 'em holler much when the folks be sold away. He say, "I have you whupped if you don't hush." They sure loved their six children though. They wouldn't want nobody buying them.

We might-a done very well if the old driver hadn't been so mean, but the least little thing we do he beat us for it and put big chains round our ankles and make us work with them on till the blood be cut out all around our ankles. Some of the masters have what they call stockades and puts their heads and feet and arms through holes in a big board out in the hot sun, but our old driver he had a bull pen. That's only thing like a jail he had. When a slave do anything he didn't like, he takes 'em in that bull pen and chains 'em down, face up to the sun, and leaves 'em there till they nearly dies.

None of us was 'lowed to see a book or try to learn. They say we git smarter than they was if we learn anything, but we slips around and gits hold of that Webster's old blue-back speller and we hides it till 'way in the night and then we lights a little pine torch,[2] and studies that spelling book. We learn it too. I can read some now and write a little too.

They wasn't no church for the slaves, but we goes to the white folks' arbor on Sunday evening, and a white man he gits up there to preach to the niggers. He say, "Now I takes my text, which is, Nigger obey your master and your mistress, 'cause what you git from them here in this world am all you ever going to git, 'cause you just like the hogs and the other animals—when you dies you ain't no more, after you been throwed in that hole." I guess we believed that for a while 'cause we didn't have no way finding out different. We didn't see no Bibles.

Sometimes a slave would run away and just live wild in the woods, but most

---

[2] Several long splinters of rich pine, of a lasting quality and making a bright light.

times they catch 'em and beats 'em, then chains 'em down in the sun till they nearly die. The only way any slaves on our farm ever goes anywhere was when the boss sends him to carry some news to another plantation or when we slips off way in the night. Sometimes after all the work was done a bunch would have it made up to slip out down to the creek and dance. We sure have fun when we do that, most times on Saturday night.

All the Christmas we had was Old Master would kill a hog and give us a piece of pork. We thought that was something, and the way Christmas lasted was 'cording to the big sweet-gum backlog what the slaves would cut and put in the fireplace. When that burned out, the Christmas was over. So you know we all keeps a-looking the whole year round for the biggest sweet gum we could find. When we just couldn't find the sweet gum, we git oak, but it wouldn't last long enough, 'bout three days on average, when we didn't have to work. Old Master he sure pile on them pine knots, gitting that Christmas over so we could git back to work.

We had a few little games we play, like Peep Squirrel Peep, You Can't Catch Me, and such like. We didn't know nothing 'bout no New Year's Day or holidays 'cept Christmas.

We had some corn-shuckings sometimes, but the white folks gits the fun and the nigger gits the work. We didn't have no kind of cotton-pickings 'cept just pick our own cotton. I's can hear them darkies now, going to the cotton patch 'way 'fore day a-singing "Peggy, does you love me now?"

One old man he sing:

> Saturday night and Sunday too
> Young gals on my mind.
> Monday morning 'way 'fore day
> Old Master got me gwine.
> Peggy, does you love me now?

Then he whoops a sort of nigger holler, what nobody can do just like them old-time darkies, then on he goes:

> Possum up a 'simmon tree,
> Rabbit on the ground.
> Lord, Lord, possum,
> Shake them 'simmons down.
> Peggy, does you love me now?

> Rabbit up a gum stump,
> Possum up a holler.
> Git him out, little boy,
> And I gives you half a dollar.
> Peggy, does you love me now?

We didn't have much looking after when we git sick. We had to take the worst stuff in the world for medicine, just so it was cheap. That old blue mass and bitter apple would keep us out all night. Sometimes he have the doctor when he thinks we going to die, 'cause he say he ain't got anyone to lose, then that calomel what that doctor would give us would pretty nigh kill us. Then they keeps all kinds of lead bullets and asafetida balls round our necks, and some carried a rabbit foot with them all the time to keep off evil of any kind.

Lord, Lord, honey! It seems impossible that any of us ever lived to see that day of freedom, but thank God we did.

When Old Master comes down in the cotton patch to tell us 'bout being free, he say, "I hates to tell you, but I knows I's got to—you is free, just as free as me or anybody else what's white." We didn't hardly know what he means. We just sort of huddle round together like scared rabbits, but after we knowed what he mean, didn't many of us go, 'cause we didn't know where to of went. Old Master he say he give us the woods land and half of what we make on it, and we could clear it and work it or starve. Well, we didn't know hardly what to do 'cause he just gives us some old dull hoes and axes to work with; but we all went to work, and as we cut down the trees and the poles he tells us to build the fence round the field and we did, and when we plants the corn and the cotton we just plant all the fence corners full too, and I never seen so much stuff grow in all my born days. Several ears of corn to the stalk, and them big cotton stalks was a-laying over on the ground. Some of the old slaves they say they believe the Lord knew something 'bout niggers after all. He lets us put corn in his crib, and then we builds cribs and didn't take long 'fore we could buy some hosses and some mules and some good hogs. Them mangy hogs what our master give us the first year was plumb good hogs after we grease them and scrub them with lye soap. He just give us the ones he thought was sure to die, but we was a-gitting going now, and 'fore long we was a-building better houses and feeling kind of happy-like. After Old Master dies, we keeps hearing talk of Texas, and me and my old man—I's done been married several years then and had one little boy—well, we gits in our covered wagon with our little mules hitched to it, and we comes to Texas. We worked as sharecroppers around Buffalo, Texas, till my old man he died. My boy was nearly grown then, so he wants to come to San Angelo and work, so here we is. He done been married long time now and git six children. Some of them work at hotels and cafés and filling stations and in homes.

ALLEN V. MANNING: MISSISSIPPI, LOUISIANA, AND TEXAS

I was born in slavery, and I belonged to a Baptist preacher. Until I was fifteen years old I was taught that I was his own chattel-property and he could do with me like he wanted to, but he had been taught that way, too, and we both believed it. I never did hold nothing against him for being hard on Negroes sometimes, and I don't think I ever would of had any trouble even if I had of growed up and died in slavery. . . .

Like I say, my master was a preacher and a kind man, but he treated the Negroes just like they treated him. He been taught that they was just like his work hosses, and if they act like they his work hosses they git along all right. But if they don't—oh, oh!

Old Master didn't have any overseer hired, but him and his boys looked after the place and had a Negro we called the driver. We-all sure hated that old black man, but I forget his name now. That driver never was allowed to think up nothing for the slaves to do but just was told to make them work hard at what the master and his boys told them to do. White folks had to set them at a job, and then old driver would whoopity and whoopity around, and egg them and egg them until they finish up, so they can go at something else. He worked hard hisself, though, and set a mighty hard pattern for the rest to keep up with. Like I say, he been taught he didn't know how to think, so he didn't try.

Old Mistress' name was Mary, and they had two daughters, Levia and Betty. Then they had three sons. The oldest was named Bill Junior, and he was plumb grown when I was a boy, but the other two, Jedson and Jim, was just a little older than me.

Old Master didn't have but two or three single Negroes, but he had several families, and most of them was big ones. My own family was pretty good size, but three of the children was born free. Pappy's name was William and Mammy's was Lucy. My brother Joe was the oldest child, and then come Adeline, Harriet, and Texana, and Betty before the surrender, and then Henry, Mattie, and Louisa after it.

When the war come along, Old Master just didn't know what to do. He always been taught not to raise his hand up and kill nobody—no matter how come—and he just kept holding out against all them that was talking about fighting, and he wouldn't go and fight. He been taught that it was all right to have slaves and treat them like he want to, but he been taught it was sinful to go fight and kill to keep them, and he lived up to what he been taught.

They was some Choctaw people lived round there, and they flew up and went right off to the war, and Mr. Trot Hand and Mr. Joe Brown that had plantations on the big road toward Quitman both went off with their grown boys right at the start, but Old Master was a preacher, and he just stayed out of it. I remember one day I was sent up to the big house, and I heard Old Master and some men out at the gate 'xpounding about the war. Some of the men had on soldier clothes, and they acted like they was mad. Somebody tell me later on that they was getting up a home guard because the Yankees done got down in Alabama not far away, but Old Master wouldn't go in with them.

Two–three days after that, it seems like, Old Master come down to the quarters and say, "Git everything bundled up and in the wagons for a long trip." The Negroes all come in, and everybody pitch in to help pack up the wagons.

Then Old Master look around and he can't find Andy. Andy was one Negro that never did act like he been taught, and Old Master's patience about wore out with him anyways.

We all know that Andy done run off again, but we didn't know where to. Leastwise all the Negroes tell Old Master that. But Old Master soon show us we done the work and he done the thinking! He just goes ahead and keeps all the Negroes busy fixing up the wagons and bundling up the stuff to travel, and keeps us all in his sight all the time, and says nothing about Andy being gone.

Then that night he sends for a white man name Clements that got some bloodhounds, and him and Mr. Clements takes time about staying awake and watching all the cabins to see nobody slips out of them. Everybody was afraid to stick their head out.

Early next morning we has all the wagons ready to drive right off, and Old Master call Andy's brother up to him. He say, "You go down to that spring and wait, and when Andy come down to the spring to fill that cedar bucket you stole outen the smokehouse for him to git water in, you tell him to come on in here. Tell him I know he is hiding out 'way down the branch where he can come up wading the water clean up to the cornfield and the melon patch, so the hounds won't git his scent, but I'm going to send the hounds down there if he don't come on in right now." Then we all knowed we was for the work and Old Master was for the thinking, 'cause pretty soon Andy come on in. He'd been right where Old Master think he is.

About that time Mr. Sears come riding down the big road. He was a deacon in Old Master's church, and he see us all packed up to leave, and so he light at the big gate and walk up to where we is. He ask Old Master where we all lighting out for, and Old Master say for Louisiana. We Negroes don't know where that is. Then Old Deacon say what Old Master going to do with Andy, 'cause there stood Mr. Clements holding his bloodhounds and Old Master had his cat-o'-nine-tails in his hand.

Old Master say just watch him, and he tell Andy if he can make it to that big black-gum tree down at the gate before the hounds git him, he can stay right up in that tree and watch us all drive off. Then he tell Andy to git!

Poor Andy just git hold of the bottom limbs when the bloodhounds grab him and pull him down onto the ground. Time Old Master and Mr. Clements git down there, the hounds done tore off all Andy's clothes and bit him all over bad. He was rolling on the ground and holding his shirt up round his throat when Mr. Clements git there and pull the hounds off of him.

Then Old Master light in on him with that cat-o'-nine-tails, and I don't know how many lashes he give him, but he just bloody all over and done fainted pretty soon. Old Deacon Sears stand it as long as he can and then he step up and grab Old Master's arm and say, "Time to stop, Brother! I'm speaking in the name of Jesus!" Old Master quit then, but he still powerful mad. I don't think he believe Andy going to make that tree when he tell him that.

Then he turn on Andy's brother and give him a good beating too, and we all drive off and leave Andy setting on the ground under a tree and Old Deacon standing by him. I don't know what ever become of Andy, but I reckon maybe he went and live with Old Deacon Sears until he was free.

When I think and remember it, it all seems kind of strange, but it seem like Old Master and Old Deacon both think the same way. They kind of understand that Old Master had a right to beat his Negro all he wanted to for running off, and he had a right to set the hounds on him if he did. But he shouldn't of beat him so hard after he told him he was going to let him off if he made the tree, and he ought to keep his word even if Andy was his own slave. That's the way both them white men had been taught, and that was the way they both lived.

Old Master had about five wagons on that trip down into Louisiana, but they was all full of stuff and only the old slaves and children could ride in them. I was big enough to walk most of the time, but one time I walked in the sun so long that I got sick, and they put me in the wagon for most the rest of the way.

We would come to places where the people said the Yankees had been and gone, but we didn't run into any Yankees. They was most to the north of us, I reckon, because we went on down to the south part of Mississippi and ferried across the big river at Baton Rouge. Then we went on to Lafayette, Louisiana, before we settled down anywhere.

All us Negroes thought that was a mighty strange place. We would hear white folks talking, and we couldn't understand what they said, and lots of the Negroes talked the same way, too. It was all full of French people around Lafayette, but they had all their menfolks in the Confederate army just the same. I seen lots of men in butternut clothes coming and going hither and yon, but they wasn't in bunches. They was mostly coming home to see their folks.

Everybody was scared all the time, and two–three times when Old Master hired his Negroes out to work, the man that hired them quit his place and went on west before they got the crop in. But Old Master got a place, and we put in a cotton crop, and I think he got some money by selling his place in Mississippi. Anyway, pretty soon after the cotton was all in, he moves again and goes to a place on Simonette Lake for the winter. It ain't a bit cold in that place, and we didn't have no fire 'cepting to cook, and sometimes a little charcoal fire in some crock pots that the people left on the place when they went on out to Texas.

The next spring Old Master loaded up again, and we struck out for Texas when the Yankees got too close again. But Master Bill didn't go to Texas, because the Confederates done come that winter and made him go to the army. I think they took him to New Orleans, and Old Master was hopping mad, but he couldn't do anything or they would make him go too, even if he was a preacher.

I think he left out of there partly because he didn't like the people at that place. They wasn't no Baptists around anywhere; they was all Catholics, and Old Master didn't like them.

About that time it look like everybody in the world was going to Texas. When we would be going down the road, we would have to walk along the side all the time to let the wagons go past, all loaded with folks going to Texas.

Pretty soon Old Master say, "Git the wagons loaded again," and this time we start out with some other people, going north. We go north a while and then turn west, and cross the Sabine River and go to Nachedoches, Texas. Me and my brother Joe and my sister Adeline walked nearly all the way, but my little sister Harriet and my mammy rid in a wagon. Mammy was mighty poorly, and just when we got to the Sabine bottoms she had another baby. Old Master didn't like it 'cause it was a girl, but he named her Texana on account of where she was born and told us children to wait on Mammy good and maybe we would git a little brother next time.

But we didn't. Old Master went with a whole bunch of wagons on out to the prairie country in Coryell County and set up a farm where we just had to break the sod and didn't have to clear off much. And the next baby Mammy had the next year was a girl. We named her Betty because Mistress just have a baby a little while before and its name was Betty.

Old Master's place was right at the corner where Coryell and McLennan and Bosque counties come together, and we raised mostly cotton and just a little corn for feed. He seem like he changed a lot since we left Mississippi, and seem like he paid more attention to us and looked after us better. But most the people that already live there when we git there was mighty hard on their Negroes. They was mostly hard drinkers and hard talkers, and they work and fight just as hard as they talk, too!

One day Old Master come out from town and tell us that we all been set free, and we can go or stay just as we wish. All of my family stay on the place, and he pay us half as shares on all we make. Pretty soon the white folks begin to cut down on the shares, and the renters git only a third and some less, and the Negroes begin to drift out to other places, but Old Master stick to the halves a year or so after that. Then he come down to a third too.

It seem like the white people can't git over us being free, and they do everything to hold us down all the time. We don't git no schools for a long time, and I never see the inside of a school. I just grow up on hard work. And we can't go round where they have the voting, unless we want to catch a whipping some night, and we have to just keep on bowing and scraping when we are round white folks like we did when we was slaves. They had us down and they kept us down. But that was the way they been taught, and I don't blame them for it none, I reckon.

When I git about thirty years old, I marry Betty Sadler close to Waco, and we come up to the Creek Nation forty years ago. We come to Muskogee first, and then to Tulsa about thirty-seven years ago.

We had ten children, but only seven are alive. Three girls and a boy live here in Tulsa, and we got one boy in Muskogee and one at Frederick, Oklahoma.

I sells milk and makes my living, and I keeps so busy I don't think back on the old days much, but if anybody ask me why the Texas Negroes been kept down so much I can tell them. If they set like I did on the bank at that ferry across the Sabine, and see all that long line of covered wagons, miles and miles of them, crossing that river and going west with all they got left out of the war, it ain't hard to understand.

Them white folks done had everything they had tore up or had to run away from the places they lived, and they brung their Negroes out to Texas, and then right away they lost them, too. They always had them Negroes, and lots of them had mighty fine places back in the old states, and then they had to go out and live in sod houses and little old boxed shotguns and turn their Negroes loose. They didn't see no justice in it then, and most of them never did until they died. The folks that stayed at home and didn't straggle all over the country had their old places to live on and their old friends around them, but them Texans was different.

So I says, when they done us the way they did, they was just doing the way they was taught. I don't blame them, because anybody will do that.

White folks mighty decent to me now, and I always tried to teach my children to be respectful and act like they think the white folks they dealing with expects them to act. That the way to git along, because some folks been taught one way and some been taught another, and folks always thinks the way they been taught.

JOANNA DRAPER: MISSISSIPPI

Most folks can't remember many things happened to 'em when they only eight years old, but one of my biggest tribulations come about that time, and I never will forget it! That was when I was took away from my own mammy and pappy and sent off and bound out to another man, 'way off two–three hundred miles away from where I live. And that's the last time I ever see either one of them, or any my own kinfolks!

Where I was born was at Hazlehurst, Mississippi. Just a little piece east of Hazlehurst, close to the Pearl River, and that place was a kind of new plantation what my master, Dr. Alexander, bought when he moved into Mississippi from up in Virginia awhile before the war.

They said my mammy brings me down to Mississippi, and I was born just right after she got there. My mammy's name was Margaret, and she was born under the Ramsons, back in Tennessee. She belonged to Dave Ramson, and his pappy had come to Tennessee to settle on war land, and he had knowed Dr. Alexander's people back in Virginia too. My pappy's name was Addison, and he always belonged to Dr. Alexander. Old Doctor bought my mammy 'cause my pappy liked her. Old Doctor lived in Tennessee a little while before he go on down to Mississippi.

Old Doctor's wife named Dinah, and she sure was a good woman, but I don't remember about Old Doctor much. He was away all the time, it seem like.

When I is about six year old, they take me into the big house to learn to be a house woman, and they show me how to cook and clean up and take care of babies. That big house wasn't very fine, but it was mighty big and cool, and made out of logs with a big hall, but it didn't have no long gallery like most the houses around there had.

They was lots of big trees in the yard, and most the ground was new ground round that place, 'cause Old Doctor just started to done farming on it when I was took away, but he had some more places not so far away, over toward the river, that was old ground and made big crops for him. I went to one of the places one time, but they wasn't nobody on 'em but niggers and a white overseer. I don't know how many niggers Old Doctor had, but Master John Deeson say he had about a hundred.

At Old Doctor's house I didn't have to work very hard. Just had to help the cooks and peel the potatoes and pick the guineas and chickens and do things like that. Sometime I had to watch the baby. He was a little boy, and they would bring him into the kitchen for me to watch. I had to git up way before daylight and make the fire in the kitchen fireplace and bring in some fresh water, and go get the milk what been down in the spring all night, and do things like that until breakfast ready. Old Master and Old Mistress come in the big hall to eat in the summer, and I stand behind them and shoo off the flies.

Old Doctor didn't have no spinning and weaving niggers 'cause he say they don't do enough work, and he buy all the cloth he use for everybody's clothes. He can do that 'cause he had lots of money. He was big rich, and he keep a whole lot of hard money in the house all the time, but none of the slaves know it but me. Sometimes I would have the baby in the mistress' room and she would git three or four big wood boxes full of hard money for us to play with. I would make fences out of the money all across the floor, to keep the baby satisfied, and when he go to sleep I would put the money back in the boxes. I never did know how much they is, but a whole lot.

Even after the war start Old Doctor have that money, and he would exchange money for people. Sometimes he would go out and be gone for a long time, and come back with a lot more money he got from somewhere.

Right at the first they made him a high officer in the war, and he done doctoring somewhere at a hospital most of the time. But he could go on both sides of the war, and sometime he would come in at night and bring Old Mistress pretty little things, and I heard him tell her he got them in the North.

One day I was fanning him, and I asked him is he been to the North, and he kick out at me and tell to shut up my black mouth, and it nearly scared me to death the way he look at me! Nearly every time he been gone and come in and tell Mistress he been in the North, he have a lot more hard money to put away in them boxes, too!

One evening 'long come a man and eat supper at the house and stay all night. He was a nice-mannered man, and I like to wait on him. The next morning I hear him ask Old Doctor what is my name, and Old Doctor start in to try to sell me to that man. The man say he can't buy me 'cause Old Doctor say he want a thousand dollars, and then Old Doctor say he will bind me out to him.

I run away from the house and went out to the cabin where my mammy and pappy was, but they tell me to go on back to the big house 'cause maybe I am just scared. But about that time Old Doctor and the man come, and Old Doctor make me go with the man. We go in his buggy a long ways off to the south, and after he stop two or three night at people's houses and put me out to stay with the niggers, he come to his own house. I ask him how far it is back home, and he say about a hundred miles or more, and laugh, and ask me if I know how far that is.

I wants to know if I can go back to my mammy sometime, and he say "Sure, of course you can, some of these times. You don't belong to me, Jo, I's just your boss and not your master."

He live in a big old rottendy house, but he ain't farming none of the land. Just as soon as he git home, he go off again, and sometimes he only come in at night for a little while.

His wife's name was Kate and his name was Mr. John. I was there about a week before I found out they name was Deeson. They had two children, a girl about my size, name Joanna like me, and a little baby boy, name Johnny. One day Mistress Kate tell me I the only nigger they got. I been thinking maybe they had some somewhere on a plantation, but she say they ain't got no plantation and they ain't been at that place very long either.

That little girl Joanna and me kind of take up together, and she was a mighty nice-mannered little girl, too. Her mammy raised her good. Her mammy was mighty sickly all the time, and that's the reason they bind me to do the work.

Mr. John was in some kind of business in the war too, but I never see him with no soldier clothes on but one time. One night he come in with them on, but the next morning he come to breakfast in just his plain clothes again. Then he go off again.

I sure had a hard row at that house. It was old and rackety, and I had to scrub off the staircase and the floors all the time, and git the breakfast for Mistress Kate and the two children. Then I could have my own breakfast in the kitchen. Mistress Kate always get the supper, though.

Some days she go off with the two children and leave me at the house all day by myself, and I think maybe I run off, but I didn't know where to go.

After I been at that place two years, Mr. John come home and stay. He done some kind of trading in Jackson, Mississippi, and he would be gone three or four days at a time, but I never did know what kind of trading it was.

About the time he come home to stay I seen the first Ku Klux I ever seen one night. I was going down the road in the moonlight, and I heard a hog grunting out in the bushes at the side of the road. I just walk right on and in a little ways I hear another hog in some more bushes. This time I stop and listen, and they's another hog grunts across the road, and about that time two mens dressed up in long white shirts steps out into the road in front of me! I was so scared the goose bumps jump up all over me 'cause I didn't know what they is! They didn't say a word to me, but just walked on past me and went on back the way I had come. Then I see two more mens step out of the woods, and I run from that as fast as I can go!

I ast Miss Kate what they is, and she say they Ku Klux, and I better not go walking off down the road any more. I seen them two, three times after that, though, but they was riding horses them times.

I stayed at Mr. John's place two more years, and he got so grumpy and his wife got so mean I make up my mind to run off. I bundle up my clothes in a little bundle and hide them, and then I wait until Miss Kate take the children and go off somewhere, and I light out on foot. I had me a piece of that hard money what Master Doctor Alexander had give me one time at Christmas. I had kept it all that time, and nobody knowed I had it, not even Joanna. Old Doctor told me it was fifty dollars, and I thought I could live on it for a while.

I never had been away from that place, not even to another plantation in all the four years I was with the Deesons, and I didn't know which-a-way to go, so I just started west.

I been walking about all evening, it seem like, and I come to a little town with just a few houses. I see a nigger man and ask him where I can git something to eat, and I say I got fifty dollars.

"What you doing with fifty dollars, child? Where you belong at, anyhow?" he ask me, and I tell him I belong to Master John Deeson, but I is running away. I explain that I just bound out to Mr. John, but Dr. Alexander my real master, and then that man tell me the first time I knowed it that I ain't a slave no more!

That man Deeson never did tell me, and his wife never did!

Well, that man asked me about the fifty dollars, and then I found out that it was just fifty cents!

I can't begin to tell about all the hard times I had working for something to eat and roaming around after that. I don't know why I never did try to git back up around Hazlehurst and hunt up my pappy and mammy, but I reckon I was just ignorant and didn't know how to go about it. Anyways, I never did see them no more.

In about three years or a little over, I met Bryce Draper on a farm in Mississippi and we was married. His mammy had had a harder time than I had. She had five children by a man that belong to her master, Mr. Bryce, and already named one of the boys—that my husband—Bryce after him, and then he take her in and sell her off away from all her children!

One was just a little baby, and the master give it laudanum, but it didn't die, and he sold her (my husband's mammy) off and lied and said she was a young girl and didn't have no husband, 'cause the man what bought her said he didn't want to buy no woman and take her away from a family. That new master's name was Draper.

The last year of the war Mr. Draper die, and his wife already dead, and he give all his farm to his two slaves and set them free. One of them slaves was my husband's mammy.

Then right away the whites come and robbed the place of everything they could haul off, and run his mammy and the other niggers off! Then she went and found her boy, that was my husband, and he live with her until she died, just before we is married.

We lived in Mississippi a long time, and then we hear about how they better to the Negroes up in the North, and we go up to Kansas, but they ain't no better there, and we come down to Indian Territory in the Creek Nation in 1898, just as they getting in that Spanish War.

We leased a little farm from the Creek Nation for $15 an acre, but when they give out the allotments we had to give it up. Then we rent 100 acres from some Indians close to Wagoner, and we farm it all with my family. We had enough to do it, too!

For children we had John and Joe, and Henry, and Jim and Robert and Will that was big enough to work, and then the girls big enough was Mary, Nellie, Izora, Dora, and the baby. Dora married Max Colbert. His people belonged to the Colberts that had Colbert's Crossing on the Red River 'way before the war, and he was a freedman and got allotment.

I lives with Dora now, and we is all happy, and I don't like to talk about the days of the slavery times, 'cause they never did mean nothing to me but misery, from the time I was eight years old.

I never will forgive that white man for not telling me I was free, and not helping me to git back to my mammy and pappy! Lots of white people done that.

KATIE ROWE: ARKANSAS

I can set on the gallery, where the sunlight shine bright, and sew a powerful fine seam when my grandchildren wants a special pretty dress for the school doings, but I ain't worth much for nothing else, I reckon.

These same old eyes seen powerful lot of tribulations in my time, and when I shuts 'em now I can see lots of little children just like my grandchildren, toting hoes bigger than they is, and they poor little black hands and legs bleeding where they scratched by the brambledy weeds, and where they got whippings 'cause they didn't git out all the work the overseer set out for 'em.

I was one of them little slave gals my own self, and I never seen nothing but work and tribulations till I was a grownup woman, just about.

The niggers had hard traveling on the plantation where I was born and raised, 'cause Old Master live in town and just had the overseer on the place, but iffen he had lived out there hisself I 'speck it been as bad, 'cause he was a hard driver his own self.

He git biling mad when the Yankees have that big battle at Pea Ridge and scatter the 'Federates all down through our country all bleeding and tied up and hungry, and he just mount on his hoss and ride out to the plantation where we all hoeing corn.

He ride up and tell old man Saunders—that the overseer—to bunch us all up round the lead row man—that my own uncle Sandy—and then he tell us the law!

"You niggers been seeing the 'Federate soldiers coming by here looking pretty raggedy and hurt and wore out," he say, "but that no sign they licked!

"Them Yankees ain't gwine git this far, but iffen they do, you all ain't gwine git free by 'em, 'cause I gwine free you before that. When they git here they gwine find you already free, 'cause I gwine line you up on the bank of Bois d'Arc Creek and free you with my shotgun! Anybody miss just one lick with the hoe, or one step in the line, or one clap of that bell, or one toot of the horn, and he gwine be free and talking to the devil long before he ever see a pair of blue britches!"

That the way he talk to us, and that the way he act with us all the time.

We live in the log quarters on the plantation, not far from Washington, Arkansas, close to Bois d'Arc Creek, in the edge of the Little River bottom.

Old Master's name was Dr. Isaac Jones, and he live in the town, where he keep four, five house niggers, but he have about two hundred on the plantation, big and little, and Old Man Saunders oversee 'em at the time of the war. Old Mistress' name was Betty, and she had a daughter name Betty about grown, and then they was three boys, Tom, Bryan, and Bob, but they was too young to go to the war. I never did see 'em but once or twice till after the war.

Old Master didn't got to the war, 'cause he was a doctor and the onliest one left in Washington, and pretty soon he was dead anyhow.

Next fall after he ride out and tell us that he gwine shoot us before he let us free, he come out to see how his steam gin doing. The gin box was a little old thing 'bout as big as a bedstead, with a long belt running through the side of the ginhouse out to the engine and boiler in the yard. The boiler burn cordwood, and it have a little crack in it where the nigger ginner been trying to fix it.

Old Master come out, hopping mad 'cause the gin shut down, and ast the ginner, Old Brown, what the matter. Old Brown say the boiler weak and it liable to bust, but Old Master jump down offen his hoss and go round to the boiler and say, "Cuss fire to your black heart! That boiler all right! Throw on some cordwood, cuss fire to your heart!"

Old Brown start to the woodpile, grumbling to hisself, and Old Master stoop down to look at the boiler again, and it blow right up and him standing right there!

Old Master was blowed all to pieces, and they just find little bitsy chunks of his clothes and parts of him to bury.

The woodpile blow down, and Old Brown land 'way off in the woods, but he wasn't killed.

Two wagons of cotton blowed over, and the mules run away, and all the niggers was scared nearly to death 'cause we knowed the overseer gwine be a lot worse, now that Old Master gone.

Before the war when Master was a young man, the slaves didn't have it so hard, my mammy tell me. Her name was Fanny and her old mammy's name was Nanny. Grandma Nanny was alive during the war yet.

How she come in the Jones family was this way: Old Mistress was just a little girl, and her older brother bought Nanny and give her to her. I think his name was Littlejohn; anyways we called him Master Littlejohn. He drawed up a paper what say that Nanny always belong to Miss Betty and all the children Nanny ever have belong to her, too, and nobody can't take 'em for a debt and things like that. When Miss Betty marry, Old Master he can't sell Nanny or any of her children neither.

That paper hold good too, and Grandmammy tell me about one time it hold good and keep my own mammy on the place.

Grandmammy say Mammy was just a little gal and was playing out in the road with three, four other little children when a white man and Old Master rid up. The white man had a paper about some kind of a debt, and Old Master say take his pick of the nigger children and give him back the paper.

Just as Grandmammy go to the cabin door and hear him say that, the man git off his hoss and pick up my mammy and put her up in front of him and start to ride off down the road.

Pretty soon Mr. Littlejohn come riding up and say something to Old Master, and see Grandmammy standing in the yard screaming and crying. He just job the spurs in his hoss and go kiting off down the road after that white man.

Mammy say he catch up with him just as he git to Bois d'Arc Creek and start to wade the hoss across. Mr. Littlejohn holler to him to come back with that little nigger 'cause the paper don't cover that child, 'cause she Old Mistress' own child, and when the man just ride on, Mr. Littlejohn throw his big old long hoss-pistol down on him and make him come back.

The man hopping mad, but he have to give over my mammy and take one the other children on the debt paper.

Old Master always kind of touchy 'bout Old Mistress having niggers he can't trade or sell, and one day he have his whole family and some more white folks out at the plantation. He showing 'em all the quarters when we all come in from the field in the evening, and he call all the niggers up to let the folks see 'em.

He make Grandmammy and Mammy and me stand to one side and then he say to the other niggers, "These niggers belong to my wife but you belong to me, and I'm the only one you is to call Master. This is Tom, and Bryan, and Bob, and Miss Betty, and you is to call 'em that, and don't you ever call one of 'em

Young Master or Young Mistress, cuss fire to your black hearts!" All the other white folks look kind of funny, and Old Mistress look 'shamed of Old Master.

My own pappy was in that bunch, too. His name was Frank, and after the war he took the name of Frank Henderson, 'cause he was born under that name, but I always went by Jones, the name I was born under.

'Long about the middle of the war, after Old Master was killed, the soldiers begin coming round the place and camping. They was Southern soldiers, and they say they have to take the mules and most the corn to git along on. Just go in the barns and cribs and take anything they want, and us niggers didn't have no sweet 'taters nor Irish 'taters to eat on when they gone neither.

One bunch come and stay in the woods across the road from the overseer's house, and they was all on hosses. They lead the hosses down to Bois d'Arc Creek every morning at daylight and late every evening to git water. When we going to the field and when we coming in, we always see them leading big bunches of hosses.

They bugle go just 'bout the time our old horn blow in the morning, and when we come in they eating supper, and we smell it and sure git hungry!

Before Old Master died he sold off a whole lot of hosses and cattle, and some niggers too. He had the sales on the plantation, and white men from around there come to bid, and some traders come. He had a big stump where he made the niggers stand while they was being sold, and the men and boys had to strip off to the waist to show they muscle and iffen they had any scars or hurt places, but the women and gals didn't have to strip to the waist.

The white men come up and look in the slave's mouth just like he was a mule or a hoss.

After Old Master go, the overseer hold one sale, but mostly he just trade with the traders what come by. He make the niggers git on the stump, though. The traders all had big bunches of slaves, and they have 'em all strung out in a line going down the road. Some had wagons and the children could ride, but not many. They didn't chain or tie 'em 'cause they didn't have no place they could run to anyway.

I seen children sold off and the mammy not sold, and sometimes the mammy sold and a little baby kept on the place and give to another woman to raise. Them white folks didn't care nothing 'bout how the slaves grieved when they tore up a family.

Old Man Saunders was the hardest overseer of anybody. He would git mad and give a whipping sometime, and the slave wouldn't even know what it was about.

My Uncle Sandy was the lead row nigger, and he was a good nigger and never would touch a drap of liquor. One night some the niggers git hold of some liquor somehow, and they leave the jug half full on the step of Sandy's cabin. Next morning Old Man Saunders come out in the field so mad he was pale.

He just go to the lead row and tell Sandy to go with him and start toward the woods along Bois d'Arc Creek, with Sandy following behind. The overseer always carry a big heavy stick, but we didn't know he was so mad, and they just went off in the woods.

Pretty soon we hear Sandy hollering, and we know old overseer pouring it on, then the overseer come back by hisself and go on up to the house.

Come late evening he come and see what we done in the day's work, and go back to the quarters with us all. When he git to Mammy's cabin, where Grandmammy live too, he say to Grandmammy, "I sent Sandy down in the woods to hunt a hoss, he gwine come in hungry pretty soon. You better make him a extra hoecake," and he kind of laugh and go on to his house.

Just soon as he gone, we all tell Grandmammy we think he got a whipping, and sure 'nough he didn't come in.

The next day some white boys finds Uncle Sandy where that overseer done killed him and throwed him in a little pond, and they never done nothing to Old Man Saunders at all!

When he go to whip a nigger he make him strip to the waist, and he take a cat-o'-nine-tails and bring the blisters, and then bust the blisters with a wide strap of leather fastened to a stick handle. I seen the blood running outen many a back, all the way from the neck to the waist!

Many the time a nigger git blistered and cut up so that we have to git a sheet and grease it with lard and wrap 'em up in it, and they have to wear a greasy cloth wrapped around they body under the shirt for three–four days after they git a big whipping!

Later on in the war the Yankees come in all around us and camp, and the overseer git sweet as honey in the comb! Nobody git a whipping all the time the Yankees there!

They come and took all the meat and corn and 'taters they want too, and they tell us, "Why don't you poor darkies take all the meat and molasses you want? You made it and it's yours much as anybody's!" But we know they soon be gone, and then we git a whipping iffen we do. Some niggers run off and went with the Yankees, but they had to work just as hard for them, and they didn't eat so good and often with the soldiers.

I never forget the day we was set free!

That morning we all go to the cotton field early, and then a house nigger come out from Old Mistress on a hoss and say she want the overseer to come into town, and he leave and go in. After while the old horn blow up at the overseer's house, and we all stop and listen, 'cause it the wrong time of day for the horn.

We start chopping again, and there go the horn again.

The lead row nigger holler, "Hold up!" And we all stop again. "We better go on in. That our horn," he holler at the head nigger, and the head nigger think so too, but he say he afraid we catch the devil from the overseer iffen we quit without him there, and the lead row man say maybe he back from town and blowing the horn hisself, so we line up and go in.

When we git to the quarters, we see all the old ones and the children up in the overseer's yard, so we go on up there. The overseer setting on the end of the gallery with a paper in his hand, and when we all come up he say come and stand close to the gallery. Then he call off everybody's name and see we all there.

Setting on the gallery in a hide-bottom chair was a man we never see before. He had on a big broad black hat like the Yankees wore, but it didn't have no yellow string on it like most the Yankees had, and he was in store clothes that wasn't homespun or jeans, and they was black. His hair was plumb gray and so was his beard, and it come 'way down here on his chest, but he didn't look like he was very old, 'cause his face was kind of fleshy and healthy-looking. I think we all been sold off in a bunch, and I notice some kind of smiling, and I think they sure glad of it.

The man say, "You darkies know what day this is?" He talk kind, and smile.

We all don't know, of course, and we just stand there and grin. Pretty soon he ask again and the head man say, "No, we don't know."

"Well, this the fourth day of June, and this is 1865, and I want you all to 'member the date, 'cause you always gwine 'member the day. Today you is free, just like I is, and Mr. Saunders and your mistress and all us white people," the man say.

"I come to tell you," he say, "and I wants to be sure you all understand, 'cause you don't have to git up and go by the horn no more. You is your own bosses now, and you don't have to have no passes to go and come."

We never did have no passes, nohow, but we knowed lots of other niggers on other plantations got 'em.

"I wants to bless you and hope you always is happy and tell you you got all the right and lief that any white people got," the man say, and then he git on his hoss and ride off.

We all just watch him go on down the road, and then we go up to Mr. Saunders and ask him what he want us to do. He just grunt and say do like we damn please, he reckon, but git off that place to do it, lessen any of us wants to stay and make the crop for half of what we make.

None of us know where to go, so we all stay, and he split up the fields and show us which part we got to work in, and we go on like we was, and make the crop and git it in, but they ain't no more horn after that day. Some the niggers lazy and don't git in the field early, and they git it took away from 'em, but they plead around and git it back and work better the rest of that year.

But we all gits fooled on that first go-out! When the crop all in, we don't git half! Old Mistress sick in town, and the overseer was still on the place, and he charge us half the crop for the quarters and the mules and tools and grub!

Then he leave, and we gits another white man, and he sets up a book, and give us half the next year, and take out for what we use up, but we all got something left over after that first go-out.

Old Mistress never git well after she lose all her niggers, and one day the white boss tell us she just drap over dead setting in her chair, and we know her heart just broke.

Next year the children sell off most the place and we scatter off, and I and

Mammy go into Little Rock and do work in the town. Grandmammy done dead.

I git married to John White in Little Rock, but he died, and we didn't have no children. Then in four, five years I marry Billy Rowe. He was a Cherokee citizen, and he had belonged to a Cherokee name Dave Rowe, and lived east of Tahlequah before the war. We married in Little Rock, but he had land in the Cherokee Nation, and we come to east of Tahlequah and lived till he died, and then I come to Tulsa to live with my youngest daughter.

Billy Rowe and me had three children—Ellie, John, and Lula. Lula married a Thomas, and it's her I lives with.

Lots of old people like me say that they was happy in slavery and that they had the worst tribulations after freedom, but I knows they didn't have no white master and overseer like we all had on our place. They both dead now, I reckon, and they no use talking 'bout the dead, but I know I been gone long ago iffen that white man Saunders didn't lose his hold on me.

It was the fourth day of June in 1865 I begins to live, and I gwine take the picture of that old man in the big black hat and long whiskers, setting on the gallery and talking kind to us, clean into my grave with me.

No, bless God, I ain't never seen no more black boys bleeding all up and down the back under a cat-o'-nine-tails, and I never go by no cabin and hear no poor nigger groaning, all wrapped up in a lardy sheet no more!

I hear my children read about General Lee, and I know he was a good man. I didn't know nothing about him then, but I know now he wasn't fighting for that kind of white folks.

Maybe they that kind still yet, but they don't show it up no more, and I got lots of white friends too. All my children and grandchildren been to school, and they git along good, and I know we living in a better world, where they ain't nobody cussing fire to my black heart!

I sure thank the good Lord I got to see it.

CHARLEY WILLIAMS: LOUISIANA

Iffen I could see better outen my old eyes, and I had me something to work with and the feebleness in my back and head would let me 'lone, I would have me plenty to eat in the kitchen all the time, and plenty tobacco in my pipe, too, bless God!

And they wouldn't be no rain trickling through the holes in the roof, and no planks all fell outen the floor on the gallery neither, 'cause this one old nigger knows everything about making all he need to git along! Old Master done showed him how to git along in this world, just as long as he live on a plantation, but living in the town is a different way of living, and all you got to have is a silver dime to lay down for everything you want, and I don't git the dime very often.

But I ain't give up! Nothing like that! On the days when I don't feel so feeble and trembly I just keep patching round the place. I got to keep patching so as to keep it where it will hold the winter out, in case I git to see another winter.

Iffen I don't, it don't grieve me none, 'cause I wants to see Old Master again anyways. I reckon maybe I'll just go up and ask him what he want me to do, and he'll tell me, and iffen I don't know how he'll show me how, and I'll try to do it to please him. And when I git it done, I wants to hear him grumble like he used to and say, "Charley, you ain't got no sense but you is a good boy. This here ain't very good but it'll do, I reckon. Git yourself a little piece of that brown sugar, but don't let no niggers see you eating it—if you do I'll whup your black behind!"

That ain't the way it going be in Heaven, I reckon, but I can't set here on this old rottendy gallery and think of no way I better like to have it!

I was a great big hulking buck of a boy when the war come along and bust up everything, and I can 'member back when everybody was living peaceful and happy, and nobody never had no notion about no war.

I was borned on the 'leventh of January, in 1843, and was old enough to vote when I got my freedom, but I didn't take no stock in all that politics and goings on at that time, and I didn't vote till a long time after Old Master passed away, but I was big enough before the war to remember everything pretty plain.

Old Master's name was John Williams, and Old Mistress' name was Miss Betty, and she was a Campbell before she married. Young Missy was named Betty after her mommy, and Young Master was named Frank, but I don't know who after. Our overseer was Mr. Simmons, and he was mighty smart and had a lot of patience, but he wouldn't take no talk nor foolishness. He didn't whup nobody very often, but he only had to whup 'em just one time! He never did whup a nigger at the time the nigger done something, but he would wait till evening and have Old Master come and watch him do it. He never whupped very hard 'cept when he had told a nigger about something and promised a whupping next time and the nigger done it again. Then that nigger got what he had been hearing 'bout!

The plantation was about as big as any. I think it had about three hundred acres, and it was about two miles northwest of Monroe, Louisiana. Then he had another one not so big, two, three miles south of the big one, kind of down in the woodsy part along the White River bottoms. He had another overseer on that place and a big passel of niggers, but I never did go down to that one. That was where he raised most of his corn and shoats and lots of sorghum cane.

Our plantation was up on higher ground, and it was more open country, but still they was lots of woods all around, and lots of the plantations had been whacked right out of the new ground and was full of stumps. Master's place was more open, though, and all the fields was good plowing.

The big road runned right along past our plantation, and it come from

Shreveport and run into Monroe. There wasn't any town at Monroe in them days, just a little crossroads place with a general store and a big hidehouse. I think there was about two big hidehouses, and you could smell that place a mile before you got into it. Old Master had a part in the store, I think.

The hidehouses was just long sheds, all open along the sides and covered over with cypress clapboards.

Down below the hidehouses and the store was just a little settlement of one or two houses, but they was a school for white boys. Somebody said there was a place where they had been an old fort, but I never did see it.

Everything boughten we got come from Shreveport and was brung in by the stage and the freighters, and that was only a little coffee or gunpowder or some needles for the sewing or some strap iron for the blacksmith or something like that. We made and raised everything else we needed right on the place.

I never did even see any quinine till after I was free. My mammy knowed just what root to go out and pull up to knock the chills right outen me. And the bellyache and the running off the same way, too.

Our plantation was a lot different from some I seen other places, like 'way east of there, around Vicksburg. Some of them was fixed up fancier, but they didn't have no more comforts than we had.

Old Master come out into that country when he was a young man, and they didn't have even so much then as they had when I was a boy. I think he come from Alabama or Tennessee, and 'way back his people had come from Virginia, or maybe North Carolina, 'cause he knowed all about tobacco on the place. Cotton and tobacco was the long crops on his big place, and, of course, lots of horses and cattle and mules.

The big house was made outen square hewed logs, and chinked with little rocks and daubed with white clay, and covered with cypress clapboards. I remember one time we put on a new roof, and the niggers hauled up the cypress logs and sawed them and frowed out the clapboards by hand.

The house had two setting-rooms on one side and a big kitchen-room on the other, with a wide passage in between, and then about was the sleeping-rooms. They wasn't no stairways 'cepting on the outside. Steps run up to the sleeping-rooms on one side from the passageway and on the other side from clean outside the house. Just one big chimney was all he had, and it was on the kitchen end, and we done all the cooking in a fireplace that was pretty nigh as wide as the whole room.

In the sleeping-rooms they wasn't no fires 'cepting in braziers made out of clay, and we toted up charcoal to burn in 'em when it was cold mornings in the winter. They kept warm with the bedclothes and the knitten clothes they had.

Master never did make a big gallery on the house, but our white folks would set out in the yard under the big trees in the shade. They was long benches made outen hewed logs and all padded with gray moss and corn-shuck padding, and they set pretty soft. All the furniture in the house was homemade, too. The beds had square posts as big around as my shank, and the frame was mortised into 'em, and holes bored in the frame and homemade rope laced in to make it springy. Then a great big mattress full of goose feathers and two–three comforts as thick as my foot with carded wool inside! They didn't need no fireplaces!

The quarters was a little piece from the big house, and they run along both sides of the road that go to the fields. All one-room log cabins, but they was good and warm, and every one had a little open shed at the side where we sleep in the summer to keep cool.

They was two or three wells at the quarters for water, and some good springs in the branch at the back of the fields. You could catch a fish now and then in that branch, but Young Master used to do his fishing in White River, and take a nigger or two along to do the work at his camp.

It wasn't very fancy at the big house, but it was mighty pretty just the same, with the gray moss hanging from the big trees, and the cool green grass all over the yard, and I can shut my old eyes and see it just like it was before the war come along and bust it up.

I can see Old Master setting out under a big tree, smoking one of his long cheroots his tobacco nigger made by hand, and fanning hisself with his big wide hat another nigger platted outen young inside corn shucks for him, and I can hear him holler at a big bunch of white geeses what's gitting in his flower beds and see 'em string off behind the old gander toward the big road.

When the day begin to crack, the whole plantation break out with all kinds of noises, and you could tell what going on by the kind of noise you hear.

Come the daybreak you hear the guinea fowls start potracking down at the edge of the woods lot, and then the roosters all start up round the barn, and the ducks finally wake up and jine in. You can smell the sowbelly frying down at the cabins in the Row, to go with the hoecake and the buttermilk.

Then pretty soon the wind rise a little, and you can hear a old bell donging way on some plantation a mile or two off, and then more bells at other places and maybe a horn, and pretty soon yonder go Old Master's old ram horn with a long toot and then some short toots, and here come the overseer down the row of cabins, hollering right and left, and picking the ham outen his teeth with a long shiny goose-quill pick.

Bells and horns! Bells for this and horns for that! All we knowed was go and come by the bells and horns!

Old ram horn blow to send us all to the field. We all line up, about seventy-five field niggers, and go by the tool shed and git our hoes, or maybe go hitch up the mules to the plows and lay the plows out on the side so the overseer can see iffen the points is sharp. Any plow gits broke or the point gits bungled up on the rocks it goes to the blacksmith nigger, then we all git on down in the field.

Then the anvil start dangling in the blacksmith shop: "Tank! Deling-ding! Tank! Deling-ding!" and that old bull tongue gitting straightened out!

Course you can't hear the shoemaker awling and pegging, and the card spinners, and the old mammy sewing by hand, but maybe you can hear the old loom going "frump, frump," and you know it all right iffen your clothes do be wearing out, 'cause you gwine git new britches pretty soon!

We had about a hundred niggers on that place, young and old, and about twenty on the little place down below. We could make about every kind of thing but coffee and gunpowder that our white folks and us needed.

When we needs a hat we gits inside corn shucks and weave one out, and makes horse collars the same way. Just tie two little soft shucks together and begin plaiting.

All the cloth 'cepting the mistress' Sunday dresses come from the sheep to the carders and the spinners and the weaver, then we dye it with butternut and hickory bark and indigo and other things and set it with copperas. Leather tanned on the place made the shoes, and I never see a store-boughten wagon wheel 'cepting among the stages and the freighters along the big road.

We made pretty, long back-combs outen cow horn, and knitting needles outen second hickory. Split a young hickory and put in a big wedge to prize it open, then cut it down and let it season, and you got good bent grain for wagon hames and chair rockers and such.

It was just like that until I was grown, and then one day come a neighbor man and say we in the war.

Little while young Master Frank ride over to Vicksburg and jine the Secesh army, but Old Master just go on like nothing happen, and we all don't hear nothing more until 'long come some Secesh soldiers and take most Old Master's hosses and all his wagons.

I been working on the tobacco, and when I come back to the barns everything was gone. I would go into the woods and git good hickory and burn it till it was all coals and put it out with water to make hickory charcoal for curing the tobacco. I had me some charcoal in the fire trenches under the curing-houses, all full of new tobacco, and overseer come and say bundle all the tobacco up and he going to take it to Shreveport and sell it before the soldiers take it too.

After the hosses all gone and most the cattle and the cotton and the tobacco gone too, here come the Yankees and spread out all over the whole country. They had a big camp down below our plantation.

One evening a big bunch of Yankee officers come up to the big house, and Old Master set out the brandy in the yard, and they act pretty nice. Next day the whole bunch leave on out of that part.

When the hosses and stuff all go Old Master sold all the slaves but about four, but he kept my pappy and mammy and my brother Jimmie and my sister Betty. She was named after Old Mistress. Pappy's name was Charley and Mammy's was Sally. The niggers he kept didn't have much work without any hosses and wagons, but the blacksmith started in fixing up more wagons, and he kept them hid in the woods till they was all fixed.

Then along come some more Yankees, and they tore everything we had up, and Old Master was afeard to shoot at them on account his womenfolks, so he tried to sneak the family out, but they cotched him and brung him back to the plantation.

We niggers didn't know that he was gone until we seen the Yankees bringing them back. The Yankees had done took charge of everything and was camping in the big yard, and us was all down at the quarters scared to death, but they was just letting us alone.

It was night when the white folks tried to go away, and still night when the Yankees brung them back, and a house nigger come down to the quarters with three–four mens in blue clothes and told us to come up to the big house.

The Yankees didn't seem to be mad with Old Master, but just laughed and talked with him, but he didn't take the jokes any too good.

Then they asked him could he dance and he said "No," and they told him to dance or make us dance. There he stood inside a big ring of them mens in blue clothes, with they brass buttons shining in the light from the fire they had in front of the tents, and he just stood and said nothing, and it look like he wasn't wanting to tell us to dance.

So some of us young bucks just step up and say we was good dancers, and we start shuffling while the rest of the niggers pat.

Some nigger women go back to the quarters and git the gourd fiddles and the clapping bones made outen beef ribs, and bring them back so we could have some music. We git all warmed up and dance like we never did dance before. I 'speck we invent some new steps that night!

We act like we dancing for the Yankees, but we trying to please Master and Old Mistress more than anything, and pretty soon he begin to smile a little, and we all feel a lot better.

Next day the Yankees move on away from our place, and Old Master start gitting ready to move out. We git the wagons we hid, and the whole passel of us leaves out for Shreveport. Just left the old place standing like it was.

In Shreveport Old Master git his cotton and tobacco money what he been afraid to have sent back to the plantation when he sell his stuff, and we strike out north through Arkansas.

That was the awfullest trip any man ever make! We had to hide from everybody until we find out if they Yankees or Secesh, and we go along little old back roads and up one mountain and down another, through the woods all the way.

After a long time we git to the Missouri line, and kind of cut off through the corner of that state into Kansas. I don't know how we ever git across some of them rivers but we did. They nearly always would be some soldiers around the fords, and they would help us find the best crossing. Sometimes we had to unload the wagons and dry out the stuff what all got wet, and camp a day or two to fix up again.

Pretty soon we git to Fort Scott, and that was where the roads forked ever' whichaways. One went on north and one east and one went down into the Indian country. It was full of soldiers coming and going back and forth to Arkansas and Fort Gibson.

We took the road on west through Kansas, and made for Colorado Springs.

Fort Scott was all run down, and the old places where they used to have the soldiers was all fell in in most places. Just old rackety walls and leaky roofs, and a big pole fence made outen poles sot in the ground all tied together, but it was falling down too.

They was lots of wagons all around what belong to the army, hauling stuff for the soldiers, and some folks told Old Master he couldn't make us niggers go with him, but we said we wanted to anyways, so we just went on west across Kansas.

When we got away on west we come to a fork, and the best road went kinda south into Mexico, and we come to a little place called Clayton, Mexico, where we camped a while and then went north.

That place is in New Mexico now, but Old Master just called it Mexico. Somebody showed me where it is on the map, and it look like it a long ways offen the road to Colorado Springs, but I guess the road just wind off down that ways at the time we went over it. It was just two or three houses made outen mud at that time, and a store where the soldiers and the Indians come and done trading.

About that time Old Master sell off some of the stuff he been taking along, 'cause the wagons loaded too heavy for the mountains and he figure he better have the money than some of the stuff, I reckon.

On the way north it was a funny country. We just climb all day long gitting up one side of one bunch of mountains, and all the nigger men have to push on the wheels while the mules pull and then scotch the wheels while the mules rest. Everybody but the white folks has to walk most the time.

Down in the valleys it was warm like in Louisiana, but it seem like the sun ain't so hot on the head, but it look like every time night come it catch us up on top of one of them mountains, and it almost as cold as in the wintertime!

All the niggers had shoes and plenty warm clothes and we wrop up at night in everything we can git.

We git to Fort Scott again, and then the Yankee officers come and ask all us niggers iffen we want to leave Old Master and stay there and work, 'cause we all free now. Old Master say we can do what we please about it.

A few of the niggers stay there in Fort Scott, but most of us say we gwine stay with Old Master, and we don't care iffen we is free or not.

When we git back to Monroe to the old place, us niggers git a big surprise. We didn't hear about it, but some Old Master's kinfolks back in Virginia done come out there and fix the place up and kept it for him while we in Colorado, and it look 'bout as good as when we left it.

He cut it up in chunks and put us niggers out on it on the halves, but he had to sell part of it to git the money to git us mules and tools and food to run on. Then after while he had to sell some more, and he seem like he git old mighty fast.

Young Master been in the big battles in Virginia, and he git hit, and then he git sick, and when he come home he just like a old man he was so feeble.

About that time they was a lot of people coming into that country from the North, and they kept telling the niggers that the thing for them to do was to be free, and come and go where they please.

They try to git the darkies to go and vote, but none of us folks took much stock by what they say. Old Master tell us plenty time to mix in the politics when the young-uns git educated and know what to do.

Just the same he never mind iffen we go to the dances and the singing and such. He always lent us a wagon iffen we want to borry one to go in, too.

Some the niggers what work for the white folks from the North act pretty uppity and big, and come pestering round the dance places and try to talk up ructions amongst us, but it don't last long.

The Ku Kluckers start riding round at night, and they pass the word that the darkies got to have a pass to go and come and to stay at the dances. They have to git the pass from the white folks they work for, and passes writ from the Northern people wouldn't do no good. That the way the Kluckers keep the darkies in line.

The Kluckers just ride up to the dance ground and look at everybody's passes, and iffen some darky there without a pass or got a pass from the wrong man, they run him home, and iffen he talk big and won't go home they whup him and make him go.

Any nigger out on the road after dark liable to run across the Kluckers, and he better have a good pass! All the dances got to bust up at about 'leven o'clock, too.

One time I seen three, four Kluckers on hosses, all wrapped up in white, and they was making a black boy git home. They was riding hosses, and he was trotting down the road ahead of 'em. Ever' time he stop and start talking, they pop the whip at his heels, and he start trotting on. He was so mad he was crying, but he was gitting on down the road just the same.

I seen 'em coming, and I gits out my pass Young Master writ so I could show it, but when they ride by one in front just turns in his saddle and look back at t'other men and nod his head, and they just ride on by without stopping to see my pass. That man knowed me, I reckon. I looks to see iffen I knowed the hoss, but the Kluckers sometime swapped they hosses round amongst 'em, so the hoss maybe wasn't hisn.

They wasn't very bad 'cause the niggers round there wasn't bad, but I hear plenty of darkies git whupped in other places 'cause they act up and say they don't have to take off they hats in the white stores and such.

Any nigger that behave hisself and don't go running round late at night and drinking never had no trouble with the Kluckers.

Young Mistress go off and git married, but I don't remember the name 'cause she live off somewhere else, and the next year, I think it was, my pappy and mammy go on a place about five miles away owned by a man named Mr. Bumpus, and I go 'long with my sister Betty and brother Jimmie to help 'em.

I live around that place and never marry till Old Mammy and Pappy both gone, and Jimmie and Betty both married and I was gitting about forty year old myself, and then I go up in Kansas and work around till I git married at last.

I was in Fort Scott, and I married Mathilda Black in 1900, and she is 73 years old now and was born in Tennessee. We went to Pittsburg, Kansas, and lived from 1907 to 1913, when we come to Tulsa.

Young Master's children writ to me once in a while and told me how they gitting 'long up to about twenty year ago, and then I never heard no more about 'em. I never had no children, and it look like my wife going outlive me, so my mainest hope when I goes on is seeing Mammy and Pappy and Old Master. Old Overseer, I 'speck, was too devilish mean to be there!

Course I loves my Lord Jesus same as anybody, but you see I never hear much about Him until I was grown, and it seem like you got to hear about religion when you little to soak it up and put much by it. Nobody could read the Bible when I was a boy, and they wasn't no white preachers talked to the niggers. We had meetings sometimes, but the nigger preacher just talk about being a good nigger and "doing to please the Master," and I always thought he meant to please Old Master, and I always wanted to do that anyways.

So that the reason I always remember the time Old Master pass on.

It was about two years after the war, and Old Master been mightly poorly all the time. One day we was working in the Bumpus field and a nigger come on a mule and say Old Mistress like to have us go over to the old place 'cause Old Master mighty low and calling mine and Pappy's and Mammy's name. Old Man Bumpus say go right ahead.

When we git to the big house, Old Master setting propped up in the bed, and you can see he mighty low and outen his head.

He been talking about gitting the oats stacked, 'cause it seem to him like it gitting gloomy-dark, and it gwine to rain, and hail gwine to catch the oats in the shocks. Some nigger come running up to the back door with an old horn Old Mistress sent him out to hunt up, and he blowed it so Old Master could hear it.

Then pretty soon the doctor come to the door and say Old Master wants the bell rung 'cause the slaves should ought to be in from the fields, 'cause it gitting too dark to work. Somebody git a wagon tire and beat on it like a bell ringing, right outside Old Master's window, and then we all go up on the porch and peep in. Everybody was snuffling kind of quiet, 'cause we can't help it.

We hear Old Master say, "That's all right, Simmons. I don't want my niggers working in the rain. Go down to the quarters and see they all dried off good. They ain't got no sense, but they all good niggers." Everybody around the bed was crying, and we all was crying too.

Then Old Mistress come to the door and say we can go in and look at him if we want to. He was still setting propped up, but he was gone.

I stayed in Louisiana a long time after that, but I didn't care nothing about it, and it look like I'm staying a long time past my time in this world, 'cause I don't care much about staying no longer, only I hates to leave Mathilda.

But any time the Lord want me I'm ready, and I likes to think when He ready He going tell Old Master to ring the bell for me to come on in.

MARY REYNOLDS: LOUISIANA

My paw's name was Tom Vaughn, and he was from the North, born free man and lived and died free to the end of his days. He wasn't no educated man, but he was what he calls himself a piano man. He told me once he lived in New York and Chicago and he built the insides of pianos and knew how to make them play in tune. He said some white folks from the South told he if he'd come with them to the South he'd find a lot of work to do with pianos in them parts, and he come off with them.

He saw my maw on the place and her man was dead. He told my massa he'd buy my maw and her three children with all the money he had, iffen he'd sell her. But Massa was never one to sell any but the old niggers who was past working in the fields and past their breeding times. So my paw married my maw and works the fields, same as any other nigger. They had six gals: Martha and Panela and Josephine and Ellen and Katherine and me.

I was born same time as Miss Dora. Massa's first wife and my maw come to their time right together. Miss Dora's maw died, and they brung Miss Dora to suck with me. It's a thing we ain't never forgot. My maw's name was Sallie and Miss Dora always looked with kindness on my maw. We sucked till we was a fair size and played together, which wasn't no common thing. None the other little niggers played with the white children. But Miss Dora loved me so good.

I was just 'bout big 'nough to start playing with a broom to go 'bout sweeping up and not even half doing it when Massa sold me. They was a old white man in Trinity, and his wife died and he didn't have chick or child or slave or nothing. Massa sold me cheap, 'cause he didn't want Miss Dora to play with no nigger young-un. That old man bought me a big doll and went off and left me all day, with the door open. I just sot on the floor and played with that doll. I used to cry. He'd come home and give me something to eat and then go to bed, and I slept on the foot of the bed with him. I was scared all the time in the dark. He never did close the door.

Miss Dora pined and sickened. Massa done what he could, but they wasn't no pertness in her. She got sicker and sicker, and Massa brung 'nother doctor. He say, "You little gal is grieving the life out her body, and she sure gwine die iffen you don't do something 'bout it." Miss Dora says over and over, "I wants Mary." Massa say to the doctor, "That a little nigger young-un I done sold." The doctor tells him he better git me back iffen he wants to save the life of his child. Massa has to give a big plenty more to git me back than what he sold me for, but Miss Dora plumps up right off and grows into fine health.

Then Massa marries a rich lady from Mississippi, and they has children for company to Miss Dora and seem like for a time she forgits me.

Massa wasn't no piddling man. He was a man of plenty. He had a big house with no more style to it than a crib, but it could room plenty people. He was a medicine doctor, and they was rooms in the second story for sick folks what come to lay in. It would take two days to go all over the land he owned. He had cattle and stock and sheep and more'n a hundred slaves and more besides. He bought the best of niggers near every time the speculators come that way. He'd make a swap of the old ones and give money for young ones what could work.

He raised corn and cotton and cane and 'taters and goobers, 'sides the peas and other feeding for the niggers. I 'member I held a hoe handle mighty unsteady when they put a old woman to larn me and some other children to scrape the fields. That old woman would be in a frantic. She'd show me and then turn 'bout to show some other little nigger, and I'd have the young corn cut clean as the grass. She say, "For the love of God, you better larn it right, or Solomon will beat the breath out you body." Old Man Solomon was the nigger driver.

Slavery was the worst days was ever seed in the world. They was things past telling, but I got the scars on my old body to show to this day. I seed worse than what happened to me. I seed them put the men and women in the stock with they hands screwed down through holes in the board and they feets tied together and they naked behinds to the world. Solomon the overseer beat them with a big whip and Massa look on. The niggers better not stop in the fields when they hear them yelling. They cut the flesh 'most to the bones, and some they was when they taken them out of stock and put them on the beds, they never got up again.

When a nigger died, they let his folks come out the fields to see him afore he died. They buried him the same day, take a big plank and bust it with a ax in the middle 'nough to bend it back, and put the dead nigger in betwixt it. They'd cart them down to the graveyard on the place and not bury them deep 'nough that buzzards wouldn't come circling round. Niggers mourns now, but in them days they wasn't no time for mourning.

The conch shell blowed afore daylight, and all hands better git out for roll call, or Solomon bust the door down and git them out. It was work hard, git beatings, and half-fed. They brung the victuals and water to the fields on a slide pulled by a old mule. Plenty times they was only a half barrel water and it stale and hot, for all us niggers on the hottest days. Mostly we ate pickled pork and corn bread and peas and beans and 'taters. They never was as much as we needed.

The times I hated most was picking cotton when the frost was on the bolls. My hands git sore and crack open and bleed. We'd have a little fire in the fields, and iffen the ones with tender hands couldn't stand it no longer, we'd run and warm our hands a little bit. When I could steal a 'tater, I used to slip it in the ashes, and when I'd run to the fire I'd take it out and eat it on the sly.

In the cabins it was nice and warm. They was built of pine boarding, and they was one long row of them up the hill back of the big house. Near one side of the cabins was a fireplace. They'd bring in two, three big logs and put on the fire, and they'd last near a week. The beds was made out of puncheons fitted in holes bored in the wall, and planks laid 'cross them poles. We had ticking mattresses filled with corn shucks. Sometimes the men build chairs at night. We didn't know much 'bout having nothing, though.

Sometimes Massa let niggers have a little patch. They'd raise 'taters or goobers. They liked to have them to help fill out on the victuals. 'Taters roasted in the ashes was the best-tasting eating I ever had. I could die better satisfied to have just one more 'tater roasted in hot ashes. The niggers had to work the patches at night and dig the 'taters and goobers at night. Then if they wanted to sell any in town, they'd have to git a pass to go. They had to go at night, 'cause they couldn't ever spare a hand from the fields.

Once in a while they'd give us a little piece of Saturday evening to wash out clothes in the branch. We hanged them on the ground in the woods to dry. They was a place to wash clothes from the well, but they was so many niggers all couldn't git round to it on Sundays. When they'd git through with the clothes on Saturday evenings, the niggers which sold they goobers and 'taters brung fiddles and guitars and come out and play. The others clap they hands and stomp they feet and we young-uns cut a step round. I was plenty biggity and liked to cut a step.

We was scared of Solomon and his whip, though, and he didn't like frolicking. He didn't like for us niggers to pray, either. We never heared of no church, but us have praying in the cabins. We'd set on the floor and pray with our heads down low and sing low, but if Solomon heared he'd come and beat on the wall with the stock of his whip. He'd say, "I'll come in there and tear the hide off you backs." But some the old niggers tell us we got to pray to God that He don't think different of the blacks and the whites. I know that Solomon is burning in hell today, and it pleasures me to know it.

Once my maw and paw taken me and Katherine after night to slip to 'nother place to a praying and singing. A nigger man with white beard told us a day am coming when niggers only be slaves of God. We prays for the end of tribulation and the end of beatings and for shoes that fit our feet. We prayed that us niggers could have all we wanted to eat and special for fresh meat. Some the old ones say we have to bear all, 'cause that all we can do. Some say they was glad to the time they's dead, 'cause they'd rather rot in the ground than have the beatings. What I hated most was when they'd beat me and I didn't know what they beat me for, and I hated them stripping me naked as the day I was born.

When we's coming back from that praying, I thunk I heared the nigger dogs and somebody on horseback. I say, "Maw, it's them nigger hounds and they'll eat us up." You could hear them old hounds and sluts a-baying. Maw listens and say, "Sure 'nough, them dogs am running and God help us!" Then she and Paw talk and they take us to a fence corner and stands us up 'gainst the rails and say don't move and if anyone comes near, don't breathe loud. They went to the woods, so the hounds chase them and not git us. Me and Katherine stand there, holding hands, shaking so we can hardly stand. We hears the hounds come nearer, but we don't move. They goes after Paw and Maw, but they circles round to the cabins and gits in. Maw say it the power of God.

In them days I weared shirts, like all the young-uns. They had collars and come below the knees and was split up the sides. That's all we weared in hot weather. The men weared jeans and the women gingham. Shoes was the worstest trouble. We weared rough russets when it got cold, and it seem powerful strange they'd never git them to fit. Once when I was a young gal, they got me a new pair and all brass studs in the toes. They was too little for me, but I had to wear them. The brass trimmings cut into my ankles and them places got miserable bad. I rubs tallow in them sore places and wrops rags round them and my sores got worser and worser. The scars are there to this day.

I wasn't sick much, though. Some the niggers had chills and fever a lot, but they hadn't discovered so many diseases then as now. Massa give sick niggers ipecac and asafetida and oil and turpentine and black fever pills.

They was a cabin called the spinning-house and two looms and two spinning wheels going all the time, and two nigger women sewing all the time. It took plenty sewing to make all the things for a place so big. Once Massa goes to Baton Rouge and brung back a yaller gal dressed in fine style. She was a seamster nigger. He builds her a house 'way from the quarters, and she done fine sewing for the whites. Us niggers knowed the doctor took a black woman quick as he did a white and took any on his place he wanted, and he took them often. But mostly the children born on the place looked like niggers. Aunt Cheyney always say four of hers was Massa's, but he didn't give them no mind. But this yaller gal breeds so fast and gits a mess of white young-uns. She larnt them fine manners and combs out they hair.

Oncet two of them goes down the hill to the dollhouse, where the Missy's children am playing. They wants to go in the dollhouse and one the Missy's boys say, "That's for white children." They say, "We ain't no niggers, 'cause we got the same daddy you has, and he comes to see us near every day and fotches us clothes and things from town." They is fussing, and Missy is listening out her chamber window. She heard them white niggers say, "He is our daddy and we call him daddy when he comes to our house to see our mama."

When Massa come home that evening, his wife hardly say nothing to him, and he ask her what the matter, and she tells him, "Since you asks me, I'm studying in my mind 'bout them white young-uns of that yaller nigger wench from Baton Rouge." He say, "Now, honey, I fotches that gal just for you, 'cause she a fine seamster." She say, "It look kind of funny they got the same kind of hair and eyes as my children, and they got a nose look like yours." He say, "Honey, you just paying 'tention to talk of little children that ain't got no mind to what they say." She say, "Over in Mississippi I got a home and plenty with my daddy, and I got that in my mind."

Well, she didn't never leave, and Massa bought her a fine, new span of surrey hosses. But she don't never have no more children, and she ain't so cordial with the Massa. That yaller gal has more white young-uns, but they don't never go down the hill no more to the big house.

Aunt Cheyney was just out of bed with a suckling baby one time, and she run away. Some say that was 'nother baby of Massa's breeding. She don't come to the house to nurse her baby, so they misses her and Old Solomon gits the nigger hounds and takes her trail. They gits near her and she grabs a limb and tries to hist herself in a tree, but them dogs grab her and pull her down. The men hollers them onto her, and the dogs tore her naked and et the breasts plumb off her body. She got well and lived to be a old woman, but 'nother woman has to suck her baby, and she ain't got no sign of breasts no more.

They give all the niggers fresh meat on Christmas and a plug tobacco all round. The highest cotton-picker gits a suit of clothes, and all the women what had twins that year gits a outfitting of clothes for the twins and a double, warm blanket.

Seems like after I got bigger, I 'member more and more niggers run away. They's 'most always cotched. Massa used to hire out his niggers for wage hands. One time he hired me and a nigger boy, Turner, to work for some ornery white trash, name of Kidd. One day Turner goes off and don't come back. Old Man Kidd say I knowed 'bout it, and he tied my wrists together and stripped me. He hanged me by the wrists from a limb on a tree and spraddled my legs round the trunk and tied my feet together. Then he beat me. He beat me worser than I ever been beat before, and I faints dead away. When I come to I'm in bed. I didn't care so much iffen I died.

I didn't know 'bout the passing of time, but Miss Dora come to me. Some white folks done git word to her. Mr. Kidd tries to talk hisself out of it, but Miss Dora fotches me home when I'm well 'nough to move. She took me in a cart and my maw takes care of me. Massa looks me over good and says I'll git well, but I'm ruint for breeding children.

After while I taken a notion to marry and Massa and Missy marries us same as all the niggers. They stands inside the house with a broom held crosswise of the door and we stands outside. Missy puts a little wreath on my head they kept there, and we steps over the broom into the house. Now, that's all they was to the marrying. After freedom I gits married and has it put in the book by a preacher.

One day we was working in the fields and hears the conch shell blow, so we all goes to the back gate of the big house. Massa am there. He say, "Call the roll for every nigger big 'nough to walk, and I wants them to go to the river and wait there. They's gwine be a show and I wants you to see it." They was a big boat down there, done built up on the sides with boards and holes in the boards and a big gun barrel sticking through every hole. We ain't never seed nothing like that. Massa goes up the plank onto the boat and comes out on the boat porch. He say, "This am a Yankee boat." He goes inside and the water wheels starts moving and that boat goes moving up the river, and they says it goes to Natchez.

The boat wasn't more'n out of sight when a big drove of soldiers comes into town. They say they's Federals. More'n half the niggers goes off with them soldiers, but I goes on back home 'cause of my old mammy.

Next day them Yankees is swarming the place. Some the niggers wants to show them something. I follows to the woods. The niggers shows them soldiers a big pit in the ground, bigger'n a big house. It is got wooden doors that lifts up, but the top am sodded and grass growing on it, so you couldn't tell it. In that pit is stock, hosses and cows and mules and money and chinaware and silver and a mess of stuff them soldiers takes.

We just sot on the place doing nothing till the white folks comes home. Miss Dora come out to the cabin and say she wants to read a letter to my mammy. It come from Louis, which is brother to my mammy, and he done follow the Federals to Galveston. A white man down there write the letter for him. It am tored in half and Massa done that. The letter say Louis am working in Galveston and wants Mammy to come with us, and he'll pay our way. Miss Dora say Massa swear, "Damn Louis. I ain't gwine tell Sallie nothing," and he starts to tear the letter up. But she won't let him, and she reads it to Mammy.

After a time Massa takes all his niggers what wants to Texas with him and Mammy gits to Galveston and dies there. I goes with Massa to the Tennessee Colony and then to Navasota. Miss Dora marries and goes to El Paso. She wrote and told me to come to her, and I always meant to go.

My husband and me farmed round for times, and then I done housework and cooking for many years. I come to Dallas and cooked for seven year for one white family. My husband died years ago. I guess Miss Dora been dead these long years. I always kept my years by Miss Dora's years, 'count we is born so close.

I been blind and 'most helpless for five year. I'm gitting mighty enfeebling, and I ain't walked outside the door for a long time back. I sets and 'members the times in the world. I 'members now clear as yesterday things I forgot for a long time. I 'members 'bout the days of slavery, and I don't 'lieve they ever gwine have slaves no more on this earth. I think God done took that burden offen his black children, and I'm aiming to praise Him for it to His face in the days of glory what ain't so far off.

ELLEN BETTS: LOUISIANA

I got borned on the Bayou Teche, clost to Opelousas. That in St. Mary's Parish, in Louisiana, and I belonged to Tolas Parsons, what had 'bout five hundred slaves, counting the big ones and the little ones, and he had God know what else. When my eyes just barely fresh open, Marse Tolas die and will the whole lot of us to he brother, William Tolas Parsons. And I tells you that Marse William am the greatest man what ever walk this earth. That's the truth. I can't lie on him when the poor man's in he grave.

When a whupping got to be done, Old Marse do it heself. He don't 'low no overseer to throw he gals down and pull up their dress and whup on their bottoms like I hear tell some of 'em do. Was he still living I 'spect one part of he hands be with him today. I knows I would.

When us niggers go down the road, folks say, "Them's Parsons' niggers. Don't hit one them niggers for God's sake, or Parsons sure eat your jacket up."

Aunt Rachel what cook in the big house for Miss Cornelia had four young-uns and them children fat and slick as I ever seen. All the niggers have to stoop to Aunt Rachel just like they curtsy to Missy. I mind the time her husband, Uncle Jim, git mad and hit her over the head with the poker. A big knot raise up on Aunt Rachel's head, and when Marse 'quire 'bout it, she say she done bump the head. She dasn't tell on Uncle Jim or Marse sure beat him. Marse sure proud them black, slick children of Rachel's. You couldn't find a yaller child on he place. He sure got no use for mixing black and white.

Marse William have the prettiest place up and down that bayou, with the fine house and fine trees and such. From where we live it's five mile to Centerville one way and five mile to Patterson t'other. They hauls the lumber from one place or t'other to make wood houses for the slaves. Sometime Marse buy the furniture, and sometime the carpenter make it.

Miss Sidney was Marse's first wife, and he had six boys by her. Then he marry the widow Cornelia, and she give him four boys. With ten children springing up quick like that and all the colored children coming 'long fast as pig litters, I don't do nothing all my days, but nurse, nurse, nurse. I nurse so many children it done went and stunted my growth, and that's why I ain't nothing but bones to this day.

When the colored women has to cut cane all day till midnight come and after, I has to nurse the babies for them and tend the white children, too. Some them babies so fat and big I had to tote the feet while 'nother gal tote the head. I was such a little one, 'bout seven or eight year old. The big folks leave some toddy for colic and crying and such, and I done drink the toddy and let the children have the milk. I don't know no better. Lawsy me, it a wonder I ain't the biggest drunker in this here country, counting all the toddy I done put in my young belly!

When late of night come, iffen them babies wake up and bawl, I set up a screech and outscreech them till they shut their mouth. The louder they bawl, the louder I bawl. Sometime when Marse hear the babies cry, he come down and say, "Why the children cry like that, Ellen?" I say, "Marse, I git so hungry and tired I done drink the milk up." When I talk sassy like that, Marse just shake he finger at me, 'cause he knowed I's a good one and don't let no little mite starve.

Nobody ever hit me a lick. Marse always say being mean to the young-uns make them mean when they grows up and nobody gwine to buy a mean nigger. Marse don't even let the children go to the big cane patch. He plant little bitty patches close to the house, and each little nigger have a patch and he work it till it got growed. Marse have the house girls make popcorn for 'em and candy.

I nurse the sick folks too. Sometime I dose with blue mass pills, and some-time Dr. Fawcett leave rhubarb and ipecac and calomel and castor oil and such. Two year after the war, I git marry and git children of my own and then I turn into the wet nurse. I wet-nursed the white children and black children, like they all the same color. Sometime I have a white one pulling the one side and a black one the other.

I wanted to git the papers for midwifing but, Law, I don't never have no time for larning in slave time. If Marse cotch a paper in you hand he sure whup you. He don't 'low no bright niggers round, he sell 'em quick. He always say, "Book larning don't raise no good sugar cane." The only larning he 'low was when they larn the colored children the Methodist catechism. The only writing a nigger ever git am when he git born or marry or die, then Marse put the name in the big book.

Law, I 'lect the time Marse marry Miss Cornelia. He went on the mail boat and brung her from New Orleans. She the prettiest woman in the world almost, 'cepting she have the biggest mouth I nearly ever seed. He brung her up to the house, and all the niggers and boys and girls and cats and dogs and such come and salute her. There she stand on the gallery, with a pretty white dress on with red stripes running up and down. Marse say to her, "Honey, see all the black folks, they 'longs to you now." She wave to us and smile on us, and next day she give her wedding dress to my ma. That the finest dress I ever seen. It was purple and green silk and all the nigger gals wear that dress when they git marry. My sister Sidney wore it and Sary and Mary.

Miss Cornelia was the finest woman in the world. Come Sunday morning she done put a bucket of dimes on the front gallery and stand there and throw dimes to the nigger children just like feeding chickens. I sure right here to testify, 'cause I's right there helping grab. Sometime she done put the washtub of buttermilk on the back gallery, and us children bring us gourds and dip up that good old buttermilk till it all git drunk up. Sometime she fotch bread and butter to the back gallery and pass it out when it don't even come mealtime.

Miss Cornelia set my ma to cutting patterns and sewing right away. She give all the women a bolt of linsey to make clothes, and Ma cut the pattern. Us all have the fine drawers down to the ankle, buttoned with pretty white buttons on the bottom. Lawsy, Ma sure cut a might of drawers, with sewing for her eleven gals and four boys, too. In the summer time we all git a bolt of blue cloth and white tape for trimming, to make Sunday dresses. For the field, all the niggers git homespun what you make jumpers out of. I 'lect how Marse say, "Don't go into the field dirty Monday morning. Scrub youself and put on the clean jumper."

Marse sure good to them gals and bucks what cutting the cane. When they git done making sugar, he give a drink call "Peach and Honey" to the women-folk and whiskey and brandy to the men. And of all the dancing and capering you ever seen! My pa was fiddler, and we'd cut the pigeon wing and cut the buck and every other kind of dance. Sometime Pa git tired and say he ain't gwine to play no more, and us gals git busy and pop him corn and make candy, so to 'tice him to play more.

Marse sure turn over in he grave did he know 'bout some that 'lasses. Them black boys don't care. I seen 'em pull rats out the sugar barrel, and they taste the sugar and say, "Ain't nothing wrong with that sugar. It still sweet." One day a pert one pull a dead scorpion out the syrup kettle, and he just laugh and say, "Marse don't want waste none this syrup," and he lick the syrup right off that scorpion's body and legs.

Lawsy me, I seen thousands and thousands sugar barrels and kettles of syrup in my day. Lord knows how much cane Old Marse have. To them cutting the cane it don't seem so much, but to them what work hour in, hour out, them sugar cane fields sure stretch from one end the earth to the other. Marse ship hogs and hogs of sugar down the bayou. I seen the river boats go down with big signs what say, "Buy this here 'lasses" on the side. And he raise a world of rice and 'taters and corn and peanuts, too.

When the work slight, us black folks sure have the balls and dinners and such. We git all day to barbecue meat down on the bayou, and the white folks come down and eat 'longside the colored.

When a black gal marry, Marse marry her hisself in the big house. He marry 'em Saturday, so they git Sunday off, too. One time the river boat come bearing the license for niggers to git marry with. Marse chase 'em off and say, "Don't you come trucking no no-'count papers round my niggers. When I marry 'em, they marry as good as if the Lord God hisself marry 'em and it don't take no paper to bind the tie." Marse don't stand no messing round, neither. A gal have to be of age and ask her pa and ma and Marse and Missy, and if they 'gree, they go ahead and git marry. Marse have the marry book to put the name down.

One time Marse take me 'long to help tote some children. He done write up to Virginny for to buy fresh hands. They a old man that hobble 'long the road, and the children start to throw rocks, and the old man turn round to one prissy one and say, "Go on, young-un, you'll be where dogs can't bark at you tomorrow." Next morning us cooking in the kitchen, and all a sudden that little boy just crumple up dead on the floor. Law, we's scared. Nobody ever bother that old man no more, for he sure lay the evil finger on you.

Marse's brother, Conrad, what was a widower, come to live on the plantation, and he had a little gal 'bout eight year old. One day she in the plum orchard playing with a rattlesnake, and Marse Conrad have the fit. The little gal won't let nobody hurt that snake and she play with him. He won't bite her. She keeps him 'bout three year, and she'd rub and grease him. One day he got sick, and they give him some brandy, but he die and Old Doc pickle him in the bottle of brandy. That gal git so full of grief they take her to the infirmary in New Orleans, and then one day she up and die.

That snake ain't all what Doc Fawcett pickle. A slave woman give birth to a baby gal what have two faces with a strip of hair running 'tween. Old Doc Fawcett pickle it in the jar of brandy. Old Doc start to court Miss Cornelia when Marse die, but she don't have none of him, and he done went straight 'way and kill hisself.

One day a little man come riding by on a little dun hoss so fast you couldn't see dat hoss's tail a-switching. He whooping and hollering. Us niggers 'gun whoop and holler, too. Then first thing you know the Yanks and the Democrats 'gun to fight right there. They a high old mountain front Marse's house, and the Yanks' gun pepper cannon ball down from the top that hill. The war met right there, and them Yanks and Democrats fit for twenty-four hours straight running.

When the bullets starts raining down, Marse calls us and slip us 'way back into the woods, where it so black and deep. Next day, when the fight over, Marse come out with great big wagons piled full of mess-poke for us to eat. That what us call hog meat. Us sure glad to 'scape from the Yankees.

When us driv back to the plantation, such a sight I never seen. Law, the things I can tell. Them Yanks have kilt men and women. I seed babies pick up from the road with their brains bust right out. One old man am drawing water, and a cannon ball shoots him right in the well. They draws him up with the fishing line. They's a old sugar boat on the bayou with blood and sugar running 'longside the busted barrels. 'Lasses run in the bayou, and blood run in the ditches. Marse have the great big orchard on the road, and it wipe clean as the whistle. Bullets wipe up everything and bust that sugar cane all to pieces. The house sot far back and 'scape the bullets, but, Law, the time they have!

They's awful, awful times after that. A old cotton dress cost five dollars, and a pound of coffee cost five dollars, and a pint cup flour cost six bits. The Yanks round all the time, and one day they comes right in the house where Miss Cornelia eating her dinner. They march round the table, just scooping up meat and 'taters and grabbing cornpone right and left. Miss Cornelia don't say a word, just smile sweet as honey-cake. I reckon them soldiers mighta took the silver and such, only she charm 'em by being so quiet and ladylike. First thing you know, them soldiers curtsy to Missy and take theirself right out the door and don't come back.

Then it seem like Marse have all the trouble in the world. He boy, Ned, die in the war, and William, what name for he pa, drink bad all the time. And after the war them Ku Kluxers what wear the false faces try to tinker with Marse's niggers. One day Uncle Dave start to town, and a Kluxer ask him where am he pass. That Kluxer clout him, but Uncle Dave outrun him in the cane. Marse grab the hoss and go 'rest that man, and Marse a judge, and he make that man pay the fine for hitting Uncle Dave. After they hears of that, them old poky faces sure scared of Old Marse, and they git out from Opelousas and stays out. When me and my husband, John, come to Texas the folks say that Louisiana masters the meanest in the world, and I say right back at 'em that they is good and mean in every spot of the earth. What more, the Louisiana masters free their niggers a year before any Texas nigger git free.

When 'mancipation come, Marse git on the big block and say, "You all is as free as I is, standing right here. Does you want to stay with me, you can, and I'll pay you for the work." All the niggers cheer and say they want to stay, but Marse die not long after, and all us niggers scatter.

I sure 'lect that day Old Marse die. He won't die till Ma gits there. He keep saying, "Where's Charity? Tell Charity to come." They fotch Ma from the cane patch, and she hold Marse's hand till he die. Us niggers went to the graveyard, and us sure cry over Old Marse.

Marse's brother, Goldham, carries all he hands back to the free country to turn 'em loose. He say the free country am the ones what's yelling 'bout slave times, so they could just take care of the niggers. Marse Goldham so big that when he stand in the door you couldn't git by him, 'thout he stand sideways.

Law, times ain't like they was in slave days. All my ten children is dead and my old man gone, and now I reckon my time 'bout 'rive. All I got to do now am pray the Lord to keep me straight; then, when the great day come, I can march the road to glory.

MARY GRAYSON: INDIAN TERRITORY

I am what we colored people call a "native." That means that I didn't come into the Indian country from somewhere in the Old South, after the war, like so many Negroes did, but I was born here in the old Creek Nation, and my master was a Creek Indian. That was eighty-three years ago, so I am told.

My mammy belonged to white people back in Alabama when she was born— down in the southern part, I think, for she told me that after she was a sizable girl her white people moved into the eastern part of Alabama where there was a lot of Creeks. Some of them Creeks was mixed up with the whites, and some of the big men in the Creeks who come to talk to her master was almost white, it looked like. "My white folks moved around a lot when I was a little girl," she told me.

When Mammy was about ten or twelve years old, some of the Creeks begun to come out to the Territory in little bunches. They wasn't the ones who was taken out here by the soldiers and contractor men—they come on ahead by themselves, and most of them had plenty of money, too. A Creek come to my mammy's master and bought her to bring out here, but she heard she was being sold and run off into the woods. There was an old clay pit, dug way back into a high bank, where the slaves had been getting clay to mix with hog-hair scrapings to make chinking for the big log houses they built for the master and the cabins they made for themselves. Well, my mammy run and hid way back in that old clay pit, and it was 'way after dark before the master and the other man found her.

The Creek man that bought her was a kind sort of a man, Mammy said, and wouldn't let the master punish her. He took her away and was kind to her, but he decided she was too young to breed, and he sold her to another Creek who had several slaves already, and he brought her out to the Territory.

The McIntosh men was the leaders in the bunch that come out at that time, and one of the bunch, named Jim Perryman, bought my mammy and married her to one of his "boys," but after he waited a while and she didn't have a baby he decided she was no good breeder and he sold her to Mose Perryman.

Mose Perryman was my master, and he was a cousin to Legus Perryman, who was a big man in the tribe. He was a lot younger than Mose, and laughed at Mose for buying my mammy, but he got fooled, because my mammy got married to Mose's slave boy Jacob, the way the slaves was married them days, and went ahead and had ten children for Mr. Mose.

Mose Perryman owned my pappy and his older brother, Hector, and one of the McIntosh men—Oona, I think his name was—owned my pappy's brother William. I can remember when I first heard about there was going to be a war. The older children would talk about it, but they didn't say it was a war all over the country. They would talk about a war going to be "back in Alabama," and I guess they had heard the Creeks talking about it that way.

When I was born we lived in the Choska [pronounced Choe-skey] bottoms, and Mr. Mose Perryman had a lot of land broke in all up and down the Arkansas River along there. After the war, when I had got to be a young woman, there was quite a settlement grew up at Choska right across the river east of where Haskell now is, but when I was a child before the war all the whole bottoms was marshy kind of wilderness except where farms had been cleared out. The land was very rich, and the Creeks who got to settle there were lucky. They always had big crops. All west of us was high ground, toward Gibson Station and Fort Gibson, and the land was sandy. Some of the McIntoshes lived over that way, and my Uncle William belonged to one of them.

We slaves didn't have a hard time at all before the war. I have had people who were slaves of white folks back in the old states tell me that they had to work awfully hard and their masters were cruel to them sometimes, but all the Negroes I knew who belonged to Creeks always had plenty of clothes and lots to eat, and we all lived in good log cabins we built. We worked the farm and tended to the horses and cattle and hogs, and some of the older women worked around the owner's house, but each Negro family looked after a part of the fields and worked the crops like they belonged to us.

When I first heard talk about the war, the slaves were allowed to go and see one another sometimes, and often they were sent on errands several miles with a wagon or on a horse, but pretty soon we were all kept at home, and nobody was allowed to come around and talk to us. But we heard what was going on.

The McIntosh men got nearly everybody to side with them about the war, but we Negroes got word somehow that the Cherokees over back of Fort Gibson was not going to be in the war and that there were some Union people over there who would help slaves to get away, but we children didn't know anything about what we heard our parents whispering about, and they would stop if they heard us listening. Most of the Creeks who lived in our part of the country, between the Arkansas and the Verdigris, and some even south of the Arkansas, belonged to the Lower Creeks and sided with the South, but down below us along the Canadian River they were Upper Creeks, and there was a good deal of talk about them going with the North. Some of the Negroes tried to get away and go down to them, but I don't know of any from our neighborhood that went to them.

Some Upper Creeks came up into the Choska bottoms talking around among the folks there about siding with the North. They were talking, they said, for Old Man Gouge, who was a big man among the Upper Creeks. His Indian name was Opoeth-le-ya-hola, and he got away into Kansas with a big bunch of Creeks and Seminoles during the war.

Before that time, I remember one night my Uncle William brought another Negro man to our cabin and talked a long time with my pappy, but pretty soon some of the Perryman Negroes told them that Mr. Mose was coming down, and they went off into the woods to talk. But Mr. Mose didn't come down. When Pappy came back, Mammy cried quite a while, and we children could hear them arguing late at night. Then my Uncle Hector slipped over to our cabin several times and talked to Pappy, and Mammy began to fix up grub, but she didn't give us children but a little bit of it, and told us to stay around with her at the cabin and not go playing with the other children.

Then early one morning, about daylight, old Mr. Mose came down to the cabin in his buggy, waving a shotgun and hollering at the top of his voice. I never saw a man so mad in all my life, before nor since!

He yelled in at Mammy to "git them children together and git up to my house before I beat you and all of them to death!" Mammy began to cry and plead that she didn't know anything, but he acted like he was going to shoot sure enough, so we all ran to Mammy and started for Mr. Mose's house as fast as we could trot.

We had to pass all the other Negro cabins on the way, and we could see that they were all empty, and it looked like everything in them had been tore up. Straw and corn shucks all over the place, where somebody had tore up the mattresses, and all the pans and kettles gone off the outside walls where they used to hang them.

At one place we saw two Negro boys loading some iron kettles on a wagon, and a little further on was some boys catching chickens in a yard, but we could see all the Negroes had left in a big hurry.

I asked Mammy where everybody had gone and she said, "Up to Mr. Mose's house, where we are going. He's calling us all in."

"Will Pappy be up there too?" I asked her.

"No. Your pappy and your Uncle Hector and your Uncle William and a lot of other menfolks won't be here any more. They went away. That's why Mr. Mose is so mad, so if any of you young-uns say anything about any strange men coming to our place I'll break your necks!" Mammy was sure scared!

We all thought sure she was going to git a big whipping, but Mr. Mose just looked at her a minute and then told her to git back to the cabin and bring all the clothes, and bed ticks and all kinds of cloth we had and come back ready to travel.

"We're going to take all you black devils to a place where there won't no more of you run away!" he yelled after us. So we got ready to leave as quick as we could. I kept crying about my pappy, but Mammy would say, "Don't you worry about your pappy, he's free now. Better be worrying about us. No telling where we all will end up!" There was four or five Creek families and their Negroes all got together to leave, with all their stuff packed in buggies and wagons, and being toted by the Negroes or carried tied on horses, jackasses, mules, and milk cattle. I reckon it was a funny-looking sight, or it would be to a person now, the way we was all loaded down with all manner of baggage when we met at the old ford across the Arkansas that led to the Creek Agency. The Agency stood on a high hill a few miles across the river from where we lived, but we couldn't see it from our place down in the Choska bottoms. But as soon as we got up on the upland east of the bottoms we could look across and see the hill.

When we got to a grove at the foot of the hill near the Agency, Mr. Mose and the other masters went up to the Agency for a while. I suppose they found out up there what everybody was supposed to do and where they was supposed to go, for when we started on it wasn't long until several more families and their slaves had joined the party, and we made quite a big crowd.

The little Negro boys had to carry a little bundle apiece, but Mr. Mose didn't make the little girls carry anything and let us ride if we could find anything to ride on. My mammy had to help lead the cows part of the time, but a lot of the time she got to ride an old horse, and she would put me up behind her. It nearly scared me to death, because I had never been on a horse before, and she had to hold on to me all the time to keep me from falling off.

Of course, I was too small to know what was going on then, but I could tell that all the masters and the Negroes seemed to be mighty worried and careful all the time. Of course, I know now that the Creeks were all split up over the war, and nobody was able to tell who would be friendly to us or who would try to poison us or kill us, or at least rob us. There was a lot of bushwhacking all through that country by little groups of men who was just out to get all they could. They would appear like they was the enemy of anybody they run across, just to have an excuse to rob them or burn up their stuff. If you said you was with the South they would be with the North, and if you claimed to be with the Yankees they would be with the South, so our party was kind of upset all the time we was passing through the country along the Canadian. That was where Old Gouge had been talking against the South. I've heard my folks say that he was a wonderful speaker, too.

We all had to move along mighty slow, on account of the ones on foot, and we wouldn't get very far in one day, then we Negroes had to fix up a place to camp and get wood and cook supper for everybody. Sometimes we would come to a place to camp that somebody knew about, and we would find it all tromped down by horses and the spring all filled in and ruined. I reckon Old Gouge's people would tear up things when they left, or maybe some Southern bush-whackers would do it. I don't know which.

When we got down to where the North Fork runs into the Canadian, we went around the place where the Creek town was. There was lots of Creeks down there who was on the other side, so we passed around that place and forded across west of there. The ford was a bad one, and it took us a long time to get across. Everybody got wet and a lot of the stuff on the wagons got wet. Pretty soon we got down into the Chickasaw country, and everybody was friendly to us, but the Chickasaw people didn't treat their slaves like the Creeks did. They was more strict, like the people in Texas and other places. The Chickasaws seemed lighter color than the Creeks, but they talked more in Indian among themselves and to their slaves. Our masters talked English nearly all the time except when they were talking to Creeks who didn't talk good English, and we Negroes never did learn very good Creek. I could always understand it, and can yet, a little, but I never did try to talk it much. Mammy and Pappy used English to us all the time.

Mr. Mose found a place for us to stop close to Fort Washita, and got us places to stay and work. I don't know which direction we were from Fort Washita, but I know we were not very far. I don't know how many years we were down in there, but I know it was over two, for we worked on crops at two different places, I remember. Then one day Mr. Mose came and told us that the war was over and that we would have to root for ourselves after that. Then he just rode away, and I never saw him after that until after we had got back up into the Choska country. Mammy heard that the Negroes were going to get equal rights with the Creeks and that she should go to the Creek Agency to draw for us, so we set out to try to get back.

We started out on foot and would go a little ways each day, and Mammy would try to get a little something to do to get us some food. Two or three times she got paid in money, so she had some money when we got back. After three or four days of walking, we came across some more Negroes who had a horse, and Mammy paid them to let us children ride and tie with their children for a day or two. They had their children on the horse, so two or three little ones would get on with a larger one to guide the horse, and we would ride a while and get off and tie the horse and start walking on down the road. Then when the others caught up with the horse they would ride until they caught up with us. Pretty soon the old people got afraid to have us do that, so we just led the horse and some of the little ones rode it.

We had our hardest times when we would get to a river or big creek. If the water was swift, the horse didn't do any good, for it would shy at the water and the little ones couldn't stay on, so we would have to just wait until someone came along in a wagon and maybe have to pay them with some of our money or some of our goods we were bringing back to haul us across. Sometimes we had to wait all day before anyone would come along in a wagon.

We were coming north all this time, up through the Seminole Nation, but when we got to Weleetka we met a Creek family of freedmen who were going to the Agency too, and Mammy paid them to take us along in their wagon. When we got to the Agency, Mammy met a Negro who had seen Pappy and knew where he was, so we sent word to him and he came and found us. He had been through most of the war in the Union army.

When he got away into the Cherokee country, some of them called the "Pins" helped to smuggle him on up into Missouri and over into Kansas, but he soon found that he couldn't get along and stay safe unless he went with the army. He went with them until the war was over and was around Gibson quite a lot. When he was there he tried to find out where we had gone but said he never could find out. He was in the battle of Honey Springs, he said, but never was hurt or sick. When we got back together, we cleared a section of land a little east of the Choska bottoms, near where Clarksville now is, and farmed until I was a great big girl.

I went to school at a little school called Blackjack school. I think it was a kind of mission school and not one of the Creek Nation schools, because my first teacher was Miss Betty Weaver and she was not a Creek but a Cherokee. Then we had two white teachers, Miss King and John Kernan, and another Cherokee was in charge. His name was Ross, and he was killed one day when his horse fell off a bridge across the Verdigris, on the way from Tullahassee to Gibson Station.

When I got to be a young woman I went to Okmulgee and worked for some people near there for several years, then I married Tate Grayson. We got our freedmen's allotments on Mingo Creek, east of Tulsa, and lived there until our children were grown and Tate died, then I came to live with my daughter in Tulsa.

PART THREE

From Can to Can't

They worked, in a manner of speaking, from can to can't, from the time they could see until the time they couldn't. They do about the same thing now.

As the testimony of experience, not opinion, the slave narratives re-create the actual conditions of slavery as distinct from the romantic conception of the plantation tradition, which still survives in life and literature. The basic assumptions of this tradition—Negro inferiority, dependence, and content—have given us the pleasantly picturesque stereotypes of Uncle Tom and Uncle Remus and the not so pleasant or picturesque ethics of Jim Crow. Traces of the slave's traditional attitude of respect and "easy-going trustfulness" are reflected in the narratives as part of the pattern of slavery which Charles S. Johnson has called the "shadow of the plantation" and which has been kept alive in the rural South through a vicious circle of cultural isolation and economic depression. Moreover, certain narrators (usually house servants) are moved by feelings of genuine loyalty and affection toward a kind master or mistress. But, except for these survivals and regressions, there is no attempt here to gloss over the physical and mental effects of slavery, as in the sentimental distortions and cheap caricatures of fiction, the stage, and popular song. Instead, the slave emerges as an individual rather than a type, a person rather than a symbol, with normal sensibilities and intelligence, portrayed as only the Negro can portray his own kind.

"To take in, or to understand the exact social status of such a people in all its bearings," wrote the publisher in his preface to an 1890 reprint of Solomon Northup's *Twelve Years a Slave*, "we can pursue no better course than to live among them, to become for a time one of them, to fall from a condition of freedom to one of bondage, to feel the scourge, to bear the marks of the brands, and the outrage of manacles." The privations, penalties, and punishments, as well as the occasional favors, privileges, and rewards, were part of an elaborate system of control by which the master made slavery acceptable to the slave. With the absolute power of the owner over his human property, slavery was nothing short of tyranny; and, like every tyrant, the master lived in constant fear of revolt and had to make favorites and spies of some slaves and examples of others. In between master and slave were the overseer and the patroller, from whom no mercy was expected, and the "nigger driver," who was apt to be "meaner than the white folks."

But, in spite of all attempts to crush it, the slave had a will of his own, which was actively, as well as passively, opposed to the master's. And it is this stubborn and rebellious will—tragic, heroic, defeated, or triumphant—that, more than all else, haunts us, as it haunted the master, "frustrating his designs by a ceaseless though perhaps invisible countermining," as Theodore D. Weld wrote in 1839. As the master saw this opposing will constantly in the "dissatisfied look, and reluctant air and unwilling movement; the constrained strokes of labor, the drawling tones, the slow hearing, the feigned stupidity, the sham pains and sickness, the short memory," so in the narratives the slave expresses his hatred of enslavement and his contempt for his enslaver in less subtle and more open ways, such as "taking" what belonged to him, escaping or assisting others to escape, secretly learning or teaching others to read and write, secret meetings, suicide, infanticide, homicide, and the like.

Here, too, caught in the same inexorable nexus of human relationships, the master appears as the victim of his own system; for, in a world torn by fear, passion, and violence, all classes were inevitably demoralized and brutalized. Here are the tragic beginnings of what was most degrading of all—slavery's legacy of race prejudice and hatred, which has left its mark on the whole country.

Count the Stars Through the Cracks

I stayed round with Master's boys a lot, and them white boys was as good to me as if I had been their brother. And I stayed up to the big house lots of nights so as to be handy for running for Old Master and Mistress. The big house was fine, but the log cabin where my mammy lived had so many cracks in it that when I would sleep down there I could lie in bed and count the stars through the cracks. Mammy's beds was ticks stuffed with dried grass and put on bunks built on the wall, but they did sleep so good. I can 'most smell that clean dry grass now.

A PRETTY CROP OF CHILDREN

I

Old Master sure thought more of his little nigger children. He used to ride in the quarters 'cause he like to see 'em come running. The cook, she was a old woman name Forney, and she had to see after feeding the children. She had a way of calling 'em up. She holler, "Tee, tee, t-e-e," and all us little niggers just come running. Old Master he ride up and say, "Forney, call up them little pickaninnies," and Old Forney she lift up her voice and holler, "Tee, t-e-e, t-e-e," and Old Master just set up on the hoss and laugh and laugh a lot to see us come running up. He like to count up how many little niggers he did have. That was fun for us, too.

II

Yes, ma'am, my white folks was proud of they niggers. Um, yessum, when they used to have company to the big house, Miss Ross would bring them to the door to show them us children. And, my blessed, the yard would be black with us children, all string up there next the doorstep looking up in they eyes. Old Missus would say, "Ain't I got a pretty crop of little niggers coming on?" The lady, she look so please like. Then Miss Ross say, "Do my little niggers want some bread to gnaw on?" And us children say, "Yessum, yessum, we do." Then she would go in the pantry and see could she find some cook bread to hand us.

OLD MISTRESS' PET

When Miss Jane's husband died, he willed the niggers to his children, and Mandy Paine owned me then. When I was one month old they said I was so white Mandy Paine thought her brother was my father, so she got me and carried me to the meat block and was going to cut my head off. When the children heard, they run and cried, "Mama's going to kill Harriet's baby." Old Mistress, Jane Davis, heard about it, and she come and paid Miss Jane $40 for me and carried me to her home, and I slept right in the bed with her till the war ceasted.

Her children was grown, and they used to come by and say, "Ma, why don't you take that nigger out of your bed?" and she'd reach over and pat me and say, "This the only nigger I got."

TURKEY BUZZARD LAID ME

. . . Well, you know, Uncle Stephen, he kinda overseer for some widow womans. He mama' husband. He come to see my mama any time he gits ready. But I find out he ain't my pappy. I knowed that since when I's a little thing. I used to go over to Massa Daniels' plantation. They tell me all 'bout it. The folks over there they used to say to me: "Who's your pappy? Who's your pappy?" I just say: "Turkey buzzard lay me and the sun hatch me," and then go on 'bout my business. Course all the time they knows, and I knows, too, that Massa Daniels was my pappy. . . .

OLD HOG ROUND THE BENCH

First thing I 'member is us was bought by Massa Colonel Pratt Washington from Massa Lank Miner. Massa Washington was pretty good man. He boys, George and John Henry, was the only overseers. Them boys treat us nice. Massa always rid up on he hoss after dinner-time. He hoss was a bay, call Sank. The fields was in the bottoms of the Colorado River. The big house was on the hill, and us could see him coming. He weared a tall beaver hat always.

The reason us always watch for him am that he boy, George, try larn us our ABC's in the field. The workers watch for Massa, and when they seed him a-riding down the hill they starts singing out, "Old hog round the bench! Old hog round the bench!"

That the signal and then everybody starts working like they have something after them. But I's too young to larn much in the field, and I can't read today and have to make the cross when I signs for my name.

DON'T LET THE SUN GO DOWN ON YOU

I come up in the way of obedience. Any time I wanted to go, had to go to Old Mistress, and she say: "Don't let the sun go down on you." And when we come home, the sun was in the trees. If you seed the sun was going down on you, you run.

I DIDN'T KNOW WHAT "SELL" MEANT

One time Old Master and another man come and took some calves off, and Pappy say Old Master taking them off to sell. I didn't know what "sell" meant, and I ast Pappy, "Is he going to bring 'em back when he git through selling them?" I never did see no money neither, until time of the war or a little before.

FANNING THE FLIES

When I got big enough for to step around, from the very first, my maw took me into the big house. It still there, 'cept it done 'bout fell down now, to what it was then. But some of Marse's folks, they lives down there still. Then, you see, they is like these white folks up round here now. They ain't got no big money like they had when I was a-running up. Time I got big enough for to run around in my shirttail, my maw, she 'lowed one night to my paw, when he was setting by the fire, "That black little nigger over there, he got to git hisself some pants 'cause I's gwine to put him up over the white folks's table." In them times the doors and windows, they never had no screen wire up to them like they is now. Folks didn't know nothing 'bout no such as that then. My master and all the other big white folks, they raised peafowls. Is you ever seed any? Well, every spring us little niggers, we cotch them wild things at night. They could fly like a buzzard. They roosted up in the pine trees, right up in the tip top. So the missus, she have us young-uns clamb up there and git 'em when they first took roost. Us would clamb down, and my maw, she would pull the long feathers outen the tails. For weeks the cocks, they wouldn't let nobody see 'em if they could help it. Them birds is sure proud. When they is got the feathers, they just struts on the fences, and the fences was rail in them days. Iffen they could see theirself in a puddle of water after a rain, they would stay there all day a-strutting and carrying on like nobody's business. Yes, sir, them was pretty birds.

After us got the feathers, the missus, she'd 'low that all the nigger gals gwine to come down in the washhouse and make fly brushes. Sometime the missus'd give some of the gals some short feathers to put in their Sunday hats. When them gals got them hats on, I used to git so disgusted with 'em I'd leave 'em at church and walk home by myself. Anyway, by that time all the new fly brushes was made, and the missus, she have fans made from the short feathers for the white folks to fan the air with on hot days. Lordy, I's strayed far from what I had started out for to tell you. But I knowed that you young folks didn't know nothing 'bout all that. In them days the dining-room was big and had the windows open all the summer long, and all the doors stayed stretched, too. Quick as the mess of victuals began to come on the table, a little nigger boy was put up in the swing, I calls it, over the table, to fan the flies and gnats offen the missus' victuals. This swing was just offen the end of the long table. Some of the white folks had steps a-leading up to it. Some of 'em just had the little boys' maws to fetch the young-uns up there till they got through; then they was fetched down again.

Well, when I got my pants, my maw fetched me in and I clumb up the steps that Marse Johnson had, to git up in his swing with. At first, they had to show me just how to hold the brush, 'cause them peacock feathers was so long iffen you didn't mind your business, the ends of them feathers would splash in the gravy or something 'nother, and then the missus' table be all spattered up. Some of the masters would whup the nigger childrens for that carelessness, but Marse Johnson, he always good to his niggers. Most the white folks good to the niggers round'bout where I comes from.

It wa'n't long 'fore I got used to it, and I never did splash the feathers in no ration. But after I got used to it, I took to a-going to sleep up there. Marse Johnson he would just git up and wake me up. All the white folks at the table joke me so 'bout being so lazy I soon stop that foolishness. My maw, she roll her eyes at me when I come down after the master had to wake me up.

That change like everything else. When I got bigger, I got to be houseboy. They took down the swing and got a little gal to stand just 'hind the missus' chair and fan them flies. The missus 'low to Marse Johnson that the style done change, when he want to know how come she took the swing down. So that is the way it is now with the women; they changes the whole house with the style. But I tells my childrens, ain't no days like the old days when I was a shaver.

RIDING OLD JOHN BACKWARDS

. . . Never whipped me but one time in my life.

I'll tell you about it. This is what they whipped me for. Me and my brother Sam had to water the horses. I didn't have to go with Sam, but I was big enough to do that. We had one old horse named John—big old horse. I would have to git up on a ten-rail fence to git on him. One day I was leading Old John back, and I got tired of walking. So when I come to a ten-rail fence, I got up on Old John. I got up on him backwards, and I didn't have hold of no bridle nor nothing because I was looking at his tail.

The others got back there before I did. Old Master said to them, "Where's Tillie?"

They said to him, "She's coming, leading Old John."

After a while they saw me coming, and one of 'em, said, "There's Tillie now."

And 'nother one, "Man, she's sitting on the horse backwards." And Old John was ambling along nipping the grass now and then, with his bridle dragging and me sitting up on his back, facing his tail and slipping and sliding with every step.

Old John was gentle. But they were scared he would throw me off. Old Missus come out the gate and met him herself, 'cause she was 'fraid the others would 'cite him and make him throw me down. She gentled him and led him up to Old Master. They was careful and gentle till they got me off that horse, and then Old Master turned and lit into me and give me a brushing.

That's the only whipping he ever give me. But that didn't do me no good. Leastwise, it didn't stop me from riding horses. I rode Old John ever' chance I could git. But I didn't ride him backwards no more.

BARBECUE AND BIG MEETING

Newt and Anderson was my young masters. They was 'long 'bout my own age. They went to school at Goshen Hill. The school was near the store, some folks called it the trading post in them days. They had barrels of liquor setting out from the store in a long row. Sold the liquor to the rich mens that carried on at the race track near by. Folks in Goshen was all rich in them days. Rogers Church, where the Carlisles, Jeters, Sims, Selbys, Glens, and lots of other folks went, too, and the slaves, was the richest country church in this part of the whole state, so I is often been told. Ebenezer, over in Maybinton, was the onliest church in the whole country that tried to strive with Rogers in the way of finery and style. The Hendersons, Maybins, Hardys, Douglasses, Cofields, Chicks, and Oxners was the big folks over there. Both the churches was Methodist.

Every summer they carried on camp meeting at Rogers. All the big Methodist preachers would come from 'way off then. They was entertained in the Carlisle big house. Missus put on the dog (as the niggers says now) then. Everything was cleaned up just 'fore the meeting like us did for the early spring cleaning. Camp meeting come just after the craps was done laid by. Then all craps was done laid by before July the fourth. It was unheard of for anybody to let the Fourth come without the craps outen the way. Times is done changed now, Lord. Then the fields was heavy with corn head high and cotton up around the darky's waist! Grass was all cleaned out of the furrows on the last go round. The fields and even the terraces was put in apple pie order for the gathering of the craps in the fall.

As you all knows, the Fourth has always been nigger day. Marse and Missus had good rations for us early on the Fourth. Then us went to barbecues after the morning chores was done. In them days the barbecues was usually held on the plantation of Marse Jim Hill in Fish Dam. That was not far from Goshen. Marse Jim had a pretty spring that is still all walled up with fine rocks. The water come outen these rocks that cold that you can't hold your hand in it for more than a minute at the longest. There is a big flat rock beyond the spring that I 'specks covers more than an acre and a half of ground. A creek run along over this rock, where the mules and the hosses could rest in the shade of the trees and drink all the water that they wanted. Wild ferns growed waist high along there then. All kinds of pretty flowers and daisies was gathered by the gals. Them was the best days that any darky has ever seed. Never had nothing to aggravate your mind then. Plenty to eat; plenty to wear; plenty wood to burn; good house to live in; and no worry 'bout where it was a-coming from!

Old Marse he give us the rations for the barbecues. Every master wanted his darkies to be thought well of at the barbecues by the darkies from all the other plantations. They had pigs barbecued, and goats; and the missus let the women-folks bake pies, cakes, and custards for the barbecue, just 'zactly like it was for the white folks' barbecue theyself!

Young ones carried on like young colts, a-frolicking in the pasture till they had done got so full of victuals that they could not eat another bite. Then they roamed on off and set down somewheres to sleep in the shade of the trees. When the sun started to going down, then the old folks begin to git ready to return back to they home plantations, for there was the master's stock and chickens to feed and put up for the night, to say nothing of the cows to milk. The master's work had to go on around the big house, 'cause all the darkies had been 'lowed to have such a pleasant day. Next day being Saturday was on this occasion not only ration day, but the day to git ready for the white folks' camp meeting which I has already called to recollection several times. . . .

As I has said once, the fields was in lay-by shape and the missus done already got the house cleaned. The childrens was put in one room to sleep, and that make more room for the preachers and guests that gwine to visit in the big house for the next six weeks. Then the plans for cooking had to be brung 'bout.

They never had no ice in them days, as you well knows; but us had a dry well under our big house. It was deep, and everything keep real cool down there. Steps led down into it, and it always be real dark down there. The rats run around down there, and the young-uns scared to go down for anything. So us carry a lightwood knot for light when us put anything in it or take anything out. There ain't no need for me to tell you 'bout the wellhouse where us kept all the milk and butter, for it was the talk of the country 'bout what nice fresh milk and butter the missus always had. A hollow oak log was used for the milk trough. Three times a day Cilla had her little boy run fresh cool well water all through the trough. That keep the milk from gwine to whey and the butter fresh and cool. In the dry well was kept the canned things and dough to set till it had done riz! When company come like they always did for the camp meetings, shoats and goats and maybe a sheep or lamb or two was kilt for barbecue out by Cilla's cabin. These carcasses was kept down in the dry well over night and put over the pit early the next morning after it had done took salt. Then there was a big box covered with screen wire that victuals was kept in in the dry well. These boxes was made rat-proof.

Whilst the meats for the company table was kept barbecued out in the yard, the cakes, pies, breads, and t'other fixings was done in the kitchen out in the big house yard. Baskets had to be packed to go to camp meeting. Tables was built up at Rogers under the big oak trees that has all been cut down now. The tables just groaned and creaked and sighed with victuals at dinner hour every day during the camp meeting.

Missus fetch her finest linens and silver and glasses to outshine them brung by t'other white folks of quality. In them days the white folks of quality in Union most all come from Goshen Hill and Fish Dam. After the white folks done et all they could hold, then the slaves what had done come to church and to help with the tables and the carriages would have the dinner on a smaller table over clost to the spring. Us had table cloths on our table also, and us et from the kitchen china and the kitchen silver.

Young gals couldn't eat much in public, 'cause it ain't stylish for young courting gals to let on like they has any appetite to speak of. I sees that am a custom that still goes amongst the womenfolks, not to eat so heavy. Colored gals tried to do just like the young white missus would do.

After everything was done et, it would be enough to pack up and fetch back home to feed all the hungry niggers what roams round here in Union now. Them was the times when everybody had 'nough to eat and more than they wanted and plenty clothes to wear!

During the preaching us darkies sot in the back of the church. Our white folks had some benches there that didn't nobody set on 'cept the slaves. Us wore the best clothes that us had. The marse give us a coat and a hat, and his sons give all the old hats and coats round. Us wore shirts and pants made from the looms. Us kept them cleaned and ironed just like the master and the young masters done theirn. Then us wore a string tie, that the white folks done let us have, to church. That 'bout the onliest time that a darky was seed with a tie. Some the oldest men even wore a cravat, that they had done got from the old master. Us combed our hair on Sunday for church. But us never bothered much with it no other time. During slavery some of the old men had short plaits of hair.

The gals come out in the starch dresses for the camp meeting. They took they hair down outen the strings for the meeting. In them days all the darky womens wore they hair in string 'cept when they 'tended church or a wedding. At the camp meetings the womens pulled off the head rags, 'cept the mammies. On this occasion the mammies wore linen head rags fresh laundered. They wore the best aprons with long streamers ironed and starched out a-hanging down they backs. All the other darky womens wore the black dresses, and they got hats from some they white lady folks, just as us mens got hats from ourn. Them womens that couldn't git no hats mostly wore black bonnets. The nigger gals and wenches did all the dressing up that they could for the meeting and also for the barbecue.

At night when the meeting done busted till next day was when the darkies really did have they freedom of spirit. As the wagon be creeping along in the late hours of moonlight, the darkies would raise a tune. Then the air soon be filled with the sweetest tune as us rid on home and sung all the old hymns that us loved. It was always some big black nigger with a deep bass voice like a frog that'd start up the tune. Then the other mens jine in, followed up by the fine little voices of the gals and the cracked voices of the old womens and the grannies. When us reach near the big house us soften down to a deep hum that the missus like! Sometimes she hist up the window and tell us sing "Swing Low, Sweet Chariot" for her and the visiting guests. That all us want to hear. Us open up, and the niggers near the big house that hadn't been to church would wake up and come out to the cabin door and jine in the refrain. From that we'd swing on into all the old spirituals that us love so well and that us knowed how to sing. Missus often 'low that her darkies could sing with heaven's inspiration. Now and then some old mammy would fall outen the wagon a-shouting Glory! and Hallelujah! and Amen! After that us went off to lay down for the night.

IF ALL SLAVES HAD BELONGED TO WHITE FOLKS LIKE OURS

I was big enough to remember well us coming back from Texas after we refugeed there when the fighting of the war was so bad at St. Charles. We stayed in Texas till the surrender, then we all come back in lots of wagons. I was sick, but they put me on a little bed, and me and all the little children rode in a "Jersey" that one of the old Negro mammies drove, along behind the wagons, and our young master, Colonel Bob Chaney, rode a great big black horse. Oh! he nice-looking on that horse! Every once and a while he'd ride back to the last wagon to see if everything was all right. I remember how scared us children was when we crossed the Red River. Aunt Mandy said, "We crossing you old Red River today, but we not going to cross you any more, 'cause we are going home now, back to Arkansas." That day when we stopped to cook our dinner I picked up a lot little blackjack acorns, and when my mammy saw them she said, "Throw them things down, child. They'll make you wormy." I cried because I thought they were chinquapins. I begged my daddy to let's go back to Texas, but he said, "No! No! We going with our white folks." My mammy and daddy belonged to Colonel Jesse Chaney, much of a gentleman, and his wife, Miss Sallie, was the best mistress anybody ever had. She was a Christian. I can hear her praying yet! She wouldn't let one of her slaves hit a tap on Sunday. They must rest and go to church. They had preaching at the cabin of some one of the slaves, and in the summertime sometimes they had it out in the shade under the trees. Yes, and the slaves on each plantation had their own church. They didn't go gallivanting over the neighborhood or country like niggers do now. Colonel Chaney had lots and lots of slaves, and all their houses were in a row, all one-room cabins. Everything happened in that one room—birth, sickness, death, and everything, but in them days niggers kept their houses clean and their door yards too. These houses where they lived was called "the quarters." I used to love to walk down by that row of houses. It looked like a town, and late of an evening as you'd go by the doors you could smell meat a-frying, coffee making, and good things cooking. We were fed good and had plenty clothes to keep us dry and warm.

Along about time for the surrender, Colonel Jess, our master, took sick and died with some kind of head trouble. Then Colonel Bob, our young master, took care of his mama and the slaves. All the grown folks went to the field to work, and the little children would be left at a big room called the nursing-home. All us little ones would be nursed and fed by an old mammy, Aunt Mandy. She was too old to go to the field, you know. We wouldn't see our mammy and daddy from early in the morning till night when their work was done, then they'd go by Aunt Mandy's and get their children and go home till work time in the morning.

Some of the slaves were house Negroes. They didn't go to work in the fields. They each one had their own job around the house, barn, orchard, milkhouse, and things like that.

When washday come, Lord, the pretty white clothes! It would take three or four women a-washing all day.

When two of the slaves wanted to get married, they'd dress up nice as they could and go up to the big house, and the master would marry them. They'd stand up before him, and he'd read out of a book called *The Discipline* and say, "Thou shalt love the Lord thy God with all thy heart, all thy strength, with all thy might and thy neighbor as thyself." Then he'd say they were man and wife and tell them to live right and be honest and kind to each other. All the slaves would be there too, seeing the wedding.

Our Miss Sallie was the sweetest best thing in the world! She was so good and kind to everybody, and she loved her slaves, too. I can remember when Uncle Tony died how she cried! Uncle Tony Wadd was Miss Sallie's favorite servant. He stayed in a little house in the yard and made fires for her, brought in wood and water, and just waited on the house. He was a little black man and white-headed as cotton, when he died. Miss Sallie told the niggers when they come to take him to the graveyard, to let her know when they got him in his coffin, and when they sent and told her she come out with all the little white children, her little grandchildren, to see Uncle Tony. She just cried and stood for a long time looking at him, then she said, "Tony, you have been a good and faithful servant." Then the Negro men walked and carried him to the graveyard out in a big grove in the field. Every plantation had its own graveyard and buried its own folks and slaves right on the place.

If all slaves had belonged to white folks like ours, there wouldn't been any freedom wanted.

HOW TO TELL THE DAVIS FROM THE BETHEA NEGROES

I tell you when I come up, it the Lord's truth, I ain't know nothing but a decent living all the time. My old missus was a dear old soul, and I been raise that way. I hear talk 'bout how some of the white folks would 'bout torture they niggers to death sometimes, but never didn't see my white folks allow nothing like that. They would whip they niggers that run away and stay in the woods, but not so worser. No, ma'am, my missus wouldn't allow no slashing round 'bout where she was. I remember my boss had one of my old missus' niggers up there in the yard one morning and say he was gwine whip him, and my missus say, "John C., you let my nigger alone." You see, my missus had her niggers and then Old Boss had his niggers 'cause when Old Missus been marry Massa John C. Bethea, she had brought her share of niggers from where she was raise in the country. It been like this: Old Missus' father had scratch the pen for everyone of his children to have so many niggers apiece for they portion of his property so long as they would look after them and treat them good. Then if there been talk that them children never do what he say do, they was to take them niggers right back to they old massa's home. But, child, they never didn't take no niggers away from my old missus 'cause she sure took care of them. Stuck to her niggers till she died.

I remember just as good there been two long row of nigger house up in the quarter, and the Bethea niggers been stay in the row on one side and the Davis niggers been stay in the row on the other side. And, honey, there been so much difference in the row on this side and the row on that side. My God, child, you could go through there and spot the Sara Davis niggers from the Bethea niggers time you see them. Wa'n't no trouble no time. All Old Missus' niggers had they brush pile 'side they house to sun they beds on and dry they washing 'cause my missus would see to it herself that they never kept no nasty living. We was raise decent, honey, and that how come me and my children is that way to this very day. There that child in the house now, she does put fresh sheet on all us bed every week just like they was white people's bed. You see, if you raise that way, you ain't gwine never be no other way. Yes, ma'am, my old missus sure took time to learn her niggers right. Honey, both these hands here was raise not to steal. I been cook for heap of these white folks 'bout here that been left everything right wide open with me and ain't nobody never hear none of them complain 'bout losing nothing to this day. No, ma'am, ain't nobody never didn't turn no key on me. I remember, if my old missus would hear talk that we been bother something that didn't belong to us, she would whip us and say, "I'm not mad, but you children have got to grow up some day, and you might have to suffer worse than this if you don't learn better while you young."

I WAS HER FAVORITE CHILD

Yes, ma'am, I remember all 'bout slavery time just as good as I know you this morning. Remember the first time them Yankees come there, I was setting down in the chimney corner, and my mammy was giving me my breakfast. Remember I been setting there with my milk and my bowl of hominy, and I hear my old grandmammy come a-running in from out the yard and say all the sky was blue as indigo with the Yankees coming right there over the hill then. Say she see more Yankees than could ever cover up all the premises 'bout there. Then I hear my missus scream and come a-running with a lapful of silver and tell my grandmammy to hurry and sew that up in the feather bed 'cause them Yankees was mighty apt to destroy all they valuables. Old Missus tell all the colored people to get away, get away and take care of themselves, and tell we children to get back to the chimney corner 'cause she couldn't protect us noways no longer. Yes, honey, I was a little child setting there in that chimney corner listening to all that scampering 'bout, and I remember that day just as good as it had been this day right here.

Oh, my God, them Yankees never bring nothing but trouble and destructiveness when they come here, child. I remember I hear tell that my old stepfather been gone to the mill to grind some corn, and when he was coming down the road, two big Yankees jump out the bushes 'side the road and tell him stop there. He say they tell him if he want to save his neck, he better get off that ox right then and get away from there. He say he been so scared he make for the woods fast as he could get there and tell that he lay down with knots under his head many a night 'fore he would venture to come out from that woods. Never hear tell of his ox and corn no more neither. Oh, honey, my old missus was a dear old soul and didn't none of her colored people have no mind to want to leave there no time.

We children never didn't know nothing 'bout no hard times in that day and time. Seems like the Lord had just open up and fix the way for us to have everything we want. Oh, honey, we children never been harness up in no little bit of place to play like these children 'bout here these days. We had all the big fields and the pretty woods to wander round and 'bout and make us playhouse in. Seems like the Lord had made the little streams just right for we children to play in and all kind of the prettiest flowers to come up right down 'side the paths us little feet had made there, but that wasn't nothing. There was flowers scatter 'bout everywhere you look in the woods and all kind of birds and squirrels and rabbits and, honey, they was live playthings. That how come we been so satisfy. I here to tell you my old missus was a dear old soul, and we children sure had a fine time coming up. She didn't never have her niggers cut up and slashed up no time. She was good to us, and we stuck to her.

In the morning 'bout this time, me and my missus would take a walk in the woods down by the creek. I remember I would be there with my mammy and Old Missus would say, "Judy, where Hester? I want her to take a walk with me this morning." I been 'bout five or six years old then, and I would get tired. I say, "Mittie, I tired, I tired." She say, "Well, set down and rest awhile." I remember there been a big old sweet gum tree setting there 'side the creek that had a place hollow out in it that looked just like a chair been made there. Old Missus would set down there and take me right down 'side her and stay there till we was rested. I go with her one day when the creek been rise way up high and there been a heap of water in the road. I say, "Mittie, I scared, I scared." She tell me there couldn't nothing hurt me, and I remember we went on and see a big black fish just a-jumping in the road. Old Missus say, "Hester, catch him, catch him." I say, "Mittie, I can't, I can't, I scared." I recollects she caught that fish and tied it with her garter and let me drag it home and tell my mammy cook it for my supper. Honey, that been a day. Never couldn't forget 'bout that.

I remember me and my old missus went to the graveyard one morning, and we found a runaway nigger hiding in a house that was standing in the grave-yard. That was an old, old slavery-time house to the graveyard, and people would go there and hide. It was just like this, honey: Generally people in the country be scared of a graveyard and wouldn't nobody go there to hunt them. I remember just as good when he see us, he squatted down right low. I say, "Mittie, looka, looka, I scared." Then she say, "Hester, I notice the clouds are growing more and more gray, and I fear we better be getting back home. I never like for a rain to catch us away from home." I know Missus say that to make me think she wasn't scared, but I never had no mind to tell her I know what been the matter that she want to hurry home. Yessum, that old house in the graveyard was one of them kind that been setting high off the ground. That the kind of house they cook underneath in slavery time. Course it was closed up when they had the kitchen down there. No, ma'am, Massa never didn't go to walk with Old Missus. He was seeing over all the plantation and Missus didn't have but one son, little John C. Bethea, and he was gone off to school. No, child, Old Missus wouldn't never allow nobody to go with her but just me.

You see, it was like this: My old missus been name Sara Davis 'fore she marry Massa John Bethea, and my mammy and grandmammy had come up with her in the country and that how come there been such a feeling 'twixt them. Yes, ma'am, I love my old missus better than I ever love honey and flour bread 'cause she was a dear old soul. You see, she was always looking to me to do something for her. Say I was her favorite child to pick up things 'bout the house and yard for her. She always had my mammy preserve me and Bob as her favorite house children. She wouldn't never allow none of them other nigger children to come nowhere round where she was 'cause them what went 'bout the missus never didn't stay to the nigger quarter no time. My grandmammy, she had to get all them other plantation children together and see that they do what the missus look for them to do.

My God, child, people never know nothing but to go to church on the big Sunday in that day and time. No, ma'am, they know that been they massa's rule, and didn't nobody have no mind to question nothing 'bout it. My old missus was a dear old soul, and she would see to it that all her niggers wash and iron and cook on Saturday 'cause she never allow no work gwine on round where she was when Sunday come, be that she know 'bout it. I remember my old massa and missus used to ride to church in they big black carriage, and they always would carry me and Bob right there in the carriage with them somehow another. Stuff us down 'tween the seats somewhere. I recollects just as bright as the stars be shining Old Missus would carry me and Bob to the same little seats we been sit in every Sunday, and then she and Old Massa would go to they certain pew in the front part of the church. Oh, honey, that was a day for them niggers to walk the road to church. That was a picnic for them. Oh, they never had to walk but 'bout four miles. Why, darling, I used to walk fourteen miles to church every Sunday and didn't think nothing 'bout it. I think that was the finest thing I know for me and my grandfather to walk fourteen miles to church over there on the hill every Sunday. I remember we would set out 'bout time the sun would be rising. Yes, ma'am, we would carry our dinner with us 'cause we know we would be till night getting back home again. It just like I been tell you, the peoples sure cook they dinner for Sunday on Saturday in that day and time. That been a mighty good thing, child, been a mighty good thing. Honey, it been the rule to follow what the Bible say do in that day and time and now it seem like the rule must be, Do like you see the other fellow is doing. Yes, ma'am, if you ain't been to church in that day and time, you sure had to report how come you ain't been there.

Yes, ma'am, I remember just as good as it was yesterday what they say when freedom come here. Oh, I hates to think 'bout that day till this one. Remember they call all the niggers up to the yard and I hear Old Missus say, "You don't no more belong to me. You can go if you want to and if you want to, you can stay." I say, "Yes, ma'am, I do want to stay, I ain't gwine leave you." That was my white mammy, and I stay there long as she live too. Didn't want no better living than I was getting right there. It been a Paradise, be that what I calls it.

I SOMETIMES WISH I COULD BE BACK ON THE OLD PLACE

. . . Then there was a white woman who was kilt by a nigger boy 'cause she beat him for sicking a dog on a fine milch cow. He was the meanest nigger boy I ever seed. I'll never forgits the way them white mens treated him after he done had his trial. They drug him through the town behind a hoss, and made him walk over sharp stones with his bare feets, that bled like somebody done cut 'em with a knife. They never give him no water all that day and kept him out in the boiling sun till they got ready to hang him. When they got ready to hang him, they put him up on a stand and chunked rocks at his naked body; they threw gravel in his eyes and broke his ribs with big rocks. Then they put a rope around his neck and strung him up till his eyes pop outen his head. I knowed it was a blessing for him to die.

But all in all, white folks, then was the really happy days for us niggers. Course we didn't have the 'vantages that we has now, but there was something back there that we ain't got now, and that's security. Yes, sir, we had somebody to go to when we was in trouble. We had a massa that would fight for us and help us and laugh with us and cry with us. We had a mistress that would nurse us when we was sick and comfort us when we had to be punished. I sometimes wish I could be back on the old place. I can see the coolhouse now, packed with fresh butter and milk and cream. I can see the spring down amongst the willows and the water a-trickling down between little rocks. I can hear the turkeys a-gobbling in the yard and the chickens a-running around in the sun and shuffling in the dust. I can see the bend in the creek just below our house, and the cows as they come to drink in the shallow water and gits their feets cool.

Yes, sir, white folks, you ain't never seed nothing like it, so you can't tell the joy you gits from looking for dewberries and a-hunting guinea eggs and setting in the shade of a peach tree, reaching up and pulling off a ripe peach and eating it slow. You ain't never seed your people gathered 'bout and singing in the moonlight or heared the lark at the break of day. You ain't never walked acrost a frosty field in the early morning and gone to the big house to build a fire for your mistress and when she wake up slow have her say to you: "Well, how's my little nigger today?"

*"God ain't ax about your color, God ax about your heart." Ben
Horry, age 85, near Murrells Inlet, South Carolina. Born
December 13, 1852, Waccamaw Neck, South Carolina.*

"Nowadays when I hear folks a-growling and a-grumbling 'bout not having this and that. . . ." Fannie Moore, age 88, Asheville, North Carolina. Born September 1, 1849, Moore, South Carolina. Slave in South Carolina.

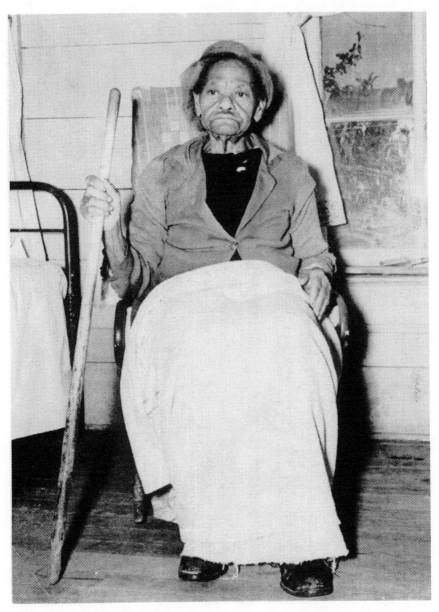

"I got the scars on my body to show to this day." Mary Reynolds,
age 105, Dallas, Texas. Born Black River, Louisiana.
Slave in Louisiana.

"I never know nothing but work." Sarah Gudger, age 121,
Asheville, North Carolina. Born September 15, 1816, near Old
Fort, McDowell County, North Carolina.

"I was one of the house servants." Charity Anderson, age 101,
Toulminville, Alabama. Born at Bell's Landing
on the Alabama River.

"Time I was ten years old I was making a regular hand 'hind the plow." Walter Calloway, age 89, Birmingham, Alabama. Born 1848, Richmond, Virginia. Slave in Virginia and Alabama.

"I was worth a heap to Marse George 'cause I had so many
children." Tempie Herndon Durham, age 103,
Durham, North Carolina.

"The souls is all white or black, 'pending on the man's life and not on his skin." Anthony Dawson, age 105, Tulsa, Oklahoma. Born July 25, 1832, near Greenville, Pitt County, North Carolina. Slave in North Carolina.

"I'm happy and satisfied now, and I hopes I see a million years to come." Richard Toler, age about 100, Cincinnati, Ohio. Born near Lynchburg, Campbell County, Virginia. Slave in Virginia.

"I ain't scared of nothing." Emma Crockett, age about 80, near
Livingston, Sumter County, Alabama.

"I belong to a full-blood Creek Indian, and I didn't know nothing but Creek talk long after the Civil War." Lucinda Davis, age about 89, Tulsa, Oklahoma.

"*I been drug about and put through the shackles so bad I done forgot some of my children's names.*" Laura Clark, age 87, near Livingston, Sumter County, Alabama. Born in North Carolina and brought to Alabama as a child.

"Mammy was a field hand. . . . She hated housework—like me."
Mollie Williams, age 84, near Terry, Hinds County, Mississippi.
Born September 15, 1853, near Utica, Mississippi.

"My mammy was a fine weaver; this is her spinning wheel."
Lucindy Lawrence Jurdon, age 79, Lee County, Alabama. Born
1858, Macon County, Georgia. Slave in Georgia.

*"I worked in the house; Mistress wa'n't going to let nobody
wash them julep glasses but me." Matilda Pugh Daniel, age 96,
near Eufaula, Barbour County, Alabama.*

"I can tell you the life of the average slave was not rosy." Martin Jackson, age 90, San Antonio, Texas. Born 1847, Victoria County, Texas.

Going High, Going Slow

At the auction the man say, "Going high, going mighty slow, a little while to go. Bid 'em in, bid 'em in. The sun am high, the sun am hot, us got to git home tonight."

TWO SELLINGS THAT DAY

Then they says they gwine sell me, 'cause Miss Nancy's father-in-law dies and they got rid of some of us. She didn't want to sell me, so she tell me to be sassy and no one would buy me. They takes me to Houston and to the market, and a man call George Fraser sells the slaves. The market was a open house, more like a shed. We all stands to one side till our turn comes. They wasn't nothing else you could do.

They stands me up on a block of wood, and a man bid me in. I felt mad. You see, I was young then, too young to know better. I don't know what they sold me for, but the man what bought me made me open my mouth while he looks at my teeth. They done all us that-a-way, sells us like you sell a hoss. Then my old master bids me goodby and tries to give me a dog, but I 'members what Miss Nancy done say and I sassed him and slapped the dog out of his hand. So the man what bought me say, "When one o'clock come, you got to sell her 'gain, she's sassy. If she done me that way I'd kill her." So they sells me twice the same day. They was two sellings that day.

OLD MAN DENMAN SAID NOT TO FRET

Old Man Denman am the great one for 'viding he property, and when Miss Lizzie marries with Mr. Creame Cramer, which am her dead sister's husband, Old Man Denman give me and two my sisters to Miss Lizzie, and he gives two more my sisters to he son. Us goes with Miss Lizzie to the Cramer place and lives in the back yard in a little room by the back door.

Everything fine and nice there till one day Miss Lizzie say to me, "Julia, go down to the well and fetch me some water," and I goes and I seed in the road a heap of men all in gray and riding hosses, coming our way. I runs back to the house and calls Miss Lizzie. She say, "What you scared for?" I tells her 'bout them men, and she say they ain't gwine hurt me none; they just wants some water. I goes back to the well and heared 'em talk 'bout a fight. I goes back to the house, and some of the mens comes to the gate and says to Mr. Cramer, "How're you, Creame?" He say, "I's all right in my health, but I ain't so good in my mind." They says, "What the matter, Creame?" He say, "I want to be in the fight so bad."

When they goes, I asks Miss Lizzie what they fighting 'bout, and she say it am 'bout money. That all I knows. Right after that Mr. Cramer goes, and we don't never see him no more. Word come back from the fighting he makes some the big high mens mad and they puts chains round he ankles and make him dig a stump in the hot sun. He ain't used to that, and it give him fever to the brain, and he dies.

When Mr. Cramer goes 'way, Miss Lizzie takes us all and goes back to Old Man Denman's. The soldiers used to pass, and all the whooping and hollering and carrying on, you ain't never heared the likes! They hollers, "Who-o-o-o, Old Man Denman, how's your chickens?" And they chunks and throws at 'em till they cripples 'em up and puts 'em in they bags, for cooking. Old Man Denman cusses at 'em something powerful.

My sister Mandy and me am down in the woods a good far piece from the house, and us keeps hearing a noise. My brother comes down and finds me and say, "Come git your dinner." When I gits there dinner am top the gate post, and he say they's soldiers in the woods and they has been persecuting a old woman on a mule. She was a nigger woman. I gits so scared I can't eat my dinner. I ain't got no heart for victuals. My brother say, "Wait for Pa; he coming with the mule, and he'll hide you out." I gits on the mule front of Pa, and us pass through the soldiers, and they grabs at us and says, "Gimme the gal, gimme the gal." Pa says I faints plumb 'way.

Us heared guns shooting round and 'bout all the time. Seems like they fit every time they git a chance. Old Man Denman's boy gits kilt, and two my sisters he property, and they don't know what to do, 'cause they has to be somebody's property and they ain't no one to 'heritance 'em. They has to go to the auction, but Old Man Denman say not to fret. At the auction the man say, "Going high, going mighty slow, a little while to go. Bid 'em in, bid 'em in. The sun am high, the sun am hot, us got to git home tonight." An old friend of Old Man Denman's hollers out he buys for William Blackstone. Us all come home, and my sisters, too, and Old Man Denman laugh big and say, "My name always been William Blackstone Denman."

SHE NEVER GOT TO KEEP HER BABIES

My mother told me that he owned a woman who was the mother of several children, and when her babies would get about a year or two of age he'd sell them, and it would break her heart. She never got to keep them. When her fourth baby was born and was about two months old, she just studied all the time about how she would have to give it up, and one day she said, "I just decided I'm not going to let Old Master sell this baby; he just ain't going to do it." She got up and give it something out of a bottle, and pretty soon it was dead. Course didn't nobody tell on her, or he'd of beat her nearly to death.

DIANA AND HER BABY

I heard the woman I lived with, a woman named Diana Wagner, tell how her mistress said, "Come on, Diana, I want you to go with me down the road a piece." And she went with her, and they got to a place where there was a whole lot of people. They were putting them up on a block and selling them just like cattle. She had a little nursing baby at home, and she broke away from her mistress and them and said, "I can't go off and leave my baby." And they had to git some men and throw her down and hold her to keep her from going back to the house. They sold her away from her baby boy. They didn't let her go back to see him again. But she heard from him after he became a young man. Some one of her friends that knowed her and knowed she was sold away from her baby met up with this boy and got to questioning him about his mother. The white folks had told him his mother's name and all. He told them, and they said, "Boy, I know your mother. She's down in Newport." And he said, "Gimme her address and I'll write to her and see if I can hear from her." And he wrote. And the white people said they heard such a hollering and shouting going on they said, "What's the matter with Diana?" And they came over to see what was happening. And she said, "I got a letter from my boy that was sold from me when he was a nursing baby." She had me write a letter to him. I did all her writing for her, and he came to see her. I didn't get to see him. I was away when he come. She said she was willing to die that the Lord let her live to see her baby again and had taken care of him through all these years.

ELIZA AND THE MAN FROM NEW YORK

I saw slaves sold. I can see that old block now. My cousin Eliza was a pretty girl, really good-looking. Her master was her father. When the girls in the big house had beaus coming to see 'em, they'd ask, "Who is that pretty gal?" So they decided to git rid of her right away. The day they sold her will always be remembered. They stripped her to be bid off and looked at. I wasn't allowed to stand in the crowd. I was laying down under a big bush. The man that bought Eliza was from New York. The Negroes had made up 'nough money to buy her off theyself, but they wouldn't let that happen. There was a man bidding for her who was a Swedelander. He always bid for the good-looking colored gals and bought 'em for his own use. He ask the man from New York, "What you gonna do with her when you git her?" The man from New York said, "None of your damn business, but you ain't got money 'nough to buy her." When the man from New York had done bought her, he said, "Eliza, you are free from now on." She left and went to New York with him. Mama and Eliza both cried when she was being showed off, and Master told 'em to shut up before he knocked their brains out.

I DON'T BELIEVE IN SLAVE TRAFFIC

My parents was Julia Ann Hodge and Cairo Hodge. I don't know my mother's last owners. When I was about eight years old, I was sold to Ben Cowen. When I was thirteen years old, I was sold to Master Anderson Harrison. My brothers, Sam and Washington, never were sold. Me and Sam Hodge, my brother, was in the war together. We struck up and knowed one another. A man bought Mama that lived at Selma, Alabama. I never seen her again to know her. After I was mustered out, I went to Birmingham, where she was drove and sold, in search of her. I heard she was taken to Selma. I went there. I give out hunting for her. It was about dusk. I saw a woman standing in the door. I asked her to tell me where I could stay. She said, "You can stay here tonight." I went in, hung my overcoat up. I started to the saloon. I met her husband with a basket on his arm coming home. I told him who I was. We went to get a drink. I offered him sherry, but he took whiskey. I got a pint of brandy, two apples, two oranges, for his wife and two little boys. I spent two nights there and two and a half days there, with my own mother but neither of us knew it then.

Fourteen years later Wash wrote to me giving me the address. I told him about this, and he said it was Mama. He told her about it. She jumped up and shouted and fell dead. I never seen her but that one time after I was sold the first time. I was about eight years old then. She had eighteen of us boys and one girl,

Diana, and then the half-brothers I seen at Selma. I had eleven brothers took off in a drove at one time and sold. They was older than I was. I don't know what become of them. I never seen my papa after I was sold. Diana died in Knoxville, Tennessee, after freedom. I seen better times in slavery than I've ever seen since, but I don't believe in slave traffic—that being sold.

FOUNDLING

Who I is, how old I is, and where I is born, I don't know. But Massa Buford told me how during the war a slave trader name William Hamilton come to Village Creek, where Massa Buford live. That trader was on his way south with my folks and a lot of other slaves, taking 'em somewheres to sell. He camped by Massa Buford's plantation and asks him, "Can I leave this little nigger here till I comes back?" Massa Buford say, "Yes," and the trader say he'll be back in 'bout three weeks, soon as he sells all the slaves. He must still be selling 'em, 'cause he never comes back so far, and there I am and my folks am took on, and I is too little to 'member 'em, so I never knows my pappy and mammy. Massa Buford says the trader comes from Missouri, but if I is born there I don't know.

The only thing I 'members 'bout all that am there am lots of crying when they tooks me 'way from my mammy. That something I never forgits.

STOLEN AND SOLD

I

The nigger stealers done stole me and my mammy outen the Choctaw Nation, up in the Indian Territory, when I was 'bout three years old. Brother Knox, Sis Hannah, and my mammy and her two stepchildren was down on the river washing. The nigger stealers driv up in a big carriage, and Mammy just thought nothing, 'cause the ford was near there and people going on the road stopped to water the horses and rest awhile in the shade. Bimeby, a man coaxes the two biggest children to the carriage and give them some kind of candy. Other children sees this and goes, too. Two other men was walking round smoking and getting closer to Mammy all the time. When he can, the man in the carriage got the two big stepchildren in with him, and me and Sis clumb in too, to see how come. Then the man holler, "Git the old one and let's git from here." With that the two big men grab Mammy, and she fought and screeched and bit and cry, but they hit her on the head with something and drug her in and throwed her on the floor. The big children begin to fight for Mammy, but one of the men hit 'em hard, and off they driv, with the horses under whip.

This was near a place called Boggy Depot. They went down the Red River, 'cross the river and on down in Louisian' to Shreveport. Down in Louisian' us was put on what they call the block and sold to the highest bidder. My mammy and her three children brung $3,000 flat. The stepchildren was sold to somebody else.

II

When Massa Langford was ruint, and they going take the store 'way from him, they was trouble, plenty of that. One day Massa send me down to he brother's place. I was there two days, and then the missy tell me to go to the fence. There was two white men in a buggy, and one of 'em say, "I thought she bigger than that." Then he asks me, "Betty, can you cook?" I tells him I been cook-helper two-three month, and he say, "You git dressed and come on down three mile to the other side the post office." So I gits my little bundle, and when I gits there he say, "Gal, you want to go 'bout twenty-six mile and help cook at the boarding-house?" He tries to make me believe I won't be gone a long time, but when I gits in the buggy they tells me Massa Langford done lost everything and he have to hide out he niggers for to keep he credickers from gitting 'em. Some of the niggers he hides in the woods, but he stole me from my sweet missy and sell me so them credickers can't git me.

When we gits to the crossroads, there the massa and a nigger man. That another slave he gwine to sell, and he hate to sell us so bad he can't look us in the eye. They puts us niggers inside the buggy, so iffen the credickers comes along they can't see us.

Finally, these slave speculators puts the nigger man and me on the train and takes us to Memphis, and when we gits there, they takes us to the nigger trader's yard. We gits there at breakfast time and waits for the boat they calls the "Ohio" to git there. The boat just ahead of this "Ohio," Old Captain Fabra's boat, was 'stroyed, and that delay our boat two hours. When it come, they was 258 niggers out of them nigger yards in Memphis what gits on that boat. They puts the niggers upstairs and goes down the river far as Vicksburg, that was the place, and then us gits offen the boat and gits on the train 'gain and that time we goes to New Orleans.

I's satisfy then I lost my people and ain't never going to see them no more in this world, and I never did. They has three big trader yard in New Orleans, and I hear the traders say that town twenty-five mile square. I ain't like it so well, 'cause I ain't like it 'bout that big river. We hears some of 'em say there's gwine to throw a long war, and us all think what they buy us for if we's gwine to be sot free. Some was still buying niggers every fall, and us think it too funny they kept on filling up when they gwine to be emptying out soon.

They have big sandbars and planks fix round the nigger yards, and they have watchmans to keep them from running 'way in the swamp. Some of the niggers they have just picked up on the road, they steals them. They calls them "wagon boy" and "wagon gal." They has one big mulatto boy they stole 'long the road that way, and he massa find out 'bout him and come and git him and take him 'way. And a woman what was a seamster, a man what knowed her seed her in the pen, and he done told her massa, and he come right down and git her. She sure was proud to git out. She was stole from 'long the road, too. You sees, if they could steal the niggers and sell 'em for the good money, them traders could make plenty money that way.

At last Colonel Fortescue, he buy me and kept me. He a fighter in the Mexican War, and he come to New Orleans to buy he slaves. He takes me up the Red River to Shreveport and then by the buggy to Liberty, in Texas.

The Colonel, he a good massa to us. He 'lows us to work the patch of ground for ourselves, and maybe have a pig or a couple of chickens for ourselves, and he always make out to give us plenty to eat.

HE SOLD HIM OVER AND OVER

There was a white man live close to us, but over in Louisian'. He had raised him a great big black man what brung fancy price on the block. The black man sure love that white man. This white man would sell Old John—that's the black man's name—on the block to some man from Georgia or other place far off. Then after while the white man would steal Old John back and bring him home and feed him good, then sell him again. After he had sold Old John some lot of times, he coaxed Old John off in the swamp one day, and Old John found dead several days later. The white folks said that the owner kilt him, 'cause a dead nigger won't tell no tales.

OLD PINCHBACK

I never knowed my age till after the war, when I's set free the second time, and then Master gits out a big book, and it shows I's twenty-five year old. It shows I's twelve when I is bought and $800 is paid for me. That $800 was stolen money, 'cause I was kidnaped, and this is how it come.

My mammy was owned by John Williams in Petersburg, in Virginia, and I come born to her on that plantation. Then my father set 'bout to git me free, 'cause he a full-blooded Indian and done some big favor for a big man high up in the courts, and he gits me set free, and then Master Williams laughs and calls me "free boy."

Then one day along come a Friday, and that a unlucky star day, and I playing round the house, and Master Williams come up and say, "Delia, will you 'low Jim walk down the street with me?" My mammy say, "All right. Jim, you be a good boy," and that the last time I ever heared her speak or ever see her. We walks down where the houses grows close together, and pretty soon comes to the slave market. I ain't seed it 'fore, but when Master Williams says, "Git up on the block," I got a funny feeling, and I knows what has happened. I's sold to Master John Pinchback, and he had the St. Vitus dance, and he likes to make he niggers suffer to make up for his squirming and twisting, and he the biggest devil on earth.

We leaves right away for Texas and goes to Master's ranch in Columbus. It was owned by him and a man call Wright, and when we gits there I's put to work without nothing to eat. That night I makes up my mind to run away, but the next day they takes me and the other niggers to look at the dogs and chooses me to train the dogs with. I's told I had to play I running away and to run five mile in any way and then climb a tree. One of the niggers tells me kind of nice to climb as high in that tree as I could if I didn't want my body tore off my legs. So I runs a good five miles and climbs up in the tree where the branches is getting small.

I sits there a long time and then sees the dogs coming. When they gits under the tree, they sees me and starts barking. After that I never got thinking of running away.

Time goes on, and the war come along, but everything goes on like it did. Some niggers dies, but more was born, 'cause Old Pinchback sees to that. He breeds niggers as quick as he can, 'cause that money for him. No one had no say who he have for wife. But the nigger husbands wasn't the only ones that keeps up having children, 'cause the masters and the drivers takes all the nigger gals they wants. Then the children was brown, and I seed one clear white one, but they slaves just the same.

The end of that war comes, and Old Pinchback says, "You niggers all come to the big house in the morning." He tells us we is free, and he opens his book and gives us all a name and tells us where we comes from and how old we is, and says he pay us 40 cents a day to stay with him. I stays 'bout a year, and there's no big change. The same houses and some got whipped, but nobody got nailed to a tree by the ears, like they used to. Finally Old Pinchback dies, and when he buried the lightning come and split the grave and the coffin wide open.

ROSE AND RUFUS

What I say am the facts. If I's one day old, I's way over ninety, and I's born in Bell County, right here in Texas, and am owned by Massa William Black. He owns Mammy and Pappy, too. Massa Black has a big plantation, but he has more niggers than he need for work on that place, 'cause he am a nigger trader. He trade and buy and sell all the time.

Massa Black am awful cruel, and he whip the colored folks and works 'em hard and feed 'em poorly. We-uns have for rations the corn meal and milk and 'lasses and some beans and peas and meat once a week. We-uns have to work in the field every day from daylight till dark, and on Sunday we-uns do us washing. Church? Shucks, we-uns don't know what that mean.

I has the correct memorandum of when the war start. Massa Black sold we-uns right then. Mammy and Pappy powerful glad to git sold, and they and I is put on the block with 'bout ten other niggers. When we-uns gits to the trading block, there lots of white folks there what come to look us over. One man shows the interest in Pappy. Him named Hawkins. He talk to Pappy, and Pappy talk to him and say, "Them my woman and childs. Please buy all of us and have mercy on we-uns." Massa Hawkins say, "That gal am a likely-looking nigger; she am portly and strong. But three am more than I wants, I guesses."

The sale start, and 'fore long Pappy am put on the block. Massa Hawkins wins the bid for Pappy, and when Mammy am put on the block, he wins the bid for her. Then there am three or four other niggers sold before my time comes. Then Massa Black calls me to the block, and the auction man say, "What am I offer for this portly, strong young wench. She's never been 'bused and will make the good breeder."

I wants to hear Massa Hawkins bid, but him say nothing. Two other men am bidding 'gainst each other, and I sure has the worriment. There am tears coming down my cheeks 'cause I's being sold to some man that would make separation from my mammy. One man bids $500, and the auction man ask, "Do I hear more? She am gwine at $500." Then someone say, "$525," and the auction man say, "She am sold for $525 to Massa Hawkins." Am I glad and 'cited! Why, I's quivering all over.

Massa Hawkins takes we-uns to his place, and it am a nice plantation. Lots better than Massa Black's. There is 'bout fifty niggers what is growed and lots of children. The first thing Massa do when we-uns gits home am give we-uns rations and a cabin. You must believe this nigger when I says them rations a feast for us. There plenty meat and tea and coffee and white flour. I's never tasted white flour and coffee, and Mammy fix some biscuits and coffee. Well, the biscuits was yum, yum, yum to me, but the coffee I doesn't like.

The quarters am pretty good. There am twelve cabins all made from logs and a table and some benches and bunks for sleeping and a fireplace for cooking and the heat. There am no floor, just the ground.

Massa Hawkins am good to he niggers and not force 'em work too hard. There am as much difference 'tween him and Old Massa Black in the way of treatment as 'twixt the Lord and the devil. Massa Hawkins 'lows he niggers have reasonable parties and go fishing, but we-uns am never tooken to church and has no books for larning. There am no education for the niggers.

There am one thing Massa Hawkins does to me what I can't shunt from my mind. I knows he don't do it for meanness, but I always holds it 'gainst him. What he done am force me to live with that nigger, Rufus, 'gainst my wants.

After I been at he place 'bout a year, the massa come to me and say, "You gwine live with Rufus in that cabin over yonder. Go fix it for living." I's 'bout sixteen year old and has no larning, and I's just ignomus child. I's thought that him mean for me to tend the cabin for Rufus and some other niggers. Well, that am start the pestigation for me.

I's took charge of the cabin after work am done and fixes supper. Now, I don't like that Rufus, 'cause he a bully. He am big and 'cause he so, he think everybody do what him say. We-uns has supper, then I goes here and there talking, till I's ready for sleep, and then I gits in the bunk. After I's in, that nigger come and crawl in the bunk with me 'fore I knows it. I says, "What you means, you fool nigger?" He say for me to hush the mouth. "This am my bunk, too," he say.

"You's teched in the head. Git out," I's told him, and I puts the feet 'gainst him and give him a shove, and out he go on the floor 'fore he know what I's doing. That nigger jump up and he mad. He look like the wild bear. He starts for the bunk, and I jumps quick for the poker. It am 'bout three feet long, and when he comes at me I lets him have it over the head. Did that nigger stop in he tracks? I's say he did. He looks at me steady for a minute, and you could tell he thinking hard. Then he go and set on the bench and say, "Just wait. You thinks it am smart, but you am foolish in the head. They's gwine larn you something."

"Hush your big mouth and stay 'way from this nigger, that all I wants," I say, and just sets and hold that poker in the hand. He just sets, looking like the bull. There we-uns sets and sets for 'bout an hour, and then he go out, and I bars the door.

The next day I goes to the missy and tells her what Rufus wants, and Missy say that am the massa's wishes. She say, "You am the portly gal, and Rufus am the portly man. The massa wants you-uns for to bring forth portly children."

I's thinking 'bout what the missy say, but say to myself, "I's not gwine live with that Rufus." That night when him come in the cabin, I grabs the poker and sits on the bench and says, "Git 'way from me, nigger, 'fore I bust your brains out and stomp on them." He say nothing and git out.

The next day the massa call me and tell me, "Woman, I's pay big money for you, and I's done that for the cause I wants you to raise me childrens. I's put you to live with Rufus for that purpose. Now, if you doesn't want whipping at the stake, you do what I wants."

I thinks 'bout Massa buying me offen the block and saving me from being separated from my folks and 'bout being whipped at the stake. There it am. What am I's to do? So I 'cides to do as the massa wish, and so I yields.

When we-uns am given freedom, Massa Hawkins tells us we can stay and work for wages or share-crop the land. Some stays and some goes. My folks and me stays. We works the land on share for three years, then moved to other land near by. I stays with my folks till they dies.

If my memorandum am correct, it am 'bout thirty year since I come to Fort Worth. Here I cooks for white folks till I goes blind 'bout ten year ago.

I never marries, 'cause one 'sperience am 'nough for this nigger. After what I does for the massa, I's never wants no truck with any man. The Lord forgive this colored woman, but he have to 'scuse me and look for some others for to 'plenish the earth.

Praying to the Right Man

Iffen you was caught, they whipped you till you said, "Oh, pray, Master!" One day a man was saying, "Oh, pray, Master! Lord, have mercy!" They'd say, "Keep whipping that nigger, goddam him." He was whipped till he said, "Oh, pray, Master! I got enough." Then they said, "Let him up now, 'cause he's praying to the right man."

THE LORD RULED HEAVEN, BUT JIM SMITH RULED THE EARTH

My uncle, Ambus Carter, was a preacher on Marse Jim Smith's place. He belonged to Marse Jim during the war, and he never did leave him. After freedom come, most of Marse Jim's niggers left him, and then he had what they called chain-gang slaves. He paid 'em out of jail for 'em to work for him. And he let 'em have money all the time so they didn't never git out of debt with him. They had to stay there and work all the time, and if they didn't work he had 'em beat. He evermore did beat 'em if they got lazy, but if they worked good, he was good to 'em. Sometimes they tried to run away. They had dogs to trail 'em with, so they always cotched 'em, and then the whipping boss beat 'em most to death. It was awful to hear 'em hollering and begging for mercy. If they hollered, "Lord, have mercy!" Marse Jim didn't hear 'em, but if they cried, "Marse Jim, have mercy!" then he made 'em stop the beating. He say, "The Lord rule Heaven, but Jim Smith rule the earth."

HE STOMPED ON THE BODY

The whippings was done by the master, and the overseer just tell the old Doc about the troubles, like the old Doc say:

"You just watch the slaves and see they works and works hard, but don't lay on with the whip, because I is the only one who knows how to do it right!"

Maybe the old master was sickened of whippings from the stories the slaves told about the plantation that joined ours on the north.

If they ever was a living devil, that plantation was his home and the owner

— 170

was it! That's what the old slaves say, and when I tell you about it, see if I is right.

That man got so mean even the white folks was scared of him, 'specially if he was filled with drink. That's the way he was most of the time, just before the slaves was freed.

All the time we hear about slaves on that place getting whipped or being locked in the stock—that one of them things where your head and hands is fastened through holes in a wide board, and you stands there all the day and all the night—and sometimes we hears of them staying in the stock for three-four weeks if they tries to run away to the North.

Sometimes we hears about some slave who is shot by that man while he is wild with the drink. That's what I'm telling about now.

Don't nobody know what made the master mad at the old slave—one of the oldest on the place. Anyway, the master didn't whip him; instead of that he kills him with the gun and scares the others so bad most of 'em runs off and hides in the woods.

The drunk master just drags the old dead slave to the graveyard, which is down in the corner away from the growing crops, and hunts up two of the young boys, who was hiding in the barn. He takes them to dig the grave.

The master stands watching every move they make, the dead man lays there with his face to the sky, and the boys is so scared they could hardly dig. The master keeps telling them to hurry with the digging.

After while he tells them to stop and put the body in the grave. They wasn't no coffin, no box, for him. Just the old clothes that he wears in the fields.

But the grave was too short, and they start to digging some more, but the master stop them. He says to put back the body in the grave, and then he jumps into the grave hisself. Right on the dead he jumps and stomps till the body is mashed and twisted to fit the hole. Then the old nigger is buried.

WE LAUGHED AT HIS FUNERAL

My old master was Dave Giles, the meanest man that ever lived. He didn't have many slaves—my mammy, and me, and my sister, Uncle Bill, and Truman. He had owned my grandma, but he give her a bad whupping, and she never did git over it and died. We all done as much work as a dozen niggers—we knowed we had to.

I seen Old Master git mad at Truman, and he buckled him down across a barrel and whupped him till he cut the blood out of him, and then he rubbed salt and pepper in the raw places. It looked like Truman would die, it hurt so bad. I know that don't sound reasonable that a white man in a Christian community would do such a thing, but you can't realize how heartless he was.

People didn't know about it, and we dasn't tell for we knowed he'd kill us if we did. You must remember he owned us body and soul, and they wasn't anything we could do about it. Old Mistress and her three girls was mean to us to.

One time me and my sister was spinning, and Old Mistress went to the wellhouse and she found a chicken snake and killed it. She brought it back, and she throwed it around my sister's neck. She just laughed and laughed about it. She thought it was a big joke.

Old Master stayed drunk all the time. I reckon that is the reason he was so fetched mean. My, how we hated him! He finally killed hisself, drinking, and I remember Old Mistress called us in to look at him in his coffin. We all marched by him slow like, and I just happened to look up and caught my sister's eye, and we both just naturally laughed. Why shouldn't we? We was glad he was dead. It's a good thing we had our laugh for Old Mistress took us out and whupped us with a broomstick. She didn't make us sorry though.

I SAID I WAS GLAD SHE WAS DEAD

Me and Zack was raised up together. He was one of the old set of children. The baby in that set. I'd set on the log across a branch and wait till Zack would break open a biscuit and sop it in ham gravy and bring it to me after he et his breakfast. One morning the sun was so bright; he run down there crying, said his mama was dead. He never brought me no biscuit. He had just got up. I was five years old. I said I was glad. Emily was the cook, and she come down there and kicked me off the log and made my nose bleed. I cried and run home. My mother picked me up in her arms, took me in her lap, and asked me about it. I told her I was glad 'cause she kept that little cowhide and whupped me with it.

IF I WERE YOU AND YOU WERE ME

To whip me she put my head between the two fence rails, and she taken the cowhide whip and beat me until I couldn't sit down for a week. Sometimes she tied our hands around a tree and tied our neck to the tree with our face to the tree, and they would get behind us with that cowhide whip with a piece of lead tied to the end, and Lord, have mercy! child, I shouted when I wasn't happy. All I could say was, "Oh, pray, Mistress, pray!" That was our way to say "Lord, have mercy!" The last whipping Old Miss give me she tied me to a tree and oh, my Lord! Old Miss whipped me that day. That was the worst whipping I ever got in my life. I cried and bucked and hollered until I couldn't. I give up for dead, and she wouldn't stop. I stop crying and said to her, "Old Miss, if I were you and you were me, I wouldn't beat you this way." That struck Old Miss's heart, and she let me go, and she did not have the heart to beat me any more.

THE CHAIN AND THE BELL

My father took me away from my mother at age of six weeks old and gave me to my grandmother, who was real old at the time. Just before she died, she gave me back to my father, who was my mammy's master. He was a old bachelor and run a saloon, and he was white, but my mammy was a Negro. He was mean to me.

Finally my father let his sister take me and raise me with her children. She was good to me, but before he let her have me he willed I must wear a bell till I was twenty-one year old, strapped round my shoulders with the bell 'bout three feet from my head in a steel frame. That was for punishment for being born into the world a son of a white man and my mammy, a Negro slave. I wears this frame with the bell where I couldn't reach the clapper, day and night. I never knowed what it was to lay down in bed and get a good night's sleep till I was 'bout seventeen year old, when my father died and my missy took the bell offen me.

Before my father gave me to his sister, I was tied and strapped to a tree and whipped like a beast by my father, till I was unconscious, and then left strapped to a tree all night in cold and rainy weather. My father was very mean. He and he sister brung me to Texas, to North Zulch, when I 'bout twelve year old. He brung my mammy, too, and made her come and be his mistress one night every week. He would have kilt every one of his slaves rather than see us go free, 'specially me and my mammy.

My missy was pretty good to me, when my father wasn't right round. But he wouldn't let her give me anything to eat but corn bread and water and little sweet 'taters, and just 'nough of that to keep me alive. I was always hungry. My mammy had a boy called Frank Adds and a girl called Marie Adds, what she give birth to by her colored husband, but I never got to play with them. Missy worked me on the farm, and there was 'bout one hundred acres and fifteen slaves to work 'em. The overseer waked us 'bout three in the morning, and then he worked us just long as we could see. If we didn't git round fast 'nough, he chain us to a tree at night with nothing to eat, and next day, if we didn't go on the run, he hit us thirty-nine licks with a belt, what was 'bout three foot long and four inches wide.

I wore the bell night and day, and my father would chain me to a tree till I nearly died from the cold and being so hungry. My father didn't 'lieve in church, and my missy 'lieved there a Lord, but I wouldn't have 'lieved her if she try larn me 'bout 'ligion, 'cause my father tell me I wasn't any more than a damn mule. I slept on a chair and tried to rest till my father died, and then I sang all day, 'cause I knowed I wouldn't be treated so mean. When Missy took that bell offen me, I think I in Heaven 'cause I could lie down and go to sleep. When I did I couldn't wake up for a long time, and when I did wake up I'd be scared to death I'd see my father with his whip and that old bell. I'd jump out of bed and run till I give out, for fear he'd come back and git me.

WHY MASTER HAD SUCH A MEAN MAN WORKING FOR HIM

Mr. Marcus Brown, the overseer, he mean sure 'nough, I tell you, and the onliest thing that keep him from beating the niggers up all the time would be Old Marse or his nephew, Mr. Bart Milton. Both of them was good and kind 'most all the time. One time that I remembers, Old Marse, he gone back to Panola County for something, and Mr. Bart Milton, he attending the camp meeting. That was the day that Mr. Marcus Brown come mighty nigh killing Henry. I'll tell you how that was, boss. It was on Monday morning that it happened. The Friday before that Monday morning all of the hands had been picking cotton, and Mr. Marcus Brown didn't think that Henry had picked enough cotton that day, and so he give Henry a lashing out in the field. That night Henry, he git mad and burn up his sack and runned off and hid in the canebrake 'long the bayou all of the next day. Mr. Marcus, he missed Henry from the field and sent Jeff and Randall to find him and bring him in. They found Henry real soon and tell him iffen he don't come on back to the field that Mr. Marcus gwine to set the hounds on him. So Henry, he comed on back then, 'cause the niggers was scared of them wild bloodhounds what they would set on 'em when they try to run off.

When Henry git back, Mr. Marcus say, "Henry, where your sack? And how come you ain't picking cotton 'stead running off like that?" Henry say he done burnt he sack up. With that Mr. Marcus lit into him like a bear, lashing him right and left. Henry broke and run then to the cookhouse where he mammy, Aunt Mary, was, and Mr. Marcus right after him with a heavy stick of wood that he picked up offen the yard. Mr. Marcus got Henry cornered in the house and near 'bout beat that nigger to death. In fact, Mr. Marcus, he really think, too, that he done kilt Henry 'cause he called Uncle Nat and said, "Nat, go git some boards and make a coffin for this nigger what I done kilt."

But Henry wasn't dead, though he was beat up terrible, and they put him in the sickhouse. For days and days Uncle Warner had to 'tend to him and wash he wounds and pick the maggots outen his sores. That was just the way that Mr.

Marcus Brown treated the niggers every time he git a chancet. He would even lash and beat the womens.

Boss, you has heared me telling that my marse was a good kind man and that his overseer, Mr. Marcus Brown, was terrible cruel and mean and would beat the niggers up every chance he git, and you ask me how come it was that the marse would have such a mean man a-working for him. Now I's gwine to tell you the reason. You know the truth is the light, boss, and this is the truth what I's gwine to say. Marse, he in love with Mr. Marcus Brown's wife, Miss Sara, and Miss Sara's young daughter, she was Marse's child. Yes, sir, she was that. Her name was Miss Harvey, that's what it was. Marse had done willed that child a big part of his property and a whole gang of niggers. He was gwine give her Tolliver, Becky, Aunt Mary, Austin, and Savannah, and a heap more 'sides that. But the war, it come on and broke Marse up, and all the darkies sot free; and after that, so I heared, Mr. Marcus Brown and Miss Sara and the young lady, Miss Harvey, they moved up North some place, and I ain't never heared no more from them.

ORDEAL BY PLANTING

Old Massa's wife's sister had a husband what kept the meanest overseer during the war that I ever is seed. . . . That man would make them niggers on the plantation plow up a great big field, big as all over yonder, and then check it for corn. And checking corn is running a straight row clean 'cross the field both ways, and it make a check 'bout two feet square. Then he'd make the niggers drap a grain of corn right in the middle of every check, and if it didn't come up straight as these here fingers on my hand, he'd snatch it up and make 'em eat it right then and there, stalk and all, 'thout ever biling it or anything. And that'll mighty near throw you in the middle of a spell of sickness, sure's you born.

But that didn't make no difference to that man. And 'stead of that, he'd nigh 'bout beat 'em to death if they 'sputed his word 'bout it, but then they didn't 'spute, 'cause they was so scared when they drapped it that it ain't gwine to come up straight like he say, that they couldn't drap it good as they could of drapped it. 'Cause they so scared they couldn't.

FILLING A BARREL WITH A THIMBLE

Before the war I 'member the overseer would say, "If you don't have that done tonight, I'll whip you tomorrow." They had one man was pretty bad, and I know they give him a thimble and a barrel and told him he had to fill up that barrel, but he couldn't do it, you know, and so they whipped him.

POOR WHITE-TRASH PATEROLLERS

My pappy name Jeff and belong to Marse Joe Woodward. He live on a plantation 'cross the other side of Wateree Crick. My mammy name Phoebe. Pappy have to git a pass to come to see Mammy, before the war. Sometime that crick git up over the bank and I, to this day, 'members one time Pappy come in all wet and drenched with water. Him had made the mule swim the crick. Him stayed over his leave that was writ on the pass. Paterollers come ask for the pass. They say: "The time done out, nigger." Pappy try to explain, but they pay no 'tention to him. Tied him up, pulled down his breeches, and whupped him right before Mammy and us children. . . . Marse Tom and Miss Jane heard the hollering of us all and come to the place they was whupping him and beg them, in the name of God, to stop, that the crick was still up and dangerous to cross, and that they would make it all right with Pappy's master. They say of Pappy: "Jeff swim 'cross. Let him git the mule and swim back." They make Pappy git on the mule and follow him down to the crick and watch him swim that swift muddy crick to the other side.

I often think that the system of paterollers and bloodhounds did more to bring on the war and the wrath of the Lord than anything else. Why the good white folks put up with them poor white-trash paterollers I never can see or understand. You never see classy buckra men a-paterolling. It was always some low-down white men, that never owned a nigger in their life, doing the paterolling and a-stripping the clothes off men like Pappy right before the wives and children and beating the blood out of him. No, sir, good white men never dirty their hands and souls in such work of the devil as that.

THEY THINK TOO HIGH OF THEMSELVES

Most them there patrollers was poor white folks, I believes. Rich folks stay in their house at night, 'less they has some sort of big frolic amongst theirselves. Poor white folks had to hustle round to make a living, so they hired out theirselves to slaveowners and rode the roads at night and whipped niggers if they catched any off their plantation without a pass. I has found that if you gives to some poor folks, white or black, something a little better than they is used to,

they is sure gwine to think too high of theirselves soon, that's right. I sure
believes that, as much as I believes I's setting in this chair talking to you.

THE LAST TIME I SAW MASTER

No, sir, he wa'n't good to none of us niggers. All the niggers round hated to
be bought by him 'cause he was so mean. When he was too tired to whup us, he
had the overseer do it; and the overseer was meaner than the massa. But, mister,
the peoples was the same as they is now. There was good ones and bad ones. I
just happened to belong to a bad one. One day I remembers my brother January
was cotched over seeing a gal on the next plantation. He had a pass, but the time
on it done give out. Well, sir, when the massa found out that he was a hour late,
he got as mad as a hive of bees. So when Brother January he come home, the
massa took down his long mule skinner and tied him with a rope to a pine tree.
He strip his shirt off and said: "Now, nigger, I'm going to teach you some
sense."
With that he started laying on the lashes. January was a big, fine-looking
nigger, the finest I ever seed. He was just four years older than me, and when the
massa begin a-beating him, January never said a word. The massa got madder
and madder 'cause he couldn't make January holler.
"What's the matter with you, nigger?" he say. "Don't it hurt?"
January, he never said nothing, and the massa keep a-beating till little
streams of blood started flowing down January's chest, but he never holler. His
lips was a-quivering and his body was a-shaking, but his mouth it never open;
and all the while I sat on my mammy's and pappy's steps a-crying. The niggers
was all gathered about, and some of 'em couldn't stand it; they had to go inside
their cabins. After while, January, he couldn't stand it no longer hisself, and he
say in a hoarse loud whisper: "Massa! Massa! have mercy on this poor nigger.". . .
Then the war came. The Yankees come in, and they pulled the fruit off the
trees and et it. They et the hams and corn, but they never burned the houses.
Seem to me like they just stay around long enough to git plenty something to
eat, 'cause they left in two or three days, and we never seed 'em since. The massa
had three boys to go to war, but there wasn't one to come home. All the children
he had was killed. Massa, he lost all his money, and the house soon begin
dropping away to nothing. Us niggers one by one left the old place, and the last
time I seed the home plantation I was a-standing on a hill. I looked back on it
for the last time through a patch of scrub pines, and it look so lonely. There
wa'n't but one person in sight, the massa. He was a-setting in a wicker chair in
the yard looking out over a small field of cotton and corn. There was four crosses
in the graveyard in the side lawn where he was a-setting. The fourth one was his

wife. I lost my old woman, too, thirty-seven years ago, and all this time, I's been a-carrying on like the massa—all alone.

HOW THAT SUIT YOU?

. . . All he niggers say Cade the good man. He hire he overseers and say, "You can correct them for they own good and make them work right, but you ain't better cut they hide or draw no blood." He git a-hold some mean overseers, but they don't tarry long. He find out they beating he niggers, and then he beat them and say, "How that suit you?"

I'LL WHIP YOU WITH CHICKEN STEW

It am years after freedom Missy Mary say to me what Massa always say, "If the nigger won't follow orders by kind treating, such nigger am wrong in the head and not worth keeping." He didn't have to rush us. We'd just dig in and do the work. One time Massa clearing some land, and it am gitting late for breaking the ground. Us always have Saturday afternoon and Sunday off. Old Jerry says to us, "Tell yous what us do—go to the clearing this afternoon and Sunday and finish for the massa. That sure make him glad."

Saturday noon come, and nobody tells the massa but us go to that clearing and sing while us work, cutting brush and grubbing stomps and burning brush. Us sing:

> Hi, ho, ug, hi, ho, ug,
> The sharp bit, the strong arm,
> Hi, ho, ug, hi, ho, ug,
> This tree am done 'fore us warm.

The massa come out, and his mouth am slipping all over he face, and he say, "What this all mean? Why you working Saturday afternoon?"

Old Jerry am a funny cuss, and he say, "Massa, O, Massa, please don't whup us for cutting down your trees."

"I's gwine whup you with the chicken stew," Massa say. And for Sunday dinner there am chicken stew with noodles and peach cobbler.

HE DIDN'T ALLOW NOBODY TO HIT THEM A LICK

My master was the best in this country. He didn't had many niggers, but he sure took good care of them what he did had. He didn't 'low nobody to hit 'em a lick. Sometime when I would git cotch up with in some devilment, the white folks would say, "Whose nigger is you?" and I say, "Marse Saddler Smith." Then they look at each other and say kinda low, "Better not do nothing to Old Smith's nigger. He'll raise the devil."

HE GLORIED IN THEIR SPUNK

Oh, them patrollers! They had a chief, and he git 'em together, and iffen they caught you without a pass and sometimes with a pass, they'd beat you. But iffen you had a pass, they had to answer to the law. One old master had two slaves, brothers, on his place. They was both preachers. Mitchell was a Hardshell Baptist and Andrew was a Missionary Baptist. One day the patroller chief was rambling through the place and found some letters writ to Mitchell and Andrew. He went to the master and said, "Did you know you had some niggers that could read and write?" Master said, "No, but I might have. Who do you 'spect?" The patroller answered, "Mitchell and Andrew." The old master said, "I never knowed Andrew to tell me a lie about nothing!"

Mitchell was called first and asked could he read and write. He was scared stiff. He said, "No, sir." Andrew was called and asked. He said, "Yes, sir." He was asked iffen Mitchell could. He said, "Sure, better'n me." The master told John Arnold, the patroller chief, not to bother 'em. He gloried in their spunk. When the old master died, he left all of his niggers a home apiece.

WHEN I GOT BACK TO MASTER HALEY

Massa Haley am kind to his colored folks, and him am kind to everybody, and all the folks likes him. The other white folks called we-uns the petted niggers. There am 'bout thirty old and young niggers and 'bout twenty pickaninnies too little to work, and the nurse cares for them while they mammies works.

I's gwine 'splain how it am managed on Massa Haley's plantation. It am sort of like the small town, 'cause everything we uses am made right there. There am the shoemaker, and he is the tanner and make the leather from the hides. Then Massa has 'bout a thousand sheep, and he gits the wool, and the niggers cards and spins and weaves it, and that makes all the clothes. Then Massa have cattle and such provide the milk and the butter and beef meat for eating. Then Massa have the turkeys and chickens and the hogs and the bees. With all that, us never was hungry.

The plantation am planted in cotton, mostly, with the corn and the wheat a little, 'cause Massa don't need much of them. He never sell nothing but the cotton.

The living for the colored folks am good. The quarters am built from logs like they's all in them days. The floor am the dirt, but we has the benches and what is made on the place. And we has the big fireplace for to cook, and we has plenty to cook in that fireplace, 'cause Massa always 'lows plenty good rations, but he watch close for the wasting of the food.

The war breaks, and that make the big change on the massa's place. He jines the army and hires a man call Delbridge for overseer. After that, the hell start to pop, 'cause the first thing Delbridge do is cut the rations. He weighs out the meat, three pound for the week, and he measure a peck of meal. And 'twa'n't enough. He half-starve us niggers, and he want more work, and he start the whippings. I guesses he starts to educate 'em. I guess that Delbridge go to hell when he died, but I don't see how the devil could stand him.

We-uns am not use to such, and some runs off. When they am cotched, there am a whipping at the stake. But that Delbridge, he sold me to Massa House, in Blanco County. I's sure glad when I's sold, but it am short gladness, 'cause here am another man what hell am too good for. He gives me the whipping, and the scars am still on my arms and my back, too. I'll carry them to my grave. He sends me for firewood, and when I gits it loaded, the wheel hits a stump, and the team jerks, and that breaks the whippletree. So he ties me to the stake, and every half hour for four hours they lays ten lashes on my back. For the first couple hours the pain am awful. I's never forgot it. Then I's stood so much pain I not feel so much, and when they takes me loose, I's just 'bout half dead. I lays in the bunk two days, gitting over that whipping, gitting over it in the body but not the heart. No, sir, I has that in the heart till this day.

After that whipping I doesn't have the heart to work for the massa. If I seed the cattle in the cornfield, I turns the back, 'stead of chasing 'em out. I guess that the reason the massa sold me to his brother, Massa John. And he am good like my first massa, he never whipped me.

Then surrender am 'nounced and Massa tells us we's free. When that takes place, it am 'bout one hour by sun. I says to myself, "I won't be here long." But I's not realize what I's in for till after I's started, but I couldn't turn back. For that means the whipping or danger from the paterollers. There I was, and I kept on gwine. No nigger am 'sposed to be off the massa's place without the pass, so I travels at night and hides during the daylight. I stays in the brush and gits water from the creeks, but not much to eat. Twice I's sure them paterollers am passing while's I's hiding.

I's twenty-one year old then, but it am the first time I's gone any place, 'cept to the neighbors, so I's worried 'bout the right way to Massa Haley's place. But the morning of the third day I comes to he place, and I's so hungry and tired and scared for fear Massa Haley not home from the army yet. So I finds my pappy, and he hides me in the cabin till a week, and then luck comes to me when Massa Haley come home. He come at night, and the next morning that Delbridge am shunt off the place, 'cause Massa Haley seed he niggers was all gaunt, and lots am run off, and the fields am not plowed right, and only half the sheep and everything left. So Massa say to that Delbridge, "There am no words can 'splain what you's done. Git off my place 'fore I smashes you."

Then I can come out from my pappy's cabin, and the old massa was glad to see me, and he let me stay till freedom am ordered. That's the happiest time in my life, when I gits back to Massa Haley.

I'D RATHER SEE THOSE MARKS ON MY OWN SHOULDERS

My mammy worked in the big house, a-spinning and a-nursing the white children. All of them called her Mammy. I 'members one thing just like it was yesterday. Miss Sarah went to Demopolis to visit with her sister, and whilst she were gone the overseer, what go by the name of Allen, whupped my mammy 'crost her back till the blood runned out.

When Miss Sarah comed back and found it out, she was the maddest white lady I ever seed. She sont for the overseer, and she say: "Allen, what you mean by whupping Mammy? You know I don't allow you to touch my house servants." She jerk her dress down and stand there looking like a soldier with her white shoulders shining and she say: "I'd rather see them marks on my own shoulders than to see 'em on Mammy's. They wouldn't hurt me no worse." Then she say: "Allen, take your family and git offen my place. Don't you let sundown catch you here." So he left. He wasn't nothing but white trash nohow.

The Slave's Chance

Before I'd be a slave
I'd be buried in my grave.

SHE RODE OFF ON A COW

She didn't work in the field. She worked at a loom. She worked so long and so often that once she went to sleep at the loom. Her master's boy saw her and told his mother. His mother told him to take a whip and wear her out. He took a stick and went out to beat her awake. He beat my mother till she woke up. When she woke up, she took a pole out of the loom and beat him nearly to death with it. He hollered, "Don't beat me no more, and I won't let 'em whip you."

She said, "I'm going to kill you. These black titties sucked you, and then you come out here to beat me." And when she left him, he wasn't able to walk.

And that was the last I seen of her until after freedom. She went out and got on an old cow that she used to milk—Dolly, she called it. She rode away from the plantation, because she knew they would kill her if she stayed.

LITTLE JOE MADE A SONG

The people that owned the plantation near us had lots of slaves. They owned lots of my kinfolks. They master would beat 'em at night when they come from the field and lock 'em up. He'd whup 'em and send 'em to the field. They couldn't visit no slaves, and no slaves was 'lowed to visit 'em. So my cousin Sallie watched him hide the keys. So she moved 'em a little further back so that he had to lean over to reach 'em. That morning soon when he come to let 'em out, she cracked him in the head with the poker and made Little Joe help put his head in the fireplace. That day in the field Little Joe made a song: "If you don't believe Aunt Sallie kilt Marse Jim, the blood is on her underdress." He just hollered it, "Aunt Sallie kilt Marse Jim." They 'zamined Aunt Sallie's underdress, so they put her in jail till the baby come, then they tried her and sentenced her to be hung, and she was.

NO OVERSEER EVER DOWNED HER

My mother had about three masters before she got free. She was a terrible working woman. Her boss went off deer hunting once for a few weeks. While he was gone, the overseer tried to whip her. She knocked him down and tore his face up so that the doctor had to 'tend to him. When Pennington came back, he noticed his face all patched up and asked him what was the matter with it. The overseer told him that he went down in the field to whip the hands and that he just thought he would hit Lucy a few licks to show the slaves that he was impartial, but she jumped on him and like to tore him up. Old Pennington said to him, "Well, if that is the best you could do with her, damned if you won't just have to take it."

Then they sold her to another man, named Jim Bernard. Bernard did a lot of big talk to her one morning. He said, "Look out there and mind you do what you told around here and step lively. If you don't, you'll get that bull whip." She said to him, "Yes, and we'll both be gitting it." He had heard about her; so he sold her to another man named Cleary. He was good to her; so she wasn't sold no more after that.

There wasn't many men could class up with her when it come to working. She could do more work than any two men. There wasn't no use for no one man to try to do nothing with her. No overseer never downed her.

SHE CHOPPED THIS MAN TO A BLOODY DEATH

One day when an old woman was plowing in the field, an overseer came by and reprimanded her for being so slow—she gave him some back talk, he took out a long closely woven whip and lashed her severely. The woman became sore and took her hoe and chopped him right across his head, and, child, you should have seen how she chopped this man to a bloody death.

SHE PULLED UP THE STUMP

Early Hurt had an overseer, named Sanders. He tied my sister Crecie to a stump to whip her. Crecie was stout and heavy. She was a grown young woman and big and strong. Sanders had two dogs with him in case he would have trouble with anyone. When he started laying that lash on Crecie's back, she pulled up that stump and whipped him and the dogs both.

Old Early Hurt came up and whipped her hisself. Said, "Oh, you're too bad for the overseer to whip, huh?"

NO MORE OVERSEERS AFTER THAT

I

Massa never had but one white overseer. He got kilt fighting. The hands was burning logs and trash, and the overseer knocked a old man down and made some of the niggers hold him while he bullwhipped him. The old man got up and knocked the overseer in the head with a big stick and then took a ax and cut off his hands and feet. Massa said he didn't ever want another white overseer, and he made my cousin overlooker after that.

II

But the oldest boy, William, got the devil in him and hires a overseer, and he rid in the fields with a quirt and rope and chair on his saddle. When he done take a notion to whip a nigger, he'd make some the men tie that nigger to the chair and beat him something scandalous. He got mad at my mother's sister, Aunt Susie Ann, and beat her till the blood run off her on the ground. She fall at his feets like she passed out, and he put up the whip and she trips him and gits the whip and whips him till he couldn't stand up. Then some the niggers throwed him off a cliff and broke his neck. His folks gits the sheriff, but Master's boys orders him off the place with a gun. There wa'n't no more overseers on the place after that.

THE RED-BONE HOUND

White folks, . . . I's gonna tell you a story 'bout a mean overseer and what happened to him during the slavery days. It all commenced when a nigger named Jake Williams got a whupping for staying out after the time on his pass done give out. All the niggers on the place hated the overseer worse than pizen, 'cause he was so mean and used to try to think up things to whup us for.

One morning the slaves was lined up ready to eat their breakfast, and Jake Williams was a-petting his old red-bone hound. 'Bout that time the overseer come up and seed Jake a-petting his hound, and he say: "Nigger, you ain't got time to be a-fooling 'long that dog. Now make him git." Jake tried to make the dog go home, but the dog didn't want to leave Jake. Then the overseer pick up a rock and slam the dog in the back. The dog, he then went a-howling off.

That night Jake, he come to my cabin and he say to me: "Heywood, I is gonna run away to a free state. I ain't a-gonna put up with this treatment no longer. I can't stand much more." I gives him my hand, and I say: "Jake, I hopes you gits there. Maybe I'll see you again sometime."

"Heywood," he says, "I wish you'd look after my hound Belle. Feed her and keep her the best you can. She a mighty good possum and coon dog. I hates to part with her, but I knows that you is the best person I could leave her with." And with that Jake slip out the door, and I seed him a-walking toward the swamp down the long furrows of corn.

It didn't take that overseer long to find out that Jake done run away, and when he did, he got out the bloodhounds and started off after him. It wa'n't long afore Jake heard them hounds a-howling in the distance. Jake, he was too tired to go any further. He circled round and doubled on his tracks so as to confuse the hounds and then he clumb a tree. 'Twa'n't long afore he seed the light of the overseer coming through the woods, and the dogs was a-gitting closer and closer. Finally they smelled the tree that Jake was in, and they started barking round it. The overseer lift his lighted pine knot in the air so's he could see Jake. He say, "Nigger, come on down from there. You done wasted 'nough of our time." But Jake, he never move nor make a sound, and all the time the dogs kept a-howling and the overseer kept a-swearing. "Come on down," he say again. "Iffen you don't I's coming up and knock you outen the tree with a stick." Jake, still he never moved, and the overseer began to climb the tree. When he got where he could almost reach Jake, he swung that stick, and it come down on Jake's leg and hurt him terrible. Jake, he raised his foot and kicked the overseer right in the mouth, and that white man went a-tumbling to the ground. When he hit the earth, them hounds pounced on him. Jake, he then lowered hisself to the bottom limbs so's he could see what had happened. He saw the dogs a-tearing at the man and he holler: "Hold him, Belle! Hold him, gal!" The leader of that pack of hounds, white folks, wa'n't no bloodhound. She was a plain old red-bone possum and coon dog, and the rest done just like she done, tearing at the overseer's throat. All the while, Jake he a-hollering from the tree for the dogs to git him. 'Twa'n't long afore them dogs tore that man all to pieces. He died right under that maple tree that he run Jake up. Jake, he and that coon hound struck off through the woods. The rest of the pack come home.

I seed Jake after us niggers was freed. That's how come I knowed all about it. It musta been six years after they killed the overseer. It was in Kentucky that I run across Jake. He was a-sitting on some steps of a nigger cabin. A hound dog was a-sitting at his side. I tells him how glad I is to see him, and then I look at the dog. "That ain't Belle?" I says. "Naw," Jake answers, "this her puppy." Then he told me the whole story. I always did want to know what happen to 'em.

A WHITE MAN'S CHANCE

Jim Williams was a patroller, and how he did like to catch a nigger off the farm without a permit so he could whip him. Jim thought he was the best man in the country and could whip the best of 'em. One night John Hardin, a big husky feller, was out late. He met Jim and knowed he was in for it. Jim said, "John, I'm gonna give you a white man's chance. I'm gonna let you fight me, and if you are the best man, well and good."

John say, "Master Jim, I can't fight with you. Come on and give me my licking and let me go on home."

But Jim wouldn't do it, and he slapped John and called him some names and told him he is a coward to fight him. All this made John awful mad, and he flew into him and give him the terriblest licking a man ever toted. He went on home, but knew he would git into trouble over it.

Jim talked around over the country about what he was going to do to John, but everybody told him that he brought it all on hisself. He never did try to git another nigger to fight with him.

GONE TO THE WOODS

If a nigger ever run off the place and come back, Master'd say, "If you'll be a good nigger, I'll not whip you this time." But you couldn't 'lieve that. A nigger run off and stayed in the woods six month. When he come back, he's hairy as a cow, 'cause he lived in a cave and come out at night and pilfer round. They put the dogs on him but couldn't cotch him. Finally he come home, and Master say he won't whip him, and Tom was crazy 'nough to 'lieve it. Master say to the cook, "Fix Tom a big dinner," and while Tom's eating, Master stand in the door with a whip and say, "Tom, I's change my mind; you have no business running off, and I's gwine take you out just like you come into the world."

Master gits a bottle whiskey and a box cigars and have Tom tied up out in the yard. He takes a chair and say to the driver, "Boy, take him down, 250 licks this time." Then he'd count the licks. When they's 150 licks, it didn't look like they is any place left to hit, but Master say, "Finish him up." Then he and the driver sot down, smoke cigars and drink whiskey, and Master tell Tom how he must mind he master. Then he lock Tom up in a log house, and Master tell all the niggers if they give him anything to eat he'll skin 'em alive. The old folks slips Tom bread and meat. When he gits out, he's gone to the woods 'gain. They's plenty niggers what stayed in the woods till surrender.

THEY LIVED IN A CAVE SEVEN YEARS

I know so many things 'bout slavery time till I never will be able to tell 'em all. . . . In them days preachers was just as bad and mean as anybody else. There was a man who folks called a good preacher, but he was one of the meanest mens I ever seed. When I was in slavery under him, he done so many bad things till God soon kilt him. His wife or children could git mad with you, and if they told him anything he always beat you. Most times he beat his slaves when they hadn't done nothing a-tall. One Sunday morning his wife told him their cook wouldn't never fix nothing she told her to fix. Time she said it he jumped up from the table, went in the kitchen, and made the cook go under the porch where he always whupped his slaves. She begged and prayed, but he didn't pay no 'tention to that. He put her up in what us called the swing, and beat her till she couldn't holler. The poor thing already had heart trouble; that's why he put her in the kitchen, but he left her swinging there and went to church, preached, and called hisself serving God. When he got back home she was dead. Whenever your master had you swinging up, nobody wouldn't take you down. Sometimes a man would help his wife, but most times he was beat afterwards.

Another master I had kept a hogshead to whup you on. This hogshead had two or three hoops round it. He buckled you face down on the hogshead and whupped you till you bled. Everybody always stripped you in them days to whup you, 'cause they didn't care who seed you naked. Some folks' children took sticks and jabbed you while you was being beat. Sometimes these children would beat you all 'cross your head, and they mas and pas didn't know what stop was.

Another way Master had to whup us was in a stock that he had in the stables. This was where he whupped you when he was real mad. He had logs fixed together with holes for your feet, hands, and head. He had a way to open these logs and fasten you in. Then he had his coachman give you so many lashes, and he would let you stay in the stock for so many days and nights. That's why he had it in the stable so it wouldn't rain on you. Every day you got that same number of lashes. You never come out able to sit down.

I had a cousin with two children. The oldest one had to nurse one of Master's grandchildren. The front steps was real high, and one day this poor child fell down these steps with the baby. His wife and daughter hollered and went on terrible, and when our master come home they was still hollering just like the baby was dead or dying. When they told him 'bout it, he picked up a board and hit this poor little child 'cross the head and kilt her right there. Then he told his slaves to take her and throw her in the river. Her ma begged and prayed, but he didn't pay her no 'tention; he made 'em throw the child in.

One of the slaves married a young gal, and they put her in the big house to work. One day Mistress jumped on her 'bout something, and the gal hit her back, Mistress said she was going to have Master put her in the stock and beat her when he come home. When the gal went to the field and told her husband 'bout it, he told her where to go and stay till he got there. That night he took his supper to her. He carried her to a cave and hauled pine straw and put in there for her to sleep on. He fixed that cave up just like a house for her, put a stove in there and run the pipe out through the ground into a swamp. Everybody always wondered how he fixed that pipe. Course they didn't cook on it till night when nobody could see the smoke. He ceiled the house with pine logs, made beds and tables out of pine poles, and they lived in this cave seven years. During this time, they had three children. Nobody was with her when these children was born but her husband. He waited on her with each child. The children didn't wear no clothes 'cept a piece tied round their waists. They was just as hairy as wild people, and they was wild. When they come out of that cave, they would run every time they seed a person.

The seven years she lived in the cave, different folks helped keep 'em in food. Her husband would take it to a certain place and she would go and git it. People had passed over this cave ever so many times, but nobody knowed these folks was living there. Our master didn't know where she was, and it was freedom 'fore she come out of that cave for good.

UNCLE ISOM

Talking 'bout niggers running away, didn't my steppappy run away? Didn't my Uncle Gabe run away? The frost would just bite they toes 'most nigh off too, whiles they was gone. They put Uncle Isom (my steppappy) in jail, and whiles he was in there he killed a white guardman. Then they put in the paper, "A nigger to kill," and our master seen it and bought him. He was a double-strengthed man, he was so strong. He'd run off, so help you God. They had the bloodhounds after him once, and he caught the hound what was leading and beat the rest of the dogs. The white folks run up on him before he knowed it and made them dogs eat his ear plumb out. But, don't you know, he got away anyhow. One morning I was sweeping out the hall in the big house, and somebody come a-knocking on the front door, and I goes to the door. There was Uncle Isom with rags all on his head. He said, "Tell Old Master here I am." I goes to Master's door and says, "Master Colonel Sam, Uncle Isom said here he am." He say, "Go round to the kitchen and tell black mammy to give you breakfast." When he was through eating, they give him three hundred lashes and, bless my soul, he run off again.

GUINEA JIM

The first thing I 'members 'bout slavery time, I wa'n't nothing but a boy, 'bout fifteen, I reckon. That's what Marse Johnnie Horn say. Us belong to Marse Ike Horn, Marse Johnnie's pa, right here on this place where us is now. But this here didn't belong to me then. This here was all Marse Ike's place. Marse Ike's gin got outa fix and we couldn't git it fixed. Colonel Lee had two gins, and one of 'em was just below old Turner house. Recollect a big old hickory tree? Well, there's where it was.

I was plenty big 'nough to drive the mules to the gin. Set on the lever and drive 'em, just like a 'lasses mill. So that night Marse Ike told us he want everybody to go with him to Colonel Lee's gin next morning, and didn't want nobody to git out and go ahead of him. That held up the ginning; made us not to go to the ginhouse till sunup.

Us got the mules and just waited. 'Twixt daylight and sunup, us all standing there at the gate, and we heared a little fine horn up the road. Us didn't know what it meant coming to the house. And bimeby Mr. Beesley, what live not far from Marse Ike, he rode up and had five dogs—five nigger dogs, what they call 'em—and soon as he come, Marse Ike's hoss was saddled up, and Marse Ike and him rode off down the road and the dogs with 'em 'head of us. Us followed 'long behind 'em, stay close as they 'low us, to see what they was up to. When they got close to the ginhouse—ginhouse right 'side the road—they stop us, and Mr. Beesley told Old Brown to go ahead. Old Brown was the lead dog and had a bell on him, and they was fasten together with a rod, just like steers. He turn 'em loose, and then he popped the whip and hollered at Old Brown and told him, "Nigger." Old Brown hollered like he hit. He want to go. And they was a fence on both sides made it a lane, so he put Old Brown over the fence on the ginhouse side and told Brown to "go ahead." He went ahead and run all around the ginhouse, and they let him in the ginroom, and he grabbled in the cotton-seed in a hole.

Then somebody holler, "Guinea Jim."

I looks and I didn't see him. Didn't nobody see him, but they know that's where he been hiding. Mr. Beesley told Old Brown he just fooling him, and Old Brown holler again, like he killing him, and Mr. Beesley say, "Go git that nigger," and Old Brown started 'way from there like he hadn't been hunting nothing, but he went around and around that gin, and Mr. Beesley told him he had to do better than that or he'd kill him, 'cause he hadn't come there for nothing.

Brown made a circle around that gin 'way down to the fence that time, and he was so fat he couldn't git through the fence. You know what sort of fence, a rail fence it was. Then he stop and bark for help. Now I seed this with my own eyes. They put Brown on top the fence, and he jump 'way out in the road, didn't stay on the fence. He jump and run up and down in the road and couldn't find no scent of Jim. You knows how they used to make them rail fences?

Well, Brown come back there, and this is the truth, so help me God. He bark, look like, for them to lift him back up on the fence, and, bless God, if that dog didn't walk that rail fence like he walking a log, as far as from here to that gate yonder, and track Jim just like he was on the ground. He fell off once, and they had to put him back, and he run his track right on to where Jim jumped off the fence, 'way out in the road. Old Brown run right across the road to the other fence and treed again on t'other side the road toward Konkabia. Old Brown walk the fence on that side the road a good piece, just like he done on the other side, and them other dogs, he hadn't never turned them loose.

When Brown he jump off that fence, he jump just as far as he can on the field side, like he gwine catch Jim like a gnat or something, and he never stop barking no more, just like he jumping a rabbit. Then Mr. Beesley turn them other dogs loose that he hadn't never turned loose, 'cause he say Old Brown done got the thing straight. And he had it straight. Them dogs run that track right on down to Konkabia and crossed it to the Blacksher side. They was a big old straw field there then, and they cross it and come on through that field, all them dogs barking just like they looking at Jim. 'Reckly, they come on Jim running with a pine brush tied behind him to drag his scent away, but it didn't bother Old Brown.

When them dogs 'gin to push him, Jim drap the brush and run back toward Konkabia. Now on Konkabia there used to be beavers worse than on Sucarnatchee now. They was a big beaver dam 'twixt the bridge and the Hale place, and Jim run to that beaver dam. You know when beavers build they dam, they cut down trees and let 'em fall in the creek, and pull in trash and brush same as folks, to dam the water up there till it's knee-deep. The dogs seen him, Old Brown looking at him, just 'fore he jump in 'bove the dam right 'mongst the trash and things they'd drug in there. Brown seed him, and he jump in right behind him. Jim just dive down under the raff and let he nose stick outa the water. Every once in a while Jim he put he head down under, he holding to a pole down there, and once Mr. Beesley seed him, he just let him stay there.

Brown would swim 'bout 'mongst the brush, backwards and forwards, and directly Mr. Beesley told Old Brown, "Go git him." Then all the men got poles and dug 'bout in the raff hunting him. They knowed he was there, and Marse Ike had a pole gigging around trying to find him too. Then he told Mr. Beesley to give him the hatchet and let him fix the pole. He sharpen the pole right sharp, then Marse Ike start to gig around with the pole and he kinda laugh to hisself, 'cause he knowed he done found Jim. 'Bout that time Jim poke he head up and say: "This here me," and everybody holler. Then he ax 'em please, for God's sake, don't let them dogs git him. They told him come on out.

You see, Jim belonged to Miss Mary Lee, Mr. John Lee's ma, and his pa was kilt in the war, so Mr. Beesley was looking out for her. Well, they took Jim outa there, and Mr. Beesley whipped him a little and told him: "Jim, you put up a pretty good fight, and I's gwine to give you a start for a run with the dogs."

Jim took out towards Miss Mary's, and Mr. Beesley held Old Brown as long as he could. They caught Jim and bite him right smart. You see they had to let 'em bite him a little to satisfy the dogs. Jim could have made it, 'cept he was all hot and wore out.

JADE HAD BIG IDEAS

One night after we had all gone to bed, I heared a noise at the window, and when I look up there was a man a-climbing in. He was a nigger. I could tell even though I could scarce see him, I knowed he was a nigger. I could hear my mistress a-breathing, and the baby was sound asleep too. I started to yell out, but I thought that the nigger would kill us, so I just kept quiet. He come in the window, and he see us a-sleeping there, and all of a sudden I knowed who it was. "Jade," I whispers, "what you a-doing here?" He come to my bed and put his rough hand over my mouth.

"Listen you black pickaninny, you tell 'em that you saw me here and I'll kill you," he say. "I throw your hide to the snakes in the swamp. Now shut up."

With that he went to the dresser and taken Mistress' money bag. After that he went to the window and climb down the ladder, and I didn't do nothing but shake myself nearly to death from fright. The next day the overseer and the pattyrollers went a-searching through the slave quarters, and they found the money bag under Jade's cot. They took him and whupped him for near fifteen minutes. We could hear him holler 'way up at the big house. Jade, he never got over that whupping. He died three days later. He was a good nigger, 'pear to me like, and the best blacksmith in the whole county. I kept a-wondering what made him want to steal that purse. Then I found out later that he was a-going to pay a white man to carry him over the line to the Northern states. Jade just had too big ideas for a nigger. I used to see Jade's ghost a-walking out in the garden in the moonlight; sometime he sit on the fence and look at his old cabin, then sometimes he stroll off down the cotton field. When the Lord git through a-punishing him for a-stealing that money, I guess he won't make us no more visits. He just go right on in heaven. That's what ghostes is, you know, peoples that can't quite git in heaven, and they had to stroll round little longer on the outside repenting.

THEY DIDN'T GET LUCY OR HER QUARTER

They say Negroes won't commit suicide, but Isom told us of a girl that committed suicide. There was a girl named Lu who used to run off and go to the dances. The patrollers would try to catch her, but they couldn't because she was too fast on her feet. One day they got after her in the daytime. She had always outrun them at night. She ran to the cabin and got her quarter which she had hid. She put the quarter in her mouth. The white folks didn't allow the slaves to handle no money. The quarter got stuck in her throat, and she went on down to the slough and drowned herself rather than let them beat her, and mark her up. Them patrollers sure would get you and beat you up. If they couldn't catch you when you were running away from them, they would come on your master's place and get you and beat you. The master would allow them to do it. They didn't let the patrollers come on the Blackshear place, but this gal was so hard-headed 'bout going out that they made a 'ception to her. And they intended to make her an example to the rest of the slaves. But they didn't get Lucy.

WHY AUNT ADELINE HUNG HERSELF

She hung herself to keep from getting a whupping. Mother raised her boy. She told Mother she would kill herself before she would be whupped. I never heard what she was to be whupped for. She thought she would be whupped. She took a rope and tied it to a limb and to her neck and then jumped. Her toes barely touched the ground. They buried her in the cemetery on the old Ed Cotton place.

BUY YOURSELF FREE

I was born in Virginia in 1847. My mother was a slave, and my grandfather was one of the early settlers in Virginia. He was born in Jamaica, and his master took him to England. When the English came to Virginia, they brought us along as servants, but when they got here, everybody had slaves, so we was slaves, too. My mother was born in the West Indies.

A man named Martin brought my grandfather here, and we took his name. And when Master was ready to die, he made a will, and it said the youngest child in the slaves must be made free, so that was my father, and he was made free when he was sixteen. That left me and my brothers and sisters all free, but all the rest of the family was slaves.

My mother was a slave near Alexandria. The master's daughter, Miss Liza, read to my mother, so she got some learning. When my mother's owner died, he left her to Miss Liza, and then my father met my mother and told her they should get married. My mother said to Miss Liza: "I'd like fine to marry Preston Martin." Miss Liza says, "You can't do that, 'cause he's a free nigger and your children would be free. You gotta marry one of the slaves." Then Miss Liza lines up ten or fifteen of the slave men for my mother to pick from, but Mother says she don't like any of 'em, she wants to marry Preston Martin. Miss Liza argues, but my mother is just stubborn, so Miss Liza says, "I'll talk to the master." He says, "I can't lose property like that, and if you can raise $1,200 you can buy yourself free." So my mother and my father saves money, and it takes a long time, but one day they goes to the master and lays down the money, and they gits married. Master don't like it, but he's promised and he can't back out.

HE BOUGHT HIMSELF

My mother was Amy Van Zandt Moore and was a Tennesseean. My father was Henry Moore, and he belonged to a old bachelor named Moore, in Alabama. Moore freed all his niggers 'fore 'mancipation except three. They was to pay a debt, and my father was Moore's choice man and was one of the three. He bought hisself. He had saved up some money, and when they went to sell him he bid $800. The auctioneer cries round to git a raise, but wouldn't nobody bid on my father 'cause he was one of Moore's "free niggers." My father done say after the war he could have buyed hisself for $1.50. So he was a free man 'fore the 'mancipation, and he couldn't live 'mong the slaves, and he had to have a guardian who was 'sponsible for his conduct till after surrender.

THE BELL AND THE LIGHT

Most of the slaves didn't know when they was born, but I did. You see, I was born on a Christmas morning—it was in 1840. I was a full-grown man when I finally got my freedom.

Before I got it, though, I helped a lot of others get theirs. Lord only knows how many; might have been as much as two-three hundred. It was 'way more than a hundred, I know.

But that all came after I was a young man—grown enough to know a pretty girl when I saw one, and to go chasing after her, too. I was born on a plantation that belonged to Mr. Jack Tabb in Mason County, just across the river in Kentucky.

Mr. Tabb was a pretty good man. He used to beat us, sure; but not nearly so much as others did, some of his own kin people, even. But he was kinda funny sometimes; he used to have a special slave who didn't have nothing to do but teach the rest of us—we had about ten on the plantation, and a lot on the other plantations near us—how to read and write and figure. Mr. Tabb liked us to know how to figure. But sometimes when he would send for us, and we would be a long time coming, he would ask us where we had been. If we told him we had been learning to read, he would near beat the daylights out of us—after getting somebody to teach us! I think he did some of that so that the other owners wouldn't say he was spoiling his slaves.

He was funny about us marrying, too. He would let us go a-courting on the other plantations near any time we liked, if we were good, and if we found somebody we wanted to marry, and she was on a plantation that belonged to one of his kinfolks or a friend, he would swap a slave so that the husband and wife could be together. Sometimes, when he couldn't do this, he would let a slave work all day on his plantation and live with his wife at night on her plantation. Some of the other owners was always talking about his spoiling us.

He wasn't a Democrat like the rest of 'em in the county; he belonged to the Know Nothing party, and he was a real leader in it. He used to always be making speeches, and sometimes his best friends wouldn't be speaking to him for days at a time.

Mr. Tabb was always specially good to me. He used to let me go all about—I guess he had to; couldn't get too much work out of me even when he kept me right under his eyes. I learned fast, too, and I think he kinda liked that. He used to call Sandy Davis, the slave who taught me, "the smartest nigger in Kentucky."

It was 'cause he used to let me go around in the day and night so much that I came to be the one who carried the running-away slaves over the river. It was funny the way I started it, too.

I didn't have no idea of ever getting mixed up in any sort of business like that until one special night. I hadn't even thought of rowing across the river myself.

But one night I had gone on another plantation courting, and the old woman whose house I went to told me she had a real pretty girl there who wanted to go across the river, and would I take her? I was scared and backed out in a hurry. But then I saw the girl, and she was such a pretty little thing, brown-skinned and kinda rosy, and looking as scared as I was feeling, so it wasn't long before I was listening to the old woman tell me when to take her and where to leave her on the other side.

I didn't have nerve enough to do it that night, though, and I told them to wait for me until tomorrow night. All the next day I kept seeing Mr. Tabb laying a rawhide across my back, or shooting me, and kept seeing that scared little brown girl back at the house, looking at me with her big eyes and asking me if I wouldn't just row her across to Ripley. Me and Mr. Tabb lost, and soon as dusk settled that night, I was at the old lady's house.

I don't know how I ever rowed the boat across the river. The current was strong, and I was trembling. I couldn't see a thing there in the dark, but I felt that girl's eyes. We didn't dare to whisper, so I couldn't tell her how sure I was that Mr. Tabb or some of the others' owners would tear me up when they found out what I had done. I just knew they would find out.

I was worried, too, about where to put her out of the boat. I couldn't ride her across the river all night, and I didn't know a thing about the other side. I had heard a lot about it from other slaves, but I thought it was just about like Mason County, with slaves and masters, overseers and rawhides; and so I just knew that if I pulled the boat up and went to asking people where to take her I would get a beating or get killed.

I don't know whether it seemed like a long time or a short time, now—it's so long ago; I know it was a long time rowing there in the cold and worrying. But it was short, too, 'cause as soon as I did get on the other side the big-eyed, brown-skin girl would be gone. Well, pretty soon I saw a tall light, and I remembered what the old lady had told me about looking for that light and rowing to it. I did; and when I got up to it, two men reached down and grabbed her. I started trembling all over again, and praying. Then, one of the men took my arm and I just felt down inside of me that the Lord had got ready for me. "You hungry, boy?" is what he asked me, and if he hadn't been holding me, I think I would have fell backward into the river.

That was my first trip; it took me a long time to get over my scared feeling, but I finally did, and I soon found myself going back across the river, with two and three people, and sometimes a whole boatload. I got so I used to make three and four trips a month.

What did my passengers look like? I can't tell you any more about it than you can, and you wasn't there. After that first girl—no, I never did see her again—I never saw my passengers. It would have to be the black nights of the moon when I would carry them, and I would meet 'em out in the open or in a house without a single light. The only way I knew who they were was to ask them: "What you say?" And they would answer, "Menare." I don't know what that word meant—it came from the Bible. I only know that that was the password I used, and all of them that I took over told it to me before I took them.

I guess you wonder what I did with them after I got them over the river. Well, there in Ripley was a man named Mr. Rankins; I think the rest of his name was John. He had a regular "station" there on his place for escaping slaves. You see, Ohio was a free state, and once they got over the river from Kentucky or Virginia, Mr. Rankins could strut them all around town, and nobody would bother 'em. The only reason we used to land 'em quietly at night was so that whoever brought 'em could go back for more, and because we had to be careful that none of the owners had followed us. Every once in a while they would follow a boat and catch their slaves back. Sometimes they would shoot at whoever was trying to save the poor devils.

Mr. Rankins had a regular station for the slaves. He had a big lighthouse in his yard, about thirty feet high, and he kept it burning all night. It always meant freedom for the slave if he could get to this light.

Sometimes Mr. Rankins would have twenty or thirty slaves that had run away on his place at a time. It must have cost him a whole lot to keep 'em and feed 'em, but I think some of his friends helped him.

Those who wanted to stay around that part of Ohio could stay, but didn't many of 'em do it, because there was too much danger that you would be walking along free one night, feel a hand over your mouth, and be back across the river and in slavery again in the morning. And nobody in the world ever got a chance to know as much misery as a slave that had escaped and been caught.

So a whole lot of 'em went on North to other parts of Ohio, or to New York, Chicago, or Canada. Canada was popular then because all of the slaves thought it was the last gate before you got all the way *inside* of heaven. I don't think there was much chance for a slave to make a living in Canada, but didn't many of 'em come back. They seem like they rather starve up there in the cold than to be back in slavery.

The army soon started taking a lot of 'em, too. They could enlist in the Union army and get good wages, more food than they ever had, and have all the little gals waving at 'em when they passed. Them blue uniforms was a nice change, too.

No, I never got anything from a single one of the people I carried over the river to freedom. I didn't want anything; after I had made a few trips I got to like it, and even though I could have been free any night myself, I figured I wasn't getting along so bad so I would stay on Mr. Tabb's place and help the others get free. I did it for four years.

I don't know to this day how he never knew what I was doing. I used to take some awful chances, and he knew I must have been up to something. I wouldn't do much work in the day, would never be in my house at night, and when he would happen to visit the plantation where I had said I was going I wouldn't be there. Sometimes I think he did know and wanted me to get the slaves away that way so he wouldn't have to cause hard feelings by freeing 'em.

I think Mr. Tabb used to talk a lot to Mr. John Fee. Mr. Fee was a man who lived in Kentucky, but Lord! how that man hated slavery! He used to always tell us (we never let our owners see us listening to him though) that God didn't intend for some men to be free and some men be in slavery. He used to talk to the owners, too, when they would listen to him, but mostly they hated the sight of John Fee.

In the night, though, he was a different man. For every slave who came through his place going across the river he had a good word, something to eat and some kind of rags, too, if it was cold. He always knew just what to tell you to do if anything went wrong, and sometimes I think he kept slaves there on his place till they could be rowed across the river. Helped us a lot.

I almost ran the business in the ground after I had been carrying the slaves across for nearly four years. It was in 1863, and one night I carried across about twelve on the same night. Somebody must have seen us, because they set out after me as soon as I stepped out of the boat back on the Kentucky side; from that time on they were after me. Sometimes they would almost catch me. I had to run away from Mr. Tabb's plantation and live in the fields and in the woods. I didn't know what a bed was from one week to another. I would sleep in a cornfield tonight, up in the branches of a tree tomorrow night, and buried in a haypile the next night. The river, where I had carried so many across myself, was no good to me; it was watched too close.

Finally, I saw that I could never do any more good in Mason County, so I decided to take my freedom, too. I had a wife by this time, and one night we quietly slipped across and headed for Mr. Rankins' bell and light. It looked like we had to go almost to China to get across that river. I could hear the bell and see the light on Mr. Rankins' place, but the harder I rowed, the farther away it got, and I knew if I didn't make it I'd get killed. But finally I pulled up by the lighthouse and went on to my freedom—just a few months before all of the slaves got theirs. I didn't stay in Ripley, though; I wasn't taking no chances. I went on to Detroit and still live there with most of ten children and thirty-one grandchildren.

The bigger ones don't care so much about hearing it now, but the little ones never get tired of hearing how their grandpa brought emancipation to loads of slaves he could touch and feel, but never could see.

BIRD IN THE AIR

There am big woods all round, and we sees lots of runawayers. One old fellow, name John, been a runawayer for four years, and the paterollers tries all they tricks, but they can't cotch him. They wants him bad, 'cause it 'spire other slaves to run away if he stays a-loose. They sots the trap for him. They know he likes good eats, so they 'ranges for a quilting and gives chitlins and lye hominy. John comes and am inside when the paterollers rides up to the door. Everybody gits quiet, and John stands near the door, and when they starts to come in, he grabs the shovel full of hot ashes and throws them into the paterollers' faces. He gits through and runs off, hollering, 'Bird in the air!"

SAVED

My mammy she work in the field all day and piece and quilt all night. Then she have to spin enough thread to make four cuts for the white folks every night. Why, sometime I never go to bed. Have to hold the light for her to see by. She have to piece quilts for the white folks, too. Why, they is a scar on my arm yet where my brother let the pine drip on me. Rich pine was all the light we ever have. My brother was a-holding the pine so's I can help Mammy tack the quilt, and he go to sleep and let it drip.

I never see how my mammy stand such hard work. She stand up for her children though. The old overseer he hate my mammy, 'cause she fight him for beating her children. Why, she git more whuppings for that than anything else. She have twelve children. I 'member I see the three oldest stand in the snow up to their knees to split rails, while the overseer stand off and grin.

My mammy she trouble in her heart about the way they treated. Every night she pray for the Lord to git her and her children out of the place. One day she plowing in the cotton field. All sudden-like she let out a big yell. Then she start singing and a-shouting and a-whooping and a-hollering. Then it seem she plow all the harder. When she come home, Marse Jim's mammy say: "What all that going on the field? You think we send you out there just to whoop and yell? No, siree, we put you out there to work, and you sure better work, else we git the overseer to cowhide you old black back."

My mammy just grin all over her black wrinkled face and say: "I's saved! The Lord done tell me I's saved. Now I know the Lord will show me the way. I ain't gwine-a grieve no more. No matter how much you all done beat me and my children, the Lord will show me the way. And some day we never be slaves." Old Granny Moore grab the cowhide and slash Mammy 'cross the back, but Mammy never yell. She just go back to the field a-singing.

PART FOUR

A War
Among the White Folks

The white folks went off to the war. They said they could whup, but the Lord said, "No," and they didn't whup. They went off laughing, and many were soon crying, and many did not come back. The Yankees come through. They took what they wanted, killed the stock, stole the horses, poured out the 'lasses, and cut up a lot of meanness. But most of 'em is dead and gone now. No matter whether they were Southern white folks or Northern white folks, they is dead now.

For the slave, time was divided into "before the war" and "after the war." The "Freedom War" was preluded by strange portents—falling stars, a "great comet," and the "elements all red as blood." These signs of coming doom fitted into the pattern of a divine punishment visited upon the South for the sins of slavery. "I often think that the system of paterollers and bloodhounds did more to bring on the war and the wrath of the Lord than anything else."

Besides the signs in the heavens, there were other indications that slavery was dying and that in the final death agony many thousands on both sides would "wade knee deep in blood and die first." The South itself was divided. Some were for humanizing slavery; others wanted it abolished, like the Reverend Dickey, who was expelled from the church and forced to leave the state for preaching freedom for the slaves. Another preacher, a Baptist, had "been taught that it was all right to have slaves and treat them like he want to, but he been taught it was sinful to go fight and kill to keep them, and he lived up to what he been taught." Miss Lucy's boy "lay out in the woods all time. He say no need in him gitting shot up and killed. He say let the slaves be free."

Similarly, the slaves were divided in their attitude toward the Yankees. Some, in their ignorance and credulousness, had been deceived and intimidated (under threat of punishment or death for giving aid and comfort to the enemy) into fearing the invaders as devils and oppressors, with horns on their head and one eye in the middle of their forehead. Most of the slaves, however, welcomed their deliverers, who in many cases brought the first news of freedom. In between were those who said with an indifference or resentment that had some basis in actual conditions but that smacks of white prejudice: "It was a war 'mong the white folks. Niggers had no say in it. . . . Niggers didn't know what the fight was 'bout."

Slaves served in both armies, but chiefly as military laborers. Many accompanied their masters as body servants or were drafted for heavy duty, such as digging trenches, throwing up breastworks, and repairing bridges. Many fugitives were pressed into service by the Union forces, and the recruiting of Negro soldiers was authorized by federal order on August 25, 1862. Like Thomas Cole, they set cannons; guarded supplies; cared for the wounded and prisoners; loaded wagons, boxcars, and boats; cleared roads; and built temporary bridges.

On the home front, slaves felt the pinch of hard times and worked harder raising food. Even the house women worked in the fields, plowing, hoeing, pulling corn and fodder, cutting cordwood, and splitting rails. Slaves also suffered the desperate cruelties of fear-maddened masters, some of whom threatened to shoot their slaves rather than set them free, or of brutal overseers left in charge by masters gone to war or of the latter's resentful wives, who justified whippings by saying: "Your master's out fighting and losing blood trying to save you from them Yankees, so you can get yourn here."

A less known but equally arduous war experience was "refugeeing," or the removal of slaves to a safe place by their masters. These long, dramatic treks through strange and difficult country were epic journeys, which trained the Negroes in migration and afforded them the satisfaction and encouragement of seeing their masters run away.

Looking back on the war as the main crisis in their lives, many slaves reckoned their ages by remembering how old they were at surrender. And in retrospect many might have echoed the regret that Negroes had not done more of the actual fighting: "If every mother's son of a black had thrown 'way his hoe and took up a gun to fight for his own freedom along with the Yankees, the war'd been over before it begun."

They Made Us Sing "Dixie"

My old master mean to us. We used to watch for him to come in the big gate, then we run and hide. He used to come to the quarters and make us children sing. He make us sing "Dixie." Sometimes he make us sing half a day. Seems like "Dixie" his main song. I tell you I don't like it now. But have mercy. He make us sing it. Seems like all the white folks like "Dixie." I's glad when he went away to war.

BACK BEFORE BREAKFAST

I

I well recollects when my master went to war. He called us all in the kitchen and told us he had to go over there and whip those sons of bitches and would be back 'fore breakfast. He didn't return for two years. I says, "Master, we sure would have waited breakfast on you a long time." He said, "Yes; they's the hardest sons of bitches to whip I ever had dealings with."

II

When the war come on, the old man Hawkens was dead. His widow had three sons, but one was married and off from her home somewhere. All three boys went to war. Her married son died in the war.

One son went to war, but he didn't want to go. He ask his mother if she rather free the Negroes or go to war. She said, "Go fight till you die, it won't be nothing but a breakfast spell." He went but come back on a furlough. He spent the rest of the time in a cave he dug down back of the field. He'd slip out and come to the house a little while at night. It was in the back woods and not very near anybody else. . . . Sister Mandy told so many times about carrying fire in a coffeepot—had a lid and handle—to the son in the cave. She'd go across there, a meadow like and a field, calling the sheep for a blind so if the cavalry spied her they would think she had a little feed for the sheep. The cavalry was close about. It was cold, and the young master would nearly freeze in his cave.

YOU CAN GET YOURN HERE

. . . Master Sam didn't never whip me, but Miss Julia whipped me every day in the morning. During the war she beat us so terrible. She say, "Your master's out fighting and losing blood trying to save you from them Yankees, so you can get yourn here." Miss Julia would take me by the ears and butt my head against the wall.

One day whiles Master was gone hunting, Mistress Julia told her brother to give Miss Harriet (me) a free whipping. She was a nigger killer. Master Colonel Sam come home, and he said, "You infernal sons of bitches, don't you know there is three hundred Yankees camped out here, and iffen they knowed you'd whipped this nigger the way you done done, they'd kill all us. Iffen they find it out, I'll kill all you all." Old rich devils! I'm here, but they is gone.

LEONARD ALLEN

I was scared of Marse Jordan, and all of the grown niggers was too, 'cept Leonard and Burrus Allen. Them niggers wasn't scared of nothing. If the devil hisself had come and shook a stick at them, they'd hit him back. Leonard was a big black buck nigger; he was the biggest nigger I ever seed. And Burrus was near 'bout as big. And they 'spised Marse Jordan worse'n pizen.

I was sort of scared of Miss Sally too. When Marse Jordan wasn't round she was sweet and kind, but when he was round she was a yes-sir, yes-sir woman. Everything he told her to do she done. He made her slap Mammy one time 'cause when she passed his coffee she spilled some in the saucer. Miss Sally hit Mammy easy, but Marse Jordan say: "Hit her, Sally, hit the black bitch like she 'zerve to be hit." Then Miss Sally draw back her hand and hit Mammy in the face, pow! then she went back to her place at the table and play like she eating her breakfast. Then when Marse Jordan leave, she come in the kitchen and put her arms round Mammy and cry, and Mammy pat her on the back, and she cry too. I loved Miss Sally when Marse Jordan wasn't round.

Marse Jordan's two sons went to the war; they went all dressed up in they fighting clothes. Young Marse Jordan was just like Miss Sally, but Marse Gregory was like Marse Jordan, even to the bully way he walk. Young Marse Jordan never come back from the war, but 'twould take more than a bullet to kill Marse Gregory. He too mean to die anyhow 'cause the devil didn't want him and the Lord wouldn't have him.

One day Marse Gregory come home on a furlough. He think he look pretty with his sword clanking and his boots shining. He was a colonel, lieutenant, or something. He was strutting round the yard showing off, when Leonard Allen say under his breath, "Look at that goddam soldier. He fighting to keep us niggers from being free."

'Bout that time Marse Jordan come up. He look at Leonard and say, "What you mumbling 'bout?"

That big Leonard wasn't scared. He say, "I say, 'Look at that goddam soldier. He fighting to keep us niggers from being free.'"

Marse Jordan's face begun to swell. It turned so red that the blood near 'bout bust out. He turned to Pappy and told him to go and bring him his shotgun. When Pappy come back, Miss Sally come with him. The tears was streaming down her face. She run up to Marse Jordan and caught his arm. Old Marse flung her off and took the gun from Pappy. He leveled it on Leonard and told him to pull his shirt open. Leonard opened his shirt and stood there big as a black giant, sneering at Old Marse.

Then Miss Sally run up again and stood 'tween that gun and Leonard.

Old Marse yell to Pappy and told him to take that woman out of the way, but nobody ain't moved to touch Miss Sally, and she didn't move neither; she just stood there facing Old Marse. Then Old Marse let down the gun. He reached over and slapped Miss Sally down, then picked up the gun and shot a hole in Leonard's chest big as your fist. Then he took up Miss Sally and toted her in the house. But I was so scared that I run and hid in the stable loft, and even with my eyes shut I could see Leonard laying on the ground with that bloody hole in his chest and that sneer on his black mouth.

THE CRACK IN THE WALL

While Master Jim is out fighting the Yanks, the mistress is fiddling round with a neighbor man, Mr. Goldsmith. I is young then, but I knows enough that Master Jim's going to be mighty mad when he hears about it.

The mistress didn't know I knows her secret, and I'm fixing to even up for some of them whippings she put off on me. That's why I tell Master Jim next time he come home.

"See that crack in the wall?" Master Jim says, "Yes," and I say, "It's just like the open door when the eyes are close to the wall." He peek and see into the bedroom.

"That's how I find out about the mistress and Mr. Goldsmith," I tells him, and I see he's getting mad.

"What do you mean?" And Master Jim grabs me hard by the arm like I was trying to get away.

"I see them in the bed."

That's all I say. The demon's got him, and Master Jim tears out of the room looking for the mistress.

Then I hears loud talking and pretty soon the mistress is screaming and calling for help, and if Old Master Ben hadn't drop in just then and stop the fight, why, I guess she be beat almost to death, that how mad the master was.

A WONDERFUL CONSIDERATION

I had a statement when I was born, but I don't 'member just now. When the war first start, I was water-toter for my master. Well, now, then I want to say that my master where I was born in Wilcox County, Alabama, his name was Higginbotham. When Mr. Higginbotham die, his son, Mr. Sam Higginbotham, was my young master. When he married, he marry in the Carroll family. My father and mother belong to Mr. Higginbotham. Mr. Sam, he move to Louisiana. When he went back to Alabama, he took sick with the cholera and die there. Mr. Sam, he marry Miss Caroline Carroll. Later on, after Mr. Sam die, Miss Caroline marry Mr. Winn. I become orphan-children property. Mr. Winn was the overseer. When I was a small boy I had playtime. I always had good owners. When I get bigger I had some time off after work in the evenings and on Sundays. Then I want to say I was hired out, and they claimed they was going to be a war. The North and the South was going to split apart. In 1861 war commence, and my mistress die. I was then staying with the Carroll family. The Carrolls were brothers of my owner. Mr. Jim and Mr. Robert was soldiers in the war. Mr. Robert was in the infantry, and Mr. Jim they took him along to drive. When they was going to Barn Chest [sic], Mr. Robert he say to me, "Fay, you go back home and tell Ma she need not be uneasy 'bout me, 'cause the Yankees is retreating to Natchitoches." So I driv back, but I didn't put up the team. When I was telling her, it was 'bout three mile over to Mosses Field.[1] When I was telling her, a big cannon shot overhead—"Boom!" She just shook and say, "Oh, Fay, git some corn and throw it to the hogs and go to Chicet." I got some corn and start to git out the crib. They shot another cannon. She say to me, "Go back and give the corn to the pigs." When I put my feets through the crib door, they shoot another shot, and I pull my feets back. She tell me to go back and feed the pigs, but I don't know if I ever git the corn to the pigs.

Mr. Carroll say that at Mansfield where they was shooting the big guns, the ladies was crying. He told 'em they needn't to cry now; when they was shooting the big guns they wasn't killing men, but when they hear the little guns shoot, then they could start crying, 'cause that mean that men was gitting kill. I dunno if you ever parch popcorn. That the way the little guns sound. He say that then they could begin crying. Our white people was coming from Shreveport to meet the Yankees from Natchitoches, aiming to go to Shreveport. If anything was a

[1] The local name for the tract of land on which the battle of Mansfield was fought, in part.

wonderful consideration it was then. Mr. Robert Carroll was stood up by a big tree there at Mansfield, and the captain, he said, "Is anybody here that know the neighborhood?" Here's the thing they want to know: When the soldiers start out, they didn't want 'em to launch out and git mix up. They sent for Mr. Carroll, 'cause he live 'bout a mile away. He was order to stand by the tree, and the captain went by waving a sword, and pretty soon the captain was killed. They kept on fighting, and after awhile a soldier come by and ax what he doing there. He said he had orders to stand there. The soldier say that the captain was killed and for him to go and help with the wounded soldiers. When the big general come from Shreveport and holler, "Charge!" the Yankees git in the corner of a rail fence. They broke right through that field old prairie, and sixty men git killed dead before they git across. Next day, coming home, I want to tell you the hosses didn't lay on this side nor on that side. They just squat down, they was dead. I think it was a wonderful consideration to bring up in memory.

One night right where the battle was fought we had to camp. It was raining and sleeting and snowing. I said, "What you going to do tonight?" Mr. James Carroll said, "We just have to stand where we camp. Just stack the guns and put out what you call the watchman." I said, "Sentinel?" and he said, "Yes." They had what you call the relief. They wasn't in bed, they was out under a tree in the cold. Every hour they'd walk 'em out 'long a runway to walk guard. It was a wonderful distressing time. The soldiers had a little song they sung:

> Eat when you're hungry,
> Drink when you're dry.
> Iffen a tree don't kill you,
> You'll live till you die.

This was 'cause they had to stand under trees, and when the Yankees shoot cannon they'd knock off limbs and tops of trees and them under the trees might git kill from the falling branches. Another song was:

> It was on the eighth of April
> They all 'member well,
> When fifes and drums were beating
> For us all to march away.

. . . I didn't quite git through 'bout the Mansfield battle. Them sixty men that was killed, they just dig a big hole and put 'em in and threw dirt on 'em. I went back after two or three days, and the bodies done swell and crack the ground. Master's plantation coming from Shreveport was on the east side of Mosses Field. We was 'bout one and a half or two mile from Mosses Field. I wasn't acquaint with many whites 'cause I was with the Carrolls, and they was always kind. I heard they was people this way and that, but I don't know 'bout that. My white folks see that I was not abused. When news of the surrender come, lots of colored folks seem to be rejoicing and sing, "I's free, I's free as a frog," 'cause a frog had freedom to git on a log and jump off when he please. Some just stayed on with their white folks. One time they say they send all the niggers back to Africa. I say they never git me. I been here, and my white folks been here, and here I going to stay. My young master say he want me for a nigger driver, so he teach me how to read and spell so I could tend to business. In time of the war Miss Caroline say the soldiers been there and take the best hoss. They sent me off with Ball, a little hoss. When I come back, I meet some soldiers. They say they going take the hoss; if they don't the Yankees come take 'em. I tell 'em they done got Master Carroll' other hoss, to leave this one. They say, "Git down, I going give you a few licks anyhow." I fall down, but they never hit me, and they say, "Maybe that Mr. Carroll whose hoss we took let this boy go on with the hoss." Miss Caroline say she wish she'd let me take Dandy; that was the best hoss.

I WISHED I NEVER RUN OFF

Massa Cole . . . die. Missy Cole, she moves to Huntsville, in Alabama. But she leave me on the plantation, 'cause I'm big and stout then. She takes my mother to cook, and that the last time I ever seed my mother. Missy Cole buys the fine house in Huntsville. My mother tells me to be good and do all the overseer tells me. I told her goodbye, and she never did git to come back to see me, and I never seed her and my brother and sister 'gain. I don't know whether they am sold or not.

I thinks to myself, that Mr. Anderson, the overseer, he'll give me that cat-o'-nine-tails the first chance he gits, but makes up my mind he won't git the chance, 'cause I's gwine run off the first chance I gits. I didn't know how to git out of there, but I's gwine North where there ain't no slaveowners. In a year or so there am 'nother overseer, Mr. Sandson, and he give me the log house and the gal to do my cooking and such. There am war talk, and we 'gins gwine to the field earlier and staying later. Corn am haul off, cotton am haul off, hogs and cattle am rounded up and haul off, and things 'gins looking bad. The war am on, but us don't see none of it. But 'stead of eating corn bread, us eats bread out of kaffir corn and maize. We raises lots of okra, and they say it gwine be parch and grind to make coffee for white folks. That didn't look good either. That winter, 'stead of killing three or four hundred hogs like we always done before, we only done one killing of a hundred seventy-five, and they not all big ones, neither. When the meat supply runs low, Mr. Sandson sends some slaves to kill a deer or wild hogs or just any kind of game. He never sends me in any them bunches, but I hoped he would, and one day he calls me to go and says not to go off the plantation too far but be sure bring home some meat. This the chance I been wanting, so when we gits to the hunting ground the leader says to scatter out, and I tells him me and 'nother man goes north and make the circle round the river and meet 'bout sundown. I crosses the river and goes north. I's gwine to the free country, where they ain't no slaves. I travels all that day and night up the river and follows the North Star. Several times I thunk the bloodhounds am trailing me, and I gits in the big hurry. I's so tired I couldn't hardly move, but I gits in a trot.

I's hoping and praying all the time I meets up with that Harriet Tubman woman. She the colored woman what takes slaves to Canada. She always travels the underground railroad, they calls it, travels at night and hides out in the day. She sure sneaks them out the South, and I think she's the brave woman.

I eats all the nuts and kills a few swamp rabbits and cotches a few fish. I builds the fire and goes off 'bout half a mile and hides in the thicket till it burns down to the coals, then bakes me some fish and rabbit. I's shaking all the time, 'fraid I'd git cotched, but I's nearly starve to death. I puts the rest the fish in my cap and travels on that night by the North Star and hides in a big thicket the next day, and along evening I hears guns shooting. I sure am scared this time, sure 'nough. I's scared to come in and scared to go out, and while I's standing there, I hears two men say, "Stick you hands up, boy. What you doing?" I says, "Uh-uh-uh, I dunno. You ain't gwine take me back to the plantation, is you?" They says, "No. Does you want to fight for the North?" I says I will, 'cause they talks like Northern men. Us walk night and day and gits in General Rosecrans' camp, and they thunk I's the spy from the South. They asks me all sorts of questions and says they'll whip me if I didn't tell them what I's spying 'bout. Finally they 'lieves me and puts me to work helping with the cannons. I feels 'portant then, but I didn't know what was in front of me, or I 'spects I'd run off 'gain.

I helps sot them cannons on this Chickamauga Mountain, in hiding places. I has to go with a man and wait on him and that cannon. First thing I knows— bang! bang! boom!—things has started, and guns am shooting faster than you can think, and I looks round for the way to run. But them guns am shooting down the hill in front of me and shooting at me, and over me and on both sides of me. I tries to dig me a hole and git in it. All this happen right now, and first thing I knows, the man am kicking me and wanting me to holp him keep that cannon loaded. Man, I didn't want no cannon, but I has to help anyway. We fit till dark, and the Rebels got more men than us, so General Rosecrans sends the message to General Woods to come help us out. When the messenger slips off, I sure wish it am me slipping off, but I didn't want to see no General Woods. I just wants to git back to that old plantation and pick more cotton. I'd been willing to do 'most anything to git out that mess, but I done told General Rosecrans I wants to fight the Rebels, and he sure was letting me do it. He wasn't just letting me do it, he was making me do it. I done got in there, and he wouldn't let me out.

White folks, there was men laying wanting help, wanting water, with blood running out them and the top or sides their heads gone, great big holes in them. I just promises the good Lord if He just let me git out that mess, I wouldn't run off no more, but I didn't know then He wasn't gwine let me out with just that battle. He gwine give me plenty more, but that battle ain't over yet, for next morning the Rebels 'gins shooting and killing lots of our men, and General Woods ain't come, so General Rosecrans orders us to 'treat and didn't have to tell me what he said, neither. The Rebels comes after us, shooting, and we runs off and leaves that cannon what I was with setting on the hill, and I didn't want that thing nohow.

We kept hotfooting till we gits to Chattanooga, and there is where we stops. Here comes one them Rebel generals with the big bunch of men and gits right on top of Lookout Mountain, right clost to Chattanooga, and wouldn't let us out. I don't know just how long, but a long time. Lots our hosses and mules starves to death, and we eats some the hosses. We all like to starve to death ourselves. Chattanooga is in the bend the Tennessee River, and on Lookout Mountain, on the east, am them Rebels and could keep up with everything we done. After a long time a General Thomas gits in some way. He finds the rough trail or wagon road round the mountain 'long the river, and supplies and men comes by boat up the river to this place and comes on into Chattanooga. More Union men kept coming, and I guess maybe six or eight generals, and they gits ready to fight. It am 'long late in fall or early winter.

They starts climbing this steep mountain, and when us gits three-fourths the way up it am foggy, and you couldn't see no place. Everything wet and the rocks am slick, and they 'gins fighting. I 'spects some shoots their own men, 'cause you couldn't see nothing, just men running and the guns roaring. Finally them Rebels fled, and we gits on Lookout Mountain and takes it.

There a long range of hills leading 'way from Lookout Mountain, nearly to Missionary Ridge. This ridge 'longside the Chickamauga River, what am the Indian name, meaning "River of Death." They fights the Rebels on Orchard Knob Hill, and I wasn't in that, but I's in the Missionary Ridge battle. We has to come out the timber and run 'cross a strip or opening up the hill. They sure kilt lots our men when we runs 'cross that opening. We runs for all we's worth and uses guns or anything we could. The Rebels turns and runs off, and our soldiers turns the cannons round what we's capture and kilt some the Rebels with their own guns.

I never did git to where I wasn't scared when we goes into the battle. This the last one I's in, and I's sure glad, for I never seed the like of dead and wounded men. We picks them up, the Rebels like the Unions, and doctors them the best we could. When I seed all that suffering, I hopes I never lives to see 'nother war. They say the World War am worse, but I's too old to go.

I sure wished lots of times I never run off from the plantation. I begs the General not to send me on any more battles, and he says I's the coward and sympathizes with the South. But I tells him I just couldn't stand to see all them men laying there dying and hollering and begging for help and a drink of water and blood everywhere you looks. Killing hogs back on the plantation didn't bother me none, but this am different.

Finally, the General tells me I can go back to Chattanooga and guard the supplies in camp there and take care the wounded soldiers and prisoners. A bunch of men is with me, and we has all we can do. We gits the orders to send supplies to some general, and it my job to help load the wagons or boxcars or boats. A train of wagons leaves sometimes. We gits all them supplies by boat, and Chattanooga am the 'stributing center. When winter comes, everybody rests awhile and waits for spring to open. The Union general sends in some more colored soldiers. There ain't been many colored men, but the last year the war there am lots. The North and the South am taking anything they can git to win the war.

When spring breaks and all the snow am gone and the trees 'gins putting out and everything 'gins to look pretty and peaceable-like, making you think you ought to be plowing and planting a crop, that when the fighting starts all over 'gain, killing men and burning homes and stealing stock and food. Then they sends me out to help clear roads and build temporary bridges. We walks miles on muddy ground, 'cross rivers, wading water up to our chins. We builds rafts and pole bridges to git the mules and hosses and cannons 'cross, and up and down hills, and cuts roads through timber.

But when they wants to battle, General Thomas always leaves me in camp to tend to supplies. He calls me a coward, and I sure glad he thunk I was. I wasn't no coward, I just couldn't stand to see all them people tore to pieces. I hears 'bout the battle in a thick forest and the trees big as my body just shot down. I seed that in the Missionary Ridge battle, too.

I shifts from one camp to 'nother and finally gits back to Chattanooga. I bet during my time I handles 'nough ammunition to kill everybody in the whole United States. I seed most the mainest generals in the Union army and some in the Rebel army.

WE WERE CONFEDERATES

. . . Us was Confederates all the while, leastwise I means my mammy and my pappy and me and all the rest of the children, 'cause Old Marse was, and Marse Jeff woulda fit 'em too and me with him iffen we had been old enough.

But the Yankees, they didn't know that we was Confederates. They just reckon we like 'most all the rest of the niggers. Us was scared of them Yankees, though, 'cause us children course didn't know what they was, and the overseer, Jim Lynch, he done told us little-uns that a Yankee was something what had one great big horn on he head and just one eye and that right in the middle of he breast. And, boss, I sure was surprised when I seen a sure 'nough Yankee and see he was a man just like any of the rest of the folks.

The war tore up things right sharp, yet and still it wasn't so bad here in Arkansas as I hear folks tell it was back in the older states like Tennessee, Alabama, and Georgia. The best I recollect the Yankees come in here 'bout July of the year, and they had a big scrap in Helena with 'em, and us could hear the cannons fifteen miles off. And then they would make their trips out foraging for stuff—corn and such—and they would take all the cotton they could find. But our mens, they would hide the cotton in the thickets and canebrakes iffen they had time, or either they would burn it up 'fore the Yankees come if they could. I 'member one day we had on hand 'bout hundred bales at the gin, and a white man come with orders to the overseer to get rid of it. So they started to hauling it off to the woods, and they hauled off 'bout fifty bales, and then they see they wasn't going to have time to git the rest to the woods, and then they commenced cutting the ties on the bales so they could set fire to them that they hadn't hid yet. And 'bout that time here come one of Mr. Tom Casteel's niggers just a-flying on a mule with a letter to the white man. Mr. Tom Casteel, he had he place just up the river from us, on the island, and when he gived the letter to the man and the man read it, he said, "The Yankees is coming!" and he lit out for the river where the boat was waiting for him and got 'way. And there was all that loose cotton on the ground, and us was scared to set fire to the cotton then. And 'bout that time the Yankees arrive and say, "Don't you burn that cotton!" And they looked all over the place and find the bales that was hid in the woods. And the next day they come and haul it off, and they say us niggers can have that what the ties been cut on. And my mammy, she set to work and likewise the other women what the Yankees say can have the loose cotton, and tie up all they can in bags. And after that us sold it to the Yankees in Helena for a dollar a pound, and that was all the money us had for a long time.

Howsomever, us all lived good 'cause there was heap of wild hogs and possums and such, and we had hid a heap of corn and us did fine. Sometimes the war boats, they would pass on the river—that is, the Yankee boats—and us would hide 'hind the trees and bushes and see them pass. We wouldn't let them see us, though, 'cause we thought they would shoot. Heap and heap of times soldiers would come by us place. When the Yankees'd come, they would ax my mammy, "Aunt Mary, is you seen any Secesh today?" And Mammy, she'd say, "No, sir," even iffen she had seen some of us mens. But when our soldiers'd come and say, "Aunt Mary, is you seen ary Yankee round here recent?" she'd always tell them the truth. They was a bunch of us soldiers, that is, the Confederates, what used to stay round in the community constant, that we knowed, but they always had to be on the dodge 'cause there was so many more Yankees than them.

Some of these men I 'member good 'cause they was us closest neighbors and some of them lived on 'jining places. There was Mr. Lum Shell, Mr. Tom Stoneham, Mr. Bob Yabee, Mr. Henry Rabb, and Mr. Tom Casteel. Them I 'member well 'cause they come to us cabin right often, and Mammy, she'd cook for 'em. And then after the niggers git they freedom, they could leave the place any time they choose. And every so often Mammy'd go to Helena, and generally she took me with her to help tote the things she git there. Old Mr. Cooledge, he had the biggest and 'bout the onliest store that there was in Helena and generally at that time. Mr. Cooledge, he was a old-like gentleman and had everything 'most in the store—boots, shoes, tobacco, medicine, and so on. Course couldn't no person go in and outen Helena at that time—that is, during war days, 'outen they had a pass and the Yankee soldier that writ the passes was named Buford. And he is the one what us always git our passes from for to git in and out. And 'twasn't so long 'fore Mr. Buford, he git to know my mammy right well and call her by her name. He, just like all the white mens, knowed her as "Aunt Mary," but him nor none of the Yankees knowed that Mammy was a Confederate. And that's something I will tell you, boss.

These soldiers that I is just named and that was us neighbors, they'd come to our cabin sometimes and say, "Aunt Mary, we want you to go to Helena for us and git some tobacco, and mebbe some medicine, and so on, and we gwine write Old Man Cooledge a note for you to take with you." And Mammy, she'd git off for town walking and 'd git the note to Old Man Cooledge. Old Man Cooledge, you see, boss, he sided with the Confederates, too, but he didn't let on that he did, but all the Confederate soldiers round there in the country, they knowed they could 'pend on him. And when my mammy'd take the note in to Old Man Cooledge, he'd fix Mammy up in some of them big wide hoop skirts and hide the things 'neath the skirts that the men sont for. Then she and sometimes me with her, us would light out for home, and course we always had our pass, and they knowed us and we easy git by the pickets and git home with the goods for those soldier men what sont us.

We've Come to Set You Free

I say, "Master, who is them soldiers?" And he say to me, "They's the Yankees, come to try to take you away from me." And I say, "Looks like to me, Master, iffen they wants to take us, they'd ask you for us." Master laughed and say, "Boy, them fellers don't axes with words. They does all they talking with cannons."

BLUE VEINS ON THEIR BELLIES

I 'member when the war started in 1861, my mammy hired me out to Mrs. Brewer, and she used to git after me and say, "You better do that good or I'll whip you. My husband gone to war now on account of you niggers, and it's a pity you niggers ever been, 'cause he may get killed and I'll never see him again."

I 'member seeing General Bragg's men and General Steele and General Marmaduke. Had a fight down at Mark's Mill. We just lived six miles from there. Seen the Yankees coming by along the big public road. The Yankees whipped and fought 'em so strong they didn't have time to bury the dead. We could see the buzzards and carrion crows. I used to hear Old Mistress say, "There goes the buzzards, done et all the meat off." I used to go to mill, and we could see the bones. Used to get out and look at their teeth. No ma'am, I wasn't scared, the white boys was with me. . . .

After a battle when the dead soldiers was laying around and didn't have on no uniform 'cause some of the other soldiers took 'em, I've heard the old folk what knowed say you could tell the Yankees from the Rebels 'cause the Yankees had blue veins on their bellies and the Rebels didn't.

YANKEES HAVE HORNS

Old Miss was name Miss Liza. She scared to stay by herself after Old Master died. I was took to be her companion. Every day she wanted me to brush her long hair and bathe her feet in cool water; she said I was gentle and didn't never hurt her. One day I was a-standing by the window, and I seen smoke—blue smoke a-rising over beyond a woods. I heared cannons a-booming and axed her what was it. She say: "Run, Mittie, and hide yourself. It's the Yanks. They's coming at last, oh, Lordy!" I was all excited and told her I didn't want to hide, I wanted to see 'em. "No," she say, right firm. "Ain't I always told you Yankees has horns on their heads? They'll get you. Go on now, do like I tells you." So I runs out the room and went down by the big gate. A high wall was there, and a tree put its branches right over the top. I clumb up and hid under the leaves. They was coming, all a-marching. The captain opened our big gate and marched them in. A soldier seen me and said, "Come on down here; I want to see you." I told him I would, if he would take off his hat and show me his horns.

FATHER DID A BOLD THING

The Yankees used to come looking for horses. One time Master Archie had sent the horses off by one of the colored slaves, who was to stay at his wife's house and hide them in the thicket. During the night, Mother hears Archie Hays hollering. She went out to see what was the matter. The Yankees had old Archie Hays out and had guns poked at his breast. He was hollering, "No, sir, I don't." And Mother came and said, "Reuben, get up and go tell them he don't know where the horses is."

Father got up and did a bold thing. He went out and said, "Wait, gentlemen, he don't know where the horses is, but if you'll wait till tomorrow morning, he'll send a man to bring them in." I don't know how they got word to him, but he brought them in the next morning and the Yankees taken them off.

WHEN DADDY LOCKED MASTER IN THE SMOKEHOUSE

When the Yankees come to see iffen they had done turn us a-loose, I am a nine-year-old nigger gal. That make me about eighty-one now. They promenade up to the gate, and the drum say a-dr-um-m-m-m-m, and the man in the blue uniform he git down to open the gate. Old Massa he see them coming, and he runned in the house and grab up the gun. When he come hustling down off the gallery, my daddy come running. He seed Old Massa too mad to know what he a-doing, so quicker than a chicken could fly he grab that gun and wrastle it outen Old Massa's hands. Then he push Old Massa in the smokehouse and lock the door. He ain't do that to be mean, but he want to keep Old Massa outen trouble. Old Massa know that, but he beat on the door and yell, but it ain't git open till them Yankees done gone.

APPLES FOR THE YANKEES, STOCK FOR THE MASTER

Of course I 'member the war. Us chaps, both niggers and white, was made to go upstairs in the big house and look out the window to see the soldiers when they come. We heard the Yankees marching before they got there, but they come from the other side of the house, facing south toward Caldwells, and we didn't see them marching in. They stopped at our house and looked around and asked if Master was at home. We told him that he wasn't there. We was eating apples, and they asked us where we got 'em. We told them that we got the apples on the place, and they asked us for some. We give them some apples; then they left. Marse had carried his fine stock about a mile off in the woods so the soldiers couldn't find them; but we didn't tell the soldiers.

MOTHER AND THE YANKEE SOLDIER

. . . Mother had lots of nice things, quilts and things, and kept 'em in a chest in her little old shack. One day a Yankee soldier climbed in the back window and took some of the quilts. He rolled 'em up and was walking out of the yard when Mother saw him and said, "Why, you nasty, stinking rascal! You say you come down here to fight for the niggers, and now you're stealing from 'em." He said, "You're a goddam liar. I'm fighting for $14 a month and the Union."

ALL RIGHT IN THEIR PLACE

I suppose them Yankees was all right in their place, . . . but they never belong in the South. Why, Miss, one of 'em ax me what was them white flowers in the field. You'd think that a gentleman with all them decorations on hisself woulda knowed a field of cotton. And as for they a-setting me free! Miss, us niggers on the Bennett place was free as soon as we was born. I always been free.

MISS MARY'S FEATHER BED

My mistress took me down to the spring back of the house. Down there it was a holler treestump, taller'n you is. She tell me to clamb up to the top of that holler tree, then she hand me a big heavy bundle, all wropped up and tied tight. It sure was heavy! Then she say: "Drap it in, Cheney." I didn't know then what she's up to, but that was the silver and jewelry she was hiding.

. . . I's setting there in the loomroom, and Mr. Thad Watt's little gal, Louise, she's standing at the window. She say: "O-o-h! Nannie! Just look down yonder!" "Baby, what is that?" I says. "Them's the Yankees coming!" "God help us!" I says, and before I can catch my breath, the place is covered. You couldn't stir 'em up with a stick. Feets sounded like muttering thunder. Them bayonets stick up like they just setting on the mouth of they guns. They swords hanging on they sides, singing a tune whilst they walk. A chicken better not pass by. Iffen he do, off come his head!

When they pass on by me, they pretty nigh shook me outa my skin. "Where's the mens?" they say and shake me up. "Where's the arms?" They shake me till my eyeballs loosen up. "Where's the silver?" Lord! Was my teeths drapping out? They didn't give me time to catch my breath. All the time, Miss Mary just look 'em in the eye and say nothing!

They took them Enfield rifles, half as long as that door, and bust in the smokehouse window. They jack me up offen my feet and drag me up the ladder and say: "Git that meat out." I kept on throwing out Miss Mary's hams and sausages till they holler, "Stop." I come backing down that ladder like a squirrel, and I ain't stop backing till I reach Miss Mary.

Yes, Lord! Them Yankees loaded up a wagon full of meat and took the whole barrel of 'lasses! Taking that 'lasses kilt us children! Our mainest 'musement was making 'lasses candy. Then us cakewalk round it. Now that was all gone. Look like them soldiers had to sharpen they swords on everything in sight. The big crepe mullen bush by the parlor window was blooming so pink and pretty, and they just stood there and whack off them blooms like folks' heads drapping on the ground.

I seed the sergeant when he run his bayonet clean through Miss Mary's bestest feather bed and rip it slam open! With that, a wind blowed up and took them feathers every whichaway for Sunday. You couldn't see where you's at. The sergeant, he just throwed his head back and laugh fit to kill hisself. Then first thing next, he done suck a feather down his windpipe. Lord, honey, that white man sure struggled. Them soldiers throwed water in his face. They shook him and beat him and roll him over, and all the time he's getting limberer and bluerer. Then they jack him up by his feets and stand him on his head. Then they pump him up and down. Then they shook him till he spit. Then he come to.

They didn't cut no more mattresses. And they didn't cut nothing much up in the parlor, 'cause that's where the lieutenant and the sergeant slept. But when they left the next day, the whole place was strewed with mutilation.

SHERMAN'S MEN

I

Sherman's army came through there looking for Jeff Davis, and they told me that they wasn't fighting any more—that I was free.

They said, "You ain't got no master and no mistress." They et dinner there. All the old folks went upstairs and turned the house over to me and the cook. And they et dinner. One of them said, "My little man, bring your hat round now and we are going to pay you," and they passed the hat round and give me a hat full of money. I thought it wasn't no good, and I carried it and give it to my old mistress, but it was good.

They asked me if I had ever seen Jeff Davis. I said, "No." Then they said, "That's him sitting there." He had on a black dress and a pair of boots and a mantilla over his shoulders and a Quaker bonnet and a black veil.

They got up from the dining table, and Sherman ordered them to "Recover arms." He had on a big black hat full of eagles, and he had stars and stripes all over him. That was Sherman's artillery. They had mules with pots and skillets, and frying pans, and axes, and picks, grubbing hoes, and spades, and so on, all strapped on those mules. And the mules didn't have no bridles, but they went on just as though they had bridles. One of the Yanks started a song when he picked up his gun.

> Here's my little gun,
> His name is number one.
> Four and five rebels,
> We'll slay 'em as they come.
> Join the band.
> The rebels understand.
> Give up all the land
> To my brother Abraham.
> Old General Lee,
> Who is he?
> He's not such a man
> As our General Grant.
> Snap Poo, Snap Peter,
> Real rebel eater.
> I left my ply stock
> Standing in the mould.

I left my family
And silver and gold.
Snap Poo, Snap Peter,
Real rebel eater,
Snap Poo, Snap Peter.

And General Sherman gave the command, "Silence!" and "Silence!" roared one man, and it rolled all down the line, "Silence, silence, silence, silence." And they all got silent.

II

I saw all of Wheeler's cavalry. Sherman come through first. He came and stayed all night. Thousands and thousands of soldiers passed through during the night. Cooper Cuck was with them. He was a fellow that used to peddle around in all that country before the war. He went all through the South and learned everything. Then he joined up with the Yankees. He come there. Nobody seen him that night. He knowed everybody knowed him. He went and hid under something somewhere. He was under the hill at daybreak, but nobody seen him. When the last of the soldiers was going out in the morning, one fellow lagged behind and rounded a corner. Then he galloped a little ways and motioned with his arms. Cooper Cuck come out from under the hill, and he and Cooper Cuck both came back and stole everything that they could lay their hands on—all the gold and silver that was in the house, and everything they could carry.

Wheeler's cavalry was about three days behind Sherman. They caught up with Sherman, but it would have been better if they hadn't, 'cause he whipped 'em and drove 'em back and went right on. They didn't have much fighting in my country. They had a little scrimmage once—thirty-six men was all they was in it. One of the Yankees got lost from his company. He come back and inquired the way to Louisville. The old boss pointed the way with his left hand, and while the fellow was looking that way, he drug him off his horse and cut his throat and took his gun offen him and killed him.

Sherman's men stayed one night and left. I mean, his officers stayed. We had to feed them. They didn't pay nothing for what they was fed. The other men cooked and ate their own grub. They took every horse and mule we had. I was sitting beside my old missus. She said: "Please don't let 'em take all our horses."

The fellow she was talking to never looked around. He just said, "Every damn horse goes."

The Yankees took my Uncle Ben with them when they left. He didn't stay but a couple of days. They got in a fight. They give Uncle Ben five horses, five sacks of silverware, and five saddles. The goods was taken in the fight. Uncle Ben brought it back with him. The boss took all that silver away from him. Uncle Ben didn't know what to do with it. The Yankees had taken all my master's, and he took Ben's. Ben give it to him. He come back 'cause he wanted to.

When Wheeler's cavalry came through, they didn't take nothing—nothing but what they et. I heard a fellow say, "Have you got anything to eat?"

My mother said, "I ain't got nothing but some chitlins."

He said, "Gimme some of those. I love chitlins."

Mother gave 'em to me to carry to him. I didn't get halfway to him before the rest of the men grabbed me and took 'em away from me and et 'em up. The man that asked for them didn't get a one.

AGGRAVATING THE YANKEES

Well, when they started off fighting at Murfreesboro, it was a continual roar. The tin pans in the cupboard rattle all time. It was distressful. The house shaking all time. All our houses jar. The earth quivered. It sound like the Judgment. Nobody felt good. Both sides foraging, one bad as the other, hungry, gitting everything you put 'way to live on. That's war. I found out all 'bout what it was. Lady, it ain't nothing but hell on this earth.

I told you I was ten miles from the war and how it roared and 'bout how the cannons shook the earth. There couldn't be a chicken nor a goose nor a ear of corn to be found 'bout our place. It was such hard times. It was both sides come git what you had. Whole heap of Yankees come in their blue suits and caps on horses up the lane. They was hunting horses. They done got every horse and colt on the place 'cepting one old mare, mother of all the stock they had on the place. Young mistress had a fuss 'bout her and led her up the steps and put her in the house.

Then when they started to leave, one old Yankee set the corner of the house on fire. We all got busy then, white folks and darkies both carrying water to put it out. We got it out, but while we doing that, mind out, they went down the lane to the road by the duck pond we had dug out. One old soldier spied a goose setting in the grass. She been so scared she never come to the house no more. Nobody knowed there was one on our place. He took his javelin and stuck it through her back. She started hollering and fluttering till the horses, nearly all of 'em, started running and some of 'em bucking. We got the fire 'bout out. We couldn't help laughing, it look so funny. I been busting I was so mad 'cause they tried take Old Beck. Three of 'em horses throwed 'em. They struck out 'cross the Jimson weeds and down through the corn patch trying to head off their horses. Them horses throwed 'em sprawling. That was the funniest sight I ever seed.

We got our water out of a cave. It was good cold limestone water. We had a long pole and a rope with a bucket on the end. We swing the pole round, let it down, then pull it back and tie it. They go to the other end and git the bucket of water. I toted 'bout all the water to both places what they used. One day I going to the cave after water. I had a habit of throwing till I got to be pretty exact 'bout hitting. I spied a hornets' nest in a tree long the lane. I knowed them soldiers be 'long back for something else, pillaging 'bout. It wasn't long, sure 'nough, they come back and went up to the house.

I got a pile of rocks in my hands. I hid down in the hazel-nut bushes. When they come by galloping, I throwed and hit that big old hornets' nest. The way they piled out on them soldiers. You could see 'em fighting far as you could see 'em with their blue caps. The horses running and bucking. I lit out to the house to see what else they carried off.

I told Marse White 'bout how I hit that hornets' nest with the first rock I throwed. He scolded me, for he said if they had seen me they would killed me. It scared him. He said, "Don't do no more capers like that." That old hornets' nest soon come down. It was big as a water bucket. Marse White call me "Son boy." I told him what terrible language they used, and 'bout some of the horses going over the lane fence. It was made outa rails piled up. Marse White sure was glad they didn't see me. He kept on saying, "Son boy, they would killed you right on the spot. Don't do nothing to 'em to aggravate 'em."

It look like we couldn't make a scratch on the ground nowhere the soldiers couldn't find it. We had a ash hopper setting all time. We made our soap and lye hominy. They took all our salt. We couldn't buy none. We put the dirt in the hopper and simmered the water down to salt. We hid that. No, they didn't find it. Our smokehouse was logs daubed with mud and straw. It was good size, 'bout as big as our cabins. It had something in it too. All the time, I tell you.

SUCH A GOOD TIME

When I used to hear the older niggers talking 'bout the Yankees coming, I was scared, 'cause I thought it was some kind of animal they was talking 'bout. My old aunty was glad to hear 'bout the Yankees coming. She just set and talk 'bout what a good time we was going to have after the Yankees come. She'd say: "Child, we going to have such a good time a-setting at the white folks' table, a-eating off the white folks' table, and a-rocking in the big rocking chair."

Something awful happen to one of the slaves though, when the Yankees did come. One of the young gals tell the Yankees where the missus had her silver, money, and jewelry hid, and they got it all. What you think happened to the poor gal? She'd done wrong I know, but I hated to see her suffer so awful for it. After the Yankees had gone, the missus and massa had the poor gal hung till she die. It was something awful to see. The Yankees took everything we had 'cept a little food, hardly 'nough to keep us alive.

THE YANKEES HUNG MASTER TWICE

. . . Oh, yes, I remember lots about the war. I remember dark days, what we called the "black days." It would be so dark you couldn't see the sun even. That was from the smoke from the fighting. You could just hear the big guns going b-o-o-m! boom! all day. Yes, I do remember seeing the Yankees. I saw 'em running fast one day past our house going back away from the fighting place. And once they hung our master. They told him they wanted his money. He said he didn't have but one dollar. They said, "We know better than that." Then they took a big rope off of one of the Yankees' saddle and took the master down in the horse lot and hung him to a big tree. They rope musta been old, for it broke. Our master was a big man, though. Then they hung him again. He told 'em he didn't have but one dollar, and they let him down and said, "Well, old man, maybe you haven't got any more money." So they let him go when the mistress and her little children come down there. He didn't have but one dollar in his pockets but had lots buried about the place in two or three places.

WHY DIDN'T YOU BRING THE MEAT WITH YOU?

I 'member when the Yankees come through. I was right to the old boss's place. It was on the river side. Miss Jane Warner, she was the missus. The place here now—where all the children raise. Mr. Rhodes got a turpentine still there now, just after you pass the house. They burn the ginhouse, the shop, the buggy-house, the turkey-house, and the fowlhouse. Start to set the cornhouse afire, but my ma say: "Please sir, don't burn the cornhouse. Give it to me and my children." So they put the fire out. I 'member when they started to break down the smokehouse door, and Old Missus come out and say: "Please don't break the door open, I got the key." So they quit. I remember when they shoot down the hog. I remember when they shoot the two geese in the yard. They choked my ma. They went to her, and they say: "Where is all the white people's gold and silver?" My ma say she don't know. "You does know!" they say and choke her till she couldn't talk. They went into the company room where the old miss was staying and start tearing up the bed. Then the captain come and the old miss say to him, "Please don't let 'em tear up my bed," and the captain went in there and tell 'em, "Come out!"

The old miss wasn't scared. But the young Miss May was sure scared. She was courting at the time. She went off and shut herself up in a room. The old miss ask the captain: "Please go in and talk to the miss, she so scared." So he went in and soon he bring her out. We children wasn't scared. But my brother run under the house. The soldiers went under there a-poking the bayonets into the ground to try to find where the silver buried, and they ran 'cross him. "What you doing under here?" they say. "I's just running the chickens out, sir," he say. "Well, you can go on out," they say. "We ain't gwine to hurt you."

I remember when they kill the hog and cook him. Cook on the fire where the little shop been. Cook him and eat him. Why didn't they cook him on the stove in the house? Didn't have no stoves. Just had to cook on the fireplace. Had an oven to fit in the fireplace. I remember when my ma saw the Yankees coming that morning, she grab the sweet potatoes that been in that oven and throw 'em in the barrel of feathers that stayed by the fireplace. Just a barrel to hold chicken feathers when you pick 'em. That's all we had to eat that day. Them Yankees put the meat in the sack and go on off. It was late then, 'bout dusk. I remember how the missus bring us all round the fire. It was dark then.

"Well, children," she say, "I's sorry to tell you, but the Yankees has carry off your ma. I don't know if you'll ever see her any more." Then we children all start crying. We still a-sitting there when my ma come back. She say she slip behind, and slip behind, slip behind, and when she come to a little pine thicket by the side of the road, she dart into it, drop the sack of meat they had her carrying, and start out for home. When we had all make over her, we say to her then: "Well, why didn't you bring the sack of meat 'long with you?"

SHE COOKED FOR THE YANKEES

I could walk when I first seed the Yankees. I run out to see 'em good. Then I run back and told Miss Becky. I said, "What is they?" She told Ma to put all us under the bed to hide us from the soldiers. One big Yankee stepped inside and says to Miss Becky, "You own any niggers?" She say, "No." Here I come outen under the bed and ask her for bread. Then the Yankee lieutenant cursed her. He made the other four come outen under the bed. They all commenced to crying, and I commenced to cry. We never seed nobody like him 'fore. We was scared to death of him. He talked so loud and bad. He loaded us in a wagon. Mama, too, went with him straight to Helena. He put us in a camp and kept us. Mama cooked for the Yankees six or seven months. She heard 'em—the white soldiers —whispering round 'bout freedom. She told 'em, "You ain't gonna keep me here no longer." She took us walking back to her old master and ax him for us a home. Then she married a man on the place. He was real old. I had five half-brothers and sisters then. I was a good-size girl then.

THOSE WHITE FOLKS HAD TO RUN AWAY

I seed the Yankees come through. I seed that. They come in the time Old Master was gone. He run off—he run away. He didn't let 'em git him. I was a little child. They stayed there all day breaking into things—breaking into the molasses and all like that. Old Mistress stayed upstairs hiding. The soldiers went down in the basement and throwed things around. Old Master was a senator; they wanted to git him. They sure did cuss him: "The ———— old senator," they would say. He took his finest horses and all the gold and silver with him somewheres. They couldn't git him. They was after senators and high-ups like that.

The soldiers tickled me. They sung. The white people's yard was just full of them playing "Yankee Doodle" and "Hang Jeff Davis on a Sour Apple Tree."

All the white people gone! Funny how they run away like that. They had to save theirselves. I 'member they took one old boss man and hung him up in a tree across a drain of water, just let his foot touch—and somebody cut him down after while. Those white folks had to run away.

HOW FATHER GOT HIS MONEY

My father had more money than many ex-slaves because he did what the Union soldiers told him. They used to give him greenbacks money and tell him to take good care of it. You see, Miss, Union money was not any good here. Everything was Confederate money. You couldn't pay for a dime's worth even with a five dollar bill of Union money then. The soldiers just keep on telling my father to take all the greenbacks he could get and hide away. There wasn't any need to hide it, nobody wanted it. Soldiers said just wait; some day the Confederate money wouldn't be any good, and greenbacks would be all the money we had. So that's how my father got his money.

GRANDMA AND THE YANKEE SOLDIERS

My grandma was a powerful Christian woman, and she did love to sing and shout. That's how come Marse Billy had her locked up in the loomroom when the Yankee mens come to our plantation. Grandma would git to shouting so loud she would make so much fuss nobody in the church could hear the preacher, and she would wander off from the gallery and go downstairs and try to go down the white folks' aisles to git to the altar where the preacher was, and they was always locking her up for 'sturbing worship, but they never could break her from that shouting and wandering round the meeting house, after she got old.

Them Yankee soldiers rode up in the big house yard and 'gun to ax me questions 'bout where Marse Billy was and where everything on the place was kept, but I was too scared to say nothing. Everything was quiet and still as could be, 'cept for Grandma a-singing and shouting up in the loomhouse all by herself. One of 'em Yankees tried the door, and he axed me how come it was locked. I told him it was 'cause Grandma had 'sturbed the Baptist meeting with her shouting. Them mens grabbed the axe from the woodpile and busted the door down. They went in and got Grandma. They axed her 'bout how come she was locked up, and she told 'em the same thing I had told 'em. They axed her if she was hungry, and she said she was. Then they took that axe and busted down the smokehouse door and told her she was free now and to help herself to anything she wanted, 'cause everything on the plantation was to belong to the slaves that had worked there. They took Grandma to the kitchen and told Ma to give her some of the white folks' dinner. Ma said, "But the white folkses ain't et yet." "Go right on," the Yankees said, "and give it to her, the best in the pot, and if they's anything left when she gets through, maybe us will let the white folkses have some of it."

Them brash men strutted on through the kitchen into the house, and they didn't see nobody else downstairs. Upstairs they didn't even have the manners to knock at Mistress' door. They just walked right on in where my sister Lucy was combing Mistress' long pretty hair. They told Lucy she was free now and not to do no more work for Mistress. Then all of 'em grabbed they big old rough hands into Mistress' hair, and they made her walk downstairs and out in the yard, and all the time they was a-pulling and jerking at her long hair, trying to make her point out to 'em where Marse Billy had done had his horses and cattle hid out. Us children was a-crying and taking on 'cause us loved Mistress, and us didn't want nobody to bother her. They made out like they was going to kill her if she didn't tell 'em what they wanted to know, but after a while they let her alone.

After they had told all the slaves they could find on the place not to do no more work and to go help theyselves to anything they wanted in the smoke-house and 'bout the big house and plantation, they rode on off, and us never seed no more of 'em. After the Yankees was done gone off, Grandma 'gun to fuss: "Now, them soldiers was telling us what ain't so, 'cause ain't nobody got no right to take what belongs to Master and Mistress." And Ma jined in: "Sure it ain't no truth in what them Yankees was a-saying," and us went right on living just like us always done till Marse Billy called us together and told us the war was over and us was free to go where us wanted to go, and us could charge wages for our work.

I JUST SAID THAT TO THE WRONG PERSON

Once the Yankee soldiers come. I was big enough to tote pails and piggins then. These soldiers made us children tote water to fill their canteens and water their horses. We toted the water on our heads. Another time we heard the Yankees was coming, and Old Master had about fifteen hundred pounds of meat. They was hauling it off to bury it and hide it when the Yankees caught them. The soldiers ate and wasted every bit of that good meat. We didn't like them a bit.

One time some Yankee soldiers stopped and started talking to me—they asked me what my name was. I say "Liza," and they say, "Liza who?" I thought a minute, and I shook my head. "Just Liza, I ain't got no other name."

He say, "Who live up yonder in that big house?" I say, "Mr. John Mixon." He say, "You are Liza Mixon." He say, "Do anybody ever call you 'nigger'?" And I say, "Yes, sir." He say, "Next time anybody call you 'nigger' you tell 'em that you is a Negro and your name is Miss Liza Mixon." The more I thought of that, the more I liked it, and I made up my mind to do just what he told me to.

My job was minding the calves back, while the cows was being milked. One evening I was minding the calves, and Old Master come along. He say, "What you doing, nigger?" I say real pertlike, "I ain't no nigger. I's a Negro and I'm Miss Liza Mixon." Old Master sure was surprised, and he picks up a switch and starts at me.

Law, but I was scared! I hadn't never had no whipping, so I run fast as I can to Grandma Gracie. I hid behind her, and she say, "What's the matter of you, child?" And I say, "Master John gwine whip me." And she say, "What you done?" And I say, "Nothing." She say she know better and 'bout that time Master John got there. He say, "Gracie, that little nigger sassed me." She say, "Lawsie, child, what does ail you?" I told them what the Yankee soldier told me to say, and Grandma Gracie took my dress and lift it over my head and pins my hands inside, and Lawsie, how she whipped me, and I dasn't holler loud either. I just said that to the wrong person.

WE'RE FIGHTING TO FREE YOU

I

O Lord, yes, that was long 'fore the war. I was right down on my master's place when it started. They said it was to free the niggers. O Lord, we was right under it in Davidson County where I come from. O Lord, yes, I knowed all about when the war started. I's a young woman, a young woman. We was treated just like dogs and hogs. We seed a hard time—I know what I'm talking about.

O God, I seed the Yankees. I saw it all. We was so scared we run under the house, and the Yankees called "Come out, Dinah." (Didn't call none of us anything but Dinah.) They said, "Dinah, we're fighting to free you and get you out from under bondage." I sure understood that, but I didn't have no better sense than to go back to Mistress.

O Lord, yes, I seed the Ku Klux. They didn't bother me 'cause I didn't stay where they could; I was 'way under the house.

Yankees burned up everything Marse John had. I looked up the Pike and seed the Yankees a-coming. They say, "We's a-fighting for you, Dinah!" Yankees walked in, child, just walked right in on us. I tell you I've seed a time. You talking 'bout war—you better wish no more war come. I know when the war started. The Secessors on this side and the Yankees on that side. Yes, Miss, I seen enough. My brother went and jined the Secessors, and they killed him time he got in the war.

II

One time the Yankees come and drunk the sweet milk and took all the butter, turkeys, and hogs and then broke the powder horn against the maple tree.

The cook say, "I'm gwine to tell Marse Joe you drink all this milk." The Yankees say, "Let the damn fool alone—here we are trying to free her and she ain't got no sense." They said there wouldn't be any more hard times after the war.

But I sure have seen some hard times. . . .

III

I saw the soldiers when they come though our place. The first start of us noticing them was this. I was always up to the white folks' house. Thad was going back to the Rebel army. Old Master told my dad to go git him a hat. He'd got him one and was riding back with Thad's hat on on top of hisn. Before he could git back, here come a man just a-riding.

Thad was eating. He look out, and then he throwed his head back and said, "Them's the Federals."

Thad finished his breakfast, and then he ran on out and got with the Federals.

He didn't join 'em. He just fooled 'em. The bridge was half a mile from our house, and the Yankee army hadn't near finished crossing it when the head of it reached us.

While they were at the house, Pa came riding up with the two hats on his head. They took the hats and threwed Pa's on the ground and tried Thad's on. They took the mare, but they give it back.

Them folks stood round there all day. Killed hogs and cooked them. Killed cows and cooked them. Took all kinds of sugar and preserves and things like that. Tore all the feathers out of the mattress looking for money. Then they put Old Miss and her daughter in the kitchen to cooking.

Ma got scared and went to bed. Directly the lieutenant come on down there and said, "Auntie, get up from there. We ain't a-going to do you no hurt. We're after helping you. We are freeing you. Aunt Dinah, you can do as you please now. You're free."

She was free!

They stayed round there all night cooking and eating and carrying on. They sent some of the meat in there to us colored folks.

Next morning they all dropped off going to take Dardanelle. You could hear the cannons roaring next day. They was all night getting away. They went on and took Dardanelle. Had all them white folks running and hiding.

The Secesh wouldn't go far. They would just hide. One night there'd be a gang of Secesh, and the next one, there'd come along a gang of Yankees. Pa was 'fraid of both of 'em. Secesh said they'd kill him if he left his white folks. Yankees said they'd kill him if he didn't leave 'em. He would hide out in the cotton patch and keep we children out there with him. Old Miss made him carry us.

We was freed and went to a place that was full of people. We had to stay in a church with about twenty other people, and two of the babies died there on account of the exposure. Two of my aunts died, too, on account of exposure then.

The soldiers didn't take anything that night but food. They left all the horses. What they took was what they could eat. But they couldn't catch the turkeys. The lieutenant stayed around all the time to make the soldiers behave themselves. The meals he made my old miss and her daughter cook was for the officers.

IV

I remember one time when the Yankees was coming through. I was up on top of a rail fence so I could see better. I said, "Just looka there at them bluebirds." When the Yankees come along, one of 'em said, "You get down from there, you little son of a bitch." I didn't wait to climb down, I just fell down from there. Old Missus come down to the quarters in her carriage—didn't have buggies in them days, just carriages—to see who was hurt. The Yankees had done told her that one of her gals had fell off the fence and got hurt. I said, "I ain't hurt, but I thought them Yankees would hurt me." She said, "They won't hurt you, they is coming through to tell you you is free." She said if they had hurt me she would just about done them Yankees up. She said Jeff Davis had done give up his seat and we was free.

PRAISE TO THE YANKEES

O my Lord, when the Yankees come through there, I hear them say it was the Republicans. Mr. Ross had done say that he hear talk that they was coming through, and he tell his niggers to hurry and hide all the plantation rations. Yes, ma'am, they dig cellars under the colored people' houses and bury what meat and barrels of flour they could, and that what they couldn't get under there, they hide it up in the loft. Mr. Ross say, "Won't none of them damn Yankees get no chance to stick they rotten tooth in my rations." We say, "Ma, you got all these rations here and we hungry." She say, "No, them ration belong to Boss, and you children better never bother them neither." Then when Mr. Ross had see to it that they had fix everything safe, he take to the swamp. That what my mammy say 'cause he know they wasn't gwine bother the womens. Lord, when them Yankees ride up to the big house, Miss Ross been scared to open her mouth 'cause the man was in the swamp. No, child, they didn't bother nothing much, but some of the rations they got hold of. Often times, they would come through and kill chickens and butcher a cow up and cook it right there. Would eat all they wanted and then when they would go to leave, they been call all the plantation niggers to come there and would give them what was left. O Lord, us was glad to get them victuals, too. Yes, ma'am, all they had left, they would give it to the poor colored people. Us been so glad, us say that us wish they would come back again. Then after they had left us plantation, they would go some other place where there was another crowd of little niggers and would left them a pile of stuff, too. Old Massa, he been stay in the swamp till he hear them Yankees been leave there, and then he come home and would keep sending to the colored people' houses to get a little bit of his rations to a time. Uncle Solomon and Sipp and Leve, they been et [as] much of Boss's rations they wanted 'cause they been know the Yankees was coming back through to free them. But my mammy, she was a widow woman, and old man Anthony Ross never left nothing to her house.

I tell you, honey, some of the colored people sure been speak praise to them Yankees. I don't know how come, but they never know no better, I say. They know and they never know. One old man been riding one of these stick horses and he been so glad, he say, "Thank God! Thank God!"

THE PRETTIEST SIGHT I EVER SAW

Prettiest thing I ever saw when the Yankees was traveling was the drums and kettledrums and them horses. It was the prettiest sight I ever saw. Them horses knowed their business, too. You couldn't go up to 'em either. They had gold bits in their mouths and looked like their bridles was covered with gold. And Yankees sitting up there with a sword.

I LOVE THE YANKEES

Mother come to Helena, Arkansas, from Lake Charles, Louisiana. I was born here since freedom. . . . I don't know nothing 'bout slavery. I know they come here. Two boats named "Tyler" and "Bragg." The Yankees took 'em up and brought 'em up to their camps to pay them to wait on them. They come. . . . She said the Yankees took the pantry-house and cleaned it up. They broke in it. I'm so glad the Yankees come. They so pretty, I love 'em. . . . I can tell 'em by the way they talk and acts. You ain't none. You don't talk like 'em. You don't act like 'em. I watched you yesterday. You don't walk like 'em. You act like the rest of these Southern women to me.

Mother said a gang of Yankees come to the quarters to haul the children off, and they said, "We are going to free you all. Come on." She said, "My husband in the field." They sont for him. He come hard as he could. They loaded men and all on them two gunboats. The boat was anchored south of Tom Henry McNeill's plantation. He didn't know they was gone. When they got here, old General Hindman had forty thousand back here in the hills. They fired in. The Yankees fired! The Yankees said they was going to drive 'em back, and they scared 'em out of here and give folks that brought in them gunboats houses to live in. Mammy went to helping the Yankees. They paid her. That was 'fore freedom. I loves the Yankees. General Hindman's house was tore down up there to build that schoolhouse. The Yankees said they was going to water their horses in the Mississippi River by twelve o'clock or take hell. I know my mammy and daddy wasn't scared 'cause the Yankees taking care of 'em and they was the ones had the cannons and gunboats too. I just love the Yankees for freeing us. They run white folks outa the houses and put colored folks in 'em. Yankees had tents here. They fed the colored folks till little after 'mancipation. When the Yankees went off they been left to root, hog, or die. White folks been free all their lives. They got no need to be poor. . . .

PART FIVE

All I Know About Freedom

But, as I was saying, the slaves was still hunting a better place and more freedom. The young folks is still hunting a better place and more freedom.

The slaves heard the news of freedom in different ways—some earlier, some later, some secretly, but all hopefully. "Everybody talk 'bout freedom and hope to git free 'fore they die." They all expected freedom and wanted it, even if "it wasn't like what they thought it would be." Nor did they all think of it in the same way. To some freedom was a word, a strange word—"When I first heard them talking about freedom, I didn't know what freedom was." To others it was a person—"Big children all laugh and say: 'All niggers free, all niggers free.' And I'd say: 'What is free?' I was looking for a man to come." To still others it was a place—"right off colored folks started on the move. They seemed to want to get closer to freedom, so they'd know what it was—like it was a place or a city."

Being free as a jay bird or a toad-frog, as they said, they obeyed the first impulse, which was one of flight or movement. Some were gone before the master was halfway through telling them they were free. Others went off and came back because they "didn't have no place to go and nothing to eat. . . . Seemed like it was four or five years before they got to places they could live." Some stayed on for a time and worked on shares, until the master died, and then they scattered.

The masters, too, reacted to emancipation in different ways. Some said: "You all go on away. . . . You have to look out for yourselves now." Others said: "Go if you wants, and stay if you wants." Some gave their Negroes a small piece of land to work. "But the mostest of them never give 'em nothing, and they sure despise them niggers what left 'em"; ". . . a heap of the marses got raging mad and just tore up truck. . . . They shot niggers down by the hundreds." Still others made the Negroes work on for several months or a year for nothing, until the government caught up with them for "carrying on with free labor." In a few cases master and slave decided to "tough it out" together, and we even hear of slaves' loaning the master money "when he was hard pushed."

The chief lesson the slaves learned from freedom was that when the master said, "You are just as free as I am," he meant: "What's mine is mine and what's yours is yours."

It seem like the white people can't git over us being free, and they do everything to hold us down all the time. We don't git no schools for a long time. . . . And we can't go round where they have the voting, unless we want to catch a whipping some night, and we have to just keep on bowing and scraping when we are round white folks like we did when we was slaves. They had us down and they kept us down.

The Reconstruction time was like this. You go up to a man and tell him you and your family want to hire for next year on his place. He say: "I'm broke, the war broke me. Move down there in the best empty house you find. You can get your provisions furnished at certain little store in the closest town about." You say: "Yes, sir." When the crop made, 'bout all you got was a little money to take to give the man what run you, and you have to stay on or starve or go get somebody else let you share crop with 'em.

No wonder it was said: "It was the poor white man who was freed by the war, not the Negroes." At the same time another war had begun in which some poor white folks and poor Negroes were to fight side by side—the war for equalization and for economic security. It was not enough now merely to say, "You could change places and work for different men." Looking back upon lives lived partly in slavery and partly in freedom, ex-slaves could say: "We soon found out that freedom could make folks proud, but it didn't make 'em rich." "I don't think a man is free unless he can vote, do you?" Nor was it enough even to say: "When you has work and some money in your pocket so you can go to the store and buy some meat and bread, then you has the best freedom there is." Neither Negroes nor whites could stop fighting for freedom until it could truly be said that "this country is a free country; no slavery now."

How Freedom Came

Every man was his own free agent. "No more master, no more mistress. You are your own free moral agent. Think and act for yourself." That is how it was declared.

LIKE FREEDOM WAS A PLACE

The end of the war, it come just like that—like you snap your fingers. . . . How did we know it! Hallelujah broke out—

> Abe Lincoln freed the nigger
> With the gun and the trigger;
> And I ain't going to get whipped any more.
> I got my ticket,
> Leaving the thicket,
> And I'm a-heading for the Golden Shore!

Soldiers, all of a sudden, was everywhere—coming in bunches, crossing and walking and riding. Everyone was a-singing. We was all walking on golden clouds. Hallelujah!

> Union forever,
> Hurrah, boys, hurrah!
> Although I may be poor,
> I'll never be a slave—
> Shouting the battle cry of freedom.

Everybody went wild. We all felt like heroes, and nobody had made us that way but ourselves. We was free. Just like that, we was free. It didn't seem to make the whites mad, either. They went right on giving us food just the same. Nobody took our homes away, but right off colored folks started on the move. They seemed to want to get closer to freedom, so they'd know what it was—like it was a place or a city. Me and my father stuck, stuck close as a lean tick to a sick kitten. The Gudlows started us out on a ranch. My father, he'd round up cattle—unbranded cattle—for the whites. They was cattle that they belonged to, all right; they had gone to find water 'long the San Antonio River and the Guadalupe. Then the whites gave me and my father some cattle for our own. My father had his own brand—7 B)—and we had a herd to start out with of seventy.

We knowed freedom was on us, but we didn't know what was to come with it. We thought we was going to get rich like the white folks. We thought we was going to be richer than the white folks, 'cause we was stronger and knowed how to work, and the whites didn't, and they didn't have us to work for them any more. But it didn't turn out that way. We soon found out that freedom could make folks proud, but it didn't make 'em rich.

Did you ever stop to think that thinking don't do any good when you do it too late? Well, that's how it was with us. If every mother's son of a black had thrown 'way his hoe and took up a gun to fight for his own freedom along with the Yankees, the war'd been over before it began. But we didn't do it. We couldn't help stick to our masters. We couldn't no more shoot 'em than we could fly. My father and me used to talk 'bout it. We decided we was too soft and freedom wasn't going to be much to our good even if we had a education.

FROM BLOODY FLAG TO WHITE

I was at Pamplin, and the Yankees and Rebels were fighting, and they were waving the bloody flag, and a Confederate soldier was up on a post, and they were shooting terribly. Guns were firing everywhere.

All a sudden they struck up "Yankee Doodle" song. A soldier came along and called to me, "How far is it to the Rebels," and I, honey, was feared to tell him! So I said: "I don't know." He called me again. Scared to death I was. I recollect gitting behind the house and pointed in the direction. You see, if the Rebels knew that I told the soldier, they would have killed me.

These were the Union men going after Lee's army, which had done been 'fore them to Appomattox.

The colored regiment came up behind, and when they saw the colored regiment they put up the white flag. You 'member 'fore this, red or bloody flag was up. Now, do you know why they raised that white flag? Well, honey, that white flag was a token that Lee had surrendered. Glory! Glory! Yes, child, the Negroes are free, and when they knew that they were free they, oh! baby! began to sing:

> Mammy, don't you cook no more,
> You are free, you are free!
> Rooster, don't you crow no more,
> You are free, you are free!

Old hen, don't you lay no more eggs,
You free, you free!

Such rejoicing and shouting you never heard in your life.

THEY GOT WHAT THEY EXPECTED

My mother said that they had been waiting a long time to hear what had become of the war, perhaps one or two weeks. One day when they were in the field molding corn, going round the corn, hoeing it, and putting a little hill around it, the conch sounded at about eleven o'clock, and they knew that the long-expected time had come. They dropped their hoes and went to the big house. They went around to the back where the master always met the servants, and he said to them, "You are all free, free as I am. You can go or come as you please. I want you to stay. If you will stay, I will give you half the crop." That was the beginning of the sharecropping system.

My mother came at once to the quarters, and when she found me she pulled the end out of a corn sack, stuck holes on the sides, put a cord through the top, pulled out the end, put it on me, put on the only dress she had, and made it back to the old home [her first master's folk].

When the slaves were freed, they got what they expected. They were glad to get it and get away with it, and that was what Mother and them did.

HE CLEANED HIS GUNS ON MY DRESS TAIL

When the war was over, Mistress' son come home, and he cleaned his guns on my dress tail. It sure stunk up my dress and made me sick too. He told Old Mistress that niggers was free now. I went and told Mammy that Old Betsy's son told her the niggers was free and what did he mean. She said, "Shhhhhh!" They never did just come out and tell us we was free. We was free in July, and Mammy left in September.

YOU BETTER HUSH

I remember the first Yankee I ever saw. They called him Captain Hogan. I had a white child in my arms. He set there and asked the boss how many Negroes did he have, and the boss said what was the news. He come out to let the Negroes know they was as free as he was and told Marse Jim to bring all of them back from Texas. I know I run and told Mama and she said, "You better hush, you'll get a whipping."

THEY LEARNED BETTER

I was living in Bartow County in North Georgia when freedom came. I don't remember how the slaves found it out. I remember them saying, "Well, they's all free." And that is all I remember. And I remember someone saying—asking a question—"You got to say 'Master'?" And somebody answered and said, "Naw." But they said it all the same. They said it for a long time. But they learned better though.

YES'M

I don't know how freedom came. I know the Yankees came through, and they'd pat we little niggers on the head and say, "Nigger, you are just as free as I am." And I would say, "Yes'm."

FREEDOM OF PEACHES

My mistress said to me when I got back home, "You're free. Go on out in the orchard and git yourself some peaches." They had a yard full of peaches. Baby, did I git me some peaches. I pulled a bushel of 'em.

THEY THREW THEIR STICKS AWAY

I heard them tell the slaves they were free. A man named Captain Barkus, who had his arm off at the elbow, called for the three nearby plantations to meet at our place. Then he got up on a platform with another man beside him and declared peace and freedom. He pointed to a colored man and yelled, "You're free as I am." Old colored folks, old as I am now, that was on sticks, throwed them sticks away and shouted.

THEY DANCED ALL NIGHT

When the war ended, white man come to the field and tell my mother-in-law she free as he is. She dropped her hoe and danced up to the turn road and danced right up into Old Master's parlor. She went so fast a bird coulda sot on her dress tail. That was in June. That night she sent and got all the neighbors, and they danced all night long.

THERE AIN'T NO ANTS BITING HER TODAY

Dr. Polk had a fine horse. He came riding through the field and said, "All you-all niggers are free now. You can stay here and work for me, or you can go to the next field and work."

I had an old aunt that they used to make set on a log. She jumped off that log and ran down the field to the quarters shouting and hollering.

The people all said, "Nancy's free; they ain't no ants biting her today." She'd been setting on that log one year. She wouldn't do no kind of work, and they make her set there all day and let the ants bite her.

IT'S NOT RECORDED

The way we first heard about freedom, one of the boys come home to stay, but no one knew that when he came. He told Sister Mandy cook him a good supper and he would tell her something good. She cooked him a good supper and set the table. He set to eat, and she ask him what it was. He told her, "All the slaves are free now."

When her son told my sister Mandy at supper table, "All the slaves are free now," Old Mistress jumped up and said, "It's not recorded! It's not recorded!"

THEY TOLD THE YANKEES "YES"

Mother said her master didn't tell them it was freedom. Other folks got told in August. They passed it round secretly. Some Yankees come, asked if they was getting paid for picking cotton in September. They told their master. They told the Yankees "Yes" 'cause they was afraid they would be run off and no place to go. They said Master Hood paid them well for their work at cotton-selling time. He never promised them nothing. She said he never told one of them to leave or to stay. He let 'em be. I reckon they got fed. . . .

HE MADE US WORK SEVERAL MONTHS AFTER THAT

I hears 'bout freedom in September, and they's picking cotton; and a white man rides up to Massa's house on a big white hoss and the houseboy tell Massa a man want see him, and he hollers: "Light, stranger." It a gov'ment man, and he have the big book and a bunch papers and say why ain't Massa turn the niggers loose. Massa say he trying to git the crop out, and he tell Massa have the slaves in. Uncle Steven blows the cow horn what they use to call to eat, and all the niggers come running, 'cause that horn mean, "Come to the big house, quick." That man reads the paper telling us we's free, but Massa make us work several months after that. He say we git 20 acres land and a mule, but we didn't git it.

DRUMS OF FREEDOM

I 'member they was gwine put us to carrying water for the hands next year, and that year we got free. My mother shouted, "Now I ain't lying 'bout that." I sure 'member when they sot the people free. They was just ready to blow the folks out to the field. I 'member old Mose would blow the bugle, and he could *blow* that bugle. If you wasn't in, you better get in. Yes, ma'am! The day freedom come, I know Mose was just ready to blow the bugle when the Yankees begun to beat the drum down the road. They knew it was all over then. That ain't no joke.

PAPA WENT OFF

I can recollect old Master Collins calling up all the niggers to his house. He told them they was free. There was a crowd of them, all sizes. Why all this took place now I don't know. Most of the niggers took what all they have on their heads and walked off. He told Mama to move up in the loomhouse; if she go off, he would kill her. We moved to the loomhouse till in 1866.

One night some of the niggers what had been Collins' slaves come and stole all Mama's children; toted us off on their backs at night. Where we come to cross the river, Uncle George Tunnel was the ferryman. He had raised Mama at his cabin at slavery. He took us to his white folks. We lived with them a year and then mama moved on Bill Cropton's place, and we lived there forty years. All the Croptons dead now.

Papa was a little chunky man. He'd steal flour and hogs. He could tote a hog on his back. My papa went on off when freedom come. They was so happy they had no sense. Mama never seen him no more. I didn't neither. Mama didn't care so much about him. He was her mate give to her. I didn't worry 'bout him nor nobody then.

The Breaking-Up and After

. . . even the best masters in slavery couldn't be as good as the worst person in freedom.

THEY KNEW WHAT HE MEANT

We never heared much about the fighting or how it was going. When the war finally was over, our old boss called us all up and had us to stand in abreast, and he stood on the gallery and he read the verdict to 'em, and said, "Now, you can just work on if you want to, and I'll treat you just like I always did." I guess when he said that they knew what he meant. There wasn't but one family left with him. They stayed about two years. But the rest was just like birds, they just flew.

OVER HALF OF THEM WERE GONE

After the war, Master Colonel Sims went to git the mail, and so he call Daniel Ivory, the overseer, and say to him, "Go around to all the quarters and tell all the niggers to come up, I got a paper to read to 'em. They're free now, so you can git you another job, 'cause I ain't got no more niggers which is my own." Niggers come up from the cabins nappy-headed, just like they gwine to the field. Master Colonel Sims, say, "Caroline [that's my mammy], you is free as me. Pa said bring you back, and I's gwine do just that. So you go on and work and I'll pay you and your three oldest children $10 a month a head and $4 for Harriet"—that's me—and then he turned to the rest and say, "Now all you-uns will receive $10 a head till the crops is laid by." Don't you know before he got halfway through, over half them niggers was gone.

WHEN CHRISTMAS CAME

I 'member when freedom come, Old Marse said, "You is all free, but you can work on and make this crop of corn and cotton; then I will divide up with you when Christmas comes." They all worked, and when Christmas come, Marse told us we could get on and shuffle for ourselves, and he didn't give us anything. We had to steal corn out of the crib. We prized the ears out between the cracks and took them home and parched them. We would have to eat on these for several days.

WHAT'S MINE IS MINE

One day . . . a few niggers was sticking sticks in the ground when the massa come up.

"What you niggers doing?" he asked.

"We is staking off the land, Massa. The Yankees say half of it is ourn."

The massa never got mad. He just look calm-like.

"Listen, niggers," he says, "what's mine is mine, and what's yours is yours. You are just as free as I and the missus, but don't go fooling around my land. I've tried to be a good master to you. I have never been unfair. Now if you wants to stay, you are welcome to work for me. I'll pay you one-third the crops you raise. But if you wants to go, you sees the gate."

The massa never have no more trouble. Them niggers just stays right there and works. Sometime they loaned the massa money when he was hard pushed. Most of 'em died on the old grounds.

YOU ALL GO ON AWAY

When freedom, my mama said Old Master called all of 'em to his house, and he said: "You all free, we ain't got nothing to do with you no more. Go on away. We don't whup you no more, go on your way." My mama said they go on off, then they come back and stand around just looking at him and Old Mistress. They give 'em something to eat and he say: "Go on away, you don't belong to us no more, you been freed."

They go away, and they kept coming back. They didn't have no place to go and nothing to eat. From what she said they had a terrible time. She said it was bad times. Some took sick and had no 'tention and died. Seemed like it was four or five years before they got to places they could live. They all got scattered.

She said they did expect something from freedom, but the only thing Old Master give Jesse was a horse and bridle and saddle. It was new. Old Master every time they go back say: "You all go on away. You been set free. You have to look out for yourselves now."

THE DEVIL AND HELL

When Young Massa went to war, they calls all the slaves to tell him good-bye. They blowed the horn. He come home two times on a furlough and says, "I's smelling and seeing the Devil." Then the next time he come home he say, "Last time I tells you 'bout smelling the Devil. I's smelling and seeing Hell now." When the war am over, he come home and say to Old Massa, "Ain't you read the 'lamation to your niggers yet?" Massa say he hasn't, and Young Massa blowed the horn and calls us all up and tells us we's free as he is and could work for who we please, but he like us to stay till the crop am out. He say he'd hire us and make a contract. Me and my mammy stays ten years, 'cause they so good it ain't no use to leave. One of the young massas am living here now, Mr. Tom, and I goes to see him.

SHE AIN'T GOT US BACK YET

All kind of war talk floating round 'fore the Yankees come. Some say the Yankees fight for freedom, and some say they'll kill all the slaves. Seems like it must have been in the middle of the war that the Yankees come by. We hears somebody holler for us to come out one night and seed the place on fire. Time we git out there, the Yankees gone. We fit the fire, but we had to tote water in buckets, and the fire burn up the ginhouse full of cotton and the cotton-house, too, and the corncrib.

The Yankees always come through at night and done what they gwine to do, and then wait for more night 'fore they go 'bout their business. Only one time they come in daylight, and some the slaves jine them and go to war.

All the talk 'bout freedom git so bad on the plantation, the massa make me put the men in a big wagon and drive 'em to Winfield. He say in Texas there never be no freedom. I driv 'em fast till night, and it take 'bout two days. But they come back home, but Massa say if he cotch any of 'em, he gwine shoot 'em.

They hang round the woods and dodge round and round till the freedom man come by.

We went right on working after freedom. Old Buck Adams wouldn't let us go. It was 'way after freedom that the freedom man come and read the paper and tell us not to work no more 'less us git pay for it. When he gone, Old Mary Adams, she come out. I 'lect what she say as if I just hear her say it. She say, "Ten years from today I'll have you all back 'gain." That ten years been over a mighty long time, and she ain't git us back yet, and she dead and gone.

They makes us git right off the place, just like you take a old hoss and turn it loose. That how us was. No money, no nothing. I git a job working for a white man on he farm, but he couldn't pay much. He didn't have nothing. He give me just 'nough to git a peck or two of meal and a little syrup.

OLD MISTRESS KEPT THE COTTON

We got free in Georgia, June 15, 1865. I'll never forget that date. What I mean is, that was the day the big freedom came. But we didn't know it and just worked on. My father was a shoemaker for Old Mistress. Only one in town, far as I recollect. He made a lot of money for Mistress. Mother was houseworker for her. As fast as us children got big enough to hire out, she leased us to anybody who would pay for our hire. I was put out with another widow woman who lived about twenty miles. She worked me on her cotton plantation. Old Mistress sold one of my sisters; took cotton for pay. I remember hearing them tell about the big price she brought because cotton was so high. Old Mistress got fifteen bales of cotton for sister, and it was only a few days till freedom came, and the man who had traded all them bales of cotton lost my sister, but Old Mistress kept the cotton. She was smart, wasn't she? She knew freedom was right there. Sister came right back to my parents.

ALL BENT OVER

All I knows 'bout how come us was sot free is that folkses said Mr. Jefferson Davis and Mr. Abraham Lincoln got to fighting 'bout us, and Mr. Lincoln's side got the best of Mr. Davis' side in the quarrel. The day they told us that us was free, there was a white man named Mr. Bruce what axed: "What you say?" They told him 'gain that all the niggers was free. He bent hisself over and never did straighten his body no more. When he died, he was still all bent over. Mr. Bruce done this to show the world how he hated to give his niggers up after they done been sot free.

MASTER LIVED A WEEK OR TWO

Jim Jackson's wife was named Mariah. They lived in a big, fine, white house. When it was freedom, a soldier come, brought a paper, and Massa Jim was setting on the porch. Tom Chapman was his overseer. They rung the big farm bell and had the oldest niggers stand in a line and us little ones in front, so we could all see. Tom Chapman read the paper and stood by the soldier. He had two big plantations. Massa Jim got sick that day and vomited and vomited. He lived a week or two weeks. They sent for Dr. Ducham, but he couldn't do him no good. He died. Massa Jim told them they could take the teams and go to town, all he ax of 'em was to feed and take care of 'em. Every one of the grown folks went and left us at home. Aunt Judy seen 'bout us like she been doing all the time. They went over to Greensboro to celebrate. They all come back. They was all ready for their breakfastes. It was twelve miles from Greensboro. Then the next day Massa Jim, or Tom Chapman one, called the grown folks to the house and told them, "You can stay and I will pay you or you can go. I pay no more doctor bills. I don't feed you no more nor give you no more clothes." Some moved and some hired to him. Some went to his father-in-law's place and some to his brother's place and around. His wife was rich. She was Dave Butler's gal. No, I mean Massa Jim's wife—Miss Mariah. That big place was what her pa give her. Massa Jim had five hundred little niggers on that place and lots more on the big plantation. He had about two thousand little niggers. We went in droves is right.

HE TOOK THE SMALLPOX

My daddy and mammy belong to Master Sam Louie, who had a big plantation over in Calhoun County. He had 'bout fifty or more grown slaves, 'sides many children of the slaves. Old Master was a good farmer; raised big crops and saved what he made. He sure was a fine businessman, but he was mighty hard on everybody he had anything to do with. He told his slaves to work hard and make him a heap of money and that he would keep it, in case of hard times. Times was all the time hard with Old Master, but the niggers never got no money. When news spread round that the Yankees was coming to free the niggers, he called all the slaves up in the yard and showed them a big sack of money, what they had made for him, and told them that he was gwine to kill all of them before the Yankees set them free and that they wouldn't need no money after they was done dead. All the slaves was mighty sad and troubled, all that day, when Old Master made that speech to them. But something happened. It 'most makes me tremble to talk to you 'bout it now. Providence, or some kind of mercy spirit, was sure walking round that plantation that night. Sometime in the night it was whispered round amongst the slaves that Old Master done took the smallpoxes and was mighty sick. Mammy said he must have been terrible sick, 'cause they buried him two days after that.

HE CUSSED TILL HE DIED

I 'member when war starts and Massa's boy, George it was, saddles up Old Bob, his pony, and left. He stays six months, and when he rid up, Massa say, "How's the war, George?" and Massa George say, "It's hell. Me and Bob has been running Yankees ever since us left." 'Fore war Massa didn't never say much 'bout slavery, but when he heared us free he cusses and say, "God never did 'tend to free niggers," and he cussed till he died. But he didn't tell us we's free till a whole year after we was, but one day a bunch of Yankee soldiers come riding up, and Massa and Missy hid out. The soldiers walked into the kitchen, and Mammy was churning and one of them kicks the churn over and say, "Git out, you's just as free as I is." Then they ransacked the place and breaks out all the window lights and when they leaves it look like a storm done hit that house. Massa come back from hiding, and that when he starts on a cussing spree what lasts as long as he lives.

MASTER GETS WORSE

I's don't know much 'bout the war. The white folks don't talk to us 'bout the war, and we-uns don't go to preaching or nothing, so we can't larn much. When freedom comes, Master says to us niggers, "All that wants to go, git now. You has nothing." And he turns them away, nothing on 'cept old rags. 'Twa'n't enough to cover their body. No hat, no shoes, no underwear.

My pappy and most the niggers goes, but I's have to stay till my pappy finds a place for me. He tells me that he'll come for me. I's have to wait over two years. The master gets worser in the disposition and goes round sort of talking to hisself, and then he gits to cussing everybody.

In 'bout a year after freedom, Master Loyed moves from Palo Pinto to Fort

Worth. He says he don't want to live in a country where the niggers am free. He kills hisself 'bout a year after they moves. After that, I's sure glad when Pappy comes for me. He had settled at Azle on a rented farm, and I's lives with him for 'bout ten years. Then I's goes and stays with my brother on Ash Creek. The three of us rents land, and us runs that farm.

THE NEWS KILLED HER DEAD

All my mother knew was that it got out that the Negroes were free. The day before the old woman told them that they were free, my grandfather, Henry Goodman, who was a teamster, Old Miss called him and told him to tell all the darkies to come up to the house the next day.

Next morning, she said, "Henry, you forgot what I told you. I want you to call all the darkies up here this morning." Henry had a voice like a foghorn. He started hollering. I wish I could holler the way he did, but I got to consider the neighbors. He hollered, " 'Tention, 'tention, hey! Miss Lucy says she wants you all up to the big house this morning. She's got something to tell you."

They all come up to the yard before the house. When they got there, she says to him—not to them; she wouldn't talk to them that morning; maybe she was too full—"Henry, you all just as free now as I am. You can stay here with Miss Lucy or you can go to work with whomsoever you will. You don't belong to Miss Lucy no more."

She had been sick for quite a bit, and she was just able to come to the door and deliver that message. Three weeks after that time, they brought her out of the house feet foremost and took her to the cemetery. The news killed her dead. That's been seventy years ago, and they just now picking up on it!

YOU GOT TO LOOK AFTER ME

When the fighting stopped, people was so glad they rung and rung the farm bells and blowed horns—big old cow horns. When Master Daniel come home, he went to my papa's house and says, "John, you free." He says, "I been free as I want to be where I is." He went on to my grandpa's house and says, "Toby, you are free!" He raised up and says, "You brought me here from Africa and North Carolina, and I going to stay with you long as ever I get something to eat. You got to look after me!" Master Daniel say, "Well, I ain't running nobody off my place long as they behave." Pretty nigh every nigger sot tight till he died of the old sets. Master Daniel say to Grandpa, "Toby, you ain't my nigger." Grandpa raise up and say, "I is, too."

DEATH OF A PLANTATION

I

The plainest thing I recollect was a big drove of the Yankee soldiers—some riding, some walking—come up to the master's house. He was a sorta old man. He was setting in the gallery. He lived in a big log house. He was reading the paper. He throwed back his head and was dead. Just scared to death. They said that was what the matter. In spite of that, they come down there and ordered us up to the house. All the niggers scared to death not to go. There lay Old Master Jim, stretched dead in his chair. They was backed up to the smokehouse door, and the horses making splinters of the door. It was three planks thick, crossed one another and bradded together with iron nails. They throwed the stuff out and say, "Come and git it. Take it to your houses." They took it. It was ours, and we didn't want it wasted. Soon as they gone, they got mighty busy bringing it back. They built 'nother door and put it up. Old Miss Caroline 'bout somewheres, scared pretty near to death. They buried Master Jim at Water Valley, Mississippi. Miss Caroline broke up and went back to Virginia. My grandma got her feather bed and died on it. 'Bout two years after that the Yankees sot fire to the house and burned it down. We all had good log houses down close together. They didn't bother us.

II

After they has argument, they never whups me when Master Billy round. Lots of time him say, "Come here, Bunch"—they calls me Bunch, 'cause I's portly—and him have something good for me to eat.

After that, it wasn't long 'fore the war starts, and the master's two boys, Billy and John, jines the army. I's powerful grieved and cries two days, and all the time Master Billy gone I worries 'bout him gitting shot. The soldiers comes and goes in the crib and takes all the corn and makes my mammy cook a meal. Master Charley cuss everything and everybody, and us watch out and keep out of his way. After two years him gits a letter from Master Billy and him say him be home soon and that John am kilt. Missy starts crying, and the master jumps up and starts cussing the war and him picks up the hot poker and say, "Free the nigger, will they? I free them." And he hit my mammy on the neck, and she starts moaning and crying and draps to the floor. There 'twas, the missy a-moaning, my mammy a-mourning, and the master a-cussing loud as him can. Him takes the gun offen the rack and starts for the field, where the niggers am a-working. My sister and I sees that, and we-uns starts running and screaming 'cause we-uns has brothers and sisters in the field. But the good Lord took a hand in that mess, and the master ain't gone far in the field when him draps all of a sudden. The death sets on the master, and the niggers comes running to him. Him can't talk or move, and they tote him in the house. The doctor comes, and the next day the master dies.

Then Master Billy comes home, and the break-up took place with freedom for the niggers. Most of 'em left as soon's they could.

The missy gits very condescending after freedom. The women was in the spinning-house and we-uns 'spects another whupping or scolding, 'cause that the usual doings when she comes. She comes in and say, "Good morning, womens," and she never said such 'fore. She say she pay wages to all what stays and how good she treat 'em. But my pappy comes and takes us over to the Widow Perry's land to work for share.

After that, the missy found Master Billy in the shed, dead, with him throat cut and the razor 'side him. There a piece of paper say he not care for to live, 'cause the nigger free, and they's all broke up.

HE COULDN'T HELP CRYING

Marse Bob knowed me better'n most the slaves, 'cause I was round the house more. One day he called all the slaves to the yard. He only had sixty-six then, 'cause he had 'vided with his son and daughter when they married. He made a little speech. He said, "I'm going to a war, but I don't think I'll be gone long, and I'm turning the overseer off and leaving Andrew in charge of the place, and I wants everything to go on, just like I was here. Now, you all mind what Andrew says, 'cause if you don't, I'll make it rough on you when I come back home." He was joking, though, 'cause he wouldn't have done nothing to them.

Then he said to me, "Andrew, you is old 'nough to be a man and look after things. Take care of Missus and see that none the niggers wants, and try to keep the place going."

We didn't know what the war was 'bout, but Master was gone four years. When Old Missus heard from him, she'd call all the slaves and tell us the news and read us his letters. Little parts of it she wouldn't read. We never heard of him gitting hurt none, but if he had, Old Missus wouldn't tell us, 'cause the niggers used to cry and pray over him all the time. We never heard tell what the war was 'bout.

When Marse Bob come home, he sent for all the slaves. He was sitting in a yard chair, all tuckered out, and shook hands all round, and said he's glad to see us. Then he said, "I got something to tell you. You is just as free as I is. You don't 'long to nobody but yourselves. We went to the war and fought, but the

Yankees done whup us, and they say the niggers is free. You can go where you wants to go, or you can stay here, just as you likes." He couldn't help but cry.

The niggers cry and don't know much what Marse Bob means. They is sorry 'bout the freedom, 'cause they don't know where to go, and they's always 'pend on Old Marse to look after them. Three families went to get farms for theyselves, but the rest just stay on for hands on the old place.

The Federals has been coming by, even 'fore Old Marse come home. They all come by, carrying they little budgets [knapsacks], and if they was walking they'd look in the stables for a horse or mule, and they just took what they wanted of corn or livestock. They done the same after Marse Bob come home. He just said, "Let them go they way, 'cause that's what they're going to do, anyway." We was scareder of them than we was of the devil. But they spoke right kindly to us colored folks. They said, "If you got a good master and want to stay, well, you can do that, but now you can go where you want to, 'cause ain't nobody going to stop you."

The niggers can't hardly git used to the idea. When they wants to leave the place, they still go up to the big house for a pass. They just can't understand 'bout the freedom. Old Marse or Missus say, "You don't need no pass. All you got to do is just take your foot in your hand and go."

It seem like the war just plumb broke Old Marse up. It wasn't long till he moved into Tyler and left my paw running the farm on a halfance with him and the nigger workers. He didn't live long, but I forgits just how long. But when Mr. Bob heired the old place, he 'lowed we'd just go 'long the way his paw has made the trade with my paw.

Young Mr. Bob 'parently done the first rascality I ever heard of a Goodman doing. The first year we worked for him we raised lots of grain and other things and fifty-seven bales of cotton. Cotton was fifty-two cents a pound, and he shipped it all away, but all he ever gave us was a box of candy and a sack of store tobacco and a sack of sugar. He said the 'signment done got lost. Paw said to let it go, 'cause we had always lived by what the Goodmans had said.

I FEEL LIKE I AM THEIRS

We niggers wouldn't know nothing about it all if it hadn't a-been for a little old black, sassy woman in the quarters that was a-talking all the time about "freedom." She give our white folks lots of trouble—she was so sassy to them, but they didn't sell her, and she was set free along with us. When they all come home from the war and Master called us up and told us we was free, some rejoiced so they shouted, but some didn't, they was sorry. Lewis come a-running over there and wanted me and the children to go on over to his white folks' place with him, and I wouldn't go—no, ma'am, I wouldn't leave my white folks. I told Lewis to go on and let me 'lone; I knowed my white folks and they was good to me, but I didn't know his white folks. So we kept living like we did in slavery, but he come to see me every day. After a few years he finally 'suaded me to go on over to the Willis place and live with him, and his white folks was powerful good to me. After a while, though, we all went back and lived with my white folks, and I worked on for them as long as I was able to work and always felt like I belonged to 'em, and, you know, after all this long time, I feel like I am theirs.

FREEDOM WASN'T NO DIFFERENCE

Freedom wasn't no difference I knows of. I works for Marse John just the same for a long time. He say one morning, "John, you can go out in the field iffen you wants to or you can git out iffen you wants to, 'cause the government say you is free. If you wants to work I'll feed you and give you clothes but can't pay you no money. I ain't got none." Humph, I didn't know nothing what money was, nohow, but I knows I'll git plenty victuals to eat, so I stays till Old Marse die and Old Miss git shut of the place. Then I gits me a job farming, and when I gits too old for that I does this and that for white folks, like fixing yards.

I's black and just a poor old nigger, but I reverence my white folks 'cause they reared me up in the right way. If colored folks pay 'tention and listen to what the white folks tell them, the world be a heap better off. Us old niggers knows that's the truth, too, 'cause we larns respect and manners from our white folks, and on the great day of judgment my white folks is gwine to meet me and shake hands with me and be glad to see me. Yes, sir, that's the truth!

BANG!

Yes, sir, everybody happy on Massa's place till war begin. He have two sons, and Willie am 'bout eighteen and Dave am 'bout seventeen. They jines the army, and after 'bout a year, Massa jine too, and, of course, that make the missy awful sad. She have to 'pend on the overseer, and it wa'n't like Massa keep things running.

In the old days, if the niggers wants the party, Massa am the big toad in the puddle. And Christmas, it am the day for the big time. A tree am fix, and some present for everyone. The white preacher talk 'bout Christ. Us have singing and 'joyment all day. Then at night, the big fire builded, and all us sot round it. There am 'bout hundred hog bladders save from hog killing. So, on Christmas night, the children takes them and puts them on the stick. First they is all blowed full of air and tied tight and dry. Then the children holds the bladder in the fire and pretty soon, "BANG!" they goes. That am the fireworks.

That all changed after Massa go to war. First the 'Federate soldiers come and takes some mules and hosses, then some more come for the corn. After while, the Yankee soldiers comes and takes some more. When they gits through, they ain't much more tooking to be done. The year 'fore surrender, us am short of rations and sometime us hungry. Us sees no battling, but the cannon bang all day. Once they bang two whole days 'thout hardly stopping. That am when Missy got touch in the head, 'cause Massa and the boys in that battle. She just walk round the yard and twist the hands and say, "They sure git kilt. They sure dead." Then when extra loud noise come from the cannon, she scream. Then word come Willie am kilt. She gits over it, but she am the different woman. For her, it am trouble, trouble, and more trouble.

She can't sell the cotton. They done took all the rations, and us couldn't eat the cotton. One day she tell us, "The war am on us. The soldiers done took the rations. I can't sell the cotton, 'cause the blockade." I don't know what am that blockade, but she say it. "Now," she say, "all you colored folks born and raise here, and us always been good to you. I can't help it 'cause rations am short, and I'll do all I can for you. Will you be patient with me?" All us stay there and holp Missy all us could.

Then Massa come home and say, "You gwine be free. Far as I cares, you is free now, and can stay here and tough it through or go where you wants. I thanks you for all the way you's done while I's gone, and I'll help you all I can." Us all stay, and it sure am tough times. Us have 'most nothing to eat, and then the Ku Klux come round there. Massa say not mix with that crowd what lose the head, just stay to home and work. Some them niggers on other plantations ain't keep the head, and they gits whupped and some gits kilt, but us does what Massa say and has no trouble with them Klux.

CLOSE MEASURING

'Nother thing I 'members when I was a little boy: That they was 'viding the corn after the surrender. Dr. DeGraffenreid measured the corn out to all of 'em what was share hands. He'd take a bushel and give 'em a bushel. When he 'most through he'd throw a ear of corn to this one, and give himself a ear; then he break a ear in two, and he take part and give them part. That was close measuring, I tell you.

WE HAVE WHITE FOLKS' EATS

When Pappy sot free by Massa Albert McKinney, he didn't have nothing—not even a shirt, so Massa Albert 'lowed him stay and work round the plantation. One day 'fore we goes back to Crosby, Pappy come down to Galveston to see Mammy and us children, 'cause he wants to take us back with him. He rid all the way on a mule, carrying a wallet what was thrown over the back of the mule like the pack saddle, and he gives it to Mammy. You know what was in that wallet? He brung a coon and possum and some corn dodger, 'cause he thinks we don't have 'nough to eat down there. Mammy she give one look at the stuff and say, "You, Tom, I's staying right here with Old Missy Cunningham, and we has white folks' eats," and she throw the whole mess 'way. I sure 'member that happening.

HE SOLD HIS FIVE BOYS

. . . I 'members day of 'mancipation. Yankees told us we was free, and they call us up from the field to sign up and see if us wanted to stay on with 'em. I stayed that year with the Moorings, then I bargain for land, but couldn't never pay for it. Turned loose 'thout nothing.

But they was a coal-black free-born nigger name George Wright had a floating mill right here on the 'Bigbee River, stayed at the point of the woods just 'bove the spring branch, and it did a good service. But he got in debt, and he sold his five boys. They was his own children, and he could sell 'em under the law. The names was Eber, Eli, Ezekiel, Enoch, and Ezra, and he sold 'em to the highest bidder right yonder front of the post office for cash. And Jack Tom was another free nigger here, and he bought some of 'em, and they others the white folks bought, and I never heard no complaint, and I seed 'em long as they lived. They was a heap of things went on. Some I likes to remember, some I don't. But I'd rather be free now. I never seed Mr. Lincoln, but when they told me 'bout him, I thought he was partly God.

THEY JUST EXPECTED FREEDOM

They just expected freedom, all I ever heard. I know they didn't expect the white folks to give them no land 'cause the man what owned the land bought it hisself 'fore he bought the hands what he put on it. They thought they was ruined bad enough when the hands left them. They kept the land, and that is about all there was left. What the Yankees didn't take they wasted and set fire to it. They set fire to the rail fences so the stock would get out—all they didn't kill and take off. Both sides was mean. But it seemed like 'cause they was fighting down here on the South's ground it was the worst here. Now that's just the way I sees it. They done one more thing too. They put any colored man in the front where he would get killed first, and they stayed sorta behind in the back lines. When they come along, they try to get the colored men to go with them, and that's the way they got treated. I didn't know where anybody was made to stay on after the war. They was lucky if they had a place to stay at. There wasn't anything to do with if they stayed. Times was awful unsettled for a long time. People what went to the cities died. I don't know, they caught diseases and changing the ways of eating and living I guess what done it. They died mighty fast for awhile. I knowed some of them, and I heard 'em talking.

That period after the war was a hard time. It sure was harder than the depression. It lasted a long time. Folks got a lots now besides what they put up with then. Seemed like they thought if they be free they never have no work to do and just have plenty to eat and wear. They found it different, and when it was cold they had no wood like they been used to. I don't believe in the colored race being slaves 'cause of the color, but the war didn't make times much better for a long time. Some of them had a worse time. So many soon got sick and died. They died of consumption and fevers and nearly froze. Some near 'bout starved. The colored folks just scattered 'bout hunting work after the war.

THEN CAME THE CALM

When freedom come, folks left home, out in the streets, crying, praying, singing, shouting, yelling, and knocking down everything. Some shot off big guns. Then come the calm. It was sad then. So many folks done dead, things tore up, and nowheres to go and nothing to eat, nothing to do. It got squally. Folks got sick, so hungry. Some folks starved nearly to death. Times got hard. We went to the washtub—onliest way we all could live. Ma was a cripple woman. Pa couldn't find work for so long when he mustered out.

I GOT ALONG HARD AFTER I WAS FREED

I got along hard after I was freed. It is a hard matter to tell you what we could find or get. We used to dig up dirt in the smokehouse and boil it and dry it and sift it to get the salt to season our food with. We used to go out and get old bones that had been throwed away and crack them open and get the marrow and use them to season the greens with. Just plenty of niggers then didn't have anything but that to eat.

Even in slavery times, there was plenty of niggers out of them three hundred slaves who had to break up old lard gourds and use them for meat. They had to pick up bones off the dunghill and crack them open to cook with. And then, of course, they'd steal. Had to steal. That the best way to git what they wanted.

RECONSTRUCTION WAS A MIGHTY HARD PULL

I was born in Edgefield County, South Carolina. I am eighty-five years old. I was born a slave of George Strauter. I remembers hearing them say, "Thank God, I's free as a jay bird." My ma was a slave in the field. I was eleven years old when freedom was declared. When I was little, Mr. Strauter whipped my ma. It hurt me bad as it did her. I hated him. She was crying. I chunked him with rocks. He run after me, but he didn't catch me. There was twenty-five or thirty hands that worked in the field. They raised wheat, corn, oats, barley, and cotton. All the children that couldn't work stayed at one house. Aunt Mat kept the babies and small children that couldn't go to the field. He had a gin and a shop. The shop was at the fork of the roads. When the war come on, my papa went to build forts. He quit Ma and took another woman. When the war close, Ma took her four children, bundled 'em up and went to Augusta. The government give out rations there. My ma washed and ironed. People died in piles. I don't know till yet what was the matter. They said it was the change of living. I seen five or six wooden, painted coffins piled up on wagons pass by our house. Loads passed every day like you see cotton pass here. Some said it was cholera and some took consumption. Lots of the colored people nearly starved. Not much to get to do and not much houseroom. Several families had to live in one house. Lots of the colored folks went up North and froze to death. They couldn't stand the cold. They wrote back about them dying. No, they never sent them back. I heard some sent for money to come back. I heard plenty 'bout the Ku Klux. They scared the folks to death. People left Augusta in droves. About a thousand would all meet and walk going to hunt work and new homes. Some of them died. I had a sister and brother lost that way. I had another sister come to Louisiana that way. She wrote back.

I don't think the colored folks looked for a share of land. They never got nothing 'cause the white folks didn't have nothing but barren hills left. About all the mules was wore out hauling provisions in the army. Some folks say they ought to done more for the colored folks when they left, but they say they was broke. Freeing all the slaves left 'em broke.

That reconstruction was a mighty hard pull. Me and Ma couldn't live. A man paid our ways to Carlisle, Arkansas, and we come. We started working for Mr. Emenson. He had a big store, teams, and land. We liked it fine, and I been here fifty-six years now. There was so much wild game, living was not so hard. If a fellow could get a little bread and a place to stay, he was all right. After I come to this state, I voted some. I have farmed and worked at odd jobs. I farmed mostly. Ma went back to her old master. He persuaded her to come back home. Me and her went back and run a farm four or five years before she died. Then I come back here.

WHO WAS FREED BY THE WAR?

When I was a boy we used to sing, "Rather be a nigger than a poor white man." Even in slavery they used to sing that. It was the poor white man who was freed by the war, not the Negroes.

FREEDMEN'S BUREAU

When freedom was on, Papa went to Atlanta and got transportation to Chattanooga. I don't know why. He met me and Mama. She picked me up and run away and met him. We went in a freight box. It had been a soldiers' home— great big house. We et on the first story out of tin pans. We had white beans or peas, crackers and coffee. Meat and wheat and cornbread we never smelt at that place. Somebody ask him how we got there, and he showed them a ticket from the Freedmen's Bureau in Atlanta. He showed that on the train every now and then. Upstairs they brought out a stack of wool blankets and started the rows of beds. Each man took his three as he was numbered. Every night the same one got his own blankets. The room was full of beds, and white guards with a gun over his shoulder guarded them all night long. We stayed there a long time— nearly a year. They tried to get jobs fast as they could and push 'em out, but it was slow work. Mama got a place to cook at—Mrs. Crutchfield's. She run a hotel in town but lived in the country. We stayed there about a year. Papa was hired somewhere else there.

I GOT MY MONEY, TOO

I went down to Augusta to the Freedmen's Bureau to see if 'twas true we was free. I reckon there was over a hundred people there. The man got up and stated to the people: "You all is just as free as I am. You ain't got no mistress and no master. Work when you want." On Sunday morning Old Master sent the house gal and tell us to all come to the house.

He said: "What I want to send for you all is to tell you that you are free. You have the privilege to go anywhere you want, but I don't want none of you to leave me now. I wants you-all to stay right with me. If you stay, you must sign to it."

I asked him: "What you want me to sign for? I is free."

"That will hold me to my word and hold you to your word," he say.

All my folks sign it, but I wouldn't sign. Master call me up and say: "Willis, why wouldn't you sign? I say: "If I is already free, I don't need to sign no paper. If I was working for you and doing for you before I got free, I can do it still, if you wants me to stay with you."

My father and mother tried to git me to sign, but I wouldn't sign. My mother said: "You oughta sign. How you know Master gwine pay?" I say: "Then I can go somewhere else."

Master pay first-class hands $15 a month, other hands $10, and then on down to $5 and $6. He give rations like they always have. When Christmas come, all come up to be paid off. Then he calls me. Ask where is me. I was standing round the corner of the house. "Come up here, Willis," he say. "You didn't sign that paper but I reckon I have to pay you too." He paid me and my wife $180. I said: "Well, you-all thought he wouldn't pay me, but I got my money, too."

I stayed to my master's place one year after the war, then I left there. Next year I decided I would quit there and go somewhere else. It was on account of my wife. You see, Master bought her off, as the highest bidder, down in Waynesboro, and she ain't seen her mother and father for fifteen years. When she got free, she went down to see 'em. Wa'n't willing to come back. 'Twas on account of Mistress and her. They both had children, five-six year old. The childrens had disagreement. Mistress slap my gal. My wife sass the mistress. But my master, he was as good a man as ever born. I wouldn't have left him for nobody, just on account of his wife and her fell out. . . .

I quit and goes over three miles to another widow lady's house, and make bargain with her. I pass right by the door. Old Boss sitting on the piazza. He say: "Hey, boy, where you gwine?" I say: "I 'cided to go." I was the foreman of the plow hands then. I saw to all the looking up, and things like that. He say: "Hold on there." He come out to the gate. 'Tell you what I give you to stay on here. I give you five acre of as good land as I got, and $30 a month to stay here and see to my business.". . .

I say, . . . "I can't, Master. It don't suit my wife round here. She won't come back. I can't stay."

He turn on me then, and busted out crying. "I didn't thought I could raise up a darky that would talk that-a-way," he said. Well, I went on off. I got the wagon and come by the house. Master say: "Now, you gwine off but don't forget me, boy. Remember me as you always done." I said: "All right."

I went over to that widow lady's house and work. Along about May I got sick. She say: "I going send for the doctor." I say: "Please ma'am, don't do that." (I thought maybe he kill me 'cause I left him.) She say: "Well, I gwine send for him." I in desperate condition. When I know anything, he walk up in the door. I was laying with my face toward the door, and I turn over.

Doctor come up to the bed. "Boy, how you getting on?" "I bad off," I say. He say: "See you is. Yeh." Lady say: "Doctor, what you think of him?" Doctor say: "Mistress, it 'most too late, but I do all I can." She say: "Please do all you can, he 'bout the best hand I got."

Doctor fix up medicine and told her to give it to me.

She say: "Uncle Will, take this medicine." I 'fraid to take it. 'Fraid he was trying to kill me. Then two men, John and Charlie, come in. Lady say: "Get this medicine in Uncle Will." One of the men hold my hand, and they gag me and put it in me. Next few days I can talk and ax for something to eat, so I git better. (I say: "Well, he didn't kill me when I took the medicine!")

I stayed there with her. . . . Next year I move right back in two miles, other side where I always live, with another lady. I stay there three year. Got along all right. When I left from there, I left there with $300 and plenty corn and hog. Everything I want, and three hundred cash dollars in my pocket!

AFTER FREEDOM

Right after freedom, my father plaited baskets and mats. He shucked mops, put handles on rakes, and did things like that in addition to his farming. He was a blacksmith all the time, too. He used to plait collars for mules. He farmed and got his harvests in season. The other things would be a help to him between times.

My father came here because he thought that there was a better situation here than in Georgia. Of course, the living was better there because they had plenty of fruit. Then he worked on a third and fourth. He got one bale of cotton out of every three he made. The slaves left many a plantation, and they would grow up in weeds. When a man would clear up the ground like this and plant it down in something, he would get all he planted on it. That was in addition to the ground that he would contract to plant. He used to plant rice, peas, potatoes, corn, and anything else he wanted too. It was all hisn so long as it was on extra ground he cleared up.

But they said, "Cotton grows as high as a man in Arkansas." Then they paid a man $2.50 for picking cotton here in Arkansas, while they just paid about 40 cents in Georgia. So my father came here. Times was good when we come here. The old man cleared five bales of cotton for himself his first year, and he raised his own corn. He bought a pony and a cow and a breeding hog out of the first year's money. He died about thirty-five years ago.

When I was coming along, I did public work after I became a grown man. First year I made crops with him and cleared two bales for myself at $12\frac{1}{2}$ cents a pound. The second year I hired out by the month at $45 per month and board. I had to buy my clothes, of course. After seven years I went to doing work as a millwright here in Arkansas. I stayed at that eighteen months. Then I steamboated.

We had a captain on that steamboat that never called any man by his name. We rolled cotton down the hill to the boat and loaded it on, and if you weren't a good man, that cotton got wet. I never wetted my cotton. But just the same, I heard what the others heard. One day after we had finished loading, I thought I'd tell him something. The men advised me not to. He was a rough man, and he carried a gun in his pocket and a gun in his shirt. I walked up to him and said, "Captain, I don't know what your name is, but I know you's a white man. I'm a nigger, but I got a name just like you have. My name's Webb. If you call 'Webb,' I'll come just as quick as I will for any other name and a lot more willing. If you don't want to say 'Webb,' you can just say 'Let's go,' and you'll find me right there." He looked at me a moment, and then he said, "Where you from?" I said, "I'm from Georgia, but I came on this boat from Little Rock." He put his arm around my shoulder and said, "Come on upstairs." We had two or three drinks upstairs, and he said, "You and your pardner are the only two men I have that is worth a damn." Then he said, "But you are right; you have a name, and you have a right to be called by it." And from then on, he quit calling us out of our names.

But I only stayed on the boat six months. It wasn't because of the captain. Them niggers was bad. They gambled all the time, and I gambled with them. But they wouldn't stop at that. They would argue and fight and cut and shoot. A man would shoot a man down and then kick him off into the river. Then when there was roll call, nobody would know what became of him. I didn't like that. I knew that I was going to kill somebody if I stayed on that boat 'cause I didn't intend for nobody to kill me. So I stopped.

After that, I went back to the man that I worked for the month for, and I stayed with him till I married. I took care of the stock. I was only married once. My wife died the fourteenth of October. We had three children, and I have one daughter living.

THAT WAS MY FREEDOM

I didn't know it was freedom till one day when I was about fourteen or fifteen years old—judging from my size and what I done. I went off to a spring to wash. I had one pot of clothes to boil and another just out of the pot to rub and rinse. A girl come to tell me Mrs. Field had company and wanted me to come cook dinner. I didn't go but told her I would be on and cook dinner soon as I could turn loose the washing. There was two colored girls and a white girl could done the cooking, but I was a good cook. The girl put on the water for me to scald the chicken soon as she went to the house. When I got there, Mrs. Field Mathis had a handful of switches corded together to beat me. I picked up the pan of boiling water to scald the chickens in. She got scared of me, told me to put the pan down. I didn't do it. I didn't aim to hurt her. I wouldn't throwed that boiling water on nothing. She sent to the store for her husband. He come, and I told him how it was about the clothes and three girls there could cook without me. He got mad at her and said: "Mary Agnes, she is as free as you are or I am. I'm not going to ever hurt her again, and you better not." That is the first I ever heard about freedom. It had been freedom a long time. I don't know how long then.

I stayed on, washed out the clothes and strung them up that evening. I ironed all the clothes and cooked the rest of the week. Mr. Field got me a good home with some colored folks. He told me if I would go there, he never would let nobody bother me and he never would mistreat me no more. I worked some for them, but they paid me. She ought to thought a heap of me the way I cooked and worked for her. That was my freedom. I was sold on a platform to Mr. Mathis.

TOBY AND GOVIE

I worked for Massa 'bout four years after freedom, 'cause he forced me to, said he couldn't 'ford to let me go. His place was near ruint, the fences burnt, and the house would have been, but it was rock. There was a battle fought near his place, and I taken Missy to a hideout in the mountains to where her father was, 'cause there was bullets flying everywhere. When the war was over, Massa come home and says, "You son of a gun, you's supposed to be free, but you ain't, 'cause I ain't gwine give you freedom." So I goes on working for him till I gits the chance to steal a hoss from him. The woman I wanted to marry, Govie, she 'cides to come to Texas with me. Me and Govie, we rides that hoss 'most a hundred miles, then we turned him a-loose and give him a scare back to his house, and come on foot the rest the way to Texas.

All we had to eat was what we could beg, and sometimes we went three days without a bite to eat. Sometimes we'd pick a few berries. When we got cold we'd crawl in a brushpile and hug up close together to keep warm. Once in awhile we'd come to a farmhouse, and the man let us sleep on cottonseed in his barn, but they was far and few between, 'cause they wasn't many houses in the country them days like now.

When we gits to Texas, we gits married, but all they was to our wedding am we just 'grees to live together as man and wife. I settled on some land, and we cut some trees and split them open and stood them on end with the tops together for our house. Then we deadened some trees, and the land was ready to farm. There was some wild cattle and hogs, and that's the way we got our start, caught some of them and tamed them.

I don't know as I 'spected nothing from freedom, but they turned us out like a bunch of stray dogs, no homes, no clothing, no nothing, not 'nough food to last us one meal. After we settles on that place, I never seed man or woman, 'cept Govie, for six years, 'cause it was a long ways to anywhere. All we had to farm with was sharp sticks. We'd stick holes and plant corn, and when it come up we'd punch up the dirt round it. We didn't plant cotton, 'cause we couldn't eat that. I made bows and arrows to kill wild game with, and we never went to a store for nothing. We made our clothes out of animal skins.

RUNNING AWAY

I was free a long time 'fore I knew it. My mistress still hired me out, till one day in talking to the woman she hired me to, "God bless her soul," she told me, "Fannie, you are free, and I don't have to pay your master for you now. You stay with me." She didn't give me no money but let me stay there and work for victuals and clothes 'cause I ain't had nowhere to go. Jesus, Jesus, God help us! Um, um, um! You children don't know. I didn't say nothing when she was telling me, but done 'cided to leave her and go back to the white folks that first own me.

I plan to 'tend a big dance. Let me see, I think it was on a Thursday night. Somehow it took and got out, you know how gals will talk, and it got to Old Bill Duffey's ears (old dog) and, baby, do you know—mind you, 'twa'n't slavery time—but the woman got so mad 'cause I runned away from her that she get a whole passel of 'em out looking for me. There was a boy who heard 'em talking and saying they was going to kill me if I were found. I will never forget this boy come up to me while I was dancing with another man and said, "Nobody knows where you are, Miss Moore. They is looking for you, and is gwine kill you, so you come on with me." Have mercy, have mercy, my Lord. Honey, you can just 'magine my feeling for a minute. I couldn't move. You know the gals and boys all got round me and told me to go with Skewball, that he would show me the way to my old mistress' house. Out we took, and we ran one straight mile up the road, then through the woods, then we had to go through a straw field. That field seem like three miles. After then, we met another skit of woods. Miss Sue, baby, my eyes (ha! ha! ha!) was bucked, and, too, if it is such a thing as being so scared your hair stand on your head, I know mine did. And that wasn't all. That boy and me puffed and sweated like bulls. Was feared to stop 'cause we might have been tracked.

At last we neared the house, and I started throwing rocks on the porch. Child, I look and heard that white woman when she hit that floor, bouncing out that bed. She must felt that I was coming back to her. She called all the men and had 'em throw a rope to me, and they drawed me up a piece to the window, then I held my arms up and they snatched me in. Honey, Skewball fled to the woods. I ain't never heard nothing 'bout him. And do you know, I didn't leave that woman's house no more for fifteen years.

PEONAGE

I

After Sherman come through Atlanta, he let the slaves go, and when he did, me and some of the other slaves went back to our old masters. Old Man Governor Brown was my boss man. After the war was over, Old Man Gordon took me and some of the others out to Mississippi. I stayed in peonage out there for 'bout forty years. I was located at just 'bout forty miles south of Greenwood, and I worked on the plantations of Old Man Sara Jones and Old Man Gordon.

I couldn't git away 'cause they watched us with guns all the time. When the levee busted, that kinda freed me. Man, they was devils; they wouldn't 'low you to go nowhere—not even to church. You done good to git something to eat. They wouldn't give you no clothes, and if you got wet you just had to lay down in what you got wet in.

And, man, they would whup you in spite of the devil. You had to ask to git water—if you didn't they would stretch you 'cross a barrel and wear you out. If you didn't work in a hurry, they would whup you with a strap that had five-six holes in it. I ain't talking 'bout what I heard—I'm talking 'bout what I done seed.

One time they sent me on Old Man Mack Williams' farm here in Jasper County, Georgia. That man would kill you sure. If that little branch on his plantation could talk it would tell many a tale 'bout folks being knocked in the head. I done seen Mack Williams kill folks, and I done seen him have folks killed. One day he told me that if my wife had been goodlooking, I never would sleep with her again 'cause he'd kill me and take her and raise childrens offen her. They used to take women away from their husbands, and put with some other man to breed just like they would do cattle. They always kept a man penned up, and they used him like a stud hoss.

When you didn't do right, Old Mack Williams would shoot you or tie a chain round your neck and throw you in the river. He'd git them other niggers to carry them to the river, and if they didn't, he'd shoot 'em down. Any time they didn't do what he said, he would shoot 'em down. He'd tell 'em to "Catch that nigger," and they would do it. Then he would tell 'em to put the chain round their neck and throw 'em in the river. I ain't heard this—I done seen it.

II

The owners went to work and notified the slaves that they were free. After the proclamation was issued, the government had agents who went all through the country to see if the slaves had been freed. They would see how the proclamation was being carried out. They would ask them, "How are you working?" "You are free." "What are you getting?" Some of them would say, "I ain't getting nothing now." Well, the agent would take that up, and they would have that owner up before the government. Maybe he would be working people for a year and giving them nothing before they found him out. There are some places where they have them cases yet. Where they have people on the place and ain't paying them nothing.

CARRYING ON WITH FREE LABOR

Yes, sir, us had a bold, driving, pushing master but not a hardhearted one. I sorry when military come and arrest him. It was this-a-way: Him try to carry on with free labor, 'bout like him did in slavery. Chester was in military district No. 2. The whole state was under that military government. Old Master went to the field and cuss a nigger woman for the way she was working, chopping cotton. She turned on him with the hoe and gashed him 'bout the head with it. Him pull out his pistol and shot her. Dr. Babcock say the wound in the woman not serious. They swore out a warrant for Master Biggers, arrest him with a squad, and take him to Charleston, where him had nigger jailors and was kicked and cuffed 'bout like a dog. They say the only thing he had to eat was corn-meal mush brought round to him and other nice white folks in a tub, and it was ladled out to them through the iron railing into the palms of their hands. Mistress stuck by him, went and stayed down there. The filthy prison and hard treatments broke him down, and when he did get out and come home, him passed over the River of Jordan, where I hopes and prays his soul finds rest.

Mistress say one time they threatened her down there, that if she didn't get up $10,000, they would send him where she would never see him again.

HOW WE GOT AWAY FROM OLD MAN BIAS

My mammy was scared of Old Tom Bias as if he was a bear. She worked in the field all day and come in at night and help with the stock. After supper they made her spin cloth. Massa fed well 'nough, but made us wear our old lowell clothes till they 'most fell off us. We was treated just like animals, but some owners treated they stock better'n Old Tom Bias handled my folks. I still got a scar over my right eye where he put me in the dark two months. We had a young cow, and when she had her first calf they sent me to milk her, and she kicked me and run me round a little pine tree, fighting and trying to hook me. Massa and Missy standing in the gate all the time, hollering to me to make the cow stand still. I got clost to her, and she kicked me off the stool, and I run to the gate, and Massa grab me and hit me 'cross the eye with a leather strap, and I couldn't see out my right eye for two months. He am dead now, but I's gwine tell the truth 'bout the way we was treated.

I could hear the guns shooting in the war. It sound like a thunderstorm when them cannons booming. Didn't nary one our menfolks go to war. I know my brother say, "Annie, when them cannons stops booming, we's gwine be all freed from Old Massa Tom's beatings."

But Massa wouldn't let us go after surrender. My mammy pretends to go to town and takes Frank and goes to Mansfield and asks the Progoe [Provost] Marshal what to do. He say we's free as Old Man Tom and didn't have to stay no more. Frank stays in town, and Mammy brings a paper from the Progoe, but she's scared to give it to Massa Tom. Me and James out in the yard making soap. I's toting water from the spring, and James fetching firewood to put round the pot. Mammy tells James to keep going next time he goes after wood, and her and me come round 'nother way and meets him down the road. That how we got 'way from Old Man Bias. Me and Mammy walks off and leaves a pot of soap biling in the backyard. We sot our pails down at the spring and cuts through the field and meets James down the big road. We left 'bout ten o'clock that morning and walks all day till it starts to git dark.

Then we comes to a white man's house and asks could we stay all night. He give us a good supper and let us sleep in his barn and breakfast next morning, and his wife fixes up some victuals in a box, and we starts to Mansfield. We was scared 'most to death when we come to that man's house, fear he'd take us back to Old Man Bias. But we had to have something to eat from somewheres. When Mammy tells him how we left Old Man Bias, he says, "That damn rascal ought to be Ku Kluxed." He told us not to be 'fraid.

We come to Mansfield and finds Frank, and Mammy hires me and James out to a white widow lady in Mansfield, and she sure a good, sweet soul. She told Mammy to come on and stay there with us till she git a job. We stayed with her two years.

HE WAS POOR AND HE HATED NEGROES

I was born in Arkansas in slavery time beyond Des Arc. My parents was sold in Mississippi. They was brought to Arkansas. I never seed my father after the closing of the war. He had been refugeed to Texas and come back here, then he went on back to Mississippi. Mama had seventeen children. She had six by my stepfather. When my stepfather was mustered out at De Valls Bluff, he come to Miss [Mrs.] Holland's and got Mama and took her on with him. I was give to Miss Holland's daughter. She married a Cargo. The Hollands raised me and my sister. I never seen Mama after she left. My mother was Jane Holland, and my father was Smith Woodson. They lived on different places here in Arkansas. I had a hard time. I was awfully abused by the old man that married Miss Betty. She was my young mistress. He was poor and hated Negroes. He said they didn't have no feeling. He drunk all the time. He never had been used to Negroes, and he didn't like 'em. He was a middle-age man, but Miss Betty Holland was in her teens.

No, Mama didn't have as hard a time as I had. She was Miss Holland's cook and washwoman. Miss Betty told her old husband, "Papa don't beat his Negroes. He is good to his Negroes." He worked overseers in the field. Nothing Miss Betty ever told him done a bit of good. He didn't have no feeling. I had to go in a trot all the time. I was scared to death of him—he beat me so. I'm scarred up all over now where he lashed me. He would strip me stark naked and tie my hands crossed and whup me till the blood ooze out and drip on the ground when I walked. The flies blowed me time and again. Miss Betty catch him gone, would grease my places and put turpentine on them to kill the places blowed. He kept a bundle of hickory switches at the house all the time. Miss Betty was good to me. She would cry and beg him to be good to me.

One time the cow kicked over my milk. I was scared not to take some milk to the house, so I went to the spring and put some water in the milk. He was snooping round somewhere and seen me. He beat me nearly to death. I never did know what suit him and what wouldn't. Didn't nothing please him. He was a poor man, never been used to nothing and took spite on me everything happened. They didn't have no children while I was there, but he did have a boy before he died. He died 'fore I left Dardanelle. When Miss Betty Holland married Mr. Cargo, she lived close to Dardanelle. That is where he was so mean to me. He lived in the deer- and bear-hunting country.

He went to town to buy them some things for Christmas good while after freedom—a couple or three years. Two men come there deer-hunting every year. One time he had beat me before them, and on their way home they went to the Freedmen's Bureau and told how he beat me and what he done it for—biggitiness. He was a biggity-acting and braggy-talking old man. When he got to town, they asked him if he wasn't hiding a little Negro girl, ask if he sent me to school. He come home. I slept on a bed made down at the foot of their bed. That night he told his wife what all he said and what all they ask him. He said he would kill whoever come there bothering about me. He been telling that about. He told Miss Betty they would fix me up and let me go stay a week at my sister's Christmas. He went back to town, bought me the first shoes I had had since they took me. They was brogan shoes. They put a pair of his sock on me. Miss Betty made the calico dress for me and made a body out of some of his pants legs and quilted the skirt part, bound it at the bottom with red flannel. She made my things nice—put my underskirt in a little frame and quilted it so it would be warm. Christmas day was a bright warm day. In the morning when Miss Betty dressed me up I was so proud. He started me off and told me how to go.

I got to the big creek. I got down in the ditch—couldn't get across. I was running up and down it looking for a place to cross. A big old mill was up on the hill. I could see it. I seen three men coming, a white man with a gun and two Negro men on horses or mules. I heard one say, "Yonder she is." Another said, "It don't look like her." One said, "Call her." One said, "Margaret." I answered. They come to me and said, "Go to the mill and cross on a foot log." I went up there and crossed and got up on a stump behind my brother-in-law on his horse. I didn't know him. The white man was the man he was sharecropping with. They all lived in a big yard-like close together. I hadn't seen my sister before in about four years. Mr. Cargo told me if I wasn't back at his house New Year's day he would come after me on his horse and run me every step of the way home. It was nearly twenty-five miles. He said he would give me the worst whupping I ever got in my life. I was going back, scared not to be back. Had no other place to live.

When New Year day come, the white man locked me up in a room in his house, and I stayed in there two days. They brought me plenty to eat. I slept in there with their children. Mr. Cargo never come after me till March. He didn't see me when he come. It started in raining and cold, and the roads was bad. When he come in March, I seen him. I knowed him. I lay down and covered up in leaves. They was deep. I had been in the woods getting sweet gum when I seen him. He scared me. He never seen me. This white man bound me to his wife's friend for a year to keep Mr. Cargo from getting me back. The woman at the house and Mr. Cargo had war nearly about me. I missed my whuppings. I never got home that whole year. It was Mrs. Brown twenty miles from Dardanelle they bound me over to. I never got no more than the common run of Negro children, but they wasn't mean to me.

When I was at Cargos', he wouldn't buy me shoes. Miss Betty would have, but in them days the man was head of his house. Miss Betty made me moccasins to wear out in the snow—made them out of old rags and pieces of his pants. I had risings on my feet, and my feet frostbite till they was solid sores. He would take his knife and stob my risings to see the matter pop 'way out. The ice cut my feet. He cut my foot on the side with a cowhide nearly to the bone. Miss Betty catch him outa sight, would doctor my feet. Seem like she was scared of him. He wasn't none too good to her. He told his wife the Freedmen's Bureau said turn that Negro girl loose. She didn't want me to leave her. He despised nasty Negroes he said. One of them fellows what come for me had been to Cargos' and seen me. He was the Negro man come to show Patsy's husband and his sharecropper where I was at. He whupped me twice before them deer hunters. They visited him every spring and fall, hunting deer, but they reported him to the Freedmen's Bureau. They knowed he was showing off. He overtook me on a horse one day, four or five years after I left there. I was on my way from school. I was grown. He wanted me to come back live with them. Said Miss Betty wanted to see me so bad. I was so scared, I lied to him and said "Yes" to all he said. He wanted to come get me a certain day. I lied about where I lived. He went to the wrong place to get me, I heard. I was afraid to meet him on the road. He died at Dardanelle before I come away. . . .

DEVILS AND GOOD PEOPLE WALKED THE ROAD

That was the way it worked. They was all kinds of white folks, just like they is now. One man in Secesh clothes would shoot you if you tried to run away. Maybe another Secesh would help slip you out to the underground and say, "God bless you, poor black devil," and some of them that was poor would help you if you could bring 'em something you stole, like a silver dish or spoons or a couple big hams. I couldn't blame them poor white folks, with the men in the war and the women and children hungry. The niggers didn't belong to them nohow, and they had to live somehow. But now and then they was a devil on earth, walking in the sight of God and spreading iniquity before him. He was the low-down Secesh that would take what a poor runaway nigger had to give for his chance to git away, and then give him 'structions that would lead him right into the hands of the patrollers and git him caught or shot!

Yes, that's the way it was. Devils and good people walking in the road at the same time, and nobody could tell one from t'other.

The Equalization War

The first war was 'bout freedom and the war right after it was equalization.

JORDAN HAD A HARD TIME

Mammy married a man named Jordan when I was a little baby. He was the overlooker and went off to the Yankees, when they come for foraging through that country the first time.

He served in the Negro regiment in the battle at Fort Piller and a lot of Secesh was killed in that battle, so when the war was over and Jordan come back home, he was a changed nigger, and all the whites and a lot of the niggers hated him. All 'cepting Old Master, and he never said a word out of the way to him. Just told him to come on and work on the place as long as he wanted to.

But Jordan had a hard time, and he brung it on hisself, I reckon.

'Bout the first thing, he went down to Wildersville Schoolhouse, about a mile from Wildersville, to a nigger and carpetbagger convention and took me and Mammy along. That was the first picnic and the first brass band I ever see. The band men was all white men, and they still had on their blue soldier clothes.

Lots of the niggers there had been in the Union army, too, and they had on parts of their army clothes. They took them out from under their coats and their wagon seats and put them on for the picnic.

There was a saloon over in Wildersville, and a lot of them went over there, but they was scared to go in, most of them. But a colored delegate named Taylor and my pappy went in and ordered a drink. The bartender didn't pay them no mind.

Then a white man named Billy Britt walked up and throwed a glass of whiskey in Jordan's face and cussed him for being in the Yankee army. Then a white man from the North named Pearson took up the fight, and him and Jordan jumped on Billy Britt, but the crowd stopped them and told Pappy to git on back to where he come from.

He got elected a delegate at the convention and went on down to Nashville and helped nominate Brownlow for governor. Then he couldn't come back home for a while, but finally he did.

Old Master was uneasy about the way things was going on, and he come out to the farm and stayed in the big house a while.

One day in broad daylight he was on the gallery, and down the road come 'bout twenty bushwhackers in Secesh clothes on horses and rid up to the gate. Old Master knowed all of them, and Captain Clay Taylor, who had been the master of the nigger delegate, was at the head of them.

They had Jordan Pyles tied with a rope and walked along on the ground betwixt two horses.

"Where you taking my nigger?" Old Master say. He run down off the gallery and out in the road.

"He ain't your nigger no more—you know that," Old Captain Taylor holler back.

"He just as much my nigger as that Taylor nigger was your nigger, and you ain't laid hands on him! Now you just have pity on my nigger!"

"Your nigger Jordan been in the Yankee army, and he was in the battle at Fort Piller and help kill our white folks, and you know it!" Old Captain Taylor say and argue on like that, but Old Master just take hold his bridle and shake his head.

"No, Clay," he say, "that boy maybe didn't kill Confederates but you and him both know my two boys killed plenty Yankees, and you forgot I lost one of my boys in the war. Ain't that enough to pay for letting my nigger alone?"

And Old Captain Taylor give the word to turn Jordan loose, and they rid on down the road.

That's one reason my stepdaddy never did leave Old Master's place, and I stayed on there till I was grown and had children.

KU KLUX

I

I never will forgit when they hung Cy Guy. They hung him for a scandalous insult to a white woman, and they comed after him a hundred strong.

They tries him there in the woods, and they scratches Cy's arm to git some blood, and with that blood they writes that he shall hang 'tween the heavens and the earth till he am dead, dead, dead, and that any nigger what takes down the body shall be hunged too.

Well, sir, the next morning there he hung, right over the road, and the sentence hanging over his head. Nobody'd bother with that body for four days, and there it hung, swinging in the wind, but the fourth day the sheriff comes and takes it down.

There was Ed and Cindy, who 'fore the war belonged to Mr. Lynch, and after the war he told 'em to move. He gives 'em a month, and they ain't gone, so the Ku Kluxes gits 'em.

It was on a cold night when they comed and drugged the niggers outen bed. They carried 'em down in the woods and whup them, then they throws 'em in the pond, their bodies breaking the ice. Ed come out and come out to our house, but Cindy ain't been seed since.

Sam Allen in Caswell County was told to move, and after a month the hundred Ku Klux come a-toting his casket, and they tells him that his time has come and iffen he want to tell his wife goodbye and say his prayers hurry up.

They set the coffin on two chairs, and Sam kisses his old woman who am a-crying, then he kneels down side of his bed with his head on the pillow and his arms throwed out front of him.

He sets there for a minute and when he riz he had a long knife in his hand. 'Fore he could be grabbed he done kill two of the Ku Kluxes with the knife, and he done gone outen the door. They ain't catch him neither, and the next night when they comed back, 'termined to git him, they shot another nigger by accident. . . .

I know one time Miss Hendon inherits a thousand dollars from her pappy's 'state, and that night she goes with her sweetheart to the gate, and on her way back to the house she gits knocked in the head with a axe. She screams, and her two nigger servants, Jim and Sam, runs and saves her, but she am robbed.

Then she tells the folkses that Jim and Sam am the guilty parties, but her little sister swears that they ain't, so they gits out of it.

After that they finds out that it am five mens—Atwater, Edwards, Andrews, Davis, and Markham. The preacher comes down to where they am hanging to preach their funeral, and he stands there while lightning plays round the dead men's heads and the wind blows the trees, and he preaches such a sermon as I ain't never heard before.

Bob Boylan falls in love with another woman, so he burns his wife and four young-uns up in their house.

The Ku Kluxes gits him, of course, and they hangs him high on the old red oak on the Hillsboro road. After they hunged him, his lawyer says to us boys, "Bury him good, boys, just as good as you'd bury me iffen I was dead."

I shook hands with Bob 'fore they hunged him, and I helped to bury him too, and we bury him nice, and we all hopes that he done gone to glory.

II

After us colored folks was 'sidered free and turned loose, the Klu Klux broke out. Some colored people started to farming, like I told you, and gathered the old stock. If they got so they made good money and had a good farm, the Klu Klux would come and murder 'em. The government builded schoolhouses, and the Klu Klux went to work and burned 'em down. They'd go to the jails and take the colored men out and knock their brains out and break their necks and throw 'em in the river.

There was a colored man they taken, his name was Jim Freeman. They taken him and destroyed his stuff and him 'cause he was making some money. Hung him on a tree in his front yard, right in front of his cabin.

There was some colored young men went to the schools they'd opened by the government. Some white woman said someone had stole something of hers, so they put them young men in jail. The Klu Klux went to the jail and took 'em out and killed 'em. That happened the second year after the war.

After the Klu Kluxes got so strong, the colored men got together and made the complaint before the law. The governor told the law to give 'em the old guns in the commissary, what the Southern soldiers had used, so they issued the colored men old muskets and said protect themselves. They got together and organized the militia and had leaders like regular soldiers. They didn't meet 'cept when they heared the Klu Kluxes was coming to get some colored folks. Then they was ready for 'em. They'd hide in the cabins, and then's when they found out who a lot of them Klu Kluxes was, 'cause a lot of 'em was kilt. They wore long sheets and covered the hosses with sheets so you couldn't recognize 'em. Men you thought was your friend was Klu Kluxes, and you'd deal with 'em in stores in the daytime, and at night they'd come out to your house and kill you. I never took part in none of the fights, but I heared the others talk 'bout them, but not where them Klu Klux could hear 'em.

One time they had twelve men in jail, 'cused of robbing white folks. All was white in jail but one, and he was colored. The Klu Kluxes went to the jailor's house and got the jail key and got them men out and carried 'em to the river bridge, in the middle. Then they knocked their brains out and threw 'em in the river.

III

The Ku Klux got after Uncle Will once. He was a brave man. He had a little mare that was a race horse. Will rode right through the bunch before they ever realized that it was him. He got on the other side of them. She [i.e., the mare] was gone! They kept on after him. They went down to his house one night. He wouldn't run for nothing. He shot two of them, and they went away. Then he was out of ammunition. People urged him to leave, for they knew he didn't have no more bullets; but he wouldn't, and they came back and killed him.

They came down to Hancock County one night, and the boys hid on both sides of the bridge. When they got in the middle of the bridge, the boys commenced to fire on them from both sides, and they jumped into the river. The darkies went on home when they got through shooting at them; but there wasn't no more Ku Klux in Hancock County. The better-thinking white folks got together and stopped it.

The Ku Klux kept the niggers scared. They cowed them down so that they wouldn't go to the polls. I stood there one night when they were counting ballots. I belonged to the County Central Committee. I went in and stood and looked. Our ballot was long; theirs was short. I stood and seen Clait Turner calling their names from our ballots. I went out and got Rube Turner, and then we both went back. They couldn't call the votes that they had put down they had. Rube saw it.

Then they said, "Are you going to contest this?"

Rube said, "Yes." But he didn't because it would have cost too much money. Rube was chairman of the committee.

The Ku Klux did a whole lot to keep the niggers away from the polls in Washington and Baldwin counties. They killed a many a nigger down there.

They hanged a Ku Klux for killing his wife, and he said he didn't mind being hung, but he didn't want a damn nigger to see him die.

But they couldn't keep the niggers in Hancock County away from the polls. There was too many of them.

YOUR OLD HORSE AIN'T NO GOOD

When the war ended up, 'most all the niggers stay with Old Master and work on the shares, until the land git divided up and sold off and the young niggers git scattered to town.

I never did have no truck with the Ku Kluckers, but I had to step mighty high to keep outen it! The sure 'nough Kluxes never did bother around us 'cause we minded our own business and never give no trouble.

We wouldn't let no niggers come round our place talking 'bout delegates and voting, and we just all stayed on the place. But they was some low white trash and some devilish niggers made out like they was Ku Klux ranging round the country, stealing hosses and taking things. Old Master said they wasn't, sure enough, so I reckon he knowed who the regular ones was.

These bunches that come around robbing got into our neighborhood, and Old Master told me I better not have my old horse at the house, 'cause if I had him they would know nobody had been there stealing and it wouldn't do no good to hide anything 'cause they would tear up the place hunting what I had and maybe whip or kill me.

"Your old hoss ain't no good, Tony, and you better kill him to make them think you already been raided on," Old Master told me, so I led him out and knocked him in the head with an axe, and then we hid all our grub and waited for the Kluckers to come 'most any night, but they never did come. I borried a hoss to use in the day and took him back home every night for about a year.

PRAYING JIM JESUS

The Yankees rode three years over the county in squads, and colored folks didn't know they was free. I have seen them in their old uniforms riding around when I was a child. White folks started talking about freedom 'fore the darkies and turning them loose with the clothes they had on and what they could tote away. No land, no home, no place; they roamed around.

When it was freedom, the thing Papa done was go to a place and start out sharecropping. Folks had no horses or mules. They had to plow new ground with oxen. I plowed when I was a girl, plowed oxen. If you had horses or mules and the Yankees come along three or four years after the war, they would swap horses, ride a piece, and if they had a chance swap horses again. Stealing went on during and long after the war.

The Ku Klux was awful in South Carolina. The colored folks had no church to go to. They gather around at folks' houses to have preaching and prayers. One night we was having it at our house, only I was the oldest and was in another room sound asleep on the bed. There was a crowd at our house. The Ku Klux come, pulled off his robe and dough face, hung it up on a nail in the room, and said, "Where's that Jim Jesus?" He pulled him out the room. The crowd run off. Mama took the three little children but forgot me and run off too. They beat Papa till they thought he was dead and throwed him in a fence corner. He was beat nearly to death, just cut all to pieces. He crawled to my bed and woke me up and back to the steps. I thought he was dead—bled to death—on the steps. Mama come back to leave and found he was alive. She doctored him up, and he lived thirty years after that. We left that morning.

The old white woman that owned the place was rich—big rich. She been complaining about the noise—singing and preaching. She called him "Praying Jim Jesus" till he got to be called that around. He prayed in the field. She said he disturbed her. Mama said one of the Ku Klux she knowed been raised up there close to Master Barton's, but Papa said he didn't know one of them that beat on him.

THE DOCTOR'S "GRAVE"

We lived in a log house during the Ku Klux days. They would watch you just like a chicken rooster watching for a worm. At night, we was scared to have a light. They would come around with the dough faces on and peer in the windows and open the door. Iffen you didn't look out, they would scare you half to death. John Good, a darky blacksmith, used to shoe the horses for the Ku Klux. He would mark the horseshoes with a bent nail or something like that; then after a raid, he could go out in the road and see if a certain horse had been rode; so he began to tell on the Ku Klux. As soon as the Ku Klux found out they was being give away, they suspicioned John. They went to him and made him tell how he knew who they was. They kept him in hiding, and when he told his tricks, they killed him.

When I was a boy on the Gilmore place, the Ku Klux would come along at night a-riding the niggers like they was goats. Yes, sir, they had 'em down on all fours a-crawling, and they would be on their backs. They would carry the niggers to Turk Creek bridge and make them set up on the banisters of the bridge, then they would shoot 'em offen the banisters into the water. I 'clare them was the awfulest days I ever is seed. A darky name Sam Scaife drifted a hundred yards in the water downstream. His folks took and got him outen that bloody water and buried him on the bank of the creek. The Ku Klux would not let them take him to no graveyard. Fact is, they would not let many of the niggers take the dead bodies of the folks nowheres. They just throwed them in a big hole right there and pulled some dirt over them. For weeks after that, you could not go near that place, 'cause it stink so far and bad. Sam's folks, they throwed a lot of Indian-head rocks all over his grave, 'cause it was so shallow, and them rocks kept the wild animals from a-bothering Sam. You can still see them rocks, I could carry you there right now.

Another darky, Eli McCollum, floated about three and a half miles down the creek. His folks went there and took him out and buried him on the banks of the stream right by the side of a Indian mound. You can see that Indian mound to this very day. It is big as my house is, over there on the Chester side.

The Ku Klux and the niggers fit at New Hope Church. A big rock marks the spot today. The church, it done burnt down. The big rock sets about seven miles east of Lockhart on the road to Chester. The darkies killed some of the Ku Klux, and they took their dead and put them in Pilgrim's Church. Then they sot fire to that church, and it burnt everything up to the very bones of the white folks. And ever since then that spot has been known as "Burnt Pilgrim." The darkies left most of the folks right there for the buzzards and other wild things to eat up, 'cause them niggers had to git away from there; and they didn't have no time for to fetch no word or nothing to no folks at home. They had a hiding place not far from "Burnt Pilgrim." A darky name Austin Sanders, he was carrying some victuals to his son. The Ku Klux cotch him, and they axed him where he was a-gwine. He 'lowed that he was a-setting some bait for coons. The Ku Klux took and shot him and left him lying right in the middle of the road with a biscuit in his dead mouth.

Doctor McCollum was one of them Ku Klux, and the Yankees sot out for to cotch him. Doc, he rid a white pony called Fannie. All the darkies, they love Doc, so they would help him for to git away from the Yankees, even though he was a Ku Klux. It's one road what forks, after you crosses Wood's Ferry. Don't nobody go over that old road now. One fork go to Leeds and one to Chester. Well, right in this fork, Mr. Buck Worthy had done built him a grave in the

Wood's Ferry Graveyard. Mr. Worthy had done built his grave hisself. It was built out of marble, and it was covered up with a marble slab. Mr. Worthy, he would take and go there and open it up and git in it on pretty days. So Old Doc, he knowed about that grave. He was going to see a sick lady one night when they got after him. He was on Old Fannie. They was about to cotch Old Doc when he reached in sight of that graveyard. It was dark. So Doc, he drive the horse on past the fork, and then he stop and hitch her in front of some dense pines. Then he took and went to that grave and slip that top slab back and got in there and pulled it over him, just leaving a little crack. Doc 'lowed he wrapped up hisself in his horse blanket, and when the Yankees left, he went to sleep in that grave and never even work up till the sun, it was a-shining in his face.

Soon after that my sister took down sick with the misery. Doc he come to see her at night. He would hide in the woods in daytime. We would fetch him his victuals. My sister was sick three weeks 'fore she died. Doc he would take some blankets and go and sleep in that grave, 'cause he knowed they would look in our house for him. They kept on a-coming to our house. Course we never knowed nothing 'bout no doctor at all. There was a nigger with wooden-bottom shoes, that stuck to them Yankees and other poor white trash round there. He 'lowed with his big mouth that he gwine to find the doctor. He told it that he had seed Fannie in the graveyard at night. Us heard it and told the doctor. Us did not want him to go near that graveyard any more. But Doc, he just laugh, and he 'lowed that no nigger was a-gwine to look in no grave, 'cause he had tried to git me to go over there with him at night and I was scared.

One night, just as Doc was a-covering up, he heard them wooden shoes a-coming; so he sot up in the grave and took his white shirt and put it over his head. He seed three shadows a-coming. Just as they got near the Doc, the moon come out from 'hind a cloud and Doc, he wave that white shirt, and he say them niggers just fell over gravestones a-gitting outen that graveyard. Doc 'lowed that he heard them wooden shoes a-gwine up the road for three miles. Well, they never did bother the doctor any more.

Doc he liked to fiddle. Old Fannie she would git up on her hind legs when the Doc would play his fiddle.

GET RID OF THE GRASS

The onliest 'sperience I had myself with the Ku Klux was one night 'fore Grandma and Auntie left. Somebody rap on our cabin door. They opened it. We got scared when we seed 'em. They had the horses wrapped up. They had on long white dresses and caps. Every one of them had a horse whip. They called me out. Grandma and Auntie so scared they hid. They told me to git 'em water.

They poured it somewhere it did not spill on the ground. Kept me toting water. Then they say, "You been a good boy?" They still drinking. One say, "Just from Hell, pretty dry." Then they told me to stand on my head. I turned summersets a few times. They tickled me round with the ends of the whips. I had on a long shirt. They laugh when I stand on my head. Old Marse White laughed. I knowed his laugh. Then I got over my scare. They say, "Who live next down the road?" I told 'em Nells Christian. They say, "What he do?" I said, "Works in the field." They all grunt, "M-m-m-m." Then they say, "Show us the way." I nearly run to death 'cross the field to keep outa the way of the white horses. The moon shining bright as day. They say, "Nells, come out here." He say, "Holy Moses." He come out. They say, "Nells, what you do?" "I farms." They say, "What you raise?" He say, "Cotton and corn." They say, "Take us to see your cotton. We just from Hell. We ain't got no cotton there." He took 'em out there where it was clean. They got down and felt it. Then they say, "What is that?" feeling the grass. Nells say, "That is grass." They say, "You raise grass, too?" He said, "No, it come up." They say, "Let us see your corn." He showed 'em the corn. They felt it. They say, "What this?" Nells say, "It grass." They say, "You raise grass here?" They all grunt, "M-m-m-m," everything Nells say. They give him one bad whupping and tell him they be back soon see if he raising grass. They said, "You raise cotton and corn but not grass on this farm." They moan, "M-m-m-m." I heard 'em say his whole family and him, too, was out by daylight with their hoes cutting the grass out their crop. I was sure glad to git back to our cabin. They didn't come back to Nells no more that I heard 'bout. The man Nells worked for musta been one in that crowd. He lived 'way over yonder.

No, I think the Ku Klux was a good thing at that time. The darkies got sassy, trifling, lazy. They was notorious. They got mean. The men wouldn't work. Their families have to work and let them roam round over the country. Some of 'em mean to their families. They woulda starved the whites out and theirselves too. I seed the Ku Klux heap-a times, but they didn't bother me no more. I heard a heap they done along after that. They say some places the Ku Klux go they make 'em git down and eat at the grass with their mouths, then they whup 'em. Sometimes they make 'em pull off their clothes and whup 'em. I sure did feel for 'em but they knowed they had no business strolling round, visiting. The Ku Klux call that whupping helping 'em git rid of the grass. Nells' master lived at what they called Caneville over 'cross the field.

KU KLUX AND CARPETBAGGERS

Seems like there wa'n't no trouble 'mongst the whites and blacks till after the war. Some white mens come down from the North and mess up with the niggers. I was a mighty little shaver, but I 'members one night after supper, my daddy and mammy and us childrens was setting under a big tree by our cabin in the quarters, when all at oncet, lickety split, here come galloping down the road what look like a whole army of ghostes. Must have been 'bout a hundred, and they was men riding hosses with the men and hosses both robed in white.

Cap'n, them mens look like they been ten feet high, and they hosses big as elephants. They didn't bother nobody at the quarters, but the leader of the crowd ride right in the front gate and up to the big dug well back of our cabin and holler to my daddy: "Come here, nigger!" Ho-oh! Course we scared. Yes, sir, look like our time done come.

My daddy went over to where he setting on his hoss at the well. Then he say: "Nigger, git a bucket and draw me some cool water." Daddy got a bucket, fill it up and hand it to him. Cap'n, would you believe it? That man just lift that bucket to his mouth and never stop till it empty. Did he have 'nough? He just smack his mouth and call for more. Just like that, he didn't stop till he drunk three buckets full. Then he just wipe his mouth and say: "Lordy, that sure was good. It was the first drink of water I's had since I was killed at the battle of Shiloh."[1]

Was we good? Cap'n, from then on there wasn't a nigger dare stick his head out the door for a week. But next day we find out they was Ku Kluxes, and they found the body of a white man hanging to a post oak over by Grand Prairie. His name was Billings, and he come from the North. He been over round Livingston messing up the niggers, telling 'em they had been promised forty acres and a mule and they ought to go 'head and take 'em from the white folks.

But that carpetbagger couldn't do nothing with Old Slick, though. Slick? Yes, sir, that what everybody call him. He hang round the courthouse at Livingston and listen to the lawyers argufy. He try to 'member all the big words them lawyers use. When that carpetbagger come to town, that nigger Slick was carrying his bag to the hotel, and when they pass the mineral well in the street, the man axed Slick: "What that water good for? Have it been tested?" Slick say: "Oh, yes, sir, that water been scanalysed by the best fenologists in the country, and they say it's three quarters carbolic acid gas and the other seven eights is hydrophobia. . . ."

Git rid of the carpetbaggers? Oh, yes, sir, they vote 'em out. Well, sir, tell you how they done that. The 'publicans done paid all the niggers' poll tax and give 'em a receipt so they could vote same as the whites. They made up to 'lect the officers at the courthouse all niggers and then send other ones to Montgomery to make the laws. Same day the election come off there was a circus in Livingston, and the Democrats 'suaded the boss man of the circus to let all Sumter County niggers in the show by showing their poll-tax receipts. Yes, sir,

[1] This familiar Ku Klux Klan trick consisted in pouring the water undetected into a leather bag or other receptacle concealed under the coat.

when the show was over, the 'lection was over too, and nobody was 'lected 'cepting white Democrats.

Course that made Sumter County a mighty unhealthy place for carpetbaggers and uppity niggers.

END OF THE KU KLUXES

Does I 'member anything 'bout the Ku Kluxes? Jesus, yes! My old master, the doctor, in going round, say out loud to people that Ku Kluxes was doing some things they ought not to do, by 'storting money out of niggers just 'cause they could.

When he was gone to Union one day, a low-down pair of white men come, with false faces, to the house and ask where Dick Bell was. Miss Nancy say her don't know. They go hunt for him. Dick made a beeline for the house. They pull out hoss pistols, first time, pow! Dick run on, second time, pow! Dick run on, third time, pow! and as Dick reach the front yard the ball from the third shot keel him over like a hit rabbit. Old Miss run out, but they git him. Her say: "I give you five dollars to let him 'lone." They say: "Not 'nough." Her say: "I give you ten dollars." They say: "Not 'nough." Her say: "I give you fifteen dollars." They say: "Not 'nough." Her say: "I give you twenty-five dollars." They take the money and say: "Us'll be back tomorrow for the other Dick." They mean Dick James.

Next day, us see them a-coming again. Dick James done load up the shotgun with buckshot. When they was coming up the front steps, Uncle Dick say to us all in the big house: "Git out the way!" The names of the men us find out afterwards was Bishop and Fitzgerald. They come up the steps, with Bishop in front. Uncle Dick open the door, slap that gun to his shoulder, and pull the trigger. That man Bishop hollers: "Oh, Lordy." He drop dead and lay there till the coroner come. Fitzgerald leap 'way. They bring Dick to jail, try him right in that courthouse over yonder. What did they do with him? Well, when Marse Bill Stanton, Marse Elisha Ragsdale, and Miss Nancy tell 'bout it all from the beginning to the end, the judge tell the jurymen that Dick had a right to protect his home and hisself and to kill that white man, and to turn him loose. That was the end of the Ku Kluxes in Fairfield.

THEY KEPT THE NEGROES FROM VOTING

I was pretty good when I was a boy. So I never had any trouble then. I was right smart size when I saw the Ku Klux. They would whip men and women that weren't married and were living together. On the first day of January, they would whip men and boys that didn't have a job. They kept the Negroes from voting. They would whip them. They put up notices: "No niggers to come out to the polls tomorrow." They would run them off of government land which they had homesteaded. Sometimes they would just persuade them not to vote. A Negro like my father, they would say to him, "Now, Brown, you are too good to get messed up. Them other niggers round here ain't worth nothing, but you are, and we don't want to see you get hurt. So you stay 'way from the polls tomorrow." And tomorrow my father would stay away, under the circumstances. They had to depend on the white people for counsel. They didn't know what to do themselves. The other niggers they would threaten them and tell them if they came out they would kill them.

VOTE AS I DAMN PLEASE

The darkies and the white folks in Union County had an insurrection over the polls about the year 1888. In them days, when you wanted to put a Republican man in, you didn't have to do much campaigning. They just went to the polls and put him in. Everybody that could vote was Republican. In the fall of 1888 they had a great trouble down there, and some of them got killed. They went around and commanded the Negroes not to go to the polls the next day. Some of the Negroes would tell them, "Well, I am going to the polls tomorrow if I have to crawl." And then some of them would say, "I'd like to know how you going to vote." The nigger would ask right back, "How you going to vote?" The white man would say, "I'm going to vote as I damn please." The nigger would say, "I'm going to do the same thing." That started the trouble.

On Sunday before the election on Monday, they went around through that county in gangs. They shot some few of the Negroes. As the Negroes didn't have no weapons to protect theirselves, they didn't have no chance. In that way, quite a few of the Negroes disbanded their homes and went into different counties and different portions of the state and different states. Henry Goodman, my grandfather, came into Hot Spring County in this way.

MY DADDY WAS IN OFFICE

I was born in Colleton County in 1867. My daddy was in office when I begin to recall things, and he keep in office, by the will of the people, until I was nearly grown. My mammy, too, was a slave, when she and Daddy marry. She die when I was 'bout twelve years old, and my only brother, Edgar, was going on ten. My daddy never marry again.

One day some white men come to see Daddy long after Mammy was gone, and they say to Daddy: "Paul, when you gwine to jump the broomstick again?" My daddy was the only one who not laugh when they say that. He reply: "I has no women in view and no wedding dream in the back of my head. I has decided a wicked woman am a big bother and a good woman am a bore. To my way of thinking, that is the only difference between them." The white folks not smile, but say: "You'll see! Just wait till the right girl come along."

Daddy just seem to make friends of all the people 'bout him, and our house, close to Smoak, was a big meeting place most of the time. Sometimes the visitors are all white men. But at other days the niggers come and talk, tell funny tales, and laugh. Most of the meetings at the house was late at night, 'cause my daddy always go to his office at Walterboro, on week days. People coming and going there, all the time. Daddy was sure popular with the people, generally speaking.

The biggest crowd I ever seen up to that time was when General M. C. Butler come to Walterboro in 1882, to speak. He had been United States senator since 1876 and was a candidate for re-election. General Butler much pleased, that day when many white leaders and Daddy call at his hotel and tell him that Daddy had been asked by his neighbors to introduce him. He say: "Well, from what I hears, Paul Jenkins can do that job as well as anybody in the state." Then he pat Daddy on the shoulder.

At the speaking, Daddy gets up, and the big crowd slaps its hands for joy, and laughs, too. Daddy not laugh much, just smile. Then he throw back his shoulders and say:

> General Butler, like Moses, led us forth at last,
> The barren wilderness he passed,
> Did on the very border stand
> Of the blessed Promised Land,
> And from the misty mountain tops of his exalted wit,
> Saw it himself and showed us it!
> That's why we am sending him back—

That was all I hear. Daddy not allowed to finish. The people riot with pleasure, and General Butler say the tribute am the finest he ever hear, and smile at Daddy sitting there on the platform with the other big folks.

At another time, Daddy has a nigger lawyer running 'gainst him for county commissioner. The lawyer's name was Amphibious McIver. They begin the campaign at Cottageville. McIver speak first. Daddy follow, and begin with:

> A bullfrog tied by its tail to a stump,
> It rear and it croak, but it couldn't make a jump!

The white folks and the niggers clap, stamp, throw hats, and laugh, finally marching up to the table to grab Daddy and carry him up the street on their shoulders. He keep saying: "Boys, why don't you let me finish my speech?" They would laugh and say: "Paul, you done made the best speech in the world!" Daddy win at the 'lection, in a big way.

My daddy learn to read, write, and cipher while he was a slave. The Jenkins family help him, he say, 'cause he always keep the peace and work as he was told to do. When he's set free, that white family help him get settled and loaned him books. He go to Charleston 'bout 1868 and buy an armful of books and studied at night or whenever he had the chance. That is why he was able to make the political races, which he make and profit by. He send me and my brother, Edgar, to school, so that we learn a good deal in books.

I Take Freedom

Freedom is better than slavery, though. I done seed both sides.

IT'S THIS WAY

What I likes best, to be slave or free? Well, it's this way. In slavery I owns nothing and never owns nothing. In freedom I's own the home and raise the family. All that cause me worriment, and in slavery I has no worriment, but I takes the freedom.

ANYBODY WHO SAYS THAT IS TELLING A LIE

A man told me a nigger woman told his wife she would rather be slave than free. Well, I think, but I might be wrong, anybody which says that is telling a lie. There is something 'bout being free, and that makes up for all the hardships. I's been both slave and free, and I knows. Course, while I was slave, I didn't have no 'sponsibility, didn't have to worry 'bout where something to eat and wear and a place to sleep was coming from, but that don't make up for being free.

A BETTER DAY

It just like this. I think this a better day we live in these times. When we belong to the white folks, we live; and after we was free, we live right on. I think being free the best time to live. Better to be loose than tied, 'cause, don't care how good your owner, you had to be under their jurisdiction. Ain't that right?

THAT'S HOW I FEEL

Well, it was a God-sent method Mr. Lincoln used to give us our freedom. Mr. Davis didn't want no war, and he 'posed it all he knowed how, but if he hadn't-a gone ahead and fit, there never would have been nothing done for us. . . .

In a way I'm satisfied with what confronts me. A person in jail or on the chain gang would rather be outside and free than in captivity. That's how I feels.

YOU CAN'T BLAME THEM FOR THIS

Lots of old slaves closes the door before they tell the truth about their days of slavery. When the door is open, they tell how kind their masters was and how rosy it all was. You can't blame them for this, because they had plenty of early discipline making them cautious about saying anything uncomplimentary about their masters. I myself was in a little different position than most slaves and, as a consequence, have no grudges or resentment. However, I can tell you the life of the average slave was not rosy. They were dealt out plenty of cruel suffering.

MORE HIS OWN SAY

A man has got more his own say now than he did have. We can do more what we want to and don't have to go to the other fellow. Slavery mighta done the other fellow some good, but I don't think it ever done the colored people no good. Some of them after freedom didn't know how to go out and work for themselves. Down at Old John Coffman's, lots of them stayed with him right along, same as if they wasn't free. They didn't want to leave here 'cause they didn't think they could live if they left him. But when they got away up here in St. Louis, they know they can make a living, without Marse John, but they got to "go up against it." Depending on somebody else is poor business. When I was working I depended on myself. If they would have freed the slaves and give them a piece of ground, I think that would have been a heap better than the way they did. Look at the Indians! They're all living. I's always been able to eat and sleep.

POOR FOLK—WHITE AND BLACK

Did you know poor whites like slaves had to git a pass? I mean, a remit like us slaves, to sell anything and to go places or do anything. Just as we colored people, they had to go to some big white man like Colonel Allen, they did. If Master wanted to, he would give them a remit or pass; and if he didn't feel like it, he wouldn't do it. It was just as he felt about it. That's what made all 'feared him. Old Master was more hard on them poor white folks than he was on us niggers.

I don't know but two sets of white folks slaves up my way; one was name Chatman, and t'other one Nellovies. These two families worked on Allen's farm as we did. Off from us, on a plot called Morgan's lot, there they lived as slaves just like us colored folks. Yes, the poor white man had some dark and tough days, like us poor niggers; I mean they were lashed and treated, some of 'em, just as pitiful and unmerciful. Lord! Lord! baby, I hope you young folks will never know what slavery is and will never suffer as your foreparents. O God! God! I'm living to tell the tale to you, honey. Yes, Jesus, you've spared me.

For, as I think, if slavery had lasted, it would have been pretty tough. As it was, some fared good, while others fared common. You know, slaves who were beat and treated bad—some of them had started gitting together and killing the white folks when they carried them out to the field to work. God is punishing some of them old suckers and their children right now for the way they use to treat us poor colored folks.

I think by Negro gitting educated he has profited, and this here younger generation is gwine to take nothing off these here poor white folks when they don't treat them right, 'cause now this country is a free country; no slavery now.

I HOPE TO SEE A MILLION YEARS TO COME

I never fit in the war; no, sir, I couldn't. My belly's been broke! But I sure did want to, and I went up to be examined, but they didn't receive me on account of my broken stomach. But I sure tried, 'cause I wanted to be free. I didn't like to be no slave. That wa'n't good times. . . . I never had no good times till I was freed.

We was never allowed no parties, and when they had goings-on at the big house, we had to clear out. I had to work hard all the time every day in the week. Had to mind the cows and calves, and when I got older I had to hoe in the field. Mr. Toler had about five hundred acres, so they tell me, and he had a lot of cows and horses and oxens, and he was a big farmer. I've done about everything in my life, blacksmith and stonemason, carpenter, everything but bricklaying. I was a blacksmith here for thirty-six years. Learned it down at Toler's. . . .

After the war I bought a fiddle, and I was a good fiddler. Used to be a fiddler for the white girls to dance. Just picked it up, it was a natural gift. I could still play if I had a fiddle. I used to play at our hoedowns, too. Played all those old-time songs—"Soldier's Joy," "Jimmy Long Josey," "Arkansas Traveler," and "Black-eye Susie."

Before the war we never had no good times. They took good care of us, though. As particular with slaves as with the stock—that was their money, you know. . . .

We had very bad eating: bread, meat, water. And they fed it to us in a trough, just like a hog. And I went in my shirt till I was sixteen, never had no clothes. And the floor in our cabin was dirt, and at night we'd just take a blanket and lay down on the floor. The dog was superior to us. They would take him in the house. . . .

I sure is glad I ain't a slave no more. I thank God that I lived to pass the years until the day of 1937. I'm happy and satisfied now, and I hopes I see a million years to come.

List of Informants
and Interviewers

The informant's age is given as at the time of the interview; that is, 1936, 1937, or 1938—most frequently, 1937. Unless otherwise specified, the informant was a slave in the state of residence. The interviewer's name, when known, is given in italics. When two names are given, the second person served either as collaborator or as editor.

Pages iii, vi
The title and the motto of the book are from a version of "When I Lay My Burden Down" recorded by Herbert Halpert for the Works Progress Administration and the Library of Congress from members of the Rust College Choir, Holly Springs, Mississippi, May 14, 1939.

Page 1
INTRODUCTION, quotation: Cato———, about 101, Dallas, Texas; born 1836 or 1837, near Pineapple, Wilcox County, Alabama; slave in Alabama

Page 7
PART ONE, MOTHER WIT, quotation: Sylvia Durant, about 72, Marion, South Carolina. *Annie Ruth Davis*

Page 9
FOOLING MASTER AND CATCHING JOHN, quotation: Harriett Robinson, 95, Oklahoma City, Oklahoma; born September 1, 1842, Bastrop, Texas; slave in Texas
FOOLING MASTER: Jake Green, 85, Livingston, Alabama. *Ruby Pickens Tartt*
CATCHING JOHN: Jake Green, 85, Livingston, Alabama. *Ruby Pickens Tartt*

Page 10
IT WAS A POSSUM A WHILE AGO: Annie Young, 86, Oklahoma City, Oklahoma; born 1851, Summers County, Tennessee; slave in Tennessee
PIG-OOIE, PIG: Lizzie Farmer, 80, McAlester, Oklahoma; born 1857, Texas; slave in Texas

Page 11
MALITIS: Mrs. Josie Jordan, 75, Tulsa, Oklahoma; born Sparta, Tennessee; slave in Tennessee

THE BOOTS THAT WOULDN'T COME OFF: Neal Upson, 81, Athens, Georgia; born near Lexington, Oglethorpe County, Georgia. *Grace McCune*

Page 12

I COME TO TELL THEM I COULDN'T COME: Uncle Hilliard Johnson, about 79, Sumter County, Alabama. *Ruby Pickens Tartt*

MASTER PUMPKIN: William M. Thomas, 87, Forth Worth, Texas; born May 17, 1850, Lauderdale County, Mississippi; slave in Mississippi

Page 13

WHAT THE PASS SAID: Clayborn Gantling, 89, Jacksonville, Florida; born January 20, 1848, Dawson, Georgia; slave in Georgia, *Rachel Austin*

Page 14

POLLY PARROT: Sophia Ward, 99, Clay County, Kentucky; born February 2, 1837. *Pearl House*

THE TERRAPIN THAT COULD TALK: Lizzie Farmer, 80, McAlester, Oklahoma; slave in Texas

TURN THE TRAY AROUND: William M. Adams, 93, Fort Worth, Texas; born San Jacinto County, Texas

Page 15

I COME FROM ABOVE, WHERE ALL IS LOVE: Mary Ella Grandberry, about 90, Sheffield, Alabama; born Barton, Alabama. *Levi D. Shelby, Jr.*

LAYING DOWN AND GETTING UP: Mingo White, Burleson, Alabama; born in Chester, South Carolina, and brought to Alabama at about the age of 5. *Levi D. Shelby, Jr.*

CUSSING MASTER: Ed McCrorey (Ed Mack), 82, Winnsboro, South Carolina. *W. W. Dixon*

Page 16

JOKE: PUTTING HAND UNDER OLD MISTRESS' DRESS: Alice Dixon, 80, El Dorado district, Arkansas. *Pernella M. Anderson*

Page 17

TALL TALES AND TALL TALK, quotation: James Henry Stith, 72, Little Rock, Arkansas; born January 26, 1866, Sparta, Hancock County, Georgia; of slave parentage. *Samuel S. Taylor*

THE PROMISED LAND: Henry Green, 90, Barton, Arkansas; born near Montgomery, Montgomery County, Alabama; slave in Alabama

BIG CORN: Tom Chisolm, 62, Columbia, South Carolina; of slave parentage. *Stiles M. Scruggs*

Page 18

THEY WERE MEN IN THOSE DAYS: Ephraim (Mike) Lawrence, about 80, Edisto Island, South Carolina. *C. S. Murray*

Page 19

SET-DOWN HOGS: Uncle Henry Barnes, 79, Prichard, Alabama; born 1858, near Suggsville, Clarke County, Alabama. *Ila B. Prine*

BAD MEN YELL: Auntie Thomas Johns, 73, Cleburne, Texas; born 1864, Burleson County, Texas; freed at the age of 2

Page 20

HOW COME, quotation: Caroline Matthews, 79, Pine Bluff, Arkansas; born and slave in Mississippi. *Mrs. Bernice Bowden*

WHY THE BOLL-WEEVIL CAME: John Love, 76, Marlin, Texas

THE BROWN BEAR AND THE PICKANINNY: Lou Turner, 89, Beaumont, Texas; born Rosedale, near Beaumont, Jefferson County, Texas

Page 21

NICODEMUS AND THE SYCAMORE TREE: George McAlilley, 84, near Winnsboro, Fairfield County, South Carolina. *W. W. Dixon*

WHY PARTRIDGES CAN'T FLY OVER TREES: Ella Kelly, 81, Winnsboro, South Carolina. *W. W. Dixon*

THE SHEEP AND THE GOATS: Anthony Dawson, 105, Tulsa, Oklahoma; born July 25, 1832, near Greenville, Pitt County, North Carolina; slave in North Carolina

Page 22

THE COON AND THE DOG: Stephen McCray, 88, Oklahoma City, Oklahoma; born 1850, Huntsville County, Alabama; slave in Alabama

YOU JUST CAN'T GET AWAY FROM WHAT THE LORD SAID: Gus (Jabbo) Rogers, about 90, Mobile County, Alabama; slave in North Carolina and Alabama. *Mary A. Poole*

Page 23

LINCOLN AND OTHERS, quotation: Mingo White, Burleson, Alabama; born in Chester, South Carolina, and brought to Alabama about the age of 5. *Levi D. Shelby, Jr.*

WHERE LINCOLN WROTE HIS NAME: I. Bob Maynard, 79, Weleetka, Oklahoma; born Falls County, Texas; slave in Texas and Mississippi. II. Alice Douglass, 77, Oklahoma City, Oklahoma; born December 22, 1860, Sumner County, Tennessee; slave in Tennessee

Page 24

WHEN LINCOLN CAME DOWN TO FREE US: I. Aunt Pinkey Howard, about 85, El Dorado district, Arkansas. *Mrs. Mildred Thompson and Mrs. Carol Graham.* II. Salena Taswell, Miami, Florida; slave in Georgia. III. Frank A. Patterson, 88,

Little Rock, Arkansas; born 1850, Raleigh, North Carolina; slave in North Carolina and Georgia. *Samuel S. Taylor.* IV. H. B. (Dad or Pappy) Holloway, 89, Little Rock, Arkansas; born free, February 15, 1848, Fort Valley, Georgia. *Samuel S. Taylor*

Page 26

MAYBE MR. LINCOLN AIN'T SO BAD: Mary Wallace Bowe, 81, Durham, North Carolina. *Travis Jordan*

WHAT FREDERICK DOUGLASS SAID: Frank A. Patterson, 88, Little Rock, Arkansas; born 1850, Raleigh, North Carolina; slave in North Carolina and Georgia. *Samuel S. Taylor*

Page 27

STEVE RENFROE: Oliver Bell, Sumter County, Alabama. *Ruby Pickens Tartt*

SAM BASS: Andy Nelson, 76, Moser Valley, Texas; born 1861, Tarrant County, Texas

Page 29

BIRDS AND BEASTS, quotation: Will Dill, 75, Spartanburg, South Carolina. *F. S. DuPre*

I'M BEING TOOK: Bill Homer, 87, Fort Worth, Texas; born June 17, 1850, near Shreveport, Caddo Parish, Louisiana; slave in Louisiana and Texas

BREAKING THE BALK: Albert Hill, 81, Fort Worth, Texas; born Walton County, Georgia; slave in Georgia

Page 30

THE PARTRIDGE AND THE FOX: Cecelia Chappel, 102, Nashville, Tennessee; born Marshall County, Tennessee

THE TORTOISE AND THE RABBIT: Rev. Lafayette Price, in his late eighties; Beaumont, Texas; born about 1850, Wilcox County, Alabama; slave in Alabama and Louisiana. *Fred Dibble*

FATAL IMITATION: Nap McQueen, 80, Beaumont, Texas; slave in Tennessee and Texas

Page 31

BARNYARD TALK: Will Dill, 75, Spartanburg, South Carolina. *F. S. DuPre*

WHAT THE FOWL SAID: Roxy Pitts, 82, Opelika, Alabama; born 1855, near Youngsboro, Alabama. *Preston Klein*

Page 32

WHAT THE BIRDS SAID: Gus Feaster, 97, Union, South Carolina. *Caldwell Sims*

WHAT THE HOUNDS SAID: H. B. (Dad or Pappy) Holloway, 89, Little Rock, Arkansas; born free, February 15, 1848, Fort Valley, Georgia. *Samuel S. Taylor*

Page 33

PASTOR AND FLOCK, quotation: Talitha Lewis, 86, Pine Bluff, Arkansas; born 1852, Goldsboro, North Carolina; slave in North Carolina. *Mrs. Bernice Bowden*

WHAT THE PREACHER SAID: I. Sarah Douglas, about 82, El Dorado, Arkansas; slave in Alabama. *Pernella M. Anderson.* II. Molly Finley, 72, Honey Creek, Arkansas; of slave parentage. *Irene Robertson.* III. Lucretia Alexander, 89, Little Rock, Arkansas; born near Hazlehurst, Copiah County, Mississippi, and brought to Arkansas at about the age of 7. *Samuel S. Taylor.* IV. Victoria McMullen, 54, Little Rock, Arkansas; of slave grandparents. *Samuel S. Taylor.* V. Waters McIntosh, 76, Little Rock, Arkansas; born July 4, 1862, Lynchburg, South Carolina; slave in South Carolina. *Samuel S. Taylor*

Page 34

GOD GOT A CLEAN KITCHEN TO PUT YOU IN: Aaron Ford, 88, Marion, South Carolina. *H. Grady Davis*

Page 35

TWO WAYS OF PREACHING THE GOSPEL: Anderson Edwards, 93, Harrison County, Texas; born March 12, 1844, Rusk County, Texas

EVERY KIND OF FISH IS CAUGHT IN A NET: Marion Johnson, El Dorado, Arkansas; born a slave in Louisiana. *Mrs. Carol Graham*

THEY'D PRAY: Talitha Lewis, 86, Pine Bluff, Arkansas; born 1852, Goldsboro, North Carolina; slave in North Carolina. *Mrs. Bernice Bowden*

Page 36

MASTER FRANK HAS COME THROUGH: Kiziah Love, 93, Colbert, Oklahoma; slave in Indian Territory

DAMN POOR PREACHER: Tom Douglas, 89, El Dorado, Arkansas; born September 15, 1847, Marion, Louisiana; slave in Louisiana. *Pernella M. Anderson*

BOOTS OR NO BOOTS: Emoline Glasgow, 78, Newberry, South Carolina. *G. L. Sumner*

Page 37

METHODIST DOGS AND BAPTIST DOGS: Siney Bonner, about 90, Birmingham, Alabama. *W. F. Jordan*

Page 38

THE POWER, quotation: William Adams, 93, Fort Worth, Texas; born San Jacinto County, Texas

A POCKET FULL OF CONJURE THINGS: Abram Sells, in his eighties, Jamestown, Texas; born near Newton, Newton County, Texas

OLD BAB, THE CONJURE MAN: Henry F. Pyles, 81, Tulsa Oklahoma; born August 15, 1856, Jackson, Tennessee; slave in Tennessee

Page 42

HOODOO: H. B. (Dad or Pappy) Holloway, 89, Little Rock, Arkansas; born free, February 15, 1848, Fort Valley, Georgia. *Samuel S. Taylor*

Page 43

THE CONJURE THAT DIDN'T WORK: Jake Green, 85, Livingston, Alabama. *Ruby Pickens Tartt*

CURED BY PRAYER: Orleans Finger, 79, Little Rock, Arkansas; born Tippa County, Mississippi; slave in Arkansas. *Samuel S. Taylor*

Page 44

I KNOW IT WAS A SIGN: Annie Page, 86, Pine Bluff, Arkansas; born 1852, Union County, Alabama. *Mrs. Bernice Bowden*

HE IS A GOOD GOD: Maggie Perkins, 81, Pine Bluff, Arkansas; born Union County, South Carolina; slave in South Carolina. *Martin and Barker*

Page 45

THE POWER: William Adams, 93, Fort Worth, Texas; born San Jacinto County, Texas

Page 48

HANTS, quotation: Lou Smith, 83, Platter, Oklahoma; slave in Texas

BLOW, GABRIEL, BLOW: Ank Bishop, 89, Livingston, Alabama; born August 16, 1849, Ward, Alabama. *Ruby Pickens Tartt*

Page 49

JOSH AND THE LORD: Willis Easter, 85, Waco, Texas; born near Nacogdoches, Nacogdoches County, Texas, and brought to Bosqueville, Texas, at the age of 2

BUT IT WAS A FAST MULE: Josh Horn, about 90, Sumter County, Alabama. *Ruby Pickens Tartt*

Page 50

THE PHANTOM RIDER: Josh Horn, about 90, Sumter County, Alabama. *Ruby Pickens Tartt*

JOSH, BLOW YOUR HORN: Josh Horn, about 90, Sumter County, Alabama. *Ruby Pickens Tartt*

Page 51

OLD JOE IS OVER THERE GETTING 'SIMMONS AND CHOPPING WOOD: Anthony Abercrombie, 100, Uniontown, Alabama; slave in Perry County, Alabama. *Susie R. O'Brien*

Page 52

RENFROE'S TREE: Henry Garry, about 75, Birmingham, Alabama; born Sumter County, Alabama. *W. F. Jordan*

THE HANTS OF BASKIN LAKE: Ella Johnson, about 85, Little Rock, Arkansas; born Helena, Arkansas. *Samuel S. Taylor*

Page 53

ALEX COMES HOME: Annie Little, 81, Mart, Texas; born January, 1856, Springfield, Missouri; slave in Missouri and Mississippi

Page 54

BUT SHE WAS AFRAID: Lydia Jones, 93, Pine Bluff, Arkansas; born and slave in Mississippi. *Mrs. Bernice Bowden*

GHOST TALK: I. John White, 121, Sand Springs, Oklahoma; born April 10, 1816; slave in Georgia and Texas. II. Florence Ruffins, Fort Worth, Texas; born De Kalb, Texas; of slave parentage

Page 55

MARSE GLENN'S MONEY: Mrs. M. E. Abrams, Whitmire, South Carolina, as told her by Uncle "Mad" Griffin, 82, Whitmire. *Caldwell Sims*

Page 57

THE SHINING SHOVEL: Gus Feaster, 97, Union, South Carolina. *Caldwell Sims*

Page 58

THE PETRIFIED MAN: Eli Harrison, 87, Fairfield County, South Carolina. *W. W. Dixon*

Page 59

ANECDOTES, quotation: Casie Jones Brown, 91, near Paragould, Greene County, Arkansas. *Velma Sample*

THE ROOSTER TEST: Neal Upson, 81, Athens, Georgia; born near Lexington, Oglethorpe County, Georgia. *Grace McCune*

THE STOLEN COAT: Perry Madden, about 79, Little Rock, Arkansas; slave in Alabama. *Samuel S. Taylor*

Page 60

THE PEDDLER AND THE PONY: Will Adams, 80, Marshall, Texas; born 1857, Harrison County, Texas

HOPPING JOHN: Susan Nelson, 80, Charleston, South Carolina. *Martha S. Pinckney*

THE LORD HAD CALLED HIM TO PREACH: Lou Smith, 83, Platter, Oklahoma; slave in Texas

Page 61

THE LORD TELLS ME WHEN IT'S RIGHT: Dellie Lewis, Mobile, Alabama. *Mary A. Poole*

IF YOU DO, THEY WILL KILL ME: Ellen Cragin, about 80, Little Rock, Arkansas; slave in Mississippi. *Samuel S. Taylor*

BOSOM AND NO SHIRT: Caroline Farrow, 80, Newberry, South Carolina. *G. L. Sumner*

MASTER SURE MADE A MESS OF THINGS THAT TIME: Chana Littlejohn, Greensboro [?], North Carolina; born near Warrenton, Warren County, North Carolina. *T. Pat Matthews*

Page 62

NO MORE HANGINGS: Elias Dawkins, 84, Gaffney, South Carolina. *Caldwell Sims*

Page 63

LOSING THE BABY: Kiziah Love, 93, Colbert, Oklahoma; slave in Indian Territory

JUST LIKE IT WAS HER OWN: Aunt Cheney Cross, about 90, near Evergreen, Conecuh County, Alabama. *Annie D. Dean*

Page 64

COLDY: William Brown, 78, North Little Rock, Arkansas; born May 3, 1861, near Old Wittsburg, Cross County, Arkansas. *Samuel S. Taylor*

THE QUILTS THAT PINCHED: Sam Word, 79, Pine Bluff, Arkansas; born February 14, 1859, near De Witt, Arkansas County, Arkansas. *Mrs. Bernice Bowden*

INDIANS DON'T TELL: Maggie Broyles, about 80, Forrest City, Arkansas; born Decatur, Tennessee; slave in Tennessee. *Irene Robertson*

Page 65

SHE PRAYED FOR FREEDOM: Nancy Anderson, 66, West Memphis, Arkansas; born Sanitobia, Mississippi; of slave parentage. *Irene Robertson*

Page 66

THE SON WHO MARRIED HIS MOTHER: Henry Brown, 80, Charleston, South Carolina. *Augustus Ladson*

BUT I CAN KILL YOU: Mother Anne Clark, 112, El Paso, Texas; born June 1, 1825, in Mississippi; slave in Louisiana; freed in Memphis

A BARREL OF MOLASSES: Mack Brantley, 80, Brinkley, Arkansas; born near Selma, Dallas County, Alabama; slave in Alabama. *Irene Robertson*

Page 67

BUZZARD ROOST: Jesse Rice, 80, Gaffney, South Carolina. *Caldwell Sims*

Page 68

JIGGING CONTEST: James W. Smith, 77, Fort Worth, Texas; born Palestine, Texas

SNIPE HUNTING: Charlie Hudson, 80, Athens, Georgia; born March 27, 1858, Elbert County, Georgia. *Sadie B. Hornsby*

Page 69

RED FLANNEL: Richard Jones (Dick Look-up), 93 [?], Union, South Carolina. *Caldwell Sims*

TRAIN GOING TO AFRICA: Will Ann Rogers, 70, Brinkley, Arkansas; born 1868, Fryers Point, Mississippi; of slave parentage. *Irene Robertson*

Page 70

ASKING OUR AGE: Hannah Brooks Wright, 85, Pine Bluff, Arkansas; born and slave in Mississippi. *Mrs. Bernice Bowden*

TELLING THEM OFF: Ella Wilson, about 100, Little Rock, Arkansas; born Atlanta, Georgia; slave in Georgia and Louisiana. *Samuel S. Taylor*

Page 71

PART TWO, LONG REMEMBRANCE, quotation: Eliza Holman, 82, Fort Worth, Texas; born near Clinton, Hinds County, Mississippi, and moved to Wise County, near Decatur, Texas, 1861; slave in Mississippi and Texas

Page 73

MILLIE EVANS: NORTH CAROLINA: Millie Evans, 87, El Dorado, Arkansas; born 1849, in North Carolina; slave in North Carolina. *Mrs. Carol Graham*

Page 77

LEE GUIDON: SOUTH CAROLINA: Lee Guidon, 89, Clarendon, Arkansas; slave in South Carolina. *Irene Robertson*

Page 81

TINES KENDRICKS: GEORGIA: Tines Kendricks, 104, Trenton, Arkansas; born near Macon, Crawford County, Georgia; slave in Georgia. *Watt McKinney*

Page 86

BEN SIMPSON: GEORGIA AND TEXAS: Ben Simpson, 90, Madisonville, Texas; born Norcross, Georgia; slave in Georgia and Texas

Page 88

MARIAH ROBINSON: GEORGIA AND TEXAS: Mariah Robinson, about 90, Meridian, Texas; born Monroe, Georgia; slave in Georgia and Texas

Page 90

NICEY KINNEY: GEORGIA: Nicey Kinney, 86, Athens, Georgia. *Grace McCune*

Page 94

CATO ———: ALABAMA: Cato ———, about 101, Dallas, Texas; born 1836 or 1837, near Pineapple, Wilcox County, Alabama; slave in Alabama

Page 99

JENNY PROCTOR: ALABAMA: Jenny Proctor, 87, San Angelo, Texas; born 1850, in Alabama; slave in Alabama

Page 103

ALLEN V. MANNING: MISSISSIPPI, LOUISIANA, AND TEXAS: Allen V. Manning, 87, Tulsa,

Oklahoma; born 1850, Clarke County, Mississippi; slave in Mississippi, Louisiana, Texas

Page 108

JOANNA DRAPER: MISSISSIPPI: Joanna Draper, 83, Tulsa, Oklahoma; born near Hazlehurst, Copiah County, Mississippi; slave in Mississippi

Page 112

KATIE ROWE: ARKANSAS: Katie Rowe, 88, Tulsa, Oklahoma; born near Washington, Hempstead County, Arkansas; slave in Arkansas

Page 118

CHARLEY WILLIAMS: LOUISIANA: Charley Williams, 94, Tulsa, Oklahoma; born January 11, 1843, near Monroe, Ouachita Parish, Louisiana; slave in Louisiana

Page 127

MARY REYNOLDS: LOUISIANA: Mary Reynolds, about 100, Dallas, Texas; born Black River, Louisiana; slave in Louisiana

Page 132

ELLEN BETTS: LOUISIANA: Ellen Betts, 84, Houston, Texas; born 1853 [?], near Opelousas, St. Landry Parish, Louisiana; slave in Louisiana

Page 137

MARY GRAYSON: INDIAN TERRITORY: Mary Grayson, 83, Tulsa, Oklahoma; born in the Creek Nation, Indian Territory

Page 143

PART THREE, FROM CAN TO CAN'T, quotation: Abbie Lindsay, 84, Little Rock, Arkansas; born June 1, 1856, Lynngrove, Louisiana; slave in Louisiana. *Samuel S. Taylor*

Page 145

COUNT THE STARS THROUGH THE CRACKS, quotation: Marion Johnson, El Dorado, Arkansas; born and slave in Louisiana. *Carol Graham*

A PRETTY CROP OF CHILDREN: I. Isaac Martin, about 86, Veth, Texas; born near Willis, Montgomery County, Texas. *Fred Dibble.* II. Mom Ryer Emmanuel, 78, Claussens, South Carolina. *Annie Ruth Davis*

Page 146

OLD MISTRESS' PET: Alice Davis, 81, Pine Bluff, Arkansas; slave in Mississippi. *Mrs. Bernice Bowden*

TURKEY BUZZARD LAID ME: Mrs. Candis Goodwin, 80, Cape Charles, Virginia; born Seaview, Virginia

OLD HOG ROUND THE BENCH: Rosina Hoard, 78, Austin, Texas; born April 9, 1859, Williamson, Texas

Page 147

DON'T LET THE SUN GO DOWN ON YOU: Jane Osbrook, 90, Pine Bluff, Arkansas; born near Camden, Ouachita County, Arkansas. *Mrs. Bernice Bowden*

I DIDN'T KNOW WHAT "SELL" MEANT: Morris Sheppard, 85, Fort Gibson, Oklahoma; born November, 1852, near Webber's Falls, Muskogee County, Oklahoma

FANNING THE FLIES: Henry Coleman, Carlisle, South Carolina. *Caldwell Sims*

Page 149

RIDING OLD JOHN BACKWARDS: Matilda Hatchett, between 98 and 100, North Little Rock, Arkansas; born near Dardanelle, Yell County, Arkansas. *Samuel S. Taylor*

BARBECUE AND BIG MEETING: Gus Feaster, 97, Union, South Carolina. *Caldwell Sims*

Page 152

IF ALL SLAVES HAD BELONGED TO WHITE FOLKS LIKE OURS: Harriett McFarlin Payne, 83, De Witt, Arkansas. *Mrs. Annie L. LaCotts*

Page 154

HOW TO TELL THE DAVIS FROM THE BETHEA NEGROES: Mom Hester Hunter, 85, Marion, South Carolina. *Annie Ruth Davis*

Page 155

I WAS HER FAVORITE CHILD: Mom Hester Hunter, 85, Marion, South Carolina. *Annie Ruth Davis*

Page 158

I SOMETIMES WISH I COULD BE BACK ON THE OLD PLACE: Aunt Nicey Pugh, 85, Prichard, Alabama. *Ila B. Prine*

Page 159

GOING HIGH, GOING SLOW, quotation: Julia Francis Daniels, 89, Dallas, Texas

TWO SELLINGS THAT DAY: Mintie Maria Miller, 85, Galveston, Texas; born 1852, Tuscaloosa, Alabama, and brought to Texas as a child

OLD MAN DENMAN SAID NOT TO FRET: Julia Francis Daniels, 89, Dallas, Texas

Page 161

SHE NEVER GOT TO KEEP HER BABIES: Lou Smith, 83, Platter, Oklahoma; slave in Texas

DIANA AND HER BABY: Adelaide J. Vaughn, 69, Little Rock, Arkansas; born Huntsville, Alabama; of slave parentage. *Samuel S. Taylor*

Page 162

ELIZA AND THE MAN FROM NEW YORK: Doc Daniel Dowdy, 81, Oklahoma City, Oklahoma; born June 6, 1856, Madison County, Georgia; slave in Georgia

I DON'T BELIEVE IN SLAVE TRAFFIC: William H. Harrison, 105, Forrest City, Arkansas; born March 4, 1832, Richmond, Virginia; slave in Virginia. *Irene Robertson*

Page 163

FOUNDLING: William Hamilton, Fort Worth, Texas; slave near Village Creek, Texas

STOLEN AND SOLD: I. Spence Johnson, about 78, Waco, Texas; born free about 1859, Choctaw Nation, Indian Territory; stolen and sold into slavery in Louisiana. II. Betty Simmons, about 100, Beaumont, Texas; born Macedonia, Alabama; slave in Alabama and Texas

Page 165

HE SOLD HIM OVER AND OVER: Spence Johnson, about 78, Waco, Texas; born free about 1859, Choctaw Nation, Indian Territory; stolen and sold into slavery in Louisiana

OLD PINCHBACK: James Green, about 97, San Antonio, Texas; born Petersburg, Virginia; slave in Virginia and Texas

Page 167

ROSE AND RUFUS: Rose Williams, over 90, Fort Worth, Texas; born Bell County, Texas

Page 170

PRAYING TO THE RIGHT MAN, quotation: Doc Daniel Dowdy, 81, Oklahoma City, Oklahoma; born June 6, 1856, Madison County, Georgia; slave in Georgia

THE LORD RULED HEAVEN, BUT JIM SMITH RULED THE EARTH: John Hill, 74, Athens, Georgia; born Walton County, Georgia. *Grace McCune*

HE STOMPED ON THE BODY: Mrs. Isabella Jackson, 79, Tulsa, Oklahoma; born and slave in Louisiana

Page 171

WE LAUGHED AT HIS FUNERAL: Annie Hawkins, 90, Colbert, Oklahoma; slave in Georgia and Texas

Page 172

I SAID I WAS GLAD SHE WAS DEAD: Mattie Fannen, 87, Forrest City, Arkansas; slave in Georgia. *Irene Robertson*

IF I WERE YOU AND YOU WERE ME: Sarah Douglas, about 82, El Dorado, Arkansas; born in Alabama; slave in Alabama and Louisiana. *Pernella M. Anderson*

Page 173

THE CHAIN AND THE BELL: J. W. Terrill, about 100, Madisonville, Texas; born DeSoto Parish, Louisiana; slave in Louisiana and Texas

Page 174

WHY MASTER HAD SUCH A MEAN MAN WORKING FOR HIM: Joe Clinton, 86, Marvell, Arkansas; born Panola County, Mississippi. *Watt McKinney*

Page 175

ORDEAL BY PLANTING: Martha Jackson, 87, Livingston, Alabama; born in 1850. *Ruby Pickens Tartt*

FILLING A BARREL WITH A THIMBLE: John H. Smith, 81, Pine Bluff, Arkansas; born 1856, in Missouri; slave in Missouri. *Mrs. Bernice Bowden*

Page 176

POOR WHITE-TRASH PATEROLLERS: Manda Walker, 80, Winnsboro, South Carolina. *W. W. Dixon*

THEY THINK TOO HIGH OF THEMSELVES: Samuel Boulware, 82, Columbia, South Carolina. *Henry Grant*

Page 177

THE LAST TIME I SAW MASTER: William Colbert, 93, Alabama; born 1844, Fort Valley, Georgia; slave in Georgia. *John Morgan Smith*

Page 178

HOW THAT SUIT YOU?: Henry Lewis, 102, Beaumont, Texas; born 1835, Pine Island, Texas

I'LL WHIP YOU WITH CHICKEN STEW: Giles Smith, 79, Fort Worth, Texas; born near Union Springs, Bullock County, Alabama; slave in Alabama

Page 179

HE DIDN'T ALLOW NOBODY TO HIT THEM A LICK: John Smith, 103, Uniontown, Alabama; slave in North Carolina and Alabama. *Susie R. O'Brien*

HE GLORIED IN THEIR SPUNK: Doc Daniel Dowdy, 81, Oklahoma City, Oklahoma; born June 6, 1856, Madison County, Georgia; slave in Georgia

WHEN I GOT BACK TO MASTER HALEY: Andy Anderson, 94, Fort Worth, Texas; born Williamson County, Texas

Page 181

I'D RATHER SEE THOSE MARKS ON MY OWN SHOULDERS: Ma Eppes, about 87, Uniontown, Alabama; born about 1850, near Faunsdale, Marengo County, Alabama. *Susie R. O'Brien*

Page 182

THE SLAVE'S CHANCE, quotation: Tom Windham, 92, Pine Bluff, Arkansas; born Indian Territory; slave in Indian Territory and Georgia. *Mrs. Bernice Bowden*

SHE RODE OFF ON A COW: Ellen Cragin, about 80, Little Rock, Arkansas; born Vicksburg, Mississippi; slave in Mississippi. *Samuel S. Taylor*

LITTLE JOE MADE A SONG: Charity Morris, 90, Camden, Arkansas; born and slave in one of the Carolinas. *Pernella M. Anderson*

Page 183

NO OVERSEER NEVER DOWNED HER: Leonard Franklin, 70, Warren, Arkansas. *Samuel S. Taylor*

SHE CHOPPED THIS MAN TO A BLOODY DEATH: "Prophet" John Henry Kemp, 80, Daytona Beach, Florida; born Oketibbeha County, Mississippi; slave in Mississippi. *L. Rebecca Baker*

SHE PULLED UP THE STUMP: Lula Jackson, 79 [?], Little Rock, Arkansas; born Sand Ridge, Russell County, Alabama; slave in Alabama. *Samuel S. Taylor*

Page 184

NO MORE OVERSEERS AFTER THAT: I. Sol Walton, 88, Marshall, Texas; born 1849, Mobile, Alabama; slave in Alabama and Louisiana. II. Dianah Watson, 102, Macedonia Community, near Marshall, Harrison County, Texas; born 1835, near New Orleans, Orleans Parish, Louisiana; slave in Louisiana

THE RED-BONE HOUND: Heywood Ford, Uniontown, Alabama. *Susie R. O'Brien*

Page 186

A WHITE MAN'S CHANCE: Morris Hillyer, 84, Alderson, Oklahoma; born Rome, Georgia; slave in Georgia

GONE TO THE WOODS: Jordon Smith, 86, Marshall, Texas; born in Georgia; slave in Georgia and Anderson County, Texas

Page 187

THEY LIVED IN A CAVE SEVEN YEARS: Leah Garrett, Richmond County, Georgia. *Louise Oliphant*

Page 188

UNCLE ISOM: Harriett Robinson, 95, Oklahoma City, Oklahoma; born September 1, 1842, Bastrop, Texas; slave in Texas

Page 189

GUINEA JIM: Josh Horn, 90, Livingston, Alabama. *Ruby Pickens Tartt*

Page 191

JADE HAD BIG IDEAS: Caroline Holland, 88, Montgomery, Alabama; born 1849, near

Mount Meigs, Montgomery County, Alabama. *Mabel Farrior, Lois Lynn, and John Morgan Smith*

Page 192

THEY DIDN'T GET LUCY OR HER QUARTER: Ida Blackshear Hutchinson, 73, Little Rock, Arkansas; born 1865, Sumter County, Alabama; of slave parentage. *Samuel S. Taylor*

WHY AUNT ADELINE HUNG HERSELF: T. W. Cotton, 80, Helena, Arkansas; born 1858. *Irene Robertson*

BUY YOURSELF FREE: James Martin, 90, San Antonio, Texas; born free, 1847, near Alexandria, Arlington County, Virginia

Page 193

HE BOUGHT HIMSELF: Jerry Moore, 89, Marshall, Texas; born May 28, 1848, Harrison County, Texas

THE BELL AND THE LIGHT: Arnold Gragston, 97, Eatonville, Florida; born 1840, Mason County, Kentucky; slave in Kentucky. *Martin Richardson*

Page 197

BIRD IN THE AIR: Walter Rimm, 80, Fort Worth, Texas; born San Patricio County, Texas

Page 198

SAVED: Fannie Moore, 88, Asheville, North Carolina; born September 1, 1849. *Marjorie Jones*

Page 199

PART FOUR, A WAR AMONG THE WHITE FOLKS, quotation: Clara Jones, about 90, Raleigh, North Carolina. *T. Pat Matthews*

Page 201

THEY MADE US SING "DIXIE," quotation: Eda Harper, 93, Pine Bluff, Arkansas; born and slave in Mississippi. *Mrs. Bernice Bowden*

BACK BEFORE BREAKFAST: I. Jerry Boykins, 92, Abilene, Texas; born Troupe County, Georgia; slave in Georgia. II. John G. Hawkens, 71, Biscoe, Arkansas; born December 9, 1866, Monroe County, Mississippi; of slave parentage. *Irene Robertson*

Page 202

YOU CAN GET YOURN HERE: Harriett Robinson, 95, Oklahoma City, Oklahoma; born September 1, 1842, Bastrop, Texas; slave in Texas

LEONARD ALLEN: Fanny Cannady, 79, Durham County, North Carolina. *Travis Jordan*

Page 203

THE CRACK IN THE WALL: Mrs. Esther Easter, 85, Tulsa, Oklahoma; born near Memphis, Shelby County, Tennessee; slave in Tennessee, Missouri, and Texas

Page 204

A WONDERFUL CONSIDERATION: Rev. Lafayette Price, in his late eighties, Beaumont, Texas; born about 1850, Wilcox County, Alabama; slave in Alabama and Louisiana. *Fred Dibble*

Page 206

I WISHED I NEVER RUN OFF: Thomas Cole, 92, Corsicana, Texas; born August 8, 1845, Jackson County, Alabama; slave in Alabama

Page 209

WE WERE CONFEDERATES: James Gill, 86, Marvell, Arkansas; slave in Alabama and Arkansas. *Watt McKinney*

Page 212

WE'VE COME TO SET YOU FREE, quotation: Andrew Moss, 85, Knoxville, Tennessee; born 1852, Wilkes County, Georgia; slave in Georgia

BLUE VEINS ON THEIR BELLIES: Hardy Miller, 85, Pine Bluff, Arkansas; born December 25, 1852, Sumter County, Georgia; slave in Georgia and Arkansas. *Mrs. Bernice Bowden*

YANKEES HAVE HORNS: Aunt Mittie Freeman, 86, North Little Rock, Arkansas; slave in Mississippi. *Beulah Sherwood Hagg*

Page 213

FATHER DID A BOLD THING: Mrs. Adrianna W. Kerns, 85, Little Rock, Arkansas. *Samuel S. Taylor*

WHEN DADDY LOCKED MASTER IN THE SMOKEHOUSE: Liza Jones, 81, Beaumont, Texas; born near Liberty, Liberty County, Texas

Page 214

APPLES FOR THE YANKEES, STOCK FOR THE MASTER: Fred James, 81, Newberry, South Carolina. *G. L. Sumner*

MOTHER AND THE YANKEE SOLDIER: Sam Word, 79, Pine Bluff, Arkansas; born February 14, 1859, near De Witt, Arkansas County, Arkansas. *Mrs. Bernice Bowden*

ALL RIGHT IN THEIR PLACE: Aunt Hannah Irwin, about 84, Eufaula [?], Alabama. *Gertha Couric*

Page 215

MISS MARY'S FEATHER BED: Aunt Cheney Cross, about 90, Evergreen, Alabama. *Annie D. Dean*

Page 216

SHERMAN'S MEN: I. Frank A. Patterson, 88, Little Rock, Arkansas; born 1850, Raleigh, North Carolina; slave in North Carolina and Georgia. *Samuel S. Taylor.* II. Claiborne Moss, 81, Little Rock, Arkansas; born June 18, 1857, Washington County, Georgia; slave in Georgia. *Samuel S. Taylor*

Page 218

AGGRAVATING THE YANKEES: Hammett Dell, 90, Brasfield, Arkansas; born October 12, 1847, near Murfreesboro, Rutherford County, Tennessee; slave in Tennessee. *Irene Robertson*

Page 219

SUCH A GOOD TIME: Margaret Hughes, 82, Columbia, South Carolina. *Everett R. Pierce*

Page 220

THE YANKEES HUNG MASTER TWICE: Margaret Hulm, 97, Humphrey, Arkansas; born March 5, 1840, Hardeman County, Tennessee; slave in Tennessee. *Mrs. Annie L. LaCotts*

WHY DIDN'T YOU BRING THE MEAT WITH YOU?: Adeline Grey, 82, Luray, South Carolina. *Phoebe Faucette*

Page 221

SHE COOKED FOR THE YANKEES: Molly Horn, 77, Holly Grove, Arkansas; slave in North Carolina and Arkansas. *Irene Robertson*

Page 222

THOSE WHITE FOLKS HAD TO RUN AWAY: Evelina Morgan, about 81, Little Rock, Arkansas; born Wedgeboro, North Carolina; slave in North Carolina. *Samuel S. Taylor*

HOW FATHER GOT HIS MONEY: Mrs. Julia A. White, 79, Little Rock, Arkansas; born 1858, Little Rock, Arkansas. *Beulah Sherwood Hagg*

GRANDMA AND THE YANKEE SOLDIERS: Martha Colquitt, 85, Athens, Georgia. *Mrs. Sarah H. Hall*

Page 224

I JUST SAID THAT TO THE WRONG PERSON: Eliza Evans, 87, McAlester, Oklahoma; slave in Selma, Alabama

WE'RE FIGHTING TO FREE YOU: I. Lizzie McCloud, about 120, Pine Bluff, Arkansas; born Davidson County, Tennessee; slave in Tennessee. *Mrs. Bernice Bowden.* II. Rosa Simmons, about 85, Pine Bluff, Arkansas; born in Tennessee; slave in Tennessee and Arkansas. *Mrs. Bernice Bowden.* III. Matilda Hatchett, between 98 and 100, North Little Rock, Arkansas; born near Dardanelle, Yell County, Arkansas. *Samuel S. Taylor.* IV. Hannah Brooks Wright, 85, Pine Bluff, Arkansas; born and slave in Mississippi. *Mrs. Bernice Bowden*

Page 227

PRAISE TO THE YANKEES: Mom Ryer Emmanuel, 78, Claussens, South Carolina. *Annie Ruth Davis*

THE PRETTIEST SIGHT I EVER SAW: Frank Larkin, 85, Pine Bluff, Arkansas; born and slave in Virginia. *Mrs. Bernice Bowden*

Page 228

I LOVE THE YANKEES: Betty Krump, Helena, Arkansas; of slave parentage. *Irene Robertson*

Page 229

PART FIVE, ALL I KNOW ABOUT FREEDOM, quotation: Martha Ann Dixon, 81, De Valls Bluff, Arkansas; born near Saratoga, Wilson County, North Carolina; slave in North Carolina. *Irene Robertson*

Page 231

HOW FREEDOM CAME, quotation: Frank A. Patterson, 88, Little Rock, Arkansas; born 1850, Raleigh, North Carolina, slave in North Carolina and Georgia. *Samuel S. Taylor*

LIKE FREEDOM WAS A PLACE: Felix Haywood, 92, San Antonio, Texas; born St. Hedwig, Texas

Page 232

FROM BLOODY FLAG TO WHITE: Mrs. Fannie Berry, Petersburg, Virginia. *Susie Byrd*

Page 233

THEY GOT WHAT THEY EXPECTED: Waters McIntosh, 76, Little Rock, Arkansas; born July 4, 1862, Lynchburg, South Carolina; slave in South Carolina. *Samuel S. Taylor*

HE CLEANED HIS GUNS ON MY DRESS TAIL: Jane Montgomery, 80, Oklahoma City, Oklahoma; born March 15, 1857, Homer, Louisiana; slave in Louisiana

Page 234

YOU BETTER HUSH: Mary Jane Hardridge, 85, Pine Bluff, Arkansas; born 1852, Jefferson County, Arkansas. *Mrs. Bernice Bowden*

THEY LEARNED BETTER: Sarah Jane Patterson, 90, Little Rock, Arkansas; born January 17, 1848, Bartow County, Georgia; slave in Georgia. *Samuel S. Taylor*

YES'M: Evelina Morgan, about 81, Little Rock, Arkansas; born Wedgeboro, North Carolina; slave in North Carolina. *Samuel S. Taylor*

FREEDOM OF PEACHES: Jeff Bailey, 76, Little Rock, Arkansas; born 1861, Monticello, Arkansas. *Samuel S. Taylor*

Page 235

THEY THREW THEIR STICKS AWAY: Lucretia Alexander, 89, Little Rock, Arkansas;

born near Hazlehurst, Copiah County, Mississippi, and brought to Arkansas at about the age of 7. *Samuel S. Taylor*

THEY DANCED ALL NIGHT: Eda Harper, 93, Pine Bluff, Arkansas; born and slave in Mississippi. *Mrs. Bernice Bowden*

THERE AIN'T NO ANTS BITING HER TODAY: Ellen Cragin, about 80, Little Rock, Arkansas; slave in Mississippi. *Samuel S. Taylor*

IT'S NOT RECORDED: John G. Hawkens, 71, Biscoe, Arkansas; born December 9, 1866, Monroe County, Mississippi; of slave parentage. *Irene Robertson*

Page 236

THEY TOLD THE YANKEES "YES": Virginia Jackson, 74, Helena, Arkansas; born Tunica, Mississippi; of slave parentage. *Irene Robertson*

HE MADE US WORK SEVERAL MONTHS AFTER THAT: Susan Merritt, 87 [?], Harrison County, Texas; born Rush County, Texas

DRUMS OF FREEDOM: Nellie Dunne, 78, Pine Bluff, Arkansas; slave in Mississippi. *Mrs. Bernice Bowden*

Page 237

PAPA WENT OFF: Linley Hadley, 77, Madison, Arkansas; born April 12, 1861, Monroe County, Mississippi; slave in Mississippi. *Irene Robertson*

Page 238

THE BREAKING-UP AND AFTER, quotation: Rev. Squires Jackson, about 95, Jacksonville, Florida; born September 14, 1841, Madison, Florida, and brought to Jacksonville at the age of 3. *Samuel Johnson*

THEY KNEW WHAT HE MEANT: Austin Grant, about 90, near Hondo, Medina County, Texas; slave in Mississippi and in Gonzales and Medina counties, Texas

OVER HALF OF THEM WERE GONE: Harriett Robinson, 95, Oklahoma City, Oklahoma; born September 1, 1842, Bastrop, Texas; slave in Texas

Page 239

WHEN CHRISTMAS CAME: Fred James, 81, Newberry, South Carolina. *G. L. Sumner*

WHAT'S MINE IS MINE: Simon Phillips, 90, Birmingham [?], Alabama; born 1847, Hale County, Alabama. *John Morgan Smith*

YOU ALL GO ON AWAY: Pauline (Pearl) Howell, 65 or 70, Brinkley, Arkansas; born Paris, Tennessee; of slave parentage. *Irene Robertson*

Page 240

THE DEVIL AND HELL: Bert Strong, 73, near Marshall, Harrison County, Texas; born 1864, Montgomery, Alabama; slave in Alabama

SHE AIN'T GOT US BACK YET: William Mathews, 89, Galveston, Texas; born December 25, 1848, Franklin Parish, near Monroe, Ouachita Parish, Louisiana; slave in Louisiana

Page 241

OLD MISTRESS KEPT THE COTTON: Henry Kirk Miller, 86, Little Rock, Arkansas; born July 25, 1851, Fort Valley, Georgia; slave in Georgia. *Beulah Sherwood Hagg*

ALL BENT OVER: Carrie Hudson, 75, Athens, Georgia; born near Ruckersville, Elbert County, Georgia. *Sadie B. Hornsby*

Page 242

MASTER LIVED A WEEK OR TWO: Mahalia Shores, 77, Marianna, Arkansas; born Greene County, Georgia; slave in Georgia. *Irene Robertson*

HE TOOK THE SMALLPOX: Isom Roberts, 80, Columbia, South Carolina. *Henry Grant*

Page 243

HE CUSSED TILL HE DIED: Anderson Edwards, 93, Harrison County, Texas; born March 12, 1844, Rusk County, Texas

MASTER GETS WORSE: Anna Miller, 85, Fort Worth, Texas; born in Kentucky; slave in Kentucky, Missouri, and Texas

Page 244

THE NEWS KILLED HER DEAD: James Reeves, 68, Little Rock, Arkansas; born in Ouachita County, Arkansas; of slave parentage. *Samuel S. Taylor*

YOU GOT TO LOOK AFTER ME: Betty Curlett, 66, Hazen, Arkansas; of slave parentage. *Irene Robertson*

Page 245

DEATH OF A PLANTATION: I. Willie Doyld, 78, Brinkley, Arkansas; slave in Mississippi. *Irene Robertson*. II. Annie Row, 86, Fort Worth, Texas; born near Rusk, Nacogdoches County, Texas

Page 246

HE COULDN'T HELP CRYING: Andrew Goodman, 97, Dallas, Texas; born near Birmingham, Alabama, and brought to Texas at the age of 3

Page 247

I FEEL LIKE I AM THEIRS: Adeline Willis, about 100, Washington, Wilkes County, Georgia; born Greene County, Georgia. *M. B. Stonestreet*

Page 248

FREEDOM WASN'T NO DIFFERENCE: John McCoy, 99, Houston, Texas; born January 1, 1838, near Houston, Harris County, Texas

BANG!: Pauline Grice, 81, North Fort Worth, Texas; born near Atlanta, Fulton County, Georgia; slave in Georgia

Page 249

CLOSE MEASURING: Oliver Bell, Livingston, Alabama. *Ruby Pickens Tartt*

Page 250

WE HAVE WHITE FOLKS' EATS: Van Moore, about 80, Houston, Texas; born near Lynchburg, Campbell County, Virginia, and brought to Harris County, near Crosby, Texas, as a baby

HE SOLD HIS FIVE BOYS: Angie Garrett, about 92, Livingston, Alabama; born about 1845, De Kalb, Mississippi; slave in Mississippi and Alabama. *Ruby Pickens Tartt*

THEY JUST EXPECTED FREEDOM: Liney Chambers, Brinkley, Arkansas; slave in Tennessee. *Irene Robertson*

Page 251

THEN CAME THE CALM: Patsy Moore, 74, Madison, Arkansas; born De Soto County, Mississippi; slave in Mississippi and Tennessee. *Irene Robertson*

I GOT ALONG HARD AFTER I WAS FREED: Thomas Ruffin, about 83, Little Rock, Arkansas; born near Raleigh, Franklin County, North Carolina; slave in North Carolina. *Samuel S. Taylor*

Page 252

RECONSTRUCTION WAS A MIGHTY HARD PULL: Warren McKinney, 85, Hazen, Arkansas; born Edgefield County, South Carolina; slave in South Carolina. *Irene Robertson*

Page 253

WHO WAS FREED BY THE WAR?: Waters McIntosh, 76, Little Rock, Arkansas; born July 4, 1862, Lynchburg, South Carolina; slave in South Carolina. *Samuel S. Taylor*

FREEDMEN'S BUREAU: Milton Ritchie, 78, Brinkley, Arkansas; born Marietta, Georgia; slave in Georgia. *Irene Robertson*

Page 254

I GOT MY MONEY, TOO: Uncle Willis Bennefield, about 101, Hepzibah, Georgia; slave in Burke County, Georgia

Page 255

AFTER FREEDOM: Ishe Webb, about 78, Little Rock, Arkansas; born Atlanta, Georgia; slave in Georgia. *Samuel S. Taylor*

Page 257

THAT WAS MY FREEDOM: Annie Griegg, 84, Madison, Arkansas; born Nashville, Tennessee; slave in Tennessee. *Irene Robertson*

TOBY AND GOVIE: Toby Jones, 87, Madisonville, Texas; born 1850, South Carolina

Page 258

RUNNING AWAY: Mrs. Fannie Berry, Petersburg, Virginia. *Susie Byrd*

Page 259

PEONAGE: I. William Ward, 105, Atlanta, Georgia. *Driskell.* II. Elijah Henry Hop-

304 — LAY MY BURDEN DOWN

kins, 81, Little Rock, Arkansas; born May 15, 1856, Barnwell County, South Carolina; slave in South Carolina and Georgia. *Samuel S. Taylor*

Page 260

CARRYING ON WITH FREE LABOR: Peter Clifton, 89, Winnsboro, South Carolina. *W. W. Dixon*

Page 261

HOW WE GOT AWAY FROM OLD MAN BIAS: Annie Osborn, 81, Marshall, Texas; born 1858, Atlanta, Georgia; slave in Georgia and Louisiana

Page 262

HE WAS POOR AND HATED NEGROES: Maggie Wesmoland, 85, Brinkley, Arkansas; born near Des Arc, Prairie County, Arkansas. *Irene Robertson*

Page 264

DEVILS AND GOOD PEOPLE WALKED THE ROAD: Anthony Dawson, 105, Tulsa, Oklahoma; born July 25, 1832, near Greenville, Pitt County, North Carolina; slave in North Carolina

Page 265

THE EQUALIZATION WAR, quotation: John Johnson, 73, near Clarendon, Monroe County, Arkansas; born near Jackson, Madison County, Tennessee; of slave parentage. *Irene Robertson*

JORDAN HAD A HARD TIME: Henry F. Pyles, 81, Tulsa, Oklahoma; born August 15, 1856, Jackson, Tennessee; slave in Tennessee

Page 266

KU KLUX: I. Ben Johnson, 85, Hecktown, Durham, North Carolina. *Mary A. Hicks.* II. Pierce Harper, 86, Galveston [?], Texas; born 1851, near Snow Hill, Greene County, North Carolina; slave in North Carolina. III. Claiborne Moss, 81, Little Rock, Arkansas; born June 18, 1857, Washington County, Georgia; slave in Georgia. *Samuel S. Taylor*

Page 269

YOUR OLD HORSE AIN'T NO GOOD: Anthony Dawson, 105, Tulsa, Oklahoma; born July 25, 1832, near Greenville, Pitt County, North Carolina; slave in North Carolina

Page 270

PRAYING JIM JESUS: Maggie Stenhouse, 72 [?], Brinkley, Arkansas; born near Pickens, Pickens County, South Carolina; of slave parentage. *Irene Robertson*

THE DOCTOR'S GRAVE: Brawley Gilmore, Union, South Carolina. *Caldwell Sims*

Page 272
GET RID OF THE GRASS: Hammett Dell, 90, Brasfield, Arkansas; born October 12, 1847, near Murfreesboro, Rutherford County, Tennessee; slave in Tennessee. *Irene Robertson*

Page 273
KU KLUX AND CARPETBAGGERS: Henry Garry, about 75, Birmingham, Alabama. *W. F. Jordan*

Page 275
END OF THE KU KLUXES: Anderson Bates, 87, Winnsboro, South Carolina. *Caldwell Sims*

Page 276
THEY KEPT THE NEGROES FROM VOTING: F. H. Brown, 75, North Little Rock, Arkansas; born in Marion County, Mississippi; slave in Mississippi. *Samuel S. Taylor*
VOTE AS I DAMN PLEASE: James Reeves, 68, Little Rock, Arkansas; born in Ouachita County, Arkansas; of slave parentage. *Samuel S. Taylor*

Page 277
MY DADDY WAS IN OFFICE: Paul Jenkins, 70, Columbia, South Carolina; born 1867, Colleton County, South Carolina; of slave parentage. *Stiles M. Scruggs*

Page 279
I TAKE FREEDOM, quotation: Henry Banner, 89 [?], Little Rock, Arkansas; born 1849 [?], Russell County, Virginia; slave in Virginia and Tennessee. *Samuel S. Taylor*
IT'S THIS WAY: Margrett Nillin, about 90, Fort Worth, Texas; born Palestine, Texas
ANYBODY WHO SAYS THAT IS TELLING A LIE: Thomas Johns, 90, Cleburne, Texas; born April 18, 1847, Chambers County, Alabama; came to Texas in 1874
A BETTER DAY: Washington Dozier, 90, Peedee, South Carolina. *Annie Ruth Davis*

Page 280
THAT'S HOW I FEEL: Charlie Hudson, 80, Athens, Georgia; born March 27, 1858, Elbert County, Georgia. *Sadie B. Hornsby*
YOU CAN'T BLAME THEM FOR THIS: Martin Johnson, 90, San Antonio, Texas; born 1847, Victoria County, Texas
MORE HIS OWN SAY: Robert Bryant, 75, Herculaneum, Missouri; born near Caledonia, Washington County, Missouri

Page 281
POOR FOLK—WHITE AND BLACK: Charles Crawley, Petersburg, Virginia; born in Lunenburg County, Virginia. *Susie Byrd*
I HOPE TO SEE A MILLION YEARS TO COME: Richard Toler, 97, Cincinnati, Ohio; born near Lynchburg, Campbell County, Virginia. *Ruth Thompson*

Index

"Abe Lincoln freed the nigger," 231
Abercrombie, Anthony, *n.,* 51, 288
Abilene (Tex.), 297
Abrams, Mrs. M. E., *n.,* 55, 289
Adam, 22
Adams, Will, *n.,* 60 (a), 289
Adams, William M., *n.,* 14 (c), 38 (a), 45, 284, 287, 288
Adultery, 203–204
Africa, 46, 69, 206, 244
Alabama, 17, 89, 94, 95, 99, 137, 138, 193, 210, 271–91, 293–99, 301–3, 305
Albany (Ga.), 79
Alderson (Okla.), 296
Alexander, Dr., *m.,* 108
Alexander, Lucretia, *n.,* 33 (III), 235 (a), 287, 300–301
Alexandria (Va.), 193, 297
Allen, Burrus, *s.,* 202
Allen, Leonard, *s.,* 202–3
Allen, Sam, *s.,* 267
Anderson, Mr., *o.,* 206
Anderson, Andy, *n.,* 179 (c), 295
Anderson, Nancy, *n.,* 65, 290
Anderson, Pernella M., *w.,* 16, 33 (b), 36 (b), 172 (b), 182 (c), 284, 287, 294, 296
Andersonville Prison, 84
Animal tales, 20–22, 29–32
Animal talk, 14, 31–32; *see also* Bird talk
Apple vinegar, making of, 75
Arkansas, 17, 86, 112, 123, 210, 262, 284–305
Arkansas River, 138
Arlington County (Va.), 297
Arson, 79
Asheville (N.C.), 297
Athens (Ga.), 90, 92, 284, 289, 290, 291, 294, 299, 302, 305
Atlanta (Ga.), 25, 259, 291, 302, 303, 304
Auctions, slave, 62, 97, 101, 115, 159, 160, 164, 165, 166, 167, 193, 254
Augusta (Ga.), 252, 254
Austin (Tex.), 86, 89, 293
Austin, Rachel, *w.,* 13, 284
Azle (Tex.), 244

Babies, 20, 63, 96, 109, 111, 131, 133, 136, 161, 187
Backlogs, 102
Bailey, Jeff, *n.,* 234 (d), 300
Baker, Rebecca L., *w.,* 183 (b), 296
Baldwin County (Ga.), 269
Banner, Henry, *n.,* 279 (a), 279
Baptists, 37, 103, 179
Baptizing, 35
Barbecues, 149, 150
Barker, *w.,* 44 (b), 288; *see also* Martin
Barkswell, Dr., *m.,* 27
Barkus, Captain, 235
Barnes, Uncle Henry, *n.,* 19 (a), 285
Barton (Ala.), 284
Bartow County (Ga.), 234
Basket plaiting, 255
Baskin Lake (Ark.), 52
Bass, Sam, 28
Bastrop (Tex.), 283, 296, 301
Bates, Anderson, *n.,* 275, 305
Baton Rouge (La.), 106
Bayou Teche (La.), 132
Bear and the pickaninny, the, 20
Beaumont (Tex.), 285, 286, 294, 295, 298
Beds, 74, 90, 94, 99–100, 120–21, 129
"Before I'd be a slave," 182
Bell, Dick, *s.,* 275
Bell, Oliver, *n.,* 27 (a), 249, 286, 302
Bells, 121, 244
Belmont (Tex.), 9
Bennefield, Uncle Willis, *n.,* 254, 303
Bernard, Jim, *m.,* 183
Berry, Buck, *m.,* 89
Berry, Caesar, *s.,* 89
Berry, Mrs. Fannie, *n.,* 232, 258, 300, 303
Bethea, John C., *m.,* 154
Betts, Ellen, *n.,* 132–37, 292
Bias, Tom, *m.,* 261
Bible, 46, 48, 60, 61, 81, 157
Biggers, Master, 260
Bird talk, 31–32
Birdville (Tex.), 27
Birmingham (Ala.), 162, 287, 288, 301, 302, 305
Biscoe (Ark.), 297, 301
Bishop, Ank, *n.,* 48 (b), 288

Black, William, *m.*, 167
Black River (La.), 292
Blackshears, the, 192
Blacksmiths, 79, 121, 122, 255, 270, 282
Blanco County (Tex.), 180
Blockade, 249
Bloodhounds, 105, 129–30, 131, 174, 176,
    184–85, 188, 189–90; *see also* Dogs
Boggy Depot (Okla.), 164
Bois d'Arc Creek (Ark.), 113
Boll-weevil story, 20
Bonner, Siney, *n.*, 37, 287
Booker, John, *m.*, 10
Boots, 11–12, 36
Bosque County (Tex.), 88, 107
Bosqueville (Tex.), 288
Boulware, Samuel, *n.*, 176 (b), 295
Bowden, Mrs. Bernice, *w.*, 20 (a), 33 (a), 35 (c),
    44 (a), 54 (a), 64 (b), 70 (a), 146 (a), 147 (a),
    175 (b), 182 (a), 201 (a), 212 (b), 214 (b),
    224 (I), 225 (II), 226 (IV), 227 (b), 234 (a),
    235 (b), 236 (c), 285–93, 295–301
Bowe, Mary Wallace, *n.*, 26 (a), 286
Boykins, Jerry, *n.*, 201 (I), 297
Boylan, Bob, *s.*, 267
Bragg, General Braxton, 212
Branding of slaves, 66, 86–87
Brantley, Mack, *n.*, 66 (c), 290
Brasfield (Ark.), 299, 305
Br'er Rabbit, 8
Brewer, Mrs., *m.*, 212
Brinkley (Ark.), 290, 301, 302, 303, 304
Britt, Billy, 265
Brooms, 74
Brown, Casie Jones, *n.*, 59 (a), 289
Brown, F. H., *n.*, 276 (a), 305
Brown, Henry, *n.*, 66 (a), 290
Brown, Joe, *m.*, 102
Brown, Marcus, *o.*, 174–75
Brown, William, *n.*, 64 (a), 290
Brownlow, Governor William G., 265
Broyles, Maggie, *n.*, 64 (c), 290
Bryant, Robert, *n.*, 280 (c), 305
Buchanan, James, 25
Buffalo (Tex.), 103
Buford, Master, 163
Bull pen, slaves in, 101
Bull Run, Battle of, 89
"Bullfrog tied by its tail to a stump, A," 278
Burials, slave, 82–83, 128, 171
Buried treasure, 54–55
Burleson (Ala.), 285
Bushwhacking, 140
Butler, General M. C., 277
Buzzards, 67, 146
Byrd, Susie, *w.*, 232, 258, 281 (a), 300, 303,
    305

Cabins, slave, 74, 89, 90, 94, 121, 129, 167,
    168

Cade, Master, 178
Calhoun County (S.C.), 242
California, 89
Camden (Ark.), 293, 296
Camp meetings, 36, 150
Canada, 196, 207
Candle-making, 74
Caneville (Tenn.), 273
Cannady, Fanny, *n.*, 202 (b), 297
Cape Charles (Va.), 292
Carlisle (Ark.), 253
Carlisle (S.C.), 293
Carpetbaggers, 265, 273–75
Cartersville (Ga.), 88
Casteel, Tom, *m.*, 210
Caswell County (N.C.), 267
Cat-o'-nine-tails, 100, 105, 116, 118, 206
Cato, *n.*, 72, 94–99, 291
Caves, 186, 201, 218
Centerville (La.), 133
Chains, slaves in, 86, 87, 101, 102, 160, 173
Chambers, Liney, *n.*, 250 (c), 303
Chaney, Bob, *m.*, 152
Chaney, Jesse, *m.*, 153
Chapman, Tom, *o.*, 242
Chappel, Cecelia, *n.*, 30 (a), 286
Charleston (S.C.), 289, 290
Chattanooga (Tenn.), 208, 209, 253
Cherokees, 118, 142
Chester (S.C.), 260, 271, 284, 285
Chicet (La.), 204
Chickamauga, Battle of, 207–9
Chickasaws, 141
Chickens, 31, 33, 34, 44, 59, 78, 95, 109
Childhood, 71, 73, 99–100, 127, 145–58
Chisolm, Tom, *n.*, 17 (c), 284
Chitlins, 218
Choctaw Nation (I.T.), 294
Choctaws, 95, 104, 163
Choska (Okla.), 138
Christian, Nells, *s.*, 273
Christmas, 96, 102, 111, 131, 239, 248, 263
Churches, 33–37, 77, 92, 157; *see also* Preachers
    and preaching
Cincinnati (Ohio), 305
Circus, 274
Civil War, 14–15, 45, 52–53, 76–77, 83–84,
    91, 97–98, 104, 109, 136, 138–39, 160, 164,
    165, 166, 167, 176, 177, 180, 199–228,
    232–33, 239–40, 245–47, 248–49, 261, 265–
    66; *see also* Confederate soldiers; Yankee
    soldiers
Clarendon (Ark.), 291, 304
Clark, Mother Anne, *n.*, 66 (b), 290
Clarksville (I.T.), 142
Claussens (S.C.), 292, 300
Clayton (N.M.), 124
Cleary, Master, 183
Cleburne (Tex.), 285
Clifton, Peter, *n.*, 260, 304
Clinton (Miss.), 291

Clinton, Joe, *n.,* 174, 295
Clothing, 63, 74–75, 91–92, 95–96, 100–101, 109, 121–22, 130, 134, 151–52
Coffman, John, *m.,* 280
Colbert (Okla.), 287, 290, 294
Colbert, William, *n.,* 177, 295
Cole, Thomas, *n.,* 206, 298
Coleman, Henry, *n.,* 147 (c), 293
Colorado River, 146
Colquitt, Martha, *n.,* 222 (c), 299
Columbia (S.C.), 284, 295, 299, 302, 305
Comanches, 88
Combahee River, 17
Confederate soldiers, 83, 106, 115, 122, 159–60, 199, 211, 225, 232, 245, 246–48, 264, 266; *see also* Civil War
Conjure, 38–47, 93; *see also* Hoodoo
Cooks and cooking, 24–25, 32, 65, 73, 74, 82, 90, 94–95, 99, 133, 150–51, 155, 187; *see also* Food
Cooledge, Mr., 211
Corn, 17–18, 79, 87, 107, 122, 155, 156, 175, 198, 233, 239, 249, 250
Corn-shucking, 51, 93, 96, 102
Corn shucks for hats and horse collars, 122
Corsicana (Tex.), 298
Coryell County (Tex.), 107
Cottageville (Ark.), 278
Cotton, 74–75, 87, 106, 107, 210, 214, 240, 241, 249, 255–56
Cotton, J. W., *n.,* 192 (b), 297
Cotton-picking, 39, 94, 102, 128, 131, 174, 236
Cotton Plant (Ark.), 69
Couric, Gertha, *w.,* 214 (c), 298
Cows, 67, 75, 77, 147, 182, 224, 261, 262
Cragin, Ellen, *n.,* 61 (b), 182 (b), 235 (c), 289, 296, 301
Cramer, Creame, *m.,* 159–60
Crawford County (Ga.), 81, 82
Crawley, Charles, *n.,* 281 (a), 305
Creek Nation, 107, 112, 137–38, 142
Cropton, Bill, 237
Crosby (Tex.), 250, 303
Cross, Aunt Cheney, *n.,* 63 (b), 215, 290, 298
Cuck, Cooper, 217
Cures, 21, 42–44, 71, 81
Curlett, Betty, *n.,* 244 (b), 302

Dallas (Tex.), 132, 283, 291, 292, 293, 302
Dances, 11–12, 18, 68, 74, 96, 102, 123, 125, 129, 135, 235, 258
Daniels, Master, 146
Daniels, Julia Francis, *n.,* 159 (a, c), 293
Dardanelle (Ark.), 226, 262, 263, 293
David, Hatton, *m.,* 90
Davidson County (Tenn.), 224
Davis, Alice, *n.,* 146 (a), 292
Davis, Annie Ruth, *w.,* 7, 145 (II), 154, 155, 227 (a), 279 (d), 283, 292, 300, 305

Davis, H. Grady, *w.,* 34, 287
Davis, Jane, *m.,* 146
Davis, Jefferson, 25, 216, 241
Davis, Sara, *m.,* 154, 157
Dawkins, Elias, *n.,* 62, 290
Dawson (Ga.), 284
Dawson, Anthony, *n.,* 21 (c), 264, 269, 285, 304
Daytona Beach (Fla.), 296
De Kalb (Miss.), 303
De Valls Bluff (Ark.), 262, 300
De Witt (Ark.), 290, 293, 298
Dean, Annie D., *w.,* 63 (b), 215, 290, 298
Decatur (Tenn.), 290
Decatur (Tex.), 291
Deeson, John, *m.,* 110
DeGraffenreid, Dr., *m.,* 249
Dell, Hammett, *s.,* 218, 272, 299, 305
Demopolis (Ala.), 181
Denman, Master, 159
Des Arc (Ark.), 262, 304
DeSoto Parish (La.), 295
Detroit (Mich.), 197
Devil, 38, 46, 47, 240, 264
Dibble, Fred, *w.,* 30 (b), 145 (I), 204, 286, 292, 298
Dill, Will, *n.,* 29 (a), 31 (a), 286
Dixon, Alice, *n.,* 16, 284
Dixon, Martha Ann, *n.,* 229, 300
Dixon, W. W., *w.,* 15 (c), 21 (a, b), 58, 176 (a), 260, 284, 285, 289, 295, 304
Dogs, 22, 32, 48, 64, 94, 159, 166, 183, 185, 188, 189; *see also* Bloodhounds
Dollard, John, 60
Douglas, Sarah, *n.,* 33 (I), 172 (b), 287, 294
Douglas, Tom, *n.,* 36 (b), 287
Douglass, Alice, *n.,* 23 (II), 285
Douglass, Frederick, 26–27
Dowdy, Doc Daniel, *n.,* 162 (a), 170 (a), 179 (b), 294, 295
Doyld, Willie, *n.,* 245 (I), 302
Dozier, Washington, *n.,* 279 (d), 305
Draper, Joanna, *n.,* 72, 108–12, 292
Drayton, John, *s.,* 18–19
Driskell, *w.,* 259 (I), 303
Drivers, Negro, 95, 101, 104, 128, 144, 206
Dunne, Nellie, *n.,* 236 (c), 301
DuPre, F. S., *w.,* 29 (a), 31 (a), 286
Durant, Sylvia, *n.,* 7, 283
Durham (N.C.), 286, 304
Dyeing, 75, 91, 122

Easter, Mrs. Esther, *n.,* 203, 298
Easter, Willis, *n.,* 49 (a), 288
"Eat when you're hungry," 205
Eatonville (Fla.), 297
Edgefield County (S.C.), 252
Edisto Island (S.C.), 285
Edwards, Anderson, *n.,* 35 (a), 243 (a), 287, 302
El Dorado (Ark.), 284, 287, 291, 292, 294

El Paso (Tex.), 132, 290
Emmanuel, Mom Ryer, *n.*, 145 (II), 227 (a), 292, 300
Eppes, Ma., *n.*, 181, 295
Eufaula (Ala.), 298
Evans, Eliza, *n.*, 224 (a), 299
Evans, Millie, *n.*, 72, 73–77, 291
Evergreen (Ala.), 290, 298

Fairfield, (S.C.), 275
Families, separation of, 85, 127–28, 161, 162–63, 167
Fannen, Mattie, *n.*, 172 (a), 294
Farmer, Lizzie, *n.*, 10 (b), 14 (b), 283, 284
Farrior, Mabel, *w.*, 191, 296–97
Farrow, Caroline, *n.*, 61 (c), 289
Faucette, Phoebe, *w.*, 220 (b), 299
Faunsdale (Ala.), 295
Feaster, Gus, *n.*, 32 (a), 57, 149 (b), 286, 289, 293
Feather beds, 155, 215, 245
Fee, John, 196–97
Fenwick Island (S.C.), 18
Fiddlers, 9, 18, 74, 89, 96, 129, 272, 282
Field hands, 18, 82, 91, 198, 252
Fillmore, Millard, 25
Finger, Orleans, *n.*, 43 (b), 288
Finley, Molly, *n.*, 33 (II), 287
Fire-making, 74
Folklore: as a weapon, 8
Food, 10, 11, 17, 19, 31–32, 33, 60, 63, 65, 73, 77, 79, 82, 95, 100, 128, 150, 151, 167, 197, 249; stealing of, 10, 12–13, 33–34, 76, 129; *see also* Cooks and cooking
Foraging and looting, 31, 78–79, 97, 115–116, 122–23, 132, 155, 177, 212–28, 243, 245, 247, 251, 265
Ford, Aaron, *n.*, 34, 287
Ford, Heywood, *n.*, 184 (b), 296
Forrest City (Ark.), 290, 294
Fort Gibson (Okla.), 138, 139, 293
Fort Piller, Battle of, 265
Fort Scott (Kan.), 123, 124, 126
Fort Valley (Ga.), 286, 287, 295, 302
Fort Washita (I.T.), 141
Fort Worth (Tex.), 169, 243–44, 284, 286, 287, 288, 289, 291, 294, 297, 302, 305
Fortescue, Colonel, *m.*, 165
Fourth of July, 150
Fox and the partridge, the, 30
Franklin, Leonard, *n.*, 183 (a), 296
Frederick (Okla.), 107
"Free Committee Men," 89
Free Negroes, 84–85, 192–93, 250
Freedmen's Bureau, 253, 254
Freedom, 77–78, 92, 171, 229–30, 238–82; masters announcing, 98, 103, 107, 117, 131–32, 137, 141, 158, 166, 238–50, 254, 257, 258; masters' violent reactions to, 85, 229, 240–45; praying for, 14–15, 66; purchasing

of, 193; Yankees and, 117, 212–28, 231–37, 242–43, 250
Freeman, Jim, *s.*, 267
Freeman, Aunt Mittie, *n.*, 212 (c), 298
Fryers Point (Miss.), 290

Gabriel's trumpet, 48
Gaffney (S.C.), 290
Gallitan (Tenn.), 23
Galveston (Tex.), 132, 250, 293, 301, 304
Games, children's, 73–74, 102
Gantling, Clayborn, *n.*, 13, 284
Gardens, slaves', 129
Garrett, Angie, *n.*, 250 (b), 303
Garrett, Leah, *n.*, 187, 296
Garry, Henry, *n.*, 52 (a), 273, 288, 305
Gaston (Ala.), 48
Gaud, Major, *m.*, 35
"General Butler, like Moses, led us forth at last," 277
Georgia, 81–94, 210, 255, 256, 284, 286, 287, 289–91, 294–300, 302–5
Ghosts, 48–58, 191
Gill, James, *n.*, 209, 298
Gilliam, Master, 36
Gilmore, Brawley, *n.*, 270 (b), 304
Glasgow, Emoline, *n.*, 36 (c), 287
Goats, 21–22, 63
Goldsboro (N.C.), 286, 287
Good, John, 270–71
Goodman, Andrew, *n.*, 246, 302
Goodman, Henry, *s.*, 244
Goodwin, Mrs. Candis, *n.*, 146 (b), 292
Goshen Hill (S.C.), 149
Gouge, Old Man (Opoeth-le-ya-hola), 139
Gourd dippers, 90, 91
Gragston, Arnold, *n.*, 193 (b), 297
Graham, Mrs. Carol, *w.*, 24 (I), 35 (b), 73, 145 (a), 285, 287, 291, 292
Grand Prairie (Ala.), 274
Grandberry, Mary Ella, *n.*, 15 (a), 284
Grant, Austin, *n.*, 238 (b), 301
Grant, Henry, *w.*, 176 (b), 242 (b), 295, 302
Graveyards, 57, 82–83, 99, 128, 156–57, 171, 271–72
Grayson, Mary, *n.*, 137–42, 292
Greeley, Horace, 24
Green, Henry, *n.*, 17 (b), 284
Green, Jake, *n.*, 9 (b, c), 43 (a), 283, 288
Green, James, *s.*, 165 (b), 294
Greensboro (Ga.), 242
Greensboro (N.C.), 289
Greenville (N.C.), 285, 304
Greenwood (Miss.), 259
Grey, Adeline, *n.*, 220 (b), 299
Grice, Pauline, *n.*, 248 (b), 302
Griegg, Annie, *n.*, 257 (a), 303
Guadalupe River, 232
Guidon, Lee, *n.*, 77–81, 291
Gunboats, Yankee, 131–32, 210

Guy, Cy, *s.*, 266

Hadley, Linley, *n.*, 237, 301
Hagg, Beulah Sherwood, *w.*, 212 (c), 222 (b), 241 (a), 298, 299, 302
Haley, Master, 179–81
Hall, Mrs. Sarah H., *w.*, 222 (c), 299
Hamilton, William, *n.*, 163 (a), 294
Hamilton, William (trader), 163
Hancock County (Ga.), 268
Hand, Trot, *m.*, 104
Hangings, 52, 62–63, 65, 78, 87, 158, 182, 192, 222, 266, 267, 269
Hants, 48–58
Hardridge, Mary Jane, *n.*, 234 (a), 300
Harper, Eda, *n.*, 201 (a), 235 (b), 297, 301
Harper, Pierce, *n.*, 267 (II), 304
Harrison, Anderson, *m.*, 162
Harrison, Eli, *n.*, 58, 289
Harrison, William H., *n.*, 162 (b), 294
Hatchet, Mathilda, *n.*, 149 (a), 225 (III), 293, 299
Hawkens, John G., *n.*, 201 (II), 235 (d), 297, 301
Hawkins, Master, 167, 201
Hawkins, Annie, *n.*, 171, 294
Hays, Archie, *m.*, 213
Haywood, Felix, *n.*, 231 (b), 300
Hazen (Ark.), 302, 303
Hazlehurst (Miss.), 108, 111, 287, 292
Helena (Ark.), 69, 210, 211, 221, 228, 300, 301
Hendon, Mistress, 267
Hepzibah (Ga.), 303
Herculaneum (Mo.), 305
"Here's my little gun," 216
Heyward, Governor, 17
"Hi, ho, ug, hi, ho, ug," 178
Hicks, Mary A., *w.*, 266 (I), 304
Higginbotham, Sam, *m.*, 204
Hill, Albert, *n.*, 29 (c), 286
Hill, John, *n.*, 170 (b), 294
Hillyer, Morris, *n.*, 186 (a), 296
Hindman, General Thomas C., 228
"His shirt am rough and his back am tough," 13
Hoard, Rosina, *n.*, 146 (c), 293
Hog bladders, used for Christmas "fireworks," 248–49
Hogs, 10, 11, 19, 64, 65, 206, 210, 221, 248–49; down, 19
Holland, Betty, *m.*, 262
Holland, Caroline, *n.*, 191, 296
Holloway, H. B., (Dad or Pappy), *n.*, 25 (IV), 32 (b), 42, 286, 287
Holly Grove (Ark.), 299
Holly Springs (Ark.), 80
Holly Springs (Miss.), 283
Holman, Eliza, *n.*, 71, 291
Homer (La.), 300
Homer, Bill, *n.*, 29 (b), 286

Hondo (Tex.), 301
Honey Creek (Ark.), 287
Honey Springs, Battle of, 142
Hood, Master, 236
Hoodoo, 42; *see also* Conjure
Hopkins, Elijah Henry, *n.*, 260 (II), 303-4
Hopping, John, 60
Horn, Josh, *n.*, 49 (b), 50 (a, b), 189, 288, 296
Horn, Molly, *n.*, 221, 299
Horns, 50, 116, 117, 121, 128, 240, 244
Hornsby, Sadie B., *w.*, 68 (b), 241 (b), 280 (a), 290, 302, 305
Horses, 11, 12, 29, 59–60, 81, 125, 149, 206, 208, 213, 217, 218, 268, 269, 272
Hot Springs County (Ark.), 276
House, Pearl, *w.*, 14 (a), 284
House boys, 11–12, 61, 95, 147–48
House hands, 153
House women, 91, 109
Houston (Tex.), 159, 292, 302, 303
Howard, Aunt Pinkey, *n.*, 24 (I), 285
Howell, Pauline (Pearl), *n.*, 239 (c), 301
Hudson, Carrie, *n.*, 241 (b), 302
Hudson, Charlie, *n.*, 68 (b), 280 (a), 290, 305
Hughes, Margaret, *n.*, 219, 299
Hulm, Margaret, *n.*, 220 (a), 299
Humor, 7–19
Humphrey (Ark.), 299
Hunger, 72, 95, 128, 129, 282; *see also* Starvation
Hunter, Mom Hester, *n.*, 154, 155, 293
Hunting, 50–51, 100, 183, 206–7, 263
Huntsville (Ala.), 206, 293
Hurt, Early, *m.*, 184
Hutchinson, Ida Blackshear, *n.*, 192 (a), 297
Hymn-singing, 152

"I fooled Old Master seven years," 9
Incest, 66
Indian Territory, 107, 112, 118, 137, 142, 163, 287, 290, 292, 294, 296
Indians, 64, 88, 165–66; *see also under individual tribes*
Indigo dye, 75
Irwin, Aunt Hannah, *n.*, 214 (c), 298
"It was on the eighth of April," 205
Ivory, Daniel, *o.*, 238

Jackson (Miss.), 110
Jackson (Tenn.), 304
Jackson, Mrs. Isabella, *n.*, 170 (c), 294
Jackson, Jim, *m.*, 242
Jackson, Lula, *n.*, 183 (c), 296
Jackson, Martha, *n.*, 175 (a), 295
Jackson, Rev. Squires, *n.*, 238 (a), 301
Jackson, Virginia, *n.*, 236 (a), 301
Jackson County (Ga.), 90
Jacksonville (Fla.), 284
James, Dick, *s.*, 275

James, Fred, *n.,* 214 (a), 239 (a), 298, 301
Jameson, Dr., *m.,* 24
Jamestown (Tex.), 287
Jasper County (Ga.), 259
Jefferson (Ga.), 90, 91, 92
Jenkins, Paul, *n.,* 277, 305
Jim Crow, 143
Johns, Auntie Thomas, *n.,* 19 (b), 285
Johns, Thomas, *n.,* 279 (c), 305
Johnson, Master, 148
Johnson, Ben, *n.,* 266 (I), 304
Johnson, Charles S., 143
Johnson, Ella, *n.,* 52 (b), 288
Johnson, Henry, *s.,* 16
Johnson, Uncle Hilliard, *n.,* 12 (a), 284
Johnson, John, *n.,* 265 (a), 304
Johnson, Marion, *n.,* 35 (b), 145 (a), 287, 292
Johnson, Martin, *n.,* 280 (b), 305
Johnson, Samuel, *w.,* 238 (a), 301
Johnson, Spence, *n.,* 163 (I), 165 (a), 294
Jokes, 7–16, 59 (a); *see also* Humor
Jones, Clara, *n.,* 199, 297
Jones, Dr. Isaac, *m.,* 113
Jones, Liza, *n.,* 213 (b), 298
Jones, Lydia, *n.,* 54 (a), 289
Jones, Marjorie, *w.,* 198, 297
Jones, Richard (Dick Look-up), *n.,* 69 (a), 290
Jones, Toby, *n.,* 257 (b), 303
Jordan, Mrs. Josie, *n.,* 11 (a), 283
Jordan, Travis, *w.,* 26 (a), 202 (b), 286, 297
Jordan, W. F., *w.,* 37, 52 (a), 273, 287, 288, 305
Juksie, 95
Jumping the broomstick, 76, 97, 101, 131; *see also* Marriage

Kansas, 112, 123–26, 142
Kelly, Ella, *n.,* 21 (b), 285
Kemp, "Prophet" John Henry, *n.,* 183 (b), 296
Kendricks, Tines, *n.,* 81–86, 291
Kentucky, 185, 196, 197, 302
Kernan, John (teacher), 142
Kerns, Mrs. Adrianna W., *n.,* 213 (a), 298
Kinney, Nicey, *n.,* 90–94, 291
Klein, Preston, *w.,* 31 (b), 286
Know-Nothing party, 194
Knoxville (Tenn.), 163, 298
Konkabia (Ala.), 190
Krump, Betty, *n.,* 228, 300
Ku Klux Klan, 27–28, 79–80, 110–11, 125, 136, 225, 249, 252, 266–76

LaCotts, Mrs. Annie L., *w.,* 152, 220 (a), 293, 299
Ladson, Augustus, *w.,* 66 (a), 290
Lafayette (La.), 106
Lake Charles (La.), 228
Langford, Master, 164
Larkin, Frank, *n.,* 227 (b), 300

Lawrence, Ephraim (Mike), *n.,* 18, 285
Lee, Robert E., 89, 118
Leeds (S.C.), 271
Lewis, Dellie, *n.,* 61 (a), 289
Lewis, Henry, *n.,* 178 (a), 295
Lewis, Talitha, *n.,* 33 (a), 35 (c), 286, 287
Lexington (Ga.), 284
Liberty (Tex.), 165
Lincoln, Abraham, 23–26, 241, 250
Lindsay, Abbie, *n.,* 143, 292
Little, Annie, *n.,* 53, 289
"Little pinch o' pepper," 38
Little Rock (Ark.), 26, 113, 118, 256, 284, 286–89, 291–93, 296–305
Littlejohn, Chana, *n.,* 61 (d), 289
Livingston (Ala.), 274, 283, 288, 295, 296, 302
Lockhart (S.C.), 271
Lookout Mountain, 208
Louie, Sam, *m.,* 242
Louisiana, 85, 103, 106, 118, 127, 132, 165, 286, 287, 290–92, 294–96, 298, 300, 301, 304
Love, John, *n.,* 20 (b), 285
Love, Kiziah, *n.,* 36 (a), 63 (a), 287, 290
Luray (S.C.), 299
Lynch, Jim, *o.,* 209
Lynchburg (Va.), 303, 305
Lynn, Lois, *w.,* 191, 297
Lynngrove (La.), 292

McAlester (Okla.), 283, 284, 299
McAlilley, George, *n.,* 21 (a), 285
McCloud, Lizzie, *n.,* 224 (I), 299
McCollum, Eli, *s.,* 271
McCoy, John, *n.,* 248 (a), 302
McCray, Stephen, *n.,* 22 (a), 285
McCrorey, Ed, (Ed Mack), *n.,* 15 (c), 284
McCune, Grace, *w.,* 11 (b), 59 (b), 90, 170 (b), 284, 289, 291, 294
Macedonia (Ala.), 294
McIntosh, Waters, *n.,* 34 (V), 233 (a), 253 (a), 287, 300, 303
McIntosh men, 138
McIver, Amphibious, 278
McKinney, Albert, *m.,* 250
McKinney, Warren, *n.,* 252, 303
McKinney, Watt, *w.,* 81, 174, 209, 291, 295, 298
McLennan County (Tex.), 107
McMullen, Victoria, *n.,* 33 (IV), 287
McNeill, Tom Henry, *m.,* 228
Macon (Ga.), 82, 291
McQueen, Nap, *n.,* 30 (c), 286
Madden, Perry, *n.,* 59 (c), 289
Madison (Ark.), 301, 303
Madison (Fla.), 301
Madisonville (Tex.), 291, 295, 303
"Malitis," 11
"Mammy, don't you cook no more," 232
Manning, Allen V., *n.,* 72, 103–8, 291–92

Mansfield (La.), 261, 262; Battle of, 204–6
Marianna (Ark.), 302
Marion (La.), 287
Marion (S.C.), 283, 287, 293
Markets, slave, 159, 165
Mark's Hill (Ga.), 212
Marlin (Tex.), 285
Marmaduke, General, 212
Marriage, 76, 97, 101, 135, 153–54, 194
Marshall (Tex.), 289, 296, 297, 301, 304
Mart (Tex.), 289
Martin, *w.*, 44 (b), 288
Martin, Master, 192
Martin, Isaac, *n.*, 145 (I), 292
Martin, James, *n.*, 192 (c), 297
Marvell (Ark.), 295, 298
Mason County (Ky.), 194
Masters and mistresses: cruel, 11, 78, 82, 85, 86–87, 101, 138, 167, 171–72, 173–74, 177, 202, 259–61; kind, 74, 82, 94, 133, 152–54, 157, 165, 167–68, 177–81
Mathews, William, *n.*, 240 (b), 301
Matthews, Caroline, *n.*, 20 (a), 285
Matthews, T. Pat, *w.*, 61 (d), 199, 289, 297
Maynard, Bob, *n.*, 23 (I), 285
Medical care, 83, 97, 103, 130, 134
Memphis (Tenn.), 164, 203
Meridian (Miss.), 90
Meridian (Tex.), 88, 89, 291
Merritt, Susan, *n.*, 236 (b), 301
Mess pork, 136
Methodists, 37, 149
Miami (Fla.), 285
Migrations, 80, 86, 88, 103, 111, 112, 117–18, 126
Miller, Anna, *n.*, 243 (b), 302
Miller, Hardy, *n.*, 212 (b), 298
Miller, Henry Kirk, *n.*, 241 (a), 302
Miller, Mintie Maria, *n.*, 159 (b), 293
Miner, Lank, *m.*, 146
Miscegenation, 130, 146, 162, 166, 173, 259–60
Missionary Ridge, Battle of, 208
Mississippi, 58, 66, 85, 103, 106, 108, 128, 131, 259, 262, 283–85, 287–92, 295–99, 301–3, 305
Missouri, 79, 142, 289, 295, 305
Mitchell, Tom, *s.*, 61–62
Mobile (Ala.), 289, 296
Mobley, Ed, *m.*, 15
Money, 95, 100, 109, 110, 111, 222
Monkey's fatal imitation, the, 30–31
Monroe (La.), 119–120, 124, 301
Montgomery (Ala.), 274, 296–97, 301
Montgomery, Jane, *n.*, 233 (b), 300
Monticello (Ark.), 300
Moore, Amy Van Zandt, *s.*, 193
Moore, Fannie, *n.*, 198, 297
Moore, Henry, *s.*, 193
Moore, Jerry, *n.*, 193 (a), 297
Moore, Patsy, *n.*, 251 (a), 303

Moore, Van, *n.*, 250 (a), 303
Morgan, Evelina, *n.*, 222 (a), 234 (c), 299, 300
Moro (Ark.), 69
Morris, Charity, *n.*, 182 (c), 296
Moser, Master, 27
Moser Valley (Tex.), 286
Moses, 23
Moss, Andrew, *n.*, 212 (a), 298
Moss, Claiborne, *n.*, 217 (II), 268 (III), 299, 304
Mother wit, 7
Mules, 16, 49–50, 79, 81, 98, 176, 177, 189, 216, 252
Mullinax, J. B., *o.*, 19
Murder: of Negroes, 19, 66, 96, 116, 171, 187, 191, 192, 203, 268; of whites, 158, 182–84
Murfreesboro (Tenn.), 218, 299, 305
Murray, Master, 18–19
Murray, C. S., *w.*, 18, 285
Murray, Joe, *s.*, 15–16
Musical instruments, 123; *see also* Fiddlers
Muskogee (Okla.), 107

Nacogdoches (Tex.), 107, 288
Nashville (Tenn.), 265, 286, 303
Natchez (Miss.), 132
Natchitoches (La.), 204
Navasota (Tex.), 132
Neel, Mr., *o.*, 77
Nelson, Andy, *n.*, 27 (b) 286
Nelson, Susan, *n.*, 60 (b), 289
New Orleans (La.), 88, 106, 134, 164–65, 296
New York, 162
Newberry (S.C.), 287, 289, 298, 301
Newport (Ark.), 161
Newton (Tex.), 287
Newton, Mistress, 16
Nicodemus, 21
Nillin, Margrett, *n.*, 279 (b), 305
Noah, 22
Norcross (Ga.), 291
North Carolina, 25, 73, 77, 244, 285, 286, 287, 289, 291, 297, 299, 300, 303, 304
North Little Rock (Ark.), 293, 298, 299, 305
North Zulch (Tex.), 173
Northrup, Solomon, *s.*, 143
Nursing white children, 133, 134, 181, 187

O'Brien, Susie R., *w.*, 51, 179 (a), 181, 184, 288, 295, 296
Ohio, 195, 196, 305
Ohio River, 194–95
Oklahoma, 107, 126, 283–85, 287, 287–90, 292–301, 304; *see also* Indian Territory
Oklahoma City (Okla.), 283, 294–97, 300, 301
Okmulgee (Okla.), 142
Old John, 8, 9–10
Old Wittsburg (Ark.), 290
Oliphant, Louise, *w.*, 187, 296
Opelika (Ala.), 286

Opelousas (La.), 132, 136, 292
Opoeth-le-ya-hola, 139
Osborn, Annie, *n.*, 261, 304
Osbrook, Jane, *n.*, 147 (a), 293
Otom, Nelse (teacher), 36
Outlaws, 27, 52, 87, 140–41
Overseers, 9, 17, 19, 77, 112–13, 119, 143–44, 146, 173, 174, 177, 178, 180, 181, 183, 184, 191, 198, 204, 206, 209, 238, 242, 246, 262
Oxen, 29, 89, 156

Page, Annie, *n.*, 44 (a), 288
Palestine (Tex.), 290, 305
Palo Pinto (Tex.), 243–44
Pamplin (Va.), 232
Paragould (Ark.), 289
Parrot story, 14
Parsons, William Tolas, *m.*, 133
Partridges, 21, 30
Passes, 13, 117, 125, 176, 177, 179, 211, 247
Patrollers, 13, 61, 97, 143–44, 176, 179, 186, 192, 264
Patterson (La.), 133
Patterson, Frank A., *n.*, 25 (III), 26 (b), 216 (I), 231 (a), 285–86, 299, 300
Patterson, Sarah Jane, *n.*, 234 (b), 300
Payne, Harriett McFarlin, *n.*, 152, 293
Peafowl, 147–48
Pearl River, 108
Peddlers, 26
Peedee (S.C.), 305
Pennington, Master, 183
Peonage, 236, 259, 260
Perkins, Maggie, *n.*, 44 (b), 288
Perryman, Mose, *m.*, 138
Persimmon beer, 78
Persimmon-picking, 51
Petersburg (Va.), 165, 300, 303, 305
Petrified man, 58
Phillips, Simon, *n.*, 239 (b), 301
Phillips, Ulrich B., 71
Phillips County (Ark.), 86
Pickens (S.C.), 304
Pierce, Everett R., *w.*, 219, 299
Pinchback, John, *m.*, 165–66
Pinckney, Martha S., *w.*, 60 (b), 289
Pine Apple (Ala.), 96, 291
Pine Bluff (Ark.), 44, 285–87, 290–93, 295–301
Pine Island (Tex.), 295
Pine-knot lights, 74, 101, 198
Pitts, Roxy, *n.*, 31 (b), 286
Pittsburg (Kan.), 126
Plantation life, 73–137 *passim*, 167–68, 179–80, 245
Platter (Okla.), 288, 293
Politics, ex-slaves in, 89, 265–78
Polk, Dr., *m.*, 235
Poll tax, 274
Poole, Mary A., *w.*, 22 (b), 61 (a), 285, 289

"Possum up a 'simmon tree," 102
Possum, 10, 100, 210
Prayer as cure, 43–44, 129, 198
Praying under the tree, 49
Preachers and preaching, 33–37, 60, 83, 89, 101, 103, 126, 149–52, 170, 179, 187, 222–23, 248, 267; *see also* Churches
Present, the attitude toward, 81, 92, 250, 251, 279–82
Price, Rev. Lafayette, *n.*, 30 (b), 204, 286, 298
Prichard (Ala.), 285, 293
Prine, Ida B., *w.*, 19 (a), 158, 285, 293
Proctor, Jenny, *n.*, 99–103, 291
Pugh, Aunt Nicey, *n.*, 158, 293
Pumpkins, stealing of, 12–13
Punishments; *see* Bull pen, slaves in; Chains, slaves in; Hangings; Murder; Stocks, slaves in; Whippings and beatings
Pyles, Henry F., *n.*, 38 (c), 265 (b), 287, 304
Pyles, Jordan, *s.*, 266

Quarters, slave, 74, 94–95, 121, 129, 145, 153, 154–55, 167, 180
Quilt-making, 197, 198
Quitman (Miss.), 104

Rabbits, 30, 100
Raccoon and the dog, the, 22
Raines, Joe, *s.*, 15
Raleigh (N.C.), 297, 299, 300, 303
Ramson, Dave, *m.*, 108
Rankins, John, 195–96
Reading and writing, 36, 60, 61, 101, 179, 194, 206, 278; *see also* Schools and schooling
Reconstruction, 80, 252–53, 265–78
Red flannel, 69, 101
Red River, 112, 153, 164
Reeves, James, *n.*, 244 (a), 276 (b), 302, 305
Refugeeing, 77, 85–86, 89, 98, 104–5, 123–24, 132, 140, 152–53; defined, 200
Renfroe, Sheriff Steve, 27, 52
Republicans, 21, 79
Reynolds, Mary, *n.*, 72, 127–32, 292
Rice, Jessie, *n.*, 67, 290
Richardson, Martin, *w.*, 193 (b), 297
Richmond (Va.), 62
"Ride and tie," 141–42
Rimm, Walter, *n.*, 197, 297
Ripley (Ohio), 195
Ritchie, Milton, *n.*, 253 (b), 303
Roberts, Isom, *n.*, 242 (b), 302
Robertson, Irene, *w.*, 33 (II), 64 (c), 65, 66 (c), 69 (b), 77, 162 (b), 172 (a), 192 (b), 201 (II), 218, 221, 228, 229, 235 (d), 236 (a), 237, 239 (c), 242 (a), 244 (b), 245 (I), 250 (c), 251 (a), 252, 253 (b), 257 (a), 262, 265 (a), 270 (a), 272, 287, 290, 291, 294, 297, 299–305

Robinson, Harriett, *n.*, 9 (a), 188, 202 (a), 238 (c), 283, 296, 297, 301
Robinson, Mariah, *n.*, 88–90, 291
Robinson, Peter, *s.*, 89
Robinson, Ridley, *m.*, 89
Rogers (S.C.), 149
Rogers, Gus (Jabbo), *n.*, 22 (b), 285
Rogers, Will Ann, *n.*, 69 (b), 290
Rooster test, 59
Rosecrans, General William S., 207, 208
Rosedale (Tex.), 285
Round Rock (Tex.), 28
Row, Annie, *n.*, 245 (II), 302
Rowe, Katie, *n.*, 72, 112–18, 292
Ruckersville (Ga.), 302
Ruffin, Thomas, *n.*, 251 (b), 303
Ruffins, Florence, *n.*, 54 (II), 289
Runaway slaves, 98, 101–2, 105, 131, 137–38, 154, 170, 171, 182–98, 206–7, 258–59
Rusk (Tex.), 302
Russ, Babb, *s.*, 38–39

Sabine River, 107–8
Sadler, Betty, *s.*, 107
St. Charles (La.), 152
St. Hedwig (Tex.), 300
Sample, Velma, *w.*, 59 (a), 289
San Angelo (Tex.), 103, 291
San Antonio (Tex.), 294, 297, 300, 305
San Antonio River, 232
Sand Ridge (Ala.), 296
Sand Springs (Okla.), 289
Sanders, Austin, *s.*, 271
Sandson, Mr., *o.*, 206
Sanitobia (Miss.), 290
Saratoga (N.C.), 300
"Saturday night and Sunday too," 102
Scaife, Sam, *s.*, 271
Schools and schooling, 36, 74, 88, 98–99; *see also* Reading and writing
Scruggs, Stiles M., *w.*, 17 (c), 277, 284, 305
Seamstresses, 130, 134
Sears, Deacon, *m.*, 105–6
Seaview (Va.), 292
Sells, Abram, *n.*, 38 (b), 287
Selma (Ala.), 162, 290, 299
Seminole Nation, 142
Sharecroppers, 107, 124, 249, 263
Sharp, Gerald, *m.*, 90–93
Sheep, 21
Sheep-shearing, 92
Sheffield (Ala.), 284
Shelby, Levi D., Jr., *w.*, 15 (a, b), 23 (a), 284, 285
Sheppard, Morris, *n.*, 147 (b), 293
Sheriffs, 27, 52, 62
Sherman, General William T., 216
Shiloh, Battle of (Ku Klux Klan trick), 272–73, 274
Shoemakers, 75, 121, 122, 179, 241

Shores, Mahalia, *n.*, 242 (a), 302
Shreveport (La.), 120, 123, 164, 204, 205
Signs and portents, 44, 84, 199
Simmons, Betty, *n.*, 164 (II), 294
Simmons, Rosa, *n.*, 225 (II), 299
Simonette Lake, 106
Simpson, Ben, *n.*, 86–87, 291
Sims, Colonel, *m.*, 238
Sims, Caldwell, *w.*, 32 (a), 55, 57, 62, 67, 69 (a), 147 (c), 149 (b), 270 (b), 275, 286, 289, 290, 293, 304
Slave trade and traffic; *see* Auctions, slave; Families, separation of; Markets, slave; Slaves, breeding of; Speculators, slave; Stealers, slave
Slaves: breeding of, 138, 166, 168–69, 259–60; given away, 88, 173; held for debt, 88, 164; inherited, 85, 159; sold by own father, 250; *see also* Burials, slave; Cabins, slave; Chains, slaves in; Quarters, slave; Runaway slaves; Stocks, slaves in
Sledge, Enoch, *s.*, 27
Sledge, Frank, *s.*, 27
Sledge, Simmy, *s.*, 27
Smith, Giles, *n.*, 178 (b), 295
Smith, James W., *n.*, 68 (a), 290
Smith, Jim, *m.*, 170
Smith, John, *n.*, 179 (a), 295
Smith, John H., *n.*, 175 (b), 295
Smith, John Morgan, *w.*, 177, 191, 239 (b), 295, 297, 301
Smith, Jordan, *n.*, 186 (b), 296
Smith, Lou, *n.*, 48 (a), 60 (c), 161 (a), 288, 289, 293
Smith, Saddler, *m.*, 179
Smoak (Ark.), 277
Smokehouses, 24–25, 31, 44, 213, 219, 220, 245, 251
Snipe hunting, 68
Snow Hill (N.C.), 304
Soap-making, 261
South Carolina, 44, 270, 283–93, 295, 298–305
Sparta (Ga.), 284
Sparta (Tenn.), 283
Spartanburg (S.C.), 286
Speculators, slave, 128, 164–65
Spinning, 74, 95, 96, 121, 130, 179–180, 181, 198, 261
Springfield (Mo.), 289
Starvation, 86, 98, 208, 251, 252, 258; *see also* Hunger
Stealers, slave, 163–65
Steamboats, 59, 135, 256
Steele, General, 212
Stenhouse, Maggie, *n.*, 270 (a), 304
Stillhouses, 78
Stith, James Henry, *n.*, 17 (a), 284
Stockades, 101
Stocks, slaves in, 128, 188
Stonestreet, M. B., *w.*, 247, 302
Strauter, George, *m.*, 252
Strong, Bert, *n.*, 240 (a), 301

Sugar-making, 135
Suggsville (Ala.), 285
Suicide, 136, 192, 244, 246
Sumner, G. L., *w.,* 36 (c), 61 (c), 214 (a),
    239 (a), 287, 289, 298, 301
Sumter County (Ala.), 27, 274–75
Syrup-making, 96

Tabb, Jack, *m.,* 194
Tahlequah (Okla.), 118
Talking animals, 14, 30–32; *see also* Animal talk;
    Bird talk
Tall tales, 17–19
Tanning, 75
Tarrant County (Tex.), 27
Tartt, Ruby Pickens, *w.,* 9 (b, c), 27 (a), 48 (b),
    49 (b), 50 (b), 175 (a), 189, 249, 250 (b),
    283, 286, 288, 295, 296, 302, 303
Taswell, Salena, *n.,* 24 (II), 285
Taylor, Captain Clay, 266
Taylor, Samuel S., *w.,* 17 (a), 25 (III, IV), 26 (b),
    32 (b), 33 (III, IV), 34 (V), 42, 43 (b), 52 (b),
    59 (c), 61 (b), 64 (a), 70 (b), 143, 149 (a),
    161 (b), 182 (b), 183 (a, c), 192 (a), 213 (a),
    216, 222 (a), 225 (III), 231 (a) 233 (a),
    234 (b, d), 235 (c), 244 (a), 251 (b), 253 (a),
    255, 260 (II), 268 (III), 276 (a, b), 279 (a),
    284, 286–93, 296–305
Teachers, 36, 89, 98–99, 142; *see also* Schools
    and schooling
Tennessee, 108, 126, 132, 210, 283, 285–87,
    290, 298, 299, 303–5
Terrapin, 14
Terrill, J. W., *n.,* 173, 295
Texas, 17, 65, 86, 88, 98, 103, 132, 166, 167,
    257, 258, 262, 283–98, 300–305
Thomas, General George H., 208–9
Thomas, William M., *n.,* 12 (b), 284
Thompson, Mrs. Mildred, *w.,* 24 (I), 285
Thompson, Ruth, *w.,* 281, 305
Tobacco, 75–76
Toler, Richard, *n.,* 281, 305
Tombigbee River, 250
Tortoise and the rabbit, the, 30
Trenton (Ark.), 291
Trickster tales, 8, 9–16
Trinity (Tex.), 127
Trinity River, 28
Tubman, Harriet, *s.,* 207
Tulsa (Okla.), 107, 118, 126, 142, 283, 285,
    287, 292, 294, 298, 304
Tunnel, Uncle George, *s.,* 237
Turner, Lou, *n.,* 20 (c), 285
Turner, Rube, 268–69
Tuscaloosa (Ala.), 293

Uncle Remus, 143
Uncle Tom, 143
Underground Railroad, 195–96, 207

Union (S.C.), 275, 286, 289, 290, 293, 304
Union County (Ark.), 276
Union County (S.C.), 77
"Union forever," 231
Union soldiers; *see* Yankee soldiers
Uniontown (Ala.), 288, 295, 296
Upper League, 79
Upson, Neal, *n.,* 11 (b), 59 (b), 284, 289

Vaughn, Adelaide J., *n.,* 161 (b), 293
Verdigris River, 142
Veth (Tex.), 292
Vicksburg (Miss.), 120, 122, 296
Village Creek (Tex.), 163, 294
Vinegar-making, 75
Virginia, 14, 15, 83, 135, 165, 192, 245, 292,
    294, 297, 300, 303, 305
Voting, 80, 125, 268–69, 274–75, 276

Waco (Tex.), 88, 89, 107, 288, 294
Wagoner (Okla.), 112
Walker, Manda, *n.,* 176 (a), 295
Walnut Spring (Tex.), 88
Walterboro (Ark.), 277
Walton, Sol, *n.,* 184 (I), 296
Ward (Ala.), 288
Ward, Sophia, *n.,* 14 (a), 284
Ward, William, *n.,* 259 (I), 303
Warner, Jane, *m.,* 220
Warren (Ark.), 296
Warrenton (N.C.), 289
Washing clothes, 75, 129
Washington (Ark.), 113, 292
Washington (Ga.), 302
Washington, Colonel Pratt, *m.,* 146
Washington County (Ga.), 269
Water, analyzing the, 274
Water Valley (Miss.), 245
Wateree Creek (S.C.), 176
Watermelon, 71
Watson, Dinah, *n.,* 184 (II), 296
Watson, Tom, 69
Waynesboro (Ga.), 254
Weaver, Betty (teacher), 142
Weaving, 121–22, 180, 181, 198
Webb, Ishe, *n.,* 255, 303
Webber's Falls (Okla.), 293
Wedgeboro (N.C.), 300
Weld, Theodore D., 144
Weleetka (Okla.), 142, 285
Wesmoland, Maggie, *n.,* 262, 304
West Memphis (Ark.), 290
Wheeler, General, 217
Whippings and beatings, 12–13, 15, 17, 19, 66,
    78, 86, 96, 112, 116, 129, 131, 133, 149,
    154, 158, 166, 167, 170–98, 201–4, 224,
    259, 270, 273
White, Master, 273
White, John, *n.,* 54 (I), 289

White, Mrs. Julia A., 222 (b), 299
White, Mingo, *n.,* 15 (b), 23 (a), 284, 285
White River, 119
Whitehead, Master, 9
Whiteside, Tom, *m.,* 78
Whitmire (S.C.), 289
Wilcox County (Ala.), 204
Wildersville (Tenn.), 265
Williams, Charley, *n.,* 118–27, 292
Williams, John, *m.,* 119, 165–66
Williams, Mack, *m.,* 259
Williams, Rose, *n.,* 167, 294
Williamson (Tex.), 293
Willis (Tex.), 292
Willis, Adeline, *n.,* 247, 302
Wilson, Ella, *n.,* 70 (b), 291
Windham, Tom, *n.,* 182 (a), 296
Winfield (Tex.), 240
Winn, Mr., *o.,* 204
Winnsboro (S.C.), 284, 295, 304, 305

Wolf, Master, 27
Wolves, 64
Wood-cutting, 18–19, 51, 80, 99
Woods, General, 207, 208
Woodward, Joe, *m.,* 176
Word, Sam, *n.,* 64 (b), 214 (b), 290, 298
Worthy, Buck, 271–72
Wright, Hannah Brooks, *n.,* 70 (a), 226 (IV), 291, 299

Yankee soldiers, 15, 17, 31, 78, 79, 80, 84, 92, 97–98, 104, 106, 113, 116, 122–23, 132, 136, 155, 177, 199, 200, 203, 209–28, 231–37, 240, 242–43, 245–48, 250, 251, 265, 266, 270; *see also* Civil War; Foraging and looting
York County (S.C.), 77
Young, Annie, *n.,* 10 (a), 283
Youngsboro (Ala.), 286